ROCKWELL LECTURES

The Rice Institute

The Structure of Christian Ethics

BY

JOSEPH SITTLER

LOUISIANA STATE UNIVERSITY PRESS
BATON ROUGE

Second printing, 1961

PREFACE

The material here presented was delivered at The Rice Institute, Houston, Texas, as a series of Rockwell Lectures. I am grateful both for the invitation to prepare these lectures, and for the thoughtful courtesy of many members of the faculty and administration of the Institute during my days in Houston.

The earliest occasion to set down an argument for the structure of Christian ethics was provided by a directive of my own Church that a Commission prepare a rather full statement for the guidance of our people as, in the midst of confusing and deepening ethical problems, they look for a solid center from which to learn what they ought to do. Large sections of my contribution to that study, which appeared in the summer of 1957 under the title *Christian Social Responsibility* (Philadelphia: Muhlenberg Press), are reproduced here by permission of the publisher.

JOSEPH SITTLER

The University of Chicago
May, 1958

v

TABLE OF CONTENTS

The Confusion in Contemporary Ethical Speech

THE effort in this first lecture is descriptive. The second and third lectures are a constructive effort to indicate the ground and the main lines of development of characteristically biblical ethics. And inasmuch as the assertions there advanced will cut across what is commonly assumed to be a proper way to derive ethical decisions from the Bible, they will commend themselves to our attention to the extent that they are shown to arise with naturalness, integrity, and clarity from the biblical material. The substance of this first lecture will be elaborated under three topics.

The Organic Nature of Biblical Speech

When a man of the twentieth century, divesting himself of the ways of thought normal to his time and place, wanders back into the speech-world and thought-world of the Bible he finds himself in a strange and puzzling land. The very structural elements of his common assumptions are there either gently laid aside in what he listens to, or are simply ignored. God, man, nature—these are the large fields of concern and enquiry now, as they have always been. But what strikes the reader of the Bible with almost the force of a palpable blow is the fact that these categories—among us separated for purposes of enquiry and description—are in the Bible but aspects of a single actuality, God himself. Our speech is specialized in order to achieve precision in the description of our world as it presents itself to us under a multitude of forms. The biblical speech is thoroughly organic.

God is the Creator. He is the fountain of life from whose eternal livingness all things are brought forth. As the up-arching lines of an exploding rocket describe parabolic arcs of light against the darkness, so does the Bible speak of all the elements, forms, forces, in the world. "The earth is the Lord's and the fulness thereof." God is not identified with the world, for he *made* it; but God is not separate from his world, either. For *He* made it. This God is never defined, his existence proved, or his nature elaborated in rational categories. God simply *is* what God manifestly does. When, for instance, the man of the Old Testament speaks about God he does not introduce his speech with an exhibition of a general truth, that there is a God, or by appeal to generalities of truth, goodness, or power in relation to which God is certified and accredited. He simply assumes that God, whose nature, will, and purpose has been made clear in his people's history, is alive, demanding and loving —and that men's lives can have no conceivable meaning or goodness save in obedient hearing and serving. What God is, that is to say, is an organic function of what God does.

The biblical speech about man has the same organic character. His existence is a subsistence. Man-in-himself is an inconceivable idea. Man *has* his existence by the Word of God. *Who* he is is organic with *whence* he is. How he should live is continuous with *where* he is—under God. If we did not so assiduously address to the first chapter of Genesis questions which are there neither raised nor answered, we should long since have heard them for what they are —a hymn to God the Creator. The fact that God made Eve, so sufficiently and delightfully different as to secure the propogation of the race, is not by any means the primary point. That he made her *at all* suggests the preliminary truth—that a solitary person is no person. Man, that is to say, is not only constituted in, by, and for organic relation to God who made him, but also for organic relation to other persons.

This radical vocabulary of relatedness characterizes every primary term of the Bible. Man is made in the image of God. He cannot become what he is if he ignores, denies, defies his structural God-relationship. And sin, too, is an organic term, for it designates a fractured relationship. God is life. Man has his life from God. If this Gift-Source of his life is repudi-

ated, man no longer has life. He is then dead—
whether the amenities of the funeral have taken
place or not. That is precisely what is said in the
statement that the wages, or outcome, of sin is death.
The New Testament speech of our Lord presupposes
this organic understanding. Man's life is a branch of
a trunk of life and it flowers when the connection is
there.

And the term *righteousness*—by us so commonly
indicative of moral probity, avoidance of glaring and
dramatic wrongdoing—is in the Bible a term that
indicates the state of a man's God-relationship. The
Hebrew term translated *righteousness* has exactly this
meaning. It means to be right, vitally related to one's
source, to live in such a way as to affirm and celebrate the God from whom one has his life. That is
why, in the Bible, men are called to be righteous
only on the ground that God is righteous. Men are
not called to an ideal, or threatened with failure to
match an elevated standard of abstract goodness.
They are called rather to be what they are, live their
true life, realize their being in their existence, and
work out their relationships on earth in organic continuity with their relationship to the Creator.

The organic terms with which the Bible speaks of
God and man inform also the biblical speech about
nature. I am not, at the moment, weighing the ade-
quacy of this speech for all aspects of natural science

investigation, although the introduction of theological ideas into scientific discourse is not so obviously ridiculous as it appeared some decades ago. The present effort is to achieve a vivid appreciation of a type of discourse characteristic of the Bible, and re-establish the category of the organic as the natural climate in which biblical terms must be heard and understood.

When, then, the Bible speaks of nature it does not introduce an entity for the description of which a new set of terms has to be invented. God made the world as he made man—by his Word. The life of nature is a given life. The entities, forms, processes of the natural world are, for the biblical writer, facts of wonder, but not of ultimate mystery. Typical of this organic continuity between God and nature is the lyrical celebration in the 104th Psalm of the inter-relatedness of the life of nature. Just as God placed his creature, man, in a garden and commanded him to " tend " it, so the world of nature—God's other creation—is spoken of as man's context in which is celebrated the same orchestration of relatedness. We are indeed dull of heart if we permit the naiveté of the lyricism to conceal from us the theology of the cosmos that sings through this Psalm. The light is God's garment, the heavens a cosmic curtain, the clouds the chariots of God, the wind and the thunder his voice. The springs, the birds, the growing grass, the grazing cattle—and consuming man—are all tied together in the bundle of Holy care.

> He causeth the grass to grow for the cattle; and herb for the service of man; That he may bring forth food out of the earth, and wine that maketh glad the heart of man; and oil to make his face to shine, and bread that strengtheneth man's heart. (Ps. 104:14)

This poem of interdependence is, however, all introductory to the consummate intention: that the million strands of dependency might illumine and confirm the shining cord of absolute dependency upon which the whole nexus hangs, through which its given life flows as a current from the Power-Source of the Holy.

> These all wait upon Thee . . . . Thou sendest forth Thy Spirit, they are created; . . . Thou hidest Thy face, they are troubled: Thou takest away their breath, they die, and return to their dust. (Ps. 104:27, 30, 29)

The Transformation of Biblical Speech in the Thought of the Church

When, to the first generation following the life of Jesus, a member of the community of faith addressed in practical terms the sodden moral life of his generation, there can still be heard through his language

8

the authentic power of the Bible's organic speech. To the Church in Rome Paul says, "I appeal to you therefore, brethren by the mercies of God, to present your bodies as a living sacrifice, holy and acceptable to God, which is your spiritual worship."

The force of the appeal rests here, not upon an abstract ethical ideal, nor upon any appeal to the self-destruction implicit in egocentricity and immorality, but as the "therefore" clearly indicates, upon a prior action of God whose force must either be confirmed and obeyed in a totally new "presentation of the body" (that is, a complete new orientation of the entire personality) or utterly rejected. Another kind of logic than that required by a cause and effect understanding of life is at work here. Side by side with the necessities of cause and effect (whose logic, in our western mental history is expressed in space terms) there is another kind of necessity. It is the inner logic of the living, the organic, the destiny-bound. And *its* logic is expressed in time terms. Entrance into the world of the second kind of discourse is simply not possible through the kind of cognition proper to the first. Where, that is to say, we read the New Testament story of the encounter of the life of God with the life of man in terms of the causality principle taken over from natural science, we not only do *not* confront and receive the ethical vitality of the New Testament message, but we positively

9

distort it. For we then impose upon a living nexus of organic powers and responses the forms of our own sensibility. The immediacies of biblical-ethical command are not communicable in the causalities of propositional speech; the vital unfolding into a new-being which is presaged by Paul's ". . . be ye transformed by the renewing of your minds . . ." is not communicable except in connection with the picture of God which grounds it—and which Paul assumes when he introduces his Apostolic counsel with the phrases, " Well, then . . . for this cause . . . therefore, brethren . . . . Because God, who is rich in mercy," and so on.

While, to be sure, this transposition of the organic vitality of Biblical speech into the abstract, intellectualized and propositional form of Western theology has been illustrated here by ethically loaded statements, the *process* was nonetheless general. And so pervasive has this process been that a great historian of Christian thought once described the entire body of Western church dogma as an " acute Hellenization of Christianity." Space does not allow a detailed examination of even the main lines of this process, but evidences of the transformative power of it can be indicated. The organic structure of the New Testament doctrine of the Church has, for most Protestant believers, become so drained of its proper character that the discovery of the living and relational language of the New Testament, due in part to the encounter and studies encouraged by the Ecumenical Movement, come as a positive shock. The Church is not, in the New Testament, a sociological quantum discoverable or mensurable by categories available anywhere in man's experience. The Church is the fellowship of the faithful which is created and bound together, *not* by men's mutual perception of a common faith in themselves, or religion, or even in God, but by the faithfulness of God become concrete in a body. This body was the actual historical appearing of a Man; and the Church, the body of Christ, is the organic household of the " members " of the body. Before the Church is the company of them that love God, it is the communion of them who acknowledge, and in that acknowledgment have their lives given a new center in One who loved them. The passive verb dominates the New Testament story! I love because I am loved; I know because I am known; I am of the Church, the body of Christ, because this body became my body; I can and must forgive because I have been forgiven; I can speak because I have been spoken to.

The confusion let loose in contemporary ethical discourse by the failure to relate ethical commands organically to the ethical Commander, reveals itself most fully in what one might call the ethics-of-the-end-of-the-sentence! The ethical teaching of Jesus, for instance, is commonly excised from his entire address to man, in word and in deed; and an effort is made to ask after the meaning and applicability of the end of a sentence, the first part of which we impatiently dismiss as having only local or occasional significance for the speaker and his first century hearers. This practice is rather like dropping in on a performance of a Bach fugue in time to hear the last page. The organic content of Jesus' address to men was not composed of highly personal epigrams consensed from the most elegant moral idealism ever envisioned by man in his quest for the good. This content was constituted, rather, by a lived-out and heroically obedient God-relationship in the fire of which all things are what they are by virtue of the Creator, all decisions are crucial in virtue of their witness to his primacy and glory, all events interpreted in terms of their transparency, recalcitrancy, or service to God's Kingly rule.

The Instrumental Evaluation of Ethics

There are evidences that our modern American enthusiasm for that aspect of Christian faith which is called *ethics* includes a covert form of idolatry—the more perilous because so disguised. There is a relation between the knowledge of God and the achievement and maintenance of human order; but God does not commonly make himself available to men who seek him primarily to achieve and maintain order. If God is sought in order to integrate the personality, the actual God is not God but the integrated personality. And when men are urged to renovate their religious values in order that the Republic may be the more firmly glued together, this covert idolatry reaches a peculiarly pernicious and untruthful pitch. There is a relation between a people who are blessed because their God is the Lord, but one does not find it recorded that God the Lord consents to be compounded into political glue.

It is instructive to examine the way the name of God, and appeals to his help, are introduced into the public political utterances of our leading politicos. The situation is described; some elements in it are announced as gratifying, others as deplorable. A vigorous program is then outlined, the hardship its execution will work upon our tax rate is confronted, and justified. And, finally, having figured out and announced what our rôle is, or ought to be, and what at the moment must be done, the entire structure of analysis and purpose is immersed in the tub of the waiting blessing of God. The performance concludes with the obvious assumption that from such commendable purposes God would not be so churlish as to withhold his effective assistance.

This understanding of Christian ethics—as a lubricant for the adjustment of the personality, and as an adhesive for public policy—does violence to the reality of both Christianity and politics. It does violence to Christianity because it makes the Holy a disposable object to be manipulated for mortal purposes; it does violence to political order because it tempts to such an identification of our purposes with the purposes of God as to engender both arrogance and insensitivity.

Nowhere, perhaps, in the recorded utterances of our English speaking men of affairs is there reflected so clearly as in President Lincoln's Second Inaugural Address the unfathomable mystery of the relationship between the purposes of God and the ethical crusades of men.

> Both (men of the North and of the South) read the same Bible, and pray to the same God; and each invokes his aid against the other . . . . The prayers of both could not be answered—that of neither has been answered fully.
>
> The Almighty has his own purposes.

It is necessary now to gather up the argument of this introductory lecture. The effort has been to expose the confusion in contemporary discourse about Christian ethics by way of an analysis of what seem to be three of its constituents. They are these: first, a failure to remain sensitive to the organic character of the biblical speech about God, man, and nature in such a way as to be aware that ethics is a function of

faith, that ethics is faith-doing, that the living continuity between man-in-God and man-among-men is
basic to the perception of the biblical revelation;
second, the transposition of organic biblical unity
of faith and life into categories of a cause and effect
structure in Christian ethical systems, with the result
that the living unity of faithful obedience has
dwindled into abstract counsels, duties, obligations;
and, third, that most religious form of idolatry whereby the Holy is understood from the point of view of,
made malleable by, and turned into an instrument of,
men's autonomous purposes.

In Oswald Spengler's *Decline of the West* is so
concise and brilliant an analogy of this confusion-
begetting process that I give here the entire paragraph:

> In a rock-stratum are embedded crystals of a
> mineral. Clefts and cracks occur, water filters
> in, and the crystals are gradually washed out so
> that in due course only their hollow mould re-
> mains. Then come volcanic outbursts which ex-
> plode the mountain; molten masses pour in,
> stiffen, and crystallize out in their turn. But
> these are not free to do so in their own special
> forms. They must fill up the space that they
> find available. Thus there are distorted forms,
> crystals whose inner structure contradicts their
> shape, stones of one kind presenting the appear-

ance of stones of another kind. The minerolo-
gists call this phenomenon *Pseudomorphosis*.[1]

In addition to the confusion-begetting factors elaborated above there is something other and something
more that has to be said. It lies deeper down and
further back; and the substance of it, while not formally a part of the foregoing analysis cannot be ignored. To ignore it would be to fail to say what has
to be said if justice is to be done to the deepest levels
where one becomes aware of ethical questions, and is
motivated to ponder them.

One does not study the Bible, teach Christian theology, live out his life, in a vacuum—even a vacuum
modified by persons who share his concern, belong
to the church, are deferential to the Christian tradition. My own career as a preacher and a teacher
of the Christian faith has been and continues to be
fulfilled in the company of as various, uninhibited,
sometimes ribald, always candid talkers as a continuous affection for literature can supply. The New
Testament letter to the Hebrews speaks of the man
of faith bearing witness to it in this world like an
athlete on a playing field of a great stadium ringed
round with a " mighty cloud of witnesses." While I,
too, work as a teacher in that stadium of the Christian centuries wherein I am instructed, consoled, and
heartened by the yet-living presences of the saints, I

am also a citizen of the world of my human brothers. There *they* sit, too, the living and the dead. They cheer and jeer, commend and criticize, throw their hats in derision and despair—and jarringly continue to talk back!

As one tries to penetrate to the structure and content of Christian ethics he cannot shut these people up, or think and act as if they were not there. They are a noisy and insistent lot. How richly our literature sparkles with works in which these men and women have made articulate their perception of the gap between man's wild, unsystematic self and the ordered thoughts, principles, institutions through which he wills to be known and honored! This literature of perception and enquiry includes ways of speaking so different and names so seemingly unrelated as Boccaccio, Cervantes, Montaigne, Blake, Hardy, Jane Austen, Hawthorne, Melville, Eliot, Cummings, Shaw, and Tennessee Williams.

What this strange crowd has in common is simply that they have each seen something wrong, or pathetic, or humorous with the way the Christian story gets itself realized in the theatre of our common human experience. The core of the story, its central affirmations, is not commonly the target of their attack or their customary sardonic comment. The story says that God has acted for man's healing, that this action became concrete in an Incarnation, that in consequence human life has available a new relation to God, a new light for seeing, a new fact and center for thinking, a new ground for forgiving and loving, a new context for acting in this world. A surprising number of this company have got that pretty straight.

The burden of the literary comment is rather in the area *between* God's action and the " Christian " behavior of the human beings supposedly determined by it. The integral character of the action seems to get lost or distorted, its organic wholeness fragmented into morsels of accredited mores. And because the authority and solemnity of the action is so vast, the failure, brokenness, hypocrisy, and humorless insensitivity of the human response provide so rich a fare for the artist as critic. It is this hiatus between the transcendent authority and origination of the ethical pattern and an all too earthly performance (often conjoined with pontifical refusal to admit as much) which is the substance of the literary commentary. *That* is what Boccaccio is documenting; Montaigne quietly smiling about; Blake bitter about. Hardy unfolds the pathetic, mad occasionalism of common incidents in such a way as to construct an attack upon the Christian assumption that God cares at all about human lives; Shaw slashes away at the ambiguities hidden away under the cover of men's moral pretensions.

That men do not perform as they profess, that

they do not live up to their announced belief—this is old and obvious stuff, and there is a sufficient literature of admonition on the subject. But the smile, or the anger, or the sardonic twist in the literature here recalled delivers a quite different and a deeper judgment. It's as if these writers suspected that some basic and horrible *misunderstanding* had occurred between God the Speaker and man the hearer. Soren Kierkegaard called it an "acoustical illusion" whereby man accredits his acoustical echo with original authority! Men set about being "ethical" under the impact and continuing power of the Gospel, within the tutorial structure of the Church, and in the light of those ordered presentations of obligation called Moral Theology. And on the way they burn witches; fight wars out of mixed purposes which they persuade themselves are not mixed at all; use venerable and holy names to designate institutions and practices which they dare not criticize, lest they threaten worldly securities; pose, posture, lie, and generally pervert the organic integrity of the life of faith.

All of this is but a way of saying that efforts to gain the truth about the Christian ethical life must operate in the two stadia of our existence as Christian men. There is the "mighty cloud of witnesses" who ensconce our unfolding days in their embattled song of faith, their firm hymn of confession and testimony to the salvatory power of God in Jesus Christ. And there is that other stadium, as big as the world, as long as man's recorded history, incessantly talking back to

> . . . the burthen of the mystery,
> . . . the heavy and the weary weight
> Of all this unintelligible world. . . .

And, between delight and despair, creating forms in language, in visual arts, and in music in which, as Mr. Peter Viereck puts it, man scrawls across his fluctuant scene the defiant " Kilroy was here! "

It is an act of almost humane piety which moves me to record here how great is the debt owed by the teacher of ethics to the company of his fellows who attend his soberer efforts with their disconcerting observations. In my own experience Miss Jane Austen has been a particularly infuriating person! Just when her age, in her tight little island, was convinced that most human problems if not in the bag were on the way to it—everything ordered, civilized, proportional—she turned loose her light, unengaged, girlish, and terribly penetrating laughter upon the whole performance! She exposed, not with a Shavian club or Trollope's broad, humorous gesture, but with genteel pricks of a knitting needle, as it were, the absurd incongruities between form and fact, the dear delusions so sweetly anesthetic to a conventional society.

This amazing spinster is an instance of the fundamentally ethical nature of the craft of the artist. The task of the artist, as artist, is not to declare directly the Gospel of God; it is rather to speak the truth about the life of man, to let real cats out of phoney bags. That is what Stendal does in the *Red and the Black*, Dostoevskii in *The Brothers Karamazov*, and Tennessee Williams in *Cat on a Hot Tin Roof*. These remind all ordered placidity that living truth is tougher than composure, that man has a gallant, godly habit of shattering, on solider ground again to build—that cracked conclusions are the casualties of his human career.

I had not been driven so deeply into the center of the ethical teaching of Jesus, had I in professorial retreat kept at arm's length this company of man's confessors. Nor would I so surely feel, as I do, that the Christian Gospel is both profounder in its analysis of the ambiguous ethical self, and alone adequate to what this analysis discloses, had I not had my ethical perceptions made articulate in the labors of the artist.

There is, for an example, Herman Melville. *Redburn* is an account in which the problem of the good and the evil, and all the disguises of both, is recorded in a young man's growing up in the wide world of men. *Moby Dick* is a wild novel in which the problem is stated with a symbolical clarity unmatched in American literature. But long after the maniacal fury of Moby Dick, when Melville in the autumnal calm of his last months groped toward an answer and felt the shape of it to be the ancient form of a cross, and a crucified man—*Billy Budd* was written, and laid away in a drawer.

W. H. Auden, in his short poem, *Herman Melville*, has celebrated the quiet, inward drama of Melville's movement toward maturity, and I close this first lecture with some lines from it.

> Towards the end he sailed into an extraordinary
>   mildness . . . .
>
> Goodness existed: that was the new knowledge
> His terror had to blow itself quite out
> To let him see it . . . .
>
> Evil is unspectacular and always human,
> And shares our bed and eats at our own table,
> And we are introduced to Goodness every day,
> Even in drawing-rooms among a crowd of faults;
> He has a name like Billy and is almost perfect
> But wears a stammer like a decoration:
> And every time they meet the same thing has to
>   happen;
> It is the Evil that is helpless like a lover
> And has to pick a quarrel and succeeds,
> And both are openly destroyed before our eyes . . . .
>
> And all the stars above him sang as in his childhood
> "All, all is vanity," but it was not the same;
> For now the words descended like the calm of
>   mountains—

—Nathaniel had been shy because his love was
selfish—
But now he cried in exultation and surrender
" The Godhead is broken like bread. We are the
pieces."

And sat down at his desk and wrote a story.[2]

The Shape of the Engendering Deed

A BRIEF look at the three terms of the title of this lecture, against the concepts of organism and morphology set forth in the first lecture, will advance us quickly and clearly into its substance. The term *shape* is used here to recall and to assert: to recall the organic and total nature of the biblical way of speaking about God and man; to assert that the same type of discourse must be continued into the field of ethics if confusion is to be avoided.

The term *deed* is used in order to bring into focus that understanding of the Scriptures which accepts them as records and witnesses to what the living God has actually done in creation, redemption, and sanctification. The reception of this deed in man's mental and moral career has, to be sure, to be related to general terms in man's vocabulary of high abstraction. And for that reason it is necessary and proper to speak of the idea of God, the structure of the God-concept, the philosophy of religion, the psychology of faith, the cultic character of the form of the Church. Each of these terms designates a discipline, some quite new, others very old, in which data and methods proper to these fields of enquiry are employed in an effort to understand the content of the specifically biblical terms, and evaluate their meaning. But the term *deed of God* is calculatedly chosen to invite the mind to ponder the particularity of the biblical speech so that the intrinsically specific quality of its referents may be grasped and honored.

The term *engendering* is used to assert that the organic relationship between God and man structured into existence in creation, incarnated into absolute involvement in redemption, persists and inwardly determines the realm of sanctification, that is, the field of Christian ethics. God's deed does not simply call, or present a pattern in front of, or evoke, or demonstrate. It *engenders*; that is, it brings into existence lives bred by its originative character. Only terms which denote a quasi-biological-organic relationship are adequate to elaborate in terms of ethics what is declared of the reality of the Christian God in his work for man's situation.

It was the perception of the necessity that all Christian speech begin with what God does and gives that moved a towering Christian scholar to make the astonishingly simple and profound statement that to be a Christian is to accept what God gives.

What God gives is the theme of the Bible. This going out from Himself in creative and redemptive action toward men is, within the Bible itself, the basic meaning of the *Word of God*. " By the Word of the Lord were the heavens made "; " The Word became flesh and dwelt among us." The Scriptures are called Word of God because they are a literature in which alone this action of the Word of God is recorded, witnessed to, and—in the hearing of the message there contained—continued. It is not strange, therefore, that the form of the Scriptures should be a drama. For drama is the form appropriate for the enunciation of movement, action, doing.

If, then, the Scriptures are a literature which depicts the action of God, is it possible so to peer into the remembered and recorded action in such a way as to evoke from among the multitudinous events, responses, utterances, the massive shape of the entire complex? It is in the confidence that this is possible that I have entitled this lecture " The Shape of the Engendering Deed."

The Bible tells man who he is and how he has gotten into his predicament. To tell him this is the intention of the stories of creation, rebellion, fall. The very dramatic character of these accounts indicates that they are God's revelation about himself, about man, nature, the ground of human community —all of these separately and in their relationship. A drama is never a slice out of life content to be only that. It is a section which reveals, like the tissue section under the eye of the pathologist, the condition of the entire organism. What is revealed in this biblical section of the situation far transcends the ancient persons, places, and events which are its

occasion. The Creator and his creature, God-will and
man-will, love creative of fellowship and lust breed-
ing estrangement, man in the garden of his peace and
man self-evicted into the relationship to nature which
now along with man "groans in travail, waiting
. . . ." These are the mighty dramatic themes which
swirl in a multitude of tender and terrible shapes
through the record of God's ancient people.

Books of prophecy, books of passionate and con-
templative song, books of history and chronicle, all,
if we listen for the motif that grounds their wonderful
variety, sing out the theme of holy conflict: God-
will and man-will. Not in abstract form or fictional-
ized persons, but richly rooted in human life and
history, in nature, and in social life, the conflict unfolds the undeviating self-giving of God and the
career of the gift among men. Old Testament history
has a grand pattern; it is the weary rhythm of rebellion, repentance, and return; and over and over
again the rhythm repeats itself. In the book of the
Judges the writer seems actually to have managed
his historical materials to accent the repetitive mo-
notony of this pattern. Old Testament song and literature of devotion swings always and with opulent
variation about the two poles: God's relentless gift
of himself in steadfast love and man's desperate
shadow-flight from love's undismissible grounding of
his life. Old Testament prophecy, attached to anec-

dotal history at a thousand points, and made articulate in many voices and many keys, has nevertheless a simple pattern. The figure of the prophet is the un-silenceable recollection of man's structurally given existence before God; and the up-welling voice of the prophet, through crusts of assumed independence and national self-sufficiency, through proudly contrived historical securities and subtly imagined individual safety, is the grave, recalling voice of God. The " whither shall I flee " of the individual singer has its large prophetic counterpart in the word addressed to the whole people, " I have called thee by thy name, thou art mine."

In the Old Testament drama God's love and mercy are never presented as simply God's feeling about apostate man. Love and mercy are rather the forms in which God's resolute will-to-restoration presses upon man. The love of God is a loving will; and the outstretched arm of the Eternal has many aspects. It is both beckoning and judging; but it is always there—the Creator of the drama, the Holy One with whom man has inescapably to do. As the Old Testament literature moves on toward its close the conflict tightens in both divine and mortal terms. In divine terms the assault of God tightens; hope is condensed from a holy nation to a remnant, and finally to the form of a Servant of the Lord. In mortal terms, the drama of alienation depicts man, ingenious in evasion and flight and self-deception, able at the last only to cry, " Oh, that thou wouldst rend the heavens, that thou wouldst come down."

Only against this background can one understand why the Evangelists of the New Testament surround the nativity of Jesus Christ with heavenly messengers and choirs, poetic condensations of the hope of Israel, the Virgin's lyrical song of acceptance. Everything seems to stand still and all things are bathed in luminous light when the new deed of God occurs in Jesus Christ. It is not in fact a strange deed if beheld from above. For God's undeviating will-to-restoration but assumes here a decisive tactic of mortal involvement. But seen from below this tactic is unique, utterly singular. For here, claim the Scriptures, is God himself in salvatory, that is, restorative action at the point and at the level of the original rupture. When the Fourth Gospel declares that the Word became flesh and dwelt among us, the new deed of God in Christ is declared in clearest terms; the involvement of the Holy Will can come to no closer engagement than this: *flesh* which is what I am, *among us* which is where I am!

Is it possible to speak of the career of Jesus of Nazareth in such a way as responsibly to include in a simple pattern the total self-giving of God, which Jesus himself, the apostles, and the faith of the Church, have declared to be the meaning of the total deed? The Scriptures themselves declare this to be possible; and, indeed, the earliest declarations of the community of faith achieve this simplicity. The parables of the Kingdom turn about a common center: God in a fresh and decisive way is at work in His world. The miracle-stories are dramatic signs which underline the impact of this liberating action of God. And the teaching of Jesus which accompanies these " signs " has its center in his announcement that a news event no less astonishing than the creation of the Cosmos has occurred. Its occurrence has brought Him with it, and thus made itself available to men on earth. The Gospels present the intention and work of Jesus in terms of an actual power-conflict in which the will of God does desperate battle with the tyrants of life that hold man in a dungeon of estrangement, cut off from his proper life, his proper ground. What these terms point to is an action of God in Jesus Christ, whereby everything that operates to separate God and man has, from God's side and by the gracious assault of his deed in Christ, been overcome.

It is within the orbit of this gracious and aggressive overcoming activity of God that the death and resurrection of Jesus is to be understood. Outside that orbit, understood only from below, that death engenders not peace but despair, not joy but bitterness. So viewed it constitutes an appalling confirmation of ultimate futility. But when understood from above, as the supreme function of God's will-to-restoration ("God was in Christ, reconciling the world unto Himself")—the death of Christ is seen as the triumphant work of restoration operative precisely at the point of desolation. In the deed of Christ on Calvary there takes place the absolute involvement of God with the absolute tragedy of man. "Herein is love, not that we love God, but that he loved us."

If the drama of restoration were to end at this point, it would accomplish no restoration. To be joined in my cell-of-dying by no other than God himself would but magnify the private pathos of mutability to the dimensions of cosmic tragedy.

"But God hath raised him up!" The meaning of that declaration of the primitive Christian community is by no means exhausted in the episode of the resurrection. The resurrection is, to be sure, the center to which such an assertion points, but the circumference of it embraces the entire God-man relationship for all time. This statement declares that the entire movement of God's loving will-to-restoration, having taken the form of the Christ-servant and having swept down into the nadir of the human situation in time and place, sweeps on, and through, and beyond it. The resurrection is the sign of the victory of Christ over death; it is also the victory-sign flying over the entire history-involved assault of God upon man's sin and alienation. The man who is the Incarnation of God's will-to-restoration disappears in death and darkness—and then reappears. It was this reappearance that gathered faith about itself, created the community of believers called the Church, and drew up into its mighty meaning all the smaller and partial meanings that emerged in tentativeness during the days of his teaching.

The term shape, or morphology, is used to speak *both* of what God does in his action in Christ, and what this Christ-action accomplishes in the believer, for two reasons. First, to insure that the continuity between the once-done deed and its continuous working be clearly designated in language; and, second, to point to the large wholeness of the action—to liberate our comprehension of the scope, movement, and pattern of what God does in Christ from imprisonment in isolated episodes of the drama. There are facts, both in the biblical record, and in the history of its interpretation, which seduce the mind from the perception of this central pattern. So richly does the biblical literature speak of man's life and fortunes, miseries and delights, so panoramic is the scope of its utterances, so inwardly suggestive and fascinating its presentation of separate episodes, that the center of the multiform drama can be obscured. It is the chief utility of contemporary biblical studies that this fragmentation has been largely overcome, and the theocentric character of the literature brought again into focus. The story is about God! And no facet of it glows in its intended color unless it be placed under that primary source of light. God is the initiator of the basic and permeative thrust, God's will-to-restoration is the dynamic power in all movement, the implacable holy love of God brackets all accounts of man's nature, his career, and his destiny. Only this angle of vision can draw up into intelligibility and coherence the myriad episodes of the story.

A particularly sharp instance of this central force is the 139th Psalm. It is there confessed that no effort of man to know himself, find himself, be himself, is a viable possibility outside the God-relationship. God's knowledge of man is prior to man's knowledge of himself; and to know ourself to be known by God is asserted to be the precondition of all wisdom and all peace.

> O Lord, thou hast searched me and known me!
> Thou knowest when I sit down and when I rise up;
>   thou discernest my thoughts from afar.
> (Ps. 139:1-2)

Flight from this prevenient knowledge leads through anxiety to frustration, to despair. Man's spirit has a three-dimensional possibility for escape—up, down, and out.

Whither shall I go from thy Spirit?
Or whither shall I flee from thy presence?
If I ascend to heaven, thou art there!
If I make my bed in Sheol, thou art there!
If I take the wings of the morning and dwell in the
    uttermost parts of the sea,
even there thy hand shall lead me,
    and thy right hand shall hold me. (Ps. 139:7-10)

Even the twilight of the subconscious and the night
of the unconscious offers no obliterating anodyne.

If I say, "Let only darkness cover me,
    and the light about me be night,"
even the darkness is not dark to thee,
    the night is bright as the day;
    for darkness is as light with thee.
For thou didst form my inward parts,
    thou didst knit me together in my mother's
    womb . . .
Thou knowest me right well;
    my frame was not hidden from thee
when I was being made in secret
    intricately wrought in the depths of the earth.
                                    (Ps. 139:11-15)

The same acknowledgment of an aggressive theocentric pattern, the same largeness of treatment, is
necessary to indicate the accomplishment of this deed
in history. If we ponder the way the early church

declared the reality of its liberated and restored life in God we are immediately struck by an obviously non-accidental congruity between the shape of God's deed and the terms used to declare the shape of the restored life of the community. The abundance of dramatic terms, and the secondary employment of spiritual, moral, religious terms, in such declarations is astounding. " Do you not know that all of us who have been baptized into Jesus Christ were baptized into his death? We were buried therefore with him by baptism into death, so that as Christ was raised from the dead by the glory of the Father, we too might walk in newness of life. For if we have been united with him in a death like his, we shall certainly be united with him in a resurrection like his— so you also must consider yourselves dead to sin and alive to God in Christ Jesus."

In his letter to the community of believers at Philippi Paul unfolds with unparalleled clarity the re-enactment–dynamics of his life as " a man in Christ." With great boldness the Apostle transposes into terms descriptive of his own life the stark historical events of the life of his Lord—suffering, death, resurrection, a new life. " For his sake I have suffered the loss of all things, and count them as refuse, in order that I may gain Christ and be found in him, not having a righteousness of my own, based on law, but that which is through faith in Christ, the righteousness from God that depends on faith; so that I may know him and the power of his resurrection, and may share his suffering, becoming like him in his death, that if possible I may attain the resurrection from the dead."

New Testament commentators, from Origen to the present, have been struck by the fact that the theological and ethical terms of Paul's speech are instant counterparts in the experience of *redemption* of the recorded cultural facts of the Synoptic record. This record is, by Paul, transposed into terms descriptive of new, operative vitalities in the life of the believer.[1]

Language like the foregoing, which is not singular but quite representative of the New Testament testimony of the new life of the community in Christ—such language is dramatic in the highest degree. The Christian life is here understood as a re-enactment from below on the part of men of the shape of the revelatory drama of God's holy will in Jesus Christ. The dynamics of this life are not abstractly indicated, nor is its creative power psychologically explicated. Suffering, death, burial, resurrection, a new life—these are actualities which plot out the arc of God's self-giving deed in Christ's descent and death and ascension; and precisely *this same shape of grace*, in its recapitulation within the life of the believer and the faithful community, is the nuclear matrix which grounds and unfolds as the Christian life.

The New Testament, to be sure, has abundant material which is immediately ethical: admonition, teaching, counsel, specific moral advice, minute directions for behavior in solitude and in the fellowship of the community. But the pastoral assumption back of all such teaching is precisely this continuity of the Christ-Life and the Christian life. Particularly illuminating is the situation to which St. Paul addresses himself in the Philippian letter. " So if there is any encouragement in Christ, any incentive of love, any participation in the Spirit—Have this mind among yourselves, which you have in Christ Jesus, who, though he was in the form of God, did not count equality with God a thing to be grasped—humbled himself and became obedient unto death . . . ."

This passage is a microcosm in which can be glimpsed the dynamics, the structure, and the sequence of Christian ethics. The Apostle feels impelled to address a concrete situation in the Philippian Christian community. No sooner, however, has he stated the problem and announced what pattern must prevail, than he buries the roots of the concrete requirement in nothing smaller than the mighty deed of God in Christ. Hence, the strange, " high christological " utterance occurring in the apostolic rejoinder to an earthy, disruptive demonstration of egocentricity. This passage gains in authority if, as Lohmeyer asserts, its represents Paul's recollection of a

37

passage from the oral tradition very early fashioned by the vitalities of liturgical speech into these memorable rhythms. There is no need, as troubled but unimaginative commentators have sometimes caused themselves, to search extra-circumstantial sources for the original home of this resounding passage. The ripples of life's concrete decisions are continuous with the huge tidal wave of God's will in Christ; and any effort to articulate a Christian ethics apart from this enactment–re-enactment structure operates with ideas foreign to the New Testament.

During the months the substance of these pages was maturing and the category of shape more and more clearly emerging as the only operational idea adequate to New Testament discourse, there was being made available to English readers, in translation, Dietrich Bonhoeffer's essays on Christian ethics. From this work the following quotation is taken:

> . . . the Holy Scriptures speak of formation in a sense which is at first entirely unfamiliar to us. Their primary concern is not with the forming of a world by means of places and programs. Wherever they speak of forming they are concerned only with the one form which has overcome the world, the form of Jesus Christ. Formation can come only from this form. But here again it is not a question of applying directly to the world the teachings of Christ or what are referred to as

38

Christian principles, so that the world might be formed in accordance with these. On the contrary, formation comes only by being drawn in into the form of Jesus Christ. It comes only as formation in His likeness, as *conformation* with the unique form of him who was made man, was crucified, and rose again.[2]

In the history of Christian thought there is no one who has so fully explicated the Christian life as a new formation engendered by the Form of the deed of God in Christ as Irenaeus. The following, from his *The Demonstration of the Apostolic Preaching* is characteristic of his method. Irenaeus operates with a series of dramatic parallels by which he illustrates how the Incarnation in history overcomes man's moral defeat. The second Adam recovers the lost dominions of the first Adam; Mary, the second Eve, overcomes by her obedience the apostasy of the first Eve; the obedient second Adam in the garden of Gethsemane overcomes the disobedient first Adam in the garden of Eden, and so on.

And, because in the original formation of Adam all of us were tied and bound up with death through his disobedience, it was right that through the obedience of Him who was made man for us we should be released from death: and because death reigned over the flesh, it was right that through the flesh it should lose its force and let man go free from its oppression. So the *Word was made flesh*, that, through that very flesh which sin had ruled and dominated, it should lose its force and be no longer in us. And therefore our Lord took that same original formation as (His) entry into flesh, so that He might draw near and contend on behalf of the fathers, and conquer by Adam that which by Adam had stricken us down.[3]

Fragments of this New Testament morphology (whereby the recapitulation-character of the Christian life is symbolized by the parallel structure of the biblical events) linger on in the liturgies of those churches which cherish continuity. The preface to the Holy Communion which is read during Lent is as follows: " Who on the Tree of the Cross didst give salvation unto mankind; that whence death arose, thence life also might rise again: and that he who by a Tree once overcame, might likewise by a Tree be overcome, through Christ our Lord; through whom with Angels etc. . . . ."

God does the redemptive and restorative deed; and God creates the response which is man's reception of it. So adequate are the God-initiated vitalities there deployed that Christian ethics is under no necessity to import into its basic structure anything at all from the rich and ennobling tradition of philosophical thought about the good, the valuable, and so on.

This is by no means to deny that philosophical ethical reflection has served by its work of analysis and the destruction of illusions, to sensitize men to the centrality and complexity of ethical problems. The continuing philosophical concern with the idea of natural law, inconclusive but persistent, is an instance of the fact that all efforts by man to know what he ought to do, drive him into trans-individual areas of his existence. Plato and Pascal have so illuminated the ambiguity of the moral personality as to place all men permanently in their debt. The truth they disclose may be submerged by arrogant pretensions or evaded by thoughtlessness, but when events revivify moral gravity this silenced truth erupts again to judge, illumine, humiliate into openness. The enormous literature of philosophical ethics is in this sense a profound and moving *confessional* which confirms the relevance of the radical drama of redemption which the Christian faith declares.

It is definitely not asserted here that the philosophical enterprise has no relevancy to the concrete tasks of Christian ethics; it is simply asserted that the faculty of reflection when functioning within the structure of the Christian ethical life must not betray that structure. The entire sequence from God's act, the re-enactment in the believer, the precise concrete duty of obedience in the tangled criss-cross of obligations that life presents—all of this is the old and ever new realm of moral philosophy. But just as it is a proper task of philosophy to reflect upon the nature and meaning of man's enquiry about God without in that enquiry coming to the knowledge of God, so it is proper to philosophical ethics to insure that the ethical implications of man's incessant enquiry about God be not ignored.

If, as we have asserted, the *shape* of the deed of God and the shape of its response is dramatically presented in the Bible, it is possible with equal clarity to discern the *content* of God's work in the Christ-deed? This is, indeed, possible, but perception of it has been clouded by a prevailing disposition in Biblical interpretation. This disposition, characterized by the dominance in popular understanding of Jesus as essentially an exemplar of humane benevolence and spirituality, has for several decades now been brought under radical criticism and reconstruction in theological and biblical studies. These studies have had slight effect upon the temper of Christian thought in the ordinary American parish. As a result the ethical reconstruction which must inevitably follow upon the repudiation of a moralistic and religious-sentimental understanding of the Gospels has not been envisioned.

What is the content of the Christ-deed, which deed is to be understood as redemptive and restorative? If one consults the works on Christian ethics which are largely influential in this decade, one discovers that the reconstruction of the biblical portrait of Christ, which has been so powerful a feature of twentieth century Protestant thought, has simply not reached out and inwardly controlled our understanding of ethics. The strength of Christ which is primarily celebrated in these works, is love. At first sight this judgment seems unassailable, for surely He manifested the strength of love, demanded it of His disciples, and empowered them for its exercise.

The discernment of this strength of love has provided the motif for interpretations of the Christian life all the way from Adolf Harnack to Reinhold Niebuhr. Adolf Harnack declared that Jesus recognized love as the single root and motive, as the entire moral principle, of man's life.

> He knows no other, and love itself, whether it takes the form of love of one's neighbor or of one's enemy, or the love of the Samaritan, is of one kind only. It must completely fill the soul; it is what remains when the soul dies to itself.[4]

Reinhold Niebuhr, despite his distinguished participation in the recovery of biblical realism which is so notable an aspect of current Christian thought, is in fundamental agreement with Harnack. Central to his argument is the phrase, " The absolutism and perfectionism of Jesus' love ethic." [5]

43

We shall get a true answer to our question about the content of Jesus' deed only when we bring this entire tradition of "love ethic" under radical question. There are many terms which indicate the innermost fire in the person and work and demand of Jesus, and love, to be sure, is one of these. Others are faith, peace, joy, hope. Each of these terms is a function of what animates them all: his career is an utterly unique and monumental realization of a human life utterly determined by the God-relationship. One must stand in awe and openness before this fact—and interpret every term declarative of it as dragging the mind into its depth. Love, for instance, is never commanded for its own sake. It is not an absolute. God is the absolute One; and the strength of love is in the love of God and the love of the neighbor in God. The unity of Jesus' person is in the fulness of his own being in his God-relationship, his absolute relation to the Absolute. Both quantitative and qualitative analysis of the Gospels reveals no other constant and central power. Professor Richard Niebuhr says very justly:

> For Jesus there is no other finally love-worthy being, no other ultimate object of devotion, than God: He is the father; there is none good save God; He alone is to be thanked; His kingdom alone is to be sought. Hence the love of God in Jesus' character and teaching is not only compati-

44

ble with anger but can be a motive to it, as when He sees the Father's house made into a den of thieves, or the Father's children outraged. Hence, it is also right and possible to underscore the significance of this virtue in Jesus, while at the same time one recognizes that according to the synoptic Gospels, He emphasized in conduct and in teaching the virtues of faith in God and humility before Him much more than love.[6]

When in the Pauline literature we confront a vital working out of what the response to God actually was in the Christian community, we become aware that the re-enactment of the Christ-life from below is in fact a tremendous drama of *faith*. It is not possible to state too strongly that the life of the believer is for Paul the actual invasion of the total personality by the Christ-life. So pervasive and revolutionary is this displacement and bestowal that terms like influence, example, command, value, are utterly incapable of even suggesting its power and its vitally recreating force. The Apostle is therefore forced to create for this experienced work of God done in Christ and actualized in faith, a quite personal vocabulary. Efforts to explicate this life-in-Christ according to philosophical and psychological concepts deliver only a series of generalizations completely inadequate to the facts which inform and ring out of the man's words and works.

For me to live is Christ—if any one is in Christ, he is a new creation, the old has passed away, the new has come—it is no longer I who live, but Christ who lives in me, and the life I now live in the flesh I live by faith in the Son of God who loved me and gave himself for me—For you have died, and your life is hid with Christ in God.[7]

In St. Paul's faith-obedience, the commandment of love to God and love to neighbor *is transposed in terms of faith*. Faith, for Paul, is the comprehensive term used to designate the life-from-below which is the creation of the whole response of the deeds and the commands of God in Christ.

This transposition whereby love from above is received, interiorized, and actualized from below in terms of *faith*, has about it nothing arbitrary or accidental. For only faith is a large enough term to point to the total commitment of the whole person which is required by the character of the revelation. The very strangeness of the deed of a God who in concrete Incarnation in the earth-scene of man's death and lovelessness dies death out of its ancient dominion, and loves love into the supreme activity of God—this very strangeness evokes as adequate to itself nothing less than a totality response which is called faith.

When one seeks for the power of God in Christ he becomes aware that he stands before a quite new and astounding possibility for human life inwardly achieved, variously expounded, dramatically illustrated in the life of Jesus himself. Faith, love, obedience, joy, hope—these are not separate virtues, qualities, or exhibitions of the fire of the God-relationship for Jesus; they are, rather, the rich vocabulary of an organic oneness with the Father announcing and doing God's will in the living continuity of obedience.

It is only in the acknowledgment of this organic continuity that the words, works, commands of Jesus can be understood so as to supply the Church both with its elemental Christology and its ethical form, force, and style.

The development of western Christology along lines which subordinate the biblical strand known as the servant-Christology to another strand known as logos-Christology has made it difficult for western Christianity to pass organically from Christology to ethics. In recent works, in Christology and in general New Testament interpretation, this is being recognized. The patristic necessity to explicate the person and work of Christ in terms appropriate to the world of the west has powerfully overlaid the primitive Christian servant-Christology with layer after layer of ontological speculation; and the result has been to obscure the functional strand in the New Testament testimony to Christ. So strong has been the insistence upon the assertion that Christ does what he does because he is who he is, that inadequate attention has been paid to the testimony that he also is affirmed to be who he is because he does what he does.

The book of the Acts is here a primary source. In the Acts Jesus is proclaimed Christ and Lord in virtue of his work as obedient, utter accomplisher of the will of God. "So let all the house of Israel understand beyond a doubt that God has made him both Lord and Christ, this very Jesus whom you have crucified." (2:36) "The God of Abraham, the God of Jacob, the God of our fathers glorified Jesus his servant." (3:12) "It was for you that God raised up his servant." (3:26)

Christian ethics is *Christological* ethics, not in the sense that such ethics are correlates derived from propositions about Christ, but in the sense that they are faithful re-enactments of that life. In the Sermon on the Mount there is dramatized this obedient life in the bestowed and accepted love of God. The fulfillment and transformation of the entire Old Testament God-relationship is here clearly recorded. Here, as in every teaching, parable, miracle of Jesus, is disclosed a faith active in love which cracks all rabbinical patterns, transcends every statutory solidification of duty, breaks out of all systematic schematizations of the good—and out of the living, perceptive, restorative passion of faith enfolds in its embrace the fluctuant, incalculable, novel emergents of human life.

48

Concerning the persistent desire to set forth the meaning of Christian ethics in terms of the " principles of Jesus," two things must be said. In the first place, the methodology which works with principles subtly belies the very nature of the truth of Christianity. The truth of Christianity is neither abstract nor propositional; it is the truth of God incarnate in a person. " Grace and truth came by Jesus Christ "— " I am the way, the truth, and the life . . . ." Truth thus acted out and bestowed in historical existence is intrinsically incapable of transmission in terms of " principles." And in the second place, the desire to extrude principles from the Christ-life may be a form of man's hidden longing to cool into palpable ingots of duty the living stuff of love, and so dismiss ". . . the Holy One with whom we have to do . . . ."

The words of the Sermon on the Mount have been and remain an embarrassment to every effort to derive Christian ethics from Jesus according to principles of ethics. The style of speech in these words of Jesus is revelatory of the ground and the living activity of the ethics of faith. Professor Karl Heim has called our attention to the nonlegislative character of these utterances, which continue to fascinate the mind with system-disintegrating and disquieting power. These words do not constitute legislation replacing the old which, clearly put forth, can then be actualized by any devout and resolute person. The *occasional* character of these utterances is the clue to the non-legal, inexhaustible, principle-transcending intent and power of them. They are like lightning flashes of God's love-gift and command which, here and there, in this instance and now in that, flash over and brilliantly illuminate the moving sea below. Or, like a gull that flies smoothly over the turbulent sea and then suddenly in a quick, sure dart swoops down and picks up something out of the waters, resumes its flight and soars on.

These teachings of Jesus are not the legislation of love (the very term contradicts the nature of love) but are rather the paradigms of love. System is proper to the inorganic; the living has a characteristic *style*. Jesus in his teaching did not attempt a systematization or exhaustive coverage of all areas of human behavior. He did not, after the manner proper to philosophers of the good, attempt to articulate general principles which, once stated, have then only to be beaten out in corollaries applicable to the variety of human life. He speaks, rather, of God and of man and of the human community in a relational and a living fashion, and on the way, in the course of his speech swoops down, now here, now there; picks up some detail, situation, instance of human pathos, error, pride, holds it up for a moment, and then moves on.

This same uncalculated *style* is characteristic of the deeds of Jesus. His words and deeds belong together.

50

Both are signs which seek to fasten our attention upon the single vitality which was the ground and purpose of his life—his God-relationship. His parables, in this sense, are spoken miracles; his miracles are acted parables. His aphorisms are verbal apertures into his mission's meaning. In the fulfillment of this mission He proceeded through the countryside as a herald, judge, and teacher, but also as a healer and a helper. And His healing and His helping have the same gull-like, unanticipated immediacy as His tales. He confronted suffering, physical and mental torment, and regarded it as a characteristic mark of this world; only God's kingdom will show once more the finished creation, untouched by pain. Jesus' cures are not done in the course of a planned mission whose purpose was to cure the ills of as many sick persons as possible. If so, we should expect more of it, more teaching about healing, and a more systematic extension of it throughout the land.

We find nothing of the sort. Rather, the pattern is —*now here, now there!* This one He touches, others He does not. His cures do not signify an arbitrary anticipation of this kingdom, which no man knows when God will send. They indicate, rather, the present and pressing existence of the available power of the kingdom, now. They, too, are signs conveying the proclamation, the power, and the promise of the kingdom. They assert and demonstrate that the kingdom is on the way, that God, through the One whom he has sent is already permitting the splendor of the kingdom to shine out, now here, now there. Now, a certain centurion—now, by chance, a priest was going down that road—and behold, a man with a withered hand! The uncontrived, episodic nature of these happenings, the way in which each is made to glow in the reflected light and instance forth the power of God's pressing kingdom, is sufficient indication that they are sparks arching out from a central impact. The kingdom is the power; and these convulsive episodes are its transforming and revivifying works.

The *occasional* character of Jesus' words and works, which is asserted to be the point of entrance into the style of the obedient life, may appear to be so fragmentary and fugitive a pattern as to be useless for the requirements of present need and the urgent necessity to articulate a clear duty to the Christian community. This protest can so persuasively occur only because a persistent moralization of Jesus' deeds and commands has almost completely incapacitated men for immediate engagement with his living voice and work. A theological method more concerned with propositional coherence than with the description of historical reality and the communication of the personal vitality of Jesus has succeeded in making virtually inaccessible to Christian ethical discourse the actual facts of Jesus' own realization of the ethics of the God-relationship.

A second objection is, that insistence upon the peculiar style of Jesus' life, his repudiation of principles in favor of a vital pattern of response, may drive the question "What ought I to do?" so deeply down into the center of Jesus' own life as to destroy clarity by sheer depth, divert from present duties by the very glory of the New Testament portrait. This apprehension discloses a grave possibility, to be sure, and must be confronted. But the more clearly it is confronted, the more certain it is that for Christian ethics there is no other way. The risk belongs to the glory. The Good Samaritan stands there, and cannot be removed or forgotten by an ever-so-understandable desire that we might replace this thundering demonstration of the immediacy of obedient love by a clearer and less disquieting catalog of duties. Jesus not only told the story of the Samaritan, but added the absolue word that men ought to go out and do likewise. This command in the context of the story grips us, as Soren Kierkegaard says, "closer than a wrestler." And it is precisely within that grip that Jesus did act! He did intervene in the sphere of illness and suffering, and set Himself, now here, now there, against the structure and the course of this world. By these occasional lightning flashes and gull-like swoops into concrete situations, He released old captivities and opened up new possibilities for human lives. The kingdom of God " in your midst " was concretely certified by liberations, restoring deeds of love.

The absolute character of the ethical commands recorded in the Sermon on the Mount, and in other fragments in the New Testament, must be taken seriously. Critical studies of the Gospel record, which strongly suggest that it reflects here and there primitive Christian preaching fused with the words of Jesus, has multiplied the evidence that these sayings are the words of the Lord. Nor is it proper so to interpret St. Paul's words about the " overcoming " of the law in such a way as to efface or otherwise avoid coming to terms with these statements. The 13th chapter of I Corinthians is a Pauline confirmation of these ethical commands, not a " spiritual " substitute for them.

A clue to their interpretation is available if we assume that they are addressed to men as the terms of a parable are. They are aimed at the same form of cognition on the part of the hearer. They endlessly fascinate and trouble the mind and the conscience, spill out boundless creative power precisely because they inwardly resist all efforts to capture their vitality in systems of ethics.

These commands were uttered to men who, in all likelihood, were no better or worse than the rest of us. If these commands are not conceptually manageable they are not thereby unintelligible or nonsensical. The Speaker intended an explosive result—and nineteen hundred years have confirmed His success. As we ponder both the capacity of man to hear God speak, and the demonic capacity of man to settle for less than the mad obedience that God requires, the form of utterance in these commands will appear as the only conceivable way the Word of God to such men as we are could be conveyed. In support of that assertion the following propositions are submitted:

1. An absolute demand is the only verbal form by which to announce and release an *indeterminate* power, communicate an indeterminate promise, diagnose and judge man's indeterminate ability to deceive and excuse himself, enunciate an indeterminate possibility.

2. To be called to stand under the will of God as absolute demand is the only possibility by which to hold lives unconditionally responsible to God, the only way fully to celebrate the Godliness of God.

3. To have to live under the absolute demand is the only way, given man's power of dissimulation and self-deception, to keep life taut with need, open to God's power, under judgment by his justice, indeterminately dependent upon his love, forgiveness, and grace.

4. To have to stand under God's absolute de-

mand is the only way to keep man open to forms and occasions of obedience that the emerging and unpredictable facts of man's involvement in social change constantly present to him for his obedience. Even relative obedience, that is to say, can only sustain itself in the light of the absolute command.

5. Only the absolute demand can sensitize man to occasions for ethical work, and energize him toward even relative achievements. And only such a demand can deliver man, in these achievements, from complacency and pride; prevent him from making an identification of the justice of man and the justice of God.

6. Only the absolute demand has the transcendent freedom to stride forever out in front of all human accomplishments, fresh and powerful with the lure of deeper and more comprehensive goals.

7. The historical-relative requires the Godly-absolute even to see and to seek the better in the existing. Any understanding of the good without God will cease even to be good. Cut off from the absolute the relative ossifies into pride, becomes inert in the memory of past achievements, or makes a sardonic idol out of more and more smooth and profitable adjustments in the social order.

The kingdom of God is not a plan, or a program, or a concept, or an idea. It is a force within whose grip every man is caught; a grip never loosened, but rather having its ultimacy illustrated by every moral achievement and approximate obedience. It is a force, a godly fascination, and veritable *Imago Dei* engraved upon man's social history. The recollective fascination, once having flashed over and personally entered into history with its " signs " to which our Gospels bear witness, can never be forgotten. Its announcement and demonstration that the alienations of human existence in solitude and in society can be healed, and that the lost territory of life in God can be recaptured—this announcement and this demonstration, the root event of all Christian ethical thinking, guarantees that a holy possibility for human life will not cease to disturb, and here and there create new possibilities for it. Uncapturable in a concept, infuriating in its resistance to system, indestructible as a fact of power and a vision of promise, the realization of this life in men's lives is both the burden and the promise of Christian faith.

If the Christian ethical life is in reality the believers' re-enactment of God's action, then it is an absolute necessity of thought that the nature of this eternal drama of gift and response, as wholly determining the reactive ethical life, be clearly seen. It is here contended that such a perception is hindered when love is made the primary term for its designation. God, to be sure, is love; but it is not possible to pass from the love of God to what is required of men without causing our thoughts to pass through and come to terms with the *form* in which this love is revealed to men. The form of the revelation demands a transposition in the understanding whereby one understands that love revealed *in this particular form* begets a response, the proper name for which is *not love but faith*. In the Synoptic Gospels, in the Fourth Gospel, and in the letters of Paul, the vocabulary of response points to faith, not to love, as the generative center. Love, to be sure, is what faith does; it is the fulness and flower of faith. But this dare not blind us to the blunt fact that the " new being " of which the New Testament is the witness, is regularly designated *faith*. Peter at Caesarea-Philippi, the centurion whose son was healed, the woman in the house of Simon the Pharisee, the primacy of the term faith in Paul's exposition of the invasive progress of the Christ-life, the central role of faith in the Fourth Gospel's account of the career of Jesus—in all of these the role ascribed to faith is startlingly obvious.

The supreme revelation of God, who is love, is Jesus. But this Jesus as he appears to sense and sight is an historical fact. Neither to men of His own time and place, nor to men of any other time and place, does His appearance and career guarantee a revelation of God. When, for instance, a disciple exclaims who Jesus is and what is His ultimate meaning for human life, Jesus himself is quick to declare that "flesh and blood" (that is, the sum total of the humanly possible estimate) "have not revealed it unto thee, but my Father which is in heaven."

The historical form of a revelation of that which is neither born of man nor verifiable by history requires that nothing less than the decision of faith shall constitute the form of the response to it. That is to say, the love of God wherewith we are loved can become life in God wherewith we love only when this given-love bears forth its giving-love in the womb of faith.

God and faith belong together as the only possible correlation, given the form of God's revelation in an historical figure and deed. The structure of Christian theology—in which faith is the determinant in all things from the doctrine of God to the doctrine of the good, ethics—arises from this controlling fact: that all gifts from God to man are given in and pass through the historical; and the historical, *qua* historical, can never beget life, certainty, redemption. The historical form of God's redemptive deed compels the faithful form of man's response. No one in the history of Christian thought has seen this more deeply, or permitted it more utterly to determine his life and thought as a Christian, than Luther.

Faith is of things which do not appear. Therefore, that there may be room for faith, it is necessary that all things which are to be believed should be hidden. They cannot, however, be hidden more remotely than under their contrary object, sense, and experience. Thus, when God makes us alive he does it by killing us; when he justifies us he does it by making us guilty; when he carries us up to heaven he does it by leading us down to hell! [8]

Professor George Forell's volume, *Faith Active in Love*, gives a thorough explication and documentation of the relation of love and faith in Luther. The Reformer asks how love of the neighbor can be the fulfilling of the love when we are commanded to love *God* above all things, even above the neighbors! The answer, Luther declares, is given by Christ himself who said that the second Commandment is like unto the first, and Christ makes of love to God and love of one's neighbor an equal love:

And for this reason, first, that God does not need our work and kindness, but points us toward our neighbor that we may do for these what we may wish to do for him. He wants only that we trust Him and hold Him to be God. For even the preaching of His glory and our praising and thanking Him take place on earth so that our neighbor may be converted and brought to God thereby. And yet all this is called love to God,

—yet really to the use and profit of our neighbor
only . . . . Here now a check is given to those
slippery and skipping souls who seek God only
in great and glorious things, who thirst after His
greatness, who bore through heaven and think
that they are serving and loving God by such
noble ways, when all the time they are betraying Him and pass by Him in their neighbors here
on earth in whom He desires to be loved and
honored . . . . For therefore did He put from
Him the form of God and put on the form of a
servant, that He might draw our love for Him
down and fasten it on our neighbors, whom we
leave lying here, and gaze the while into heaven,
thinking to show God great love and service.[9]

There are two reasons why this fundamental fact
of biblically witnessed revelation has got to fight its
way through to us who, within the tradition of the
Reformers, might be expected to be more easily per-
meable to it. First is the fact that the situation in
which Luther and the Reformers articulated the centrality of faith has tended to imprison the meaning of
the term within the situation of the sixteenth century.
When faith, that is to say, is understood exclusively
in terms of an alternative to works, it is both reduced
and intellectualized. It is reduced because it is imprisoned within the category of the individual relation to God and there effectually stifled, so that it

may fail to exercise its creative power throughout the whole of the Christian ethical life. And, second, the assertion that the just shall live by *faith* means also that by faith the just shall *live!* The entire ethical dynamics of this affirmation is intellectualized when its vitality is transposed into theological propositions which are then believed adequately responded to if they win the mind's assent.

Both these tragic developments have characterized post-Reformation theology and have clouded the perception that a Christian can only live his life in virtue of the same gift in which he has his life. If a man is restored to God when he accepts what God gives (faith), then his restored life must be lived out in faith. If faith is the most comprehensive term for the God-relationship of the believer, then faith must be the comprehensive term for the life-relationship and activity of the believer. If a believer has a " new being " in faith in Christ, then his entire new " existence " is empowered by the same gift.

The believer is commanded to love, to be sure, but this love is formed in faith, just as the love of God who is in heaven is communicated in the faith-demanding historical deed of Jesus. The continuity of the love wherewith we are loved and the love which we are commanded to exercise, passes through the passion of faith. Only in this way can the relation of God's love for man and this loved-man's love for his fellow man be made clear and persuasive. For faith alone can rescue from nonsense the command to love. Nothing is more certain than that love cannot be commanded. If love, nevertheless, *is* commanded by Jesus, then some life-transforming new relationship in virtue of which the absurdity is overcome must exist. And precisely such a convulsive event in the God-relationship of men is the central declaration of the Gospel. " In this is love, not that we loved God, but that He loved us. . . ." Faith is here presented as a function of the love of God; it is a term descriptive of how man, now that God has taken the initiative, can be newly related to him. This biblical meaning of faith is totally obscured if the term is filled from below with materials taken from man's spiritual possibilities as these are historically manifested in man's general religious quest.

It was the experience of the holy particularity and the transforming power of this Godly love that inwardly shaped the literature of the New Testament. This love of God calls and draws men to its adoration and service. As the New Testament unfolds we see that faith is the name given that surrendering obedience-from-below which permits itself henceforth to have its life fashioned by this given love of God from above. The ultimate form of the giving, a death on the cross, is so contradictory and hidden a way for God to bestow his gift that faith alone is a response adequate to it. Love and faith are not, in the New Testament, alternative or opposing terms. Faith is the name for the new God-relationship whereby the will of God, who himself establishes the relationship, is made actual. And that will is love. Faith active in love is alone faith; and love is the function of faith horizontally just as prayer is the function of faith **vertically.**

The Content of the Engendered Response

THE scope of a vitality is governed by its nature. Boyle's law of gases asserts that a gas tends to fill all available space. It is of the nature of the gospel of redemption that all space, all personal relationships, all structures of society are the field of its energy. The gospel of the Word of God made flesh makes mankind the object of the gospel; the gospel in the concrete figure of the man Jesus whose existence was filled out within our mortal conditions—born of a woman, betrayed, denied, crucified—makes the entire earthly life of every man the operational area of this gospel. The gospel as redemptive event on the field of history makes the configuration of historical events the matrix of this gospel's working. The thrust of the redemptive action of God is into the structure of mankind, society, the family, and all economic orders. The scope of that redemptive activity, restoring to God in faith and active in love, can clearly be no more restricted than its originating action.

These clearly biblical facts stand in contradiction to two dangers that have often crippled Christian expositions of ethics. The first is the practice of dividing ethics into the categories of personal and social. Aside from psychological and sociological facts which reveal

65

the severe limitations if not the actual absurdity of such a division, it is clearly not biblical in its understanding of God the Creator and man the creature. Man is created in community, and for community. The proverb " Ein Mensch ist kein Mensch " (A solitary man is no man) bluntly puts a truth which is central to biblical teaching. God's covenant is with a people; one of Jesus' most impassioned statements of his mission is in the word " gather "; and the obedience of primitive faith immediately understood its proper form in terms of a community of " the called " to " membership " in a " fellowship " which is " the household of faith " and which is " his body, the Church."

The second danger that operates to delimit the scope of the Christian life in its ethical vitality is one that has existed from the first days of the Christian era but confronts the believer today with peculiar power. It is the life-situation of millions of western men in their actual daily experience: the emergence and peril of the power-struggle between conflicting ideologies; the destruction, as a consequence of the technizing of material existence, of symbolic forms in which men traditionally have actualized their individuality and significance; the permeation of the realms of value, meaning, and all self-consciousness by the relentless momentum-to-bigness that characterizes the huge collectivities of politics, social life, the economic order. The stuff that men make meanings of can become so mechanized, rationalized, and "packaged," that the natural facts and processes of nature are concealed by the transformation of technology. While the workings of nature continue to exist and determine, they are rendered too febrile to support symbolic weight. A bottle of homogenized, pasteurized, and colorfully packaged milk may be safer for the body, but it contributes little to a child's empathy with the suggested Creator and Sustainer of "the cattle on a thousand hills." Our generation is just young enough to know with immediate comprehension and delight what Dylan Thomas is talking about in the first stanza of his *Fern Hill*:

> Now as I was young and easy under the apple boughs
> About the lilting house and happy as the grass was
>   green,
>   The night above the dingle starry,
>   Time let me hail and climb
>   Golden in the heyday of his eyes,
> And honoured among wagons I was prince of the
>   apple towns
> And once below a time I lordly had the trees and leaves
>   Trail with daisies and barley
>   Down the rivers of the windfall light.[1]

And we are old enough, and have lived long enough with apples packed in the State of Washington on

Monday and consumed in Illinois on Friday, to know what A. E. Housman's lad is living through when he says:

> Into my heart an air that kills
> From yon far country blows . . .
> What are those blue remembered hills,
> What spires, what farms are those? [2]

This life-situation can be described in such a way as virtually to identify it with the demonic and hence exhort men to withdraw from any engagement with the very forms of society within which they are placed. Such a course is both futile and wrong: futile because it flees the facts, and wrong because it tempts men to suppose that both the power of the divine redemption and the power of human creativity are restricted to venerated ways of ordering the human community. It is ironical that certain proponents of this position nostalgically assess as better than existing structures of community life circumstances which are historical memories precisely because they failed to meet the needs of millions of men! Accurate descriptions of contemporary life which point out its perils and corruptions, its thrust toward the " thingification " of man, are to be regarded as challenges to the scope and creativity of ethical life, and not as excuses for failure or devout rationalizations for lack of positive effort.

68

There is a strain in Protestant piety which makes it particularly susceptible to the temptation to interpret the counsel to keep oneself "unspotted from the world" in terms of quietism. The very historical matrix within which Protestant Christianity arose guarantees that the actual situation of the solitary individual before God should be insisted upon as the impact-point of the message of alienation, forgiveness, restoration. Insistence upon the inescapable responsibility of the individual has both prophetic power and peril. Its power is in its truth; its peril is in its tendency to make a false stopping point out of a true starting point, to force a definition of scope out of a point of impact, to restrict responsibility to the dimension within which that responsibility was learned.

The gospel itself is the corrective of all restrictive distortions of the gospel. The same gospel which demands intense inwardness as the theater of faith points to the world as a field of faith. The same Lord who meets, judges, heals, and forgives, in the solitary and naked aloneness of the self, plunges that self into the actuality of the world as its proper place for faithful activity in love.

The content of Christian ethics is disclosed in ever new and fresh ways as men's actual situations are confronted by God's revelation in Christ. When this assertion is taken seriously, certain old problems which have confused Christian ethical teaching are seen in a new way. The will of God, for instance, declared to be supremely revealed in Jesus Christ, cannot now be identified with the Ten Commandments. The Ten Commandments are now seen to be disclosures of the Creator—creature structure of existence, of the holy Source of all that is, of the requirements that inhere in the human situation simply by virtue of its source in God and the structure which he has given it. Because God is Creator his reality is not to be denied by idolatrous substitution of any earthly source, good, value or purpose as ultimate. (I am the Lord Thy God, thou shall have no other gods before me.) Because God is the Creator the given structures of dual sexuality, marriage, family, the reality and needs of child-life are to be honored and protected. (Honor thy father and thy mother. Thou shall not commit adultery.) The integrity of personal life is not to be violated. Because God is the Creator, men's lives and those things which they fashion and use for support and delight are to be respected. (Thou shall not kill; thou shall not steal; thou shall not covet.)

The Ten Commandments, as the law of God, are a verbalization of the given structures of creation. They stand above all men, believers and non-believers alike, as an accurate transcript of the facts—that the world is of God, that ultimate relations among men and things are grounded in him. The Stoic-immanental concept of *natural law* with which many systems of philosophical ethics operate is not introduced here because it is not needed. The perceptions and needs that require this concept are, in Christian ethics, completely confronted, and their space filled by the doctrine of God the Creator. The deed of God in Christ, however, occurred in a world which had and knew the Ten Commandments. If the deed is redemptive in intention and in fact, that does not deny or abrogate the revelation of God the Creator, but rather fulfills in the strategy of redemption what man regularly fractures in the structure of creation. Redemption does not destroy creation but realizes it. Grace does not destroy nature but fulfills it. This fulfilling and realization is generated in men who by faith in God's new beginning with them in the second Adam, Christ, are given what the New Testament calls a " new being."

This faith, this " new being " in Christ, is not only a restoration to fellowship with God in the forgiveness of sins, but an entirely new placement and activity in the midst of the world. Here and now in this living situation the believer is both forgiven and commanded. The forgiveness is of God's love, and the command is to actualize in history the same love which accepts, forgives, and restores the believer.

The content of this love is disclosed to the believer in his own obedience to it. " He that does the will shall know the truth." " If you love me you will keep my commandments." This does not mean that because the believer loves his Lord he has formal cause to keep the Lord's commandments; it means, rather, that the commandment and the actualization of the love of Christ are in organic continuity. To love is to serve; and to love Christ is to serve him where he presents himself in his identification with needy men for our service.

What then is the specific content of this faith-active-in-love at the point where Christ meets us in man? The moment the question is put that way (which is the way the New Testament puts it) we comprehend what is meant by the assertion that Christian ethics discloses its content at the point of God's revelation of himself in Christ. Only now are we ready for that concentration of content which confronts us in such a passage as Matthew 25:31-46. In this teaching Jesus presents himself for the service of faithful love in absolute identification with human need—loneliness, estrangement, hunger, thirst. There faith sees him, there faith must obey him.

Christian ethics is the actualization of justification. For justification, being certified or made righteous in the God-relationship, bestows positive liberation to serve. This liberation exists inwardly because, as Luther puts it, " God has taken care of my salvation in Christ," and I am henceforth free as before God. This liberation exists outwardly because the energies which men futilely devote to the pleasing of God are now called out and exercised where God's purposes and family require them. When the self is known, loved, forgiven, then the self is set free in disciplined service to the will of God. And this will of God is now confronted both as a known and as an unknown. It is known in Christ who is the incarnate concretion of God's ultimate and relentless will-to-restoration; and it remains unknown in the fact that the actual service of this will is presented to the believer not as a general program given in advance but as an ever-changing and fluctuant obligation to the neighbor in the midst of history's life.

Corollary to this known (which is the love of God as giver and restorer) and corollary to the unknown (which is the precise form the love of the neighbor requires in novel situations) is what Alexander Miller has called "An absolute element and an element of calculation." He comments, "But Christian ethics differs from idealist ethics in that its absolute is an absolute loyalty and not an absolute principle. While the Christian calculation differs from typical pragmatism in that while there is always a hidden absolute in pragmatism, an unadmitted presupposition about what is good for man, in the Christian scheme the calculation is grounded in a very precise understanding of what is good for man, determined by the revelation of God in Christ: 'Live life, then,' says St.

Paul, ' not as men who do not know the meaning and purpose of life, but as those who do.' " [3]

It is now possible to speak somewhat more specifically of the dynamics of Christian ethical decision and to indicate how these operate. If not by appeal to principles, or in patternless dependency upon the mercurial stuff of one's chance observations and occasionally animated affections—then what alternative remains?

Christian ethical decision is generated between the two poles of faith and the facts of life. Each of these acts upon the other: facts act upon faith to reveal to it the forms available as its field of action; faith acts upon facts to discover their meaning and peril and promise for men.

Facts without faith are blind; faith without facts is empty. Facts are never *mere* facts. They are what they are plus an indeterminate, undetermined potential. And one aspect of faith is certainly this, that it bestows upon its child sensitiveness to dimensions of possibility that are not otherwise discerned. Faith does not diminish the facticity of facts; but faith enlarges and penetrates the world of fact with its peculiar livingness. The quality of this creativity, Christianly known, is not disclosed when its source is sought in man's natural vitalities, or in the reason's power whereby old stasis is made malleable to the mind's vision; but ultimately it is found in the power of

that love which " so loved the world " that it endlessly creates new fields for its realization in history.

The confused and often contradictory nature of
the facts with which we are confronted presses obedience down to the operational level of faith. Faith
interprets facts in terms of their specifically human
content. That is why the facts of human misery in
post-war Europe discovered to millions of Christians
in prosperous America a contemporary field for the
operation of their faith; and faith penetrated these
facts with its unique dimension, revealing in this
anguish not only men needing coats and calories, but
human beings whose lives could be restored to meaning by nothing less than personal identification with
them in their hurt by fellow children of the crucified
object of the common faith. It is precisely the salvatory power of this uniquely faithful deed of love,
whose content included the ancient word and the
sacraments, which was not understood by those who
would adequately treat all crucifixions with calories.

This means that the will to help must devise the
means to help in ways determined by the actual collectivities within which men are deepeningly involved, and within which interdependency each man
is related to all men by a thousand cords. Needs that
are shaped by structures must be met by help that
also is structured! The requirement of justice is not
only not ignored by Christian ethics, but is in an even

more urgent sense an actually effective way to bring the help of the group-concern to bear upon the needs which are created, in part, by the group way of life.

That faith should seek to realize its proper obedience in alliance with the struggle for and the use of the instruments of justice does not by any means constitute a distortion of the gift and primacy of faithful ethics; it is, rather, faith's realistic acceptance of the root-fact of collective life—that the quest for justice is a drive built into all human relationships. It is there, not primarily as an ideal envisioned by human reflection, but as a vision engendered by a dimension of man's self as a creation of the Creator.

There are, indeed, needs of the neighbor, uninvolved with patterns of group life; these confront the believer with a demand for concern which is immediate, simple, urgent. But deepening areas of contemporary man's need are shaped by and involved with his existence in the huge collectives of economy, politics, community organization. Love must grasp the kind of hand that need holds out. The quest for justice is, on the one hand, an effort to understand the peculiar requirements of human life in its mobile career, and, on the other hand, to create instruments of positive law to certify these requirements, set limits to forces that would ignore them, and order collective life toward a tolerable balance of goods.

This means that love and justice are not two forms of the obedience of faith; they are modes of life's responsibility for lives. The apparently impersonal arrangements which justice makes to serve a need may cover the face of the need with pipes, valves, and pumps. But the need, the stuff, and the arrangements are not thereby bereft of the holiness that all faithful obedience has. A cup of cold water for my neighbor's need can no longer be actualized by simply sensitizing mercy or multiplying cups. The town pump for a few dozen has been displaced by a gigantic water supply system for millions; and concern that justice should prevail in the procurement, distribution, availability, and price of water is the hard, pragmatic face that love wears. And justice and technical competence are the hands it must work with. Justice is not identical with love; and the potencies and ingenuities of love are not exhausted in the struggle for justice. But justice is a primary instrument of love and a field for its operation. This has always been so, as the prophets of Israel so passionately insisted; it is so now and with a heightened urgency.

Just as it is necessary to relate faith-active-in-love and the quest for justice, so it is necessary at the same time to assert that this relationship is not an identity. For while the God-relationship, which is both source and content of faith and love, acknowledges the requirements of justice as also from God, the nobility of the quest for justice can exist and trouble men's lives without such a recognition. Justice can exist without any acknowledgment of the God-relationship; but the God-relationship cannot exist without concern for justice.

A comparison of the terms *justice* and *righteousness* will clarify the point. Justice is a term whose referent is an ideal balance of goods, duties, satisfactions within the human community. This ideal, and some effort to realize it, is not foreign to any culture whose story is available to us. To account for the existence of the ideal of justice it has not been necessary to postulate a divine source. Vitalities operative within empirical society have been powerfully generative of the quest for and the creation of various structures of justice. With such accounts the Christian understanding of the Creator cannot be satisfied; and in its doctrine of God the Creator and Redeemer, it has insisted upon relating justice to the creative and restorative will of God.

But the biblical term *righteousness* is grounded precisely in a postulate that justice need not propose. Righteousness is a term used to designate human life sprung from, determined by, and accountable to the life of God. It is a thoroughly theonomous term. That is why, although faith-active-in-love ought to relate itself to all in human life which seeks justice, this faith can never account for itself nor be at rest with the achievements of justice.

If, then, faith is to be active in love, and if justice in the huge and impersonal collectivities of contemporary life is love operating at a distance, how are the energies of love to be related to that practical ordering of life in community which is called politics? Preliminary to any effort to speak to this question must be a comment about the term politics. The term indicates that nexus of practical arrangements for the creation of order, the enhancement of community values, the protection of life, and the provision of necessary services that every community is absolutely required to bring into existence under one form of government or another. The tradition in Christianity whereby this function is held to be " ordained of God " is thoroughly biblical; and the frequent lamentations of the pious over the dirt in politics may constitute but a devout mechanism whereby one avoids coming to terms with the problem at all. While most Christians today, to be sure, would admit that the Gospel is relevant to the realm of politics, they turn in revulsion from the actual operation of political parties and the devious devices required for the formation of practical policies. To involve themselves in jockeying, trading, calculation, compromise, baby kissing, and boodle-splitting requires a rough handling of ethical " principles." And in avoiding this danger they successfully avoid any contribution to public order. This attitude makes a certain sense if Christianity and the duties of the Christian man are identified with loyalty to a set of principles; but such an identification is both a reduction and a perversion of the Christian faith.

The state may sometimes make pretensions beyond the finite and mortal end and function for which it is ordained; and these pretensions are in continuity with that general disposition to idolatry which tempts men always and everywhere. Nevertheless, the state, ordained of God for limited and finite ends, is the necessary means by which the will to the good becomes effective for the correction of collective injustice and the restraint of inordinate greed. Luther's view of the state, in so far as it was tied to the peculiar political situation of his time, ought no longer be used as an adequate guide in our engagement with present problems. But he had an understanding of the function of state as a " mask of God " which far transcends his practical conclusions from princely-state circumstances of the sixteenth century, and is intrinsically more inclusive of the facts of human evil and political creativity than the state-view of either Geneva or Rome. For his call to men everywhere and in every circumstance to realize their vocation as the faithful service of God in daily work, shattered the false separation of sacred and secular, recognized the duties of the common life as valid structures for Godly service, and celebrated the entire creation as a field in which every believer is summoned to be a " little Christ " to his neighbor's need.

In this situation, in politics as in every other sphere, Christian ethics is given its content as it makes pragmatic selections among available alternatives to enhance and serve the common good, approximates ever more sensitively the demands of justice, and finds methods to allay tensions and curb inordinate desires. In this faithful process (which is the mortally ultimate situation!) the believer never transcends the fact that he is *simul justus et peccator* (simultaneously justified man and sinner). This is to say that ethical decisions are never delivered from, and ethical achievements never add up to, a position elevated above faith's obedient placement within, and joyful acceptance of, man's creaturely situation. Just as no achievement can place a man beyond the daily need of God's judgment, grace, and forgiveness, so that no ethical decision is ever wholly true, just, or good—so, also, men's efforts will forever stand under both the thrust and the limitation of the same situation. A particularly poignant illustration of this necessity confronts us as we consider efforts presently being made toward some kind of precarious peace among the nations. Here is the dilemma: because history—in this, like human life in general—can never wholly redeem, redress, cancel out, or compensate for past wrongs, the very efforts for present and future peace constitute a kind of " betrayal " of millions of men who are dead by the power of the evil, whose countrymen's torments remain, and whose loss of freedom may be permanent. But the present facts are of such a nature that the attempt to right what has been wrong would seemingly involve two vaster terrors: a struggle more full of pain and death than the one whose effects the nations seek to redress, and world-wide acceptance of the fateful use of now available weapons which might well obliterate the very possibility of anything resembling normal human life and freedom for the entire planet. But in the very moment one so concludes, he is aware that this apparently " Christian," rational, humane concern represents also a pious façade back of which lurks a hope not to disturb prosperity, the securities of one's own career and family. It is in part a kind of highly commendable " long view " which permits one to have his ethical cake and eat it, too!

The heartbreaking choices which confront us so sharply in the affairs of nations are but the transcript of the situation which is structural in the solitary life of the believing individual. In a recent book, *The Cruel Sea*, a dramatic instance of this is presented. The commander of a destroyer, convoying a fleet of merchant ships, has finally located the submarine which had sunk several ships and caused the loss of hundreds of lives. The sonar-device which located the hidden submarine indicated that it was precisely at the point where, on the surface of the water, some hundreds of men, previously torpedoed, were swimming about. To drop a depth bomb for the destruction of the submarine would at the same time mean the destruction of the men swimming in the water. There was but an instant to make his choice, and the commander made it knowing that no choice available could be anything but death-dealing. The subsequent tormented statement of the commander, " One must do what one must do—and say one's prayers," is an eloquent condensation of the ethical situation. " One must *do* "—for inactivity, refusal to do anything, is already to do something. And that something is not good. ". . . what one *must* do " is not an open choice; definite alternatives are absolutely given. Both are deadly. ". . . and say one's prayers " is an acknowledgment of deepest piety that no decision fulfills the will of God or releases man from that relation to God which dares to live only by the daily forgiveness of sins.

When the God-relationship is centrally informed by faith, then the actual situation of decision-pressed man is saved from the despair which would inevitably overtake him if this relationship were simply compounded of love. For love, no matter how deeply

83

accepted from God, obediently directed toward men, firmly held to as the motivation of action, both reveals and compels the acceptance of pragmatic choices, *all* possible variations of which are fraught with inadequacy, pain, and denial. In this sense love is the tutor of faith! Even the " law of love," no less than the law of Moses, is a schoolmaster who leads the believer to Christ. For, in Christ, the believing lover of men-in-Christ now stands with his Lord and supreme Lover precisely in his crucifixion! " I am crucified with Christ " is a term expressive not only of the Christian recapitulation of the Christ-life in the large, but a symbol of the inner content of numberless ethical decisions in their actual heartbreaking character. A Christian ethics must, therefore, work where love reveals need. It must do this work in faith which comes from God and not as accumulating achievements to present to God. In this working it must seek limited objectives without apology, and support failure without despair. It can accept ambiguity without lassitude, and seek justice without identifying justice and love.

Ours is a generation upon which two forces from opposite directions are beating with such fury that we are in danger of ethical paralysis between them. From the one side we are the heirs of an ethical analysis which properly insists upon the will of God as transcendent to the relativity of all cultural life, reveals the ambiguity of everything human, the admixture of self-interest in everything human, the lurking demonic in every positive course. The result of this penetrating effort to speak the truth about man as sinner in his modern situation has been that decisiveness before gigantic evils and shrieking human injustices has been paralyzed by the sheer fullness with which every man's evil has been revealed, and ethical complexity has been so elaborately analyzed as to stun the conscience.

From the other side, we are a generation before whose eyes every primal meaning of " The grace of the Lord Jesus Christ, the love of God, and the communion of the Holy Ghost" has been blasted by spirits organized into effective powers and threatening to reshape all existence into a one-dimensional denial of that God-relationship which constitutes humanity. Between these two forces—an analysis which reveals involvement and humble arrogance, and the fact of millions of men enslaved, betrayed, liquidated —the Christian believer is tempted to stand in horrified but inert repentance.

The repentance must remain, for it is the constant heartbeat of the man of faith in history; but the stasis must be overcome. We are sinners, to be sure, but precisely such sinners as are addressed by the word of St. John, that if a man see his brother in need and shut up his bowels of compassion, how dwelleth the love of God in him? Unless we can discover a way, both to acknowledge the facts, act in faith and love, and accept the consequences of our action, our generation will constitute a huge portrait of repentant believers with furrowed brows and inert hands.

The way of advance is to understand that it is a function of faith itself to discern the differences between facts and then act upon what it discerns. Faith without discrimination between facts is a sentiment that encourages brutality; faith without acts (works!) is dead. There is, to be sure, no human fact in which sin is not involved. But within some structures of fact there are alive, free, and operative forces of grace, insights of elemental justice, recreating energies of love. In politics, as in theology, freedom is a precondition of regeneration. It is a fact that the Negro community in American life has been exploited, contemptuously handled, overtly insulted by public law. It is also a fact that within American public life concerned men and institutions have been free to combat injustice, illumine ignorance, plead and work for equality of treatment.

The body of fact presented, for instance, by the Soviet reading of history and man, is a body of fact of a quite different order. It is a legitimate and necessary function of faith to discern this difference. For this closed matrix of dogma and force permits no operational space for the very forces which alone could corrode its idolatry, disintegrate its monodimensional dogma about man and history, and force it open to the powers of grace, justice, and love.

We began with the assertion that to be a Christian is to accept what God gives. We end with a reiteration of that assertion now so elaborated, it is hoped, as to disclose how the structure of Christian ethics grows organically out of the fact and the content of the endlessly giving God. The Christian man is to accept what God gives as Creator: the world with its needs, problems, possibilities; its given orders of family, community, state, economy. Each of these is invested with the promise and potency of grace, and each of these is malleable to the perverse purposes of evil.

The Christian is to accept what God gives as Redeemer: the earth and all human life as the place where God's glory became flesh and dwelt among us, and, therefore, the holy place for life in forgiveness, in the obedience of faith, in the works of love. " Man becomes man because God became man." God has given the form of himself and his will in a man; and the ethical life is the birth-pangs attending the new-being of man in history, ". . . until Christ be formed in you."

The Christian is to accept what God gives as Holy Spirit the Sanctifier. This acceptance includes the gifts that God gives from above; and the tasks which he gives in the world around. This gift and these tasks belong together. The gift is celebrated in the doing of the tasks; the tasks are undertaken in faith as witnesses to the gift.

NOTES TO THE TEXT

CHAPTER I

[1] *The Decline of the West: Perspectives of World History,* authorized translation with notes by Charles Francis Atkinson (New York: Alfred A. Knopf), II, 189.

[2] *The Collected Poetry of W. H. Auden* (New York: Random House, 1945), 145-46.

CHAPTER II

[1] See, for example, James S. Stewart, *A Man in Christ* (New York: Harper & Brothers, n. d.); and, Charles H. Dodd, *The Meaning of Paul for Today* (New York: George H. Doran Company, 1920); and Anders Nygren, *Commentary on Romans* (Philadelphia: Muhlenberg Press, 1949).

[2] *Ethics* (New York: Macmillan Company, 1955), 18.

[3] *The Demonstration of the Apostolic Preaching,* trans. from the Armenian by J. A. Robinson ("Translations of Christian Literature," Series IV, *Oriental Texts* [New York: Macmillan Company, 1920]), 21 ff.

[4] *What is Christianity?* (New York: G. P. Putnam's Sons, 1901), 78 f.

[5] *An Interpretation of Christian Ethics* (New York: Harper and Brothers, 1935), 39. This work is cited because its argument is that phase of Niebuhr's thought which is best known and most influential. It would be quite unjust, however, not to call attention to the deepening criticism and correction of this simple " love ethic " in Niebuhr's later work. In his book *The Self and the Dramas of History* (New York: Charles Scribner's Sons, 1955) is clear evidence of Niebuhr's supplanting of *love* by *faith* as the fulcrum in his continuing argument; and in Vol. II of the *Library of Living Theology,* edited by Charles W. Kegley and Robert W. Bretall (New York: Macmillan Company, 1956), there are several essays which question his earlier agreement with Harnack, and acknowledge the maturer Christianity of his later and current writings.

[6] *Christ and Culture* (New York: Harper and Brothers, 1951), 16. Professor Niebuhr's use of the term " virtue " in this work

would lead to confusion were it not clearly apparent in the entire discussion that the word is used in its original meaning of *strength*, and is devoid of the content common to its use in the older philosophical ethics.

[7] Cf. Phil. 1:21, II Cor. 5:17, Gal. 2:20, and Col. 3:3.

[8] Weimar edition, 18:633.

[9] *Faith Active in Love: An Investigation of Principles Underlying Luther's Social Ethics* (New York: American Press, 1954).

CHAPTER III

[1] *The Collected Poems of Dylan Thomas* (New York: New Directions, 1953), 175-80.

[2] *A Shropshire Lad* (New York: Shakespeare House, 1951), 62.

[3] Alexander Miller, *The Renewal of Man* (New York: Doubleday & Company, Inc., 1955), 44.

DATE DUE

a

MEMOIRS OF MARMONTEL

VOLTAIRE

F. JENKINS HÉLIOG. PARIS

MEMOIRS

OF

MARMONTEL

WRITTEN BY HIMSELF

INCLUDING

*ANECDOTES OF THE MOST DISTINGUISHED LITERARY AND
POLITICAL CHARACTERS WHO APPEARED IN FRANCE
DURING THE LAST CENTURY*

TRANSLATED FROM THE FRENCH

IN TWO VOLUMES—VOLUME II

LONDON

H. S. NICHOLS

3 SOHO SQUARE AND 62A PICCADILLY W.

MDCCCXCV

Printed and Published by
H. S. NICHOLS,
3 SOHO SQUARE, LONDON, W.

CONTENTS TO VOL. II

BOOK VIII

BOOK IX

BOOK X

BOOK XI

BOOK XII

BOOK XIII

BOOK XIV

BOOK XV

BOOK XIX

BOOK XX

MEMOIRS

OF

MARMONTEL

BOOK VIII

As soon as Diderot and I were alone, and at such a distance from the company as not to be heard, he began his narrative in these words:

"Were it not that you know a part of what I have to say, I should observe the same silence with you as I have done with the public, respecting the origin and motive of the injury done me by a man whom I loved, and whom I still pity, for I believe him to be most unhappy. It is cruel for me to be calumniated in an atrocious manner, under the treacherous mask of friendship, and to be betrayed without being able to defend myself; but such is my situation. You will soon see that my reputation is not the only one interested. Since, therefore, I cannot defend my honour, but at the expense of another's, it is my duty to be silent, and I am silent. Rousseau abused me without mentioning the true reason; but it was impossible for me to answer him without alluding to it. I must have divulged what he has passed over in silence; and he was very sure that I would do no such thing. He was perfectly certain that I would allow him to reap the fruits of his injurious conduct, rather than disclose to the public a secret which is not my own; in this respect, therefore, Rousseau is an unfair aggressor—he strikes a disarmed man.

"You know what an unhappy passion Rousseau had conceived for Madame ——. He was one day so rash as to declare it in a manner which could not fail to wound her. Shortly after, Rousseau called upon me at Paris. 'I am a madman; I am undone,' said he; 'listen to what has happened.' And he gave me an account of his adventure. 'Well,' said I, 'where is the misfortune?' 'Do not you see that she will presently write to —— that I have attempted to seduce her, to carry her off from him? and can you doubt that he will accuse me of insolence and treachery? I have thus made him my mortal enemy for life.' 'Not at all,' said I, coolly; '—— is a reasonable man; he knows you; he is well aware that you are neither a Cyrus nor a Scipio. After all, where is the great offence? a moment of error, of delirium! You must write him yourself, without delay, and make a full acknowledgment; and while you urge in excuse an intoxication with which he cannot be unacquainted, you must beg him to forgive you this moment of error. Be assured, the only effect will be to make him love you the more.'

"Rousseau was transported, and took me in his arms. 'You restore me to life,' said he; 'the advice you give me reconciles me with myself; I will write this very evening.' From that time he appeared more tranquil; and I made no doubt of his having done that upon which we had agreed.

"But some time after, —— arrived, and called upon me. He did not explain himself, but showed such deep indignation against Rousseau, that I at first thought Rousseau had not written to him. 'Have you not received a letter from him?' said I. 'Yes,' said he, 'a letter which deserves the severest chastisement.'

"'Sir,' said I, 'how can you feel so much resent-

ment on account of a moment of folly, which he acknowledges, and entreats you to forgive? If this letter offends
you, it is I whom you must accuse; for it was by my
advice that he wrote it.' 'And do you know,' said he,
'what this letter contains?' 'I know that it contains a
confession, excuses, and a petition for forgiveness.' 'It
contains no such thing. It is a compound of treachery
and insolence; it is a masterpiece of art, with the view
of throwing upon Madame —— the blame from which
he wishes to free himself.' 'You amaze me,' said I;
'this was not at all what he promised.' In order to
appease him, I then gave a plain account of the grief
and repentance which Rousseau seemed to feel at having
offended him, and the resolution he had formed of asking
forgiveness; by that means I easily brought —— to
regard him with pity.

"To this explanation, Rousseau gave the name of
treachery. . As soon as he learned that I had made
an acknowledgment in his name, which he had not
made himself, he exhibited an excess of rage, accusing
me of having betrayed him. On learning this, I went
to him. 'For what purpose are you come?' said he.
'I am come,' said I, 'to know whether you are a wicked
man or a fool.' 'Neither the one nor the other,' said
he; 'but my heart is wounded, inflamed against you.
I will never see you again.' 'What have I done?'
said I. 'You have dived,' said he, 'into the recesses
of my soul; you have extracted my secret, and have
divulged it. You have exposed me to the contempt,
to the hatred of a man who will never forgive me.' I
allowed his rage to evaporate; and after he was weary
of loading me with reproaches, I said, 'We are alone;
and between us two, your eloquence is vain. Your
judges here are reason, truth, my conscience and your
own. Will you examine them?' He made no answer,
but threw himself into his elbow-chair, covered his eyes
with his hands, and I continued:

" ' On the day,' said I, ' on which we agreed that
you should be ingenuous in your letter to —— you
were, according to your own account, reconciled to
yourself; what, then, made you change your resolution?
You answer not; I will answer for you. When you
were under the necessity of taking up your pen and
making the humble acknowledgment of an unhappy
error—although the confession would have done you
honour—your devilish pride got up. Yes, your pride;
you accused me of treachery, and I have endured it; you
must now allow me to accuse you of pride, for otherwise
your conduct would only be meanness. Pride then whis-
pered that it was unworthy of your character to write to
any man in a humble tone, and to ask forgiveness of a
happy rival; that it was not you who ought to be accused,
but she, whose seducing graces, whose alluring coquetry,
whose flattering sweetness had won your heart. Then,
artfully embellishing this fine excuse, you did not perceive that by imputing the arts of a coquette to a woman
of delicacy and feeling, and holding up the picture to a
man who esteems and loves her, you were wounding
two hearts at once.' ' Well,' exclaimed he, ' suppose I
have been unjust, imprudent, senseless, how does this
justify you for having betrayed my confidence, and
revealed the secret of my soul?' ' It follows from this,'
said I, ' that the deceit is all on your side; that your
conduct alone induced me to defend you as I have done.
Why did you not tell me that you had changed your
opinion? I would not have spoken of your repentance;
I would not have supposed myself repeating the very
words of your letter. You concealed from me your
having done what you knew I would not have approved
of; and when this conduct of yours produced its natural
effect, you treat it as a crime. Go! your heart is capable
only of hatred, since, in the most sincere and tender
friendship, you seek for occasions of indulging that
passion.'

"'Courage! barbarian,' said he; 'you will soon completely overwhelm a weak and miserable man. I had no consolation remaining on earth but my own esteem, and you have torn it from me.' Never in his life was Rousseau so eloquent and so interesting as then in his affliction. Deeply affected by the state in which I saw him, my eyes were filled with tears; when he saw me weep, he was himself affected, and took me in his arms.

"Now, then, we were reconciled, and he continued to read to me his 'New Eloise,' which he had completed; while I went on foot twice or thrice a week from Paris to his hermitage in order to hear it read, and to answer as a friend to the confidence of my friend. Our rendezvous was in the wood of Montmorency; I arrived in a violent perspiration, and he always complained when I made him wait. Now just at this time appeared the letter on public amusements, with that fine passage from Solomon, in which he accuses me of having injured and betrayed him."

"What!" cried I, "in the midst of perfect harmony—after a full reconciliation! It is incredible." "It is, indeed, and yet it is true. Rousseau had determined to break with me, and with my friends; he had missed the most favourable opportunity. What, indeed, could be more convenient than to advance accusations, from which I could not justify myself. Vexed at having lost this advantage, he resumed it, persuading himself that my apparent reconciliation had been only affected, and that I had imposed upon him." "What a man!" exclaimed I, again; "and yet he believes his own heart to be good." Diderot replied, "It should be so, for he has naturally much feeling, and he loves men very well, so long as they appear only in the distance. He hates only those who come near him, because his pride makes him believe that they all envy him; that they serve only to humble, that they flatter only to injure

him; and that even those who pretend to love him, are
accomplices in this conspiracy. This is his malady. He
is rendered interesting by misfortunes, by talents, by the
goodness and uprightness which is at the bottom of his
soul, and he would have friends if he believed in them.
He will never have any, or they will love him without
any return; for he will always view them with distrust."

This fatal mistrust, which led him so rashly and so
hastily not only to suspect but to believe his friends
guilty of whatever is most atrocious, most mean, and
most infamous; which made him accuse them of meanness and perfidy, with no other proof than the reveries
of an ardent and gloomy imagination, whose vapours
troubled his wretched head, and whose malignant influence soured and poisoned his gentlest affections. In
short, this delirium of a suspicious and timid mind,
rendered ferocious by misfortune, was, indeed, the malady
of Rousseau and the torment of his soul.

Instances of this were every day seen in the injurious
manner in which he broke off all intercourse with the
persons who were most devoted to him, accusing them
sometimes of laying snares for him, sometimes of coming
to his house only as spies, to betray and sell him to his
enemies. I know particulars on this subject which are
perfectly incredible. But the most astonishing of all
was the monstrous ingratitude with which he repaid the
tender and active friendship of the virtuous David Hume,
and the deep malignity with which insult was added to
injury in the calumnies which he raised against him.

You will find in the very collection of the works of
Rousseau this monument of his shame. You will there
see the artful manner in which he prepared his calumny;
you will see the absurd proofs by which he thought himself able to convict his most sincere friend—the most
honourable and best of men—of deceit, of duplicity, of the
blackest treachery; you will read, not without indignation, in the relation which he gives of his own conduct

towards his benefactor, the following stroke of raillery, which is the sublimity of insolence :

> " First blow on the cheek of my patron.
> Second blow on the cheek of my patron.
> Third blow on the cheek of my patron."

I believe the general opinion completely fixed upon the subject of these two men ; but if anything more were wanting to confirm the idea which is entertained of the character of David Hume, the following are facts to which I have been witness :

On the recommendation of my Lord Maréchal, and of the Countess de Boufflers, Hume offered to procure Rousseau a free and peaceful retreat in England. Rousseau having accepted this generous offer, they were on the point of setting out, when Hume, who was acquainted with the Baron d'Holbach, told him that he was taking Rousseau into his own country. " Sir," said the baron, " you are cherishing a serpent in your bosom ; I give you warning, you will feel its bite."

The baron himself had invited Rousseau to his house, and had paid a great deal of attention to him ; his house was the rendezvous of those who were then called philosophers, and, in the full security with which honourable minds are inspired by the inviolable sacredness of the hospitable roof under which they meet, d'Holbach and his friends had admitted Rousseau to their most intimate acquaintance. Now, you may see in his " Emile " the manner in which he stigmatized them. Assuredly, although the brand of atheism, which he fixed upon their society, had been just, it would have been an odious breach of trust. But with respect to the greater number, he well knew it to be a mere calumny; he knew that the theism of his vicar had zealous proselytes among them. The baron, therefore, had come to know him at his own expense. But honest David Hume thought he saw more passion than truth in the warning which the baron gave him. He made no hesitation, therefore, in carrying Rousseau along with him to his native country, and in rendering him all the good offices of friendship. He believed, and it was natural he should, that he had made happy the most feeling and best of men; he expressed his pleasure in all the letters he wrote to the Baron d'Holbach, and was constantly endeavouring to remove the bad opinion which the baron entertained of Rousseau. He extolled the goodness of heart, the candour, the ingenuousness of his friend. "I am vexed to think," said he, "that you should be unjust towards him. Believe me, Rousseau is far from being a bad man. The more I see him, the more I esteem and love him." By every post the letters from Hume to the baron repeated the same praises; and the latter, after reading them, always said, "He does not know him yet; wait a little, and he will know him." Accordingly, not long after, he receives a letter from Hume beginning thus: "You are quite in the right, my lord; Rousseau is a monster." "Ay," said the baron coolly, and without any surprise, "he knows him now!"

How had so sudden a change happened in the opinion of the one, and in the conduct of the other. You will see it in the statement of facts published by the two parties. Here I think it my duty to declare and attest, that, at the very time when Rousseau was accusing Hume of betraying and dishonouring him at London, the same Hume, full of candour and of zealous friendship for him, was attempting to erase the fatal impressions which he had left at Paris, and to restore him to the good opinion of those who viewed him with the utmost aversion and contempt.

What ravage had this excessive pride made in a soul naturally mild and tender! Considering the information and talents which he possessed, how weak, how wretchedly little, was this vanity, so restless, so gloomily suspicious, and, at the same time, so angry and vindictive,

which was irritated with the very thought of an attempt
being made to wound it, which supposed such an attempt
even without the slightest ground, and never forgave it.
An important lesson for those whose minds have any
propensity to this vice! without it, no one would have
been more beloved or respected than Rousseau; but it
poisoned his life, it rendered benefits odious, benefactors
insupportable, and gratitude burdensome to him; it made
him repel friendship with insult; it made him live unhappy and die almost abandoned. Let me pass to more
pleasing objects with which I have a nearer concern.

Neither the agreeable life which I spent at Paris,
nor that, still more agreeable, which I spent in the country, deprived my dear Odde and my sister of the delightful fortnight which was annually reserved for them. I
passed it with them at Saumur; and there, indeed, it
was that all the sensibility of my soul was called forth
to enjoyment. By this couple, who loved each other
more than light and life, I saw myself loved and revered as the source of their happiness. I could not
satiate myself with the inexpressible pleasure of con-
templating my own work in the happiness of two pure
souls, whose every vow invoked upon my head the
blessings of heaven. Their tenderness penetrated, their
piety transported my soul. Their behaviour exhibited
genuine virtue in all its simplicity. To this continual
enjoyment was added that of seeing them beloved and
honoured in their city. Madame Odde was quoted as
the model of her sex; the name of M. Odde was syn-
onymous with justice and truth. If any dispute arose
between the branch of the court of excise established
at Saumur and the company of farmers-general, Odde
was referred to as their umpire. I was witness to this
confidence, acquired by a man who was another self.
I was witness to the love of the people for a man who
exercised a severe employment without a single complaint being ever urged against him, so skilful was his

humanity in softening its rigour.   I myself shared in the
respect with which they were regarded.   Their friends
did not know how best to entertain me; and all the
days which we spent together were days of rejoicing.
You would not have been born, my children, had my
worthy sister lived — I would have gone and spent my
old age with her; but she carried in her bosom the
seeds of that malady which has been fatal to all my
family; and this hope, which I had indulged, was soon
cruelly torn from me.

In one of these happy visits which I paid at Saumur,
I was led, by the vicinity of Ormes, to pay a visit to the
Count d'Argenson, formerly minister of war, whom the
King had sent thither into exile.   I had not forgotten the
kindness he expressed for me during the period of his
glory.   When I was very young, I had written a little
poem upon the establishment of the military school, the
principal honour of which belonged to him; and he had
taken pleasure in recommending this proof of my zeal.
He had presented me, at his table, to the nobility who
served in the army, as a young man who had a right to
their gratitude and protection.   He received me in his
exile with extreme sensibility.   Oh! my children, what
an incurable malady is that of ambition !   How dismal is
the life of a disgraced minister !   Already worn out by
labour, chagrin completed the ruin of his health.   His
body was torn with the gout, his soul was still more
cruelly torn with recollection and regret; and amid the
agreeable reception, which he was so kind as to give
me, I could not but see that he was a victim to grief
of every kind.

Taking a walk with him in his gardens, I perceived
at a distance a marble statue; I asked whom it represented.   " It is one," said he, " at which I have no longer
courage to look "; and as we turned away, " Ah ! Marmontel," said he, " if you knew the zeal with which I
have served him, if you knew how often he assured me

that we should spend our lives together, and that I had not a better friend in the world than he! Such are the promises of kings, such is their friendship," and as he said these words, his eyes were filled with tears.

In the evening, during the time of supper, we remained alone in the drawing-room. This drawing-room was hung with pictures representing the battles at which he had been present along with the King. He showed me the place in which they had been stationed during the action; he repeated what the King had said—he had not forgotten a single word. "Here," said he, talking of one of these battles, "I believed for two hours that my son was dead. The King was so kind as to appear affected by my grief. How changed is he now! nothing of mine affects him any longer!" These ideas haunted him; and when he was left a moment to himself, he sank, as it were, into an abyss of grief. Then his daughter-in-law, Madame de Voyer, went immediately and sat down by him, pressed him in her arms, and caressed him; while he like a child, dropping his head upon the bosom, or upon the knees of his comforter, bathed them in tears, which he made no attempt to conceal.

This poor man, who, on account of his gout, lived only on boiled fish, was by that means, too, deprived of the only pleasure of the senses which could have been agreeable to him; for he was an epicure. But the most austere regimen did not procure even an alleviation of his sufferings. On leaving him, I could not forbear expressing how deeply I sympathised in his afflction. "You give me an additional regret," said he, "at not having done something for you which I could once have done so easily." Shortly after, he obtained permission to remove to Paris. I saw him arrive there at the point of death, and received his last sighs.

On some future occasion, my children, I will give you very curious details relative to the cause of his disgrace, and that of his antagonist, M. de Machault, which happened on the same day. A motive of delicacy prevents me from inserting these particulars in memoirs which might accidentally escape out of your possession. But instead of this serious anecdote, I will give you a very diverting one ; for my narrative must now and then be a little enlivened.

My friend Vaudesir had a small estate near Angers, from which his unhappy son, Saint-James, took his name. As he knew that I went every year to visit my sister at Saumur, by the way of Angers, he once offered to take me thither in his post-chaise, on condition that three days of my journey should be spent at St. James, whither he was going. I willingly agreed to this engagement, and I met at St. James the flower of the wits from the Angerine Academy ; among others, an abbé, who bore much resemblance to the Abbé Beau-Genie of the *Mercure-Galant*. He had just signalised himself by so singular a piece of folly that I could not believe it. " Will you believe it," said Vaudesir, " if he tells it himself ? Only assist me in getting him to do it, and you shall see." Towards the end of dinner, I brought the abbé on the field by talking of his academy; and Vaudesir, taking up the conversation, gave it a magnificent character. " Next to the French Academy," said he, " we have not such an illustrious and well-constituted body. The son of M. de Contades has just been received into it. The abbé spoke in the name of the academy, and with the greatest success." " The abbé would doubtless add the panegyric of the father to that of the son." " Certainly," said the abbé ; " I took care not to omit that ; and I paid a just tribute of praise to the marshal." " The field," said I, " was rich and vast ; yet there was one step not easily got over." " Ay," said he, smiling, " the affair of Minden ; that certainly was the critical point. But I extricated myself very happily. In the first place, I spoke of the actions which had deservedly raised the Marshal de Contades to the command of

armies; I enumerated all the glorious actions he had
previously performed; and when I came to the battle
of Minden, I said only two words, 'Contades appears,
Contades is conquered'; and then I went on with
another subject." Being like to burst for want of vent
to my laughter, I endeavoured to change the conversation. "These words," said I, "remind me of those of
Cæsar, after defeating the son of Mithridates, 'I came,
I saw, I conquered.'" "True," said the abbé, "my
phrase has even been thought somewhat more laconic."
The grave and emphatic manner in which he pronounced
his folly was so diverting that Vaudesir and I found great
difficulty in keeping our gravity, and dared not look at
each other, lest we should burst into laughter.

Madame Geoffrin was not pleased with these
journeys, and my consequent absence. During the
whole summer, I did not attend the Academy. She
heard complaints made; she thought I incurred censure
by yielding my fees to the attentive academicians—
which, with regard to the d'Olivets, was certainly a very
ill-founded apprehension — and I frequently received
warm reprimands upon what she termed the inconsistency of my conduct. "Really," said she, "what can
be more ridiculous than first to be so anxious to belong
to the Academy, and after your admission, not to attend."
My excuse was the example of the greater number, who
attended still worse than I. But she urged, with reason,
that I was one of those whose academical functions re-
required constant attendance. She had also a little
private interest of her own in these remonstrances; for
she spent the summer at Paris, and during this time she
did not wish her literary society to be dispersed. I listened
to her advice with a respectful modesty, and next day I
set out as if nothing had been said. It was natural
enough that her kindness to me should be cooled by
this behaviour; but a dinner, at which I made myself
agreeable, reconciled us; and on serious occasions she

resumed her affection for me. I experienced this in two
illnesses which seized me at her house. One was the
same fever which has attacked me five times in my life,
and which will carry me off at last : it came on at the
time that my "Art of Poetry" was printing. I wished
to add a few articles more, and in consequence of my
head being full of this employment, the delirium which
attended my feverish paroxysms became more oppressive. My friends were uneasy about my situation ;
Madame Geoffrin was anxious. Geriglan, a little physician, whom she kept for her servants, cured me very well.

My other illness was a singular kind of rheum ; it
was a viscous humour, which obstructed the organ of
respiration, and which, notwithstanding all the effort
of a violent cough, I was unable to expectorate. You
may suppose that, after having seen all my family die
of chest complaints, I had some reason to think that
my turn was now come. I actually believed so ; and
being deprived of sleep, growing thinner every day—in
short, feeling myself waste away, I no longer doubted
that the last stage of the disease would be soon announced by the usual symptom. I formed my resolution
accordingly, and thought only of finding a subject for
some work to occupy my thoughts, which, after employing my last moments, might leave behind me some
traces worthy of myself.

I had been presented with a print of Belisarius,
from the picture of Vandyck ; it often attracted my
eyes, and I wondered that the poets had made no use
of so moral, so interesting a subject. I conceived a
desire to treat it myself in prose ; and as soon as this
idea had struck my mind, my illness was suspended
as by a sudden charm. Oh ! wonderful power of imagination ! The pleasure of inventing my story, of arranging and unfolding it, the interest which was excited
in me by the first glimpse of the situations and of the
scenes which I had imagined, captivated my attention,

and withdrew it from myself, so as to render credible
all that I had heard of ecstatic transports. My chest
was oppressed; I breathed with difficulty; I had fits
of convulsive coughing—yet I scarcely observed them.
My friends called upon me and spoke of my illness; I
answered like a man who had something else in his
head; I was thinking of Belisarius. The want of sleep,
which had hitherto been so uneasy to me, was no longer
attended with the same wearisome restlessness. My
nights, like my days, were spent in meditating upon the
adventures of my hero. I was not the less exhausted;
and this continual study would have completed the loss
of my strength, had not a remedy been found for my
illness. I was acquainted with a Florentine physician,
of the name of Gatti, celebrated as the promoter of
inoculation, skilful in his art, and a very agreeable man;
he it was who came and saved me. "The object," said
he, "is to dissolve that thick and glutinous humour
which encumbers your lungs, and the remedy is agreeable; you must drink oxymel. All I did then was to
boil together excellent honey and vinegar; and I was
very soon cured by the salutary use of the syrup formed
from this mixture. It was now more than three months
since I thought myself dying; but, during these three
months, I had made some progress in my work. The
only chapters that remained to compose were those which
required research. All the labour of the imagination was
finished, and that was the most interesting.

This work bears a graver character than my other
writings, because, in composing it, I believed myself
uttering my last words—*novissima verba*, according to the
expression of the ancients. The first trial I made of it
was upon the soul of Diderot; the second upon that of
the hereditary Prince, now Duke of Brunswick. Diderot
was very well pleased with the moral part; but he
thought the political part too concise, and prevailed upon
me to extend it. The Prince of Brunswick, who was

travelling in France, after having made war against us with chivalric loyalty and heroic valour, was enjoying at Paris that high esteem to which his virtues entitled him—a homage more flattering than those customary respects which are paid to persons of his birth and rank. He expressed a desire to be present at a private meeting of the French Academy, an honour which till then had been bestowed only on crowned heads. At this meeting I read a large extract from " Belisarius " ; and had the pleasure of seeing, at the images which I had presented, the countenance of the young hero take fire and his eyes fill with tears.

He took particular pleasure in the society of literary men, and you will soon see how much he valued it. Helvetius asked him to dine with us, and he owned that never in his life had he enjoyed a dinner so much. It was not likely that I should have been particularly noticed, yet so it happened. Helvetius having told the Prince that he thought him like the Pretender, and the Prince having answered that this remark had actually been made by a number of persons, I said, in a half-whisper, " A few additional features of resemblance would have made Prince Edward King of England." These words were heard ; the Prince felt them, and I saw a modest blush on his countenance.

Though the reading of " Belisarius " had succeeded so well at the Academy, I was sure that it would have very bad success with the Sorbonne. But this was not what gave me anxiety ; and provided the Court and the Parliament should take no part in the quarrel, I was very well pleased to have a skirmish with the theological faculty. I took every precaution, therefore, that I might have it only to fear.

The Abbé Terray was not yet in the ministry, but he was a member of the Parliament, and possessed the greatest interest with that body. I went with Madame Gaulard, his friend, to spend some time at his country-

seat of La Motte, and there I read "Belisarius" to him.
His sensibility was naturally small, yet, on this occasion,
he showed a good deal. After having interested him, I
disclosed my apprehensions of hostility from the Sorbonne, and asked him if he thought the Parliament would
condemn my book in case of its receiving their censure.
He assured me that the Parliament would take no part in
the business, and promised to be my defender in case any
person should attack me.

This was not all. A privilege was necessary, with
the assurance of its not being revoked. I had no personal
interest with old Maupeou, then keeper of the seals. But
Madame Merlin, my bookseller's wife, was known and
protected by him. I made her feel his pulse, and he promised us every kind of favour.

I had still precautions to take with a view to the
Court, and here the dangerous part of my book was not
theology. I dreaded being accused of allusions, of ill-
natured applications, and of having had someone else
than Justinian in view when I drew the picture of a weak
and deluded monarch. Unhappily, there was but too
much analogy between the two reigns: of this the King
of Prussia was so sensible, that when he had received my
book, he wrote with his own hand, at the foot of a letter
from his secretary Lecat, "I have just read the beginning
of your 'Belisarius'; you are a bold man." Others might
say the same; and if my enemies attacked me from this
quarter, I was undone.

There was no possibility, however, of taking any
direct precautions against this danger. The least anxiety
shown on my part would have roused their vigilance and
have led to a public accusation. No one would have
ventured either to encourage me or to promise assistance,
and the first advice that I should have received would
have been to throw my work into the fire, or to omit
everything which could be capable of such an application;
and how much must I then have omitted!

I assumed an air the very reverse of anxiety. I wrote to the Count de Saint-Florentin, minister of the King's household, that I was on the eve of publishing a work, the subject of which appeared to me worthy of interesting the heart of the King; that I was exceedingly desirous of being allowed to dedicate it to His Majesty; and that, when I should give it to him (the minister) to examine, I would beg him to solicit this favour for me. With that view, I asked a moment's audience, and he granted it.

When I communicated my manuscript, I owned to him, confidentially, that there was a chapter with which bigoted theologians might not be satisfied. " It is, therefore," said I, " very desirable for me that the secret should not leak out; and I beg you, my lord, not to allow my manuscript to go out of your closet." As he entertained a friendship for me, he promised this, and kept his word. But some days after, on returning my work, which he had read, or made somebody read to him, he said that " the religion of ' Belisarius ' would not be relished by theologians; that probably my book would be censured, and that, on that account only, he dared not propose that the King should accept of the dedication." Upon which I begged him to be so good as to keep my secret, and withdrew quite satisfied.

What, indeed, was my object? I wished to have somebody at Court who could bear witness to the design I had entertained of dedicating my work to the King, which would be a proof that nothing had been farther from my thoughts than to write a satire upon his reign; than which nothing could be more true. With such a means of defence, my apprehensions from this quarter too were dispelled. But I was obliged to pass under the eyes of a censor; and, instead of one, two were given me, for the literary censor dared not undertake to approve of what concerned theology.

"Belisarius" was thus subjected to the examination

of a doctor of the Sorbonne. He was called Chevrier. Eight days after I had given him my work, I called upon him. He returned it to me, and praised it highly ; but when I threw my eyes on the last sheet, his approbation did not appear. "Be so good then," said I, "as to write two words here." He answered with a smile. "What! sir," urged I, "do you not approve of it?" "No, sir ; God forbid!" replied he, mildly. "And may I know, at least, what appears to you so reprehensible?" "Little in detail, but much when taken all together ; and the author knows too well the spirit in which he wrote his book, to expect that I should give it my approbation." I was going to urge him to explain himself. "No, sir," said he ; "you understand me very well ; I understand you, too ; let us not lose time in saying more ; but seek another censor." Luckily, I found one who was less difficult, and "Belisarius" was printed.

As soon as it appeared, the Sorbonne was in an uproar ; and the sage doctors determined to pass sentence upon it. This censure was still regarded by many as a very formidable affair ; and among this number were many of my friends. The alarm spread among them. Some advised me, if possible, to appease the fury of these doctors ; others, more firm, more jealous of my philosophical honour, exhorted me not to bend. I desired both not to be uneasy, told my secret to no one, and began with watching the judgment of the public.

My book was eagerly purchased ; the first edition was sold off ; I pushed on the second, I hastened the third. Nine thousand copies were circulated before the Sorbonne had extracted what they meant to censure ; and, thanks to the noise they made on the subject of the fifteenth chapter, no other was spoken of ; it was as good to me as the tail of Alcibiades's dog. I was delighted to see the service the doctors were doing me, by turning the attention of men into another direction. The thing for me was to appear neither timid nor rebellious, and to gain

time till the editions of my book were multiplied and
spread over Europe. I stood, therefore, in a defensive
attitude, without appearing either to dread the Sorbonne,
or to brave it ; when a man who, since that time, has
had powerful enemies to encounter, the Abbé Georgel,
came and invited me to take the archbishop as a mediator, assuring me that if I called upon him I should meet
with a good reception, and that he knew him to be disposed to negotiate an accommodation between me and
the faculty. Nothing suited my plan better than a system of conciliation. I called upon the prelate ; he received me with a paternal look, and always called me " My
dear M. Marmontel." I was affected by the kindness
which seemed to be expressed by these friendly words.
I have since learnt that it was his lordship's usual address to people of little consequence.

I assured him of my sincerity, my respect for religion, my desire to leave no obscurity upon my doctrine
and that of my book, and I asked, as a favour, permission
to give an explanation to the doctors, in his presence,
upon every point which appeared to them reprehensible
in this book. He seemed to be pleased with this character of a mediator, of a restorer of peace. He promised
to act accordingly, and desired me, on my side, to call
upon the syndic of the faculty, Dr. Riballier, and to give
my explanation to him.

I called upon Riballier. Our conversations and my
correspondence with him are printed ; to these I refer
you.

The other doctors, who were assembled by the
archbishop at his house of Conflans, to which I went
to confer with them, were not quite so unfair as Riballier. But, in our conferences, they, too, indulged in
the habit of falsifying passages and perverting their
meaning. I armed myself with patience and moderation, rectified the text which they had altered, explained to them my thoughts, and offered to insert

these explanations as notes to my book. The archbishop was very well satisfied, but these gentlemen
were not. The Abbé le Fevre, an old caviller, who
was only known in the school by the name of "La
Grande Cateau," at length concluded with saying, "All
your explanations are in vain ; the fifteenth chapter of
your book must absolutely disappear; it is there that
the venom lies."

" If what you ask were possible," replied I, "perhaps
I might do it for the sake of peace. But there are now
forty thousand copies of my book spread over Europe,
and, in all the editions which have been and will be
finished, the fifteenth chapter is and will always be
printed. Where, then, would be the use of publishing
an edition in which it is omitted ? This mutilated
edition would be published by nobody ; it would be
money lost both to myself and my bookseller." " Well,
then," said he, " your book will be censured without
mercy." " Yes, sir," said I, " I expect no mercy if it be
you who compose the censure. But his lordship will
bear witness for me that I have done everything which
you could reasonably require, in order to soften your
anger."

" Yes, my dear M. Marmontel," said the archbishop,
" I have been satisfied in many respects with your
sincerity and docility. But there is one article upon
which I demand a formal recantation ; it is that of
toleration." " If your lordship," said I, " will just cast
your eyes upon some lines which I wrote this morning,
you will see an express declaration of my private opinion
upon this subject, and of the grounds upon which it
rests." I presented him with this note, which you will
find printed at the end of " Belisarius." He silently
read it and handed it over to the doctors. "Very good,"
said they ; " commonplace arguments, repeated a thousand times, and a thousand times refuted ; the refuse of
the schools." "You treat very contemptuously," said I,

"the authority of the Fathers of the Church and that
of St. Paul, by whom my reasonings are supported."
They replied that the writings of the Fathers of the
Church were an arsenal in which all parties found arms,
and that the passage of St. Paul, which I alleged, proved
nothing.

"Well," enquired I, "since your authority is to be
the only law, what do you ask?" "The right of the
sword," said they, "to exterminate heresy, irreligion,
impiety, and to bring the whole world under the yoke of
the true faith."

This was what I expected, that I might retire in good
order and entrench myself in a post where they could not
attack me. "Præmunitum, atque ex omni parte causæ
septum." [1] ("De Or.," l. 3.) I, therefore, replied that
"the sword was one of those carnal weapons which St.
Paul had censured when he said, 'Arma militiæ nostræ
non carnalia sunt'";[2] and after these words I was going
away. The prelate retained me, and squeezing my hands
within his, conjured me, with a tenderness which was
truly laughable, to subscribe this atrocious dogma. "No,
my lord," said I; "had I signed it, I should have thought
my pen dipped in blood; I should have thought myself
approving all the cruelties committed in the name of
religion." "So," said Le Fevre, with his doctorial insolence, "you attach great importance and authority to
your own opinion?" "I know, sir," said I, "that my
authority is nothing; but I set some value upon my conscience, which forbids me, in the name of humanity and of
religion itself, to approve persecution. 'Defendenda re-
ligio est, non occidendo, sed moriendo; non sævitia, sed
patientia,—si sanguine, si tormentis, si malo religionem
defendere velis; jam non defendetur, sed polluetur atque

---

1 " Fortified and hedged in on every side."
2 " Our arms are not fleshly."

violabitur.'[1] This is the opinion of Lactantius; it is
also that of Tertullian and of St. Paul; and you will
permit me to believe that these were at least as good
men as you."

" Come," said he to his brethren, " there is no more
to be said. The gentleman wishes to be censured, and
he shall be so." Thus ended our conferences, from which
I had extracted the most precious result. It was now no
little theological chicanery in which I should have been
exposed to their scholastic wranglings; it was a matter
of controversy brought to the plainest and most striking
terms. They have attempted, I could say, to make me
acknowledge the right of imposing belief by force, of
employing the sword, tortures, the scaffold and the
flames; they have attempted to make me approve of
preaching the gospel sword in hand. This is the abominable doctrine to which I have refused to subscribe. Such
is the ground on which the Abbé le Fevre has declared
that I should be censured without mercy. This statement, which I took care to spread through the city, the
Court, the Parliament and the councils, rendered the
Sorbonne odious; at the same time my friends exerted
themselves in order to render it ridiculous, and for that I
could perfectly rely on them.

The first operation of the theological faculty had
been to extract from my book the propositions that were
worthy of condemnation. It was an object of emulation
who should have the glory of discovering the greatest
number. They searched them out curiously, like pearls,
everyone zealously adding to the heap. Having collected
thirty-seven, and thinking this number sufficient, they
published the list under the title of " Indiculus."[2]

1 " Religion must be defended, not by killing, but by death; not
by cruelty, but by patience : if you attempt to defend religion by
bloodshed, by tortures, by evildoing, it will be no longer defended,
but will be violated and polluted."

2 A short catalogue or list.

Voltaire added the epithet of "Ridiculus." Never did adjective and substantive agree better together; "Indiculus Ridiculus" seemed made for each other, and they continued inseparable. M. Turgot played upon the folly of the doctors in a different manner. As he was himself a good theologian, and a still better logician, he laid it down, first, as an evident and universally acknowledged principle, that of two contradictory propositions, if one is false the other is necessarily true. He then exposed, upon two opposite and parallel columns, the thirty-seven propositions censured by the Sorbonne, and the thirty-seven contradictory propositions most correctly made out. There could be no medium; the faculty, while it condemned the one, necessarily adopted and professed the others. Now, among the latter, there was not a single one which was not either horrible or ludicrously absurd. This ray of light thrown upon the doctrine of the Sorbonne, struck them like a thunderbolt. In vain did they attempt to withdraw their "Indiculus"; it was too late, the blow was given.

Voltaire undertook to drag through the mire the syndic Riballier, and his scribe Cogé, a professor at the same college (Mazarin), of which Riballier was principal, and who had written, from his dictating, a calumnious libel against "Belisarius" and myself. At the same time, Voltaire, with those arms of ridicule which he wielded so skilfully, fell with his utmost might upon the whole Sorbonne; and his little sheets, which came from Geneva, and which circulated rapidly through Paris, amused the public at the expense of the faculty. Some of my friends, who understood both reasoning and raillery, were also so charitable as to undertake my defence; so that, before the decree of the theological tribunal appeared, it was already disgraced and scouted.

While the Sorbonne, rendered still more furious by these attacks, were labouring with all their might to make "Belisarius" a heretic, a deist, an enemy to the throne and to the altar (for these were the two great weapons with which they fought), I was constantly receiving letters from the Sovereigns of Europe, and from the wisest and most enlightened men, in which they extolled my book, which, they said, ought to be the breviary of kings. The Empress of Russia had translated it into her native language, and had dedicated the translation to an archbishop of that country. The Empress-Queen of Hungary, who was so strict with respect to writings levelled against religion, had, in spite of the Archbishop of Vienna, ordered it to be printed in her dominions. I neglected not, as you may well suppose, to make the Court and Parliament acquainted with this universal success; and neither the one nor the other felt any desire to share the ridicule of the Sorbonne.

Things being in this state, I found my presence no longer necessary in Paris; so that the time which was employed by the doctors in manufacturing their decree of censure, was spent by me in fulfilling the sacred duties of friendship.

Madame Filleul was dying of a slow fever, occasioned by a sharp humour in her blood, for which Bouvart, the most skilful of our physicians, had ordered the waters and baths of Aix-la-Chapelle. She was attended by the young Countess de Seran; but, in the state in which the patient was, the assistance of a male friend was necessary. Their friend Bouret besought me to accompany them. I considered it as a duty; and as soon as they heard my reply, Madame de Seran wrote me the following note:

"Is it indeed true that you are coming with us to the waters? No, I cannot believe it. It was the object of my utmost desire, but I did not dare to make it an object of hope. Your employments, your business, your pleasures, are all against it. Give me the assurance yourself, if you wish me to be convinced of it; and if you give it, believe that I will value this mark of friendship above all

those which I have met with in life. Madame Filleul
dares not hope it any more than I. But you would,
perhaps, be determined by the desire she shows, and the
gratitude she expresses."

I set out with them. Madame Filleul was so ill,
and Madame de Seran so fully expected to see her friend
die on the road, that she advised me to provide myself
with mourning. We arrived at Aix-la-Chapelle with
this courageous woman, who, though she had scarcely a
breath of life remaining, continued still to laugh at our
assumed gaiety. We sent for the physician belonging to
the waters; he found her too weak to bear the bath, and
began with getting her to make a very mild trial of the
waters. Their virtue was such as to produce an eruption
of the humour, which restored the patient to life, and in a
few days she recovered her strength and was able to bear
the bath. Then a prodigious change was wrought by a
kind of miracle. The eruption became complete over her
whole body, and the patient was so far recovered as to be
able to walk out, so that we could not but admire the progress of her recovery, her appetite and the increase of
strength. Alas! notwithstanding all our remonstrances
and our prayers, she abused this speedy recovery, and
would no longer observe the moderate regimen which was
prescribed; yet, notwithstanding her intemperance, she
would have been saved had it not been for the fatal imprudence of which, without our knowledge, she was guilty,
just as her cure was completed. M. de Marigny, whose
sister was dead, wishing to take a wife to his own mind,
such as he thought would make him happy, had married
the eldest daughter of Madame Filleul, the idol of us all;
the beautiful, the sprightly, the charming Julia. In compliance with the desire which his wife felt to see her
mother, he brought her to us, and, at the same time, set
out along with Cochin, the celebrated artist, on a tour
through Holland and Brabant, with the view of seeing
the pictures of the Dutch and Flemish schools.

I have described to you the character of this respectable, interesting and unfortunate man. In his young wife were united all the charms which can be desired in a person of her age, as well in point of external appearance, as of mind and character, mildness, ingenuity, kindness, gaiety and wit — nay, even very sound, good sense, and all cultivated with the greatest care. But, tormented as he was by a gloomy and suspicious self-love, scarce was he married when he took it into his head to be jealous of the tenderness which she felt for her mother, and of the friendship which united her from childhood with Madame de Seran. He was witness to their mutual sensibility at meeting; but he concealed the vexation it occasioned, and the short time he spent with us was not darkened by any cloud. He even expressed very affectionate sentiments for Madame Filleul. "I leave," said he, "our dear Julia with you. It is perfectly right that she should pay attention to her mother's health. I will come in a short time and carry her back, hoping then to find your health, which is so valuable to us all, completely restored." He said also agreeable things to the Countess de Seran, and left us all convinced of his being perfectly tranquil. But in his character, the least particle of ill-humour was like a leaven which quickly fermented and communicated its own nature to the whole mass of thought. As soon as he was alone and left to himself, he figured his wife, now she was with her mother, forgetting him, feeling more at liberty, and expressing to us her pleasure at his absence. "She did not love him, she did not live for him, and he was far from being the object most dear to her in the world." Such were the reflections which revolved in his wretched brain. He had more than once communicated to me the dismal secret. Yet the letters he wrote during the whole of his tour were very agreeable, and till his return we discovered nothing of what was going on in his mind. Let us leave him to his travels and talk a little of the life which we led at Aix-la-Chapelle.

Though we could not prevent Madame Filleul, who was naturally lively, wilful, and fond of good living, from doing everything that was possible to retard her cure ; yet the virtue of the waters and baths was sufficient to expel the new sources of acrimony which she every day poured into her blood, in the form of rich sauces and ragoûts, whose seasoning was absolute poison for her. She boasted of being cured ; and though we were not quite so much convinced of it as she was, we thought we had much reason to rejoice. Our ladies, therefore, took all the amusements of the watering-place, which I shared with them. In the afternoon we walked ; and in the evening we went to the dance at the Ridotto, where there was very high gaming ; but none of us played. The dances were all English, both very pretty and very well executed. It was a curious spectacle for me to see these chains of men and women, from all the northern nations — Russians, Poles, Germans, and particularly English — assembled and drawn together by the common attraction of pleasure. I need not tell you that two French ladies of singular beauty, the eldest of whom was just twenty, drew attention and homage wherever they appeared. When their admirers, therefore, were attending them, either in the morning walk to the waters, or sometimes at their own house, I had solitary hours. I spent these in composition. I was writing " The Incas."

At this time, two of our French bishops came to the waters and took lodgings in our neighbourhood. One of these, Broglio, Bishop of Noyon, was ill ; the other, who was Marboeuf, Bishop of Autun, and since minister for the Church, came to attend him. They were curious to see the author of the book which the Sorbonne was then censuring. They called upon me, and invited me to walk with them. I saw clearly that these prelates wished to wrestle with me, and as I liked the game very well, I willingly entered the ring.

They began, as you may suppose, with talking of "Belisarius." They expected to find me much alarmed at the decree which the Sorbonne was about to fulminate, and they were much surprised to see me so tranquil under their anathema. "Belisarius," said I, "is an old soldier, a worthy man and a Christian at heart; he loves his religion sincerely and cordially; he believes all that is taught in the Gospel and rejects only what that volume does not contain. Belisarius refuses only to believe in the 'gloomy phantoms of superstition, and in the monstrous horrors of fanaticism. I have proposed to the Sorbonne to render this distinction evident by explanatory notes added to my book. They have refused this conciliatory proposition; they have required me to expunge the fifteenth chapter from a book of which forty thousand copies are already circulated — a childish demand, for a mutilated edition, which no one will purchase, could have had no effect but to ruin me. In short, they have obstinately demanded that I should acknowledge the doctrine of civil intolerance, the right of the sword, the lawfulness of proscription, of exile, of the dungeon, the dagger, the rack, and the flames, for forcing men to believe in the religion of the. Lamb; so that, in the lamb of the Gospel, I could discover only the tiger of the Inquisition. I have adhered to the doctrine of Lactantius, of Tertullian, of St. Paul, and to the spirit of the Gospel. This is the reason why the Sorbonne is now busy manufacturing a decree of censure, which it will fulminate against Belisarius, Lactantius, Tertullian, St. Paul, and everyone who thinks as they do. Take care of yourselves, my lords, for you may happen to be of the number."

"But what occasion," said the Bishop of Autun, "have philosophers to speak of theology?" "What occasion," replied I, "have theologians to tyrannise over men's minds, and excite princes to employ force in doing violence to men's belief? Are princes qualified

to judge upon subjects of faith and doctrine ? "   " No,
certainly," said he ; " princes are not judges."   " But
you would have them for your executioners."   " I know
not," replied he, " why the theologians should now be
accused of a kind of persecution which is no longer practised. Never did the Church use her power with so much
moderation."   " It is true, my lord," said I, " that the
Church does use it more temperately ; this she does with
a view of preserving it."   " Why then," urged he,
" should you fix upon this time for attacking it ? "
" Because," replied I, " we write not for the present
moment only ; because it is to be feared that the future
may resemble the past ; and because, when the waters
are low, it is the proper time for labouring at the dykes."
" Ah ! " said he, " they who overturn the dykes are the
pretended philosophers ; and they aim at nothing less
than the destruction of religion."   " Only," replied I,
" let this charitable, beneficent and peaceful religion
retain its own character, and I will venture to assure you
that the unbeliever himself will not dare to attack it.
Neither its pure doctrines nor its morality, nor even its
mysteries, raise enemies against it. But a number of
intelligent men revolt at the violent and fanatical
opinions with which it has been contaminated by a dark
and inhuman theology. Let it be freed from this mixture ; let it be restored to its primitive sanctity ; and
then those who attack it will be the open enemies of the
unhappy, the oppressed and the weak, whom it comforts
and supports."

　　" You may say what you please," replied the bishop ;
" its doctrine is fixed, the edifice is well cemented, and
we will never suffer a single stone to be removed."   I
desired them to observe that the art of mining was
carried to a great height ; that, by means of a little
powder, very high and solid towers were overturned
from their foundations, and even the hardest rocks were
broken.   " Heaven forbid," continued I, " that I should

wish the accomplishment of this prophecy. I sincerely love, I revere from the bottom of my soul, this consolatory religion; but, if ever it perishes from among us, theological fanaticism will be the sole cause, and, with its own hand, will have struck the mortal blow."

He then went to a little distance from me, and I thought I heard him whispering to the Bishop of Noyon, "It will last longer than we." He was mistaken. He then returned to me, and urged, "If you love religion, why should you join those who are planning its destruction?" "I join those only," replied I, "who love it like myself, and who desire it to appear as it came down from heaven—pure, without mixture, and without stain; 'Sicut aurora consurgens, pulchra ut luna, electa ut sol.'"[1] He added, smiling, "'Terribilis ut castrorum acies ordinata.'"[2] "Yes," replied I, "it is terrible to the wicked, to the fanatical, to the impious; but its terrors are all in the future, and are inspired by arms of its own, which are neither sword nor fire." This was nearly the tenor of our first conversation.

At another time, as he constantly repeated that the philosophers took too much liberty: "It is true, my lord," said I, "that they sometimes contrive to supply your place in very exalted functions; but they are such only as you yourselves do not deign to perform." "What functions?" enquired he. "Those of preaching upon the house-tops truths which are too seldom told to sovereigns, to their ministers, to the flatterers who surround them. Since the exile of Fénélon, or, if you please, since the short course of affecting morality which Massillon gave to Louis XV. when a child—instructions which were useless from being premature—have public vices and public crimes found one courageous assailant

---

[1] "As the rising dawn, beautiful as the moon, resplendent as the sun."

[2] "Terrible as an army drawn up in order of battle."

among the priesthood? In the pulpit you venture, indeed, to touch upon little weaknesses, upon ordinary frailties ; but who dares to attack the desolating passions, the scourges of nations—in short, the moral fountains whence flow the sufferings of humanity? Who dares to call pride, ambition, vainglory, false zeal, the furious desire of reigning, and of conquering—who dares to call them to account before God and man for the tears and blood of their innumerable victims?" I then supposed a Chrysostom in the pulpit; and while I enlarged on the subjects which would call forth his eloquence, perhaps I was eloquent myself.

However this may be, my two prelates, after having twice or thrice felt my pulse, found the disease incurable ; till one day, showing the manuscript of "The Incas" on my table, I said to them, "Here is a work which will reduce your doctors to the alternative either of burning the Gospel, or of respecting in Las Casas, the apostle of the Indies, the same sentiments and the same doctrine which they condemn in Belisarius." They then saw that there was nothing more to hope ; and their zeal being damped, or rather their curiosity satisfied, I was left at liberty to dispose of the time which we were throwing away ; they in attempting to make me a theological philosopher, and I in attempting to make them philosophical theologians.

"The Incas," which still required a good deal of labour, was interrupted for some time, and gave place to a memorial in which I undertook to plead the cause of the peasantry of the North, and which is printed in the collection of my works.

I had just read in the *Gazette* that a person, whose name was concealed, proposed to the Economical Society of St. Petersburg, a prize of a thousand ducats for the best work upon the following question : " Is it advantageous for a State that the peasant should be a proprietor of land, or should he possess only movable goods ? and how far is it for the advantage of the State, that the right of the peasant over his property should extend ? "

I had no doubt that this question was proposed by the Empress of Russia herself ; and since she wished the truth on this great subject to be known in her dominions, I resolved to declare it without reserve. One of the Russian ministers, M. de Saldern, had come to Aix-la-Chapelle for the benefit of the waters. I saw him often, and he spoke of Northern affairs as frankly as can be done by a prudent minister. It was through him that my memorial reached its destination. It did not, as I had foreseen, obtain the prize; but I received assurances of its having made a considerable impression.

Thus my solitary hours were filled up, and usefully employed. But a mode of spending my time, which was no less interesting, and, to confess the truth, still more attractive than study, was the conversation of the three ladies, whose characters were all different, but so well agreeing, that their colours united and blended with each other like those of the rainbow. Now, it is from this harmonious mixture of sentiments and thoughts that the charm of conversation results. Unanimity of sentiment, though agreeable at first, becomes in the end tiresome. Accordingly, Madame Filleul used to say that she liked difference of opinion ; that nothing else was genuine and sincere ; that Nature never made any two things exactly alike; neither two eggs, nor two leaves of trees, nor two minds and characters ; and that, wherever there appeared to be a constant similarity of feelings and opinions, there was dissimulation and complaisance on one side, and frequently on both.

One of the three, Madame de Seran, had admitted me to her confidence; and the subject of this confidence was of such a nature as to give rise to interesting private conversations. She might, had she chosen, have succeeded to Madame de Pompadour. She carried on a constant correspondence with the King ; he wrote her by every post ; and these letters and replies were all shown to me. The thread of this little story had been formed as follows :

Madame de Seran was the daughter of a M. de Bulioud, a man of good family, but of no fortune, who had formerly been governor of the pages to the Duke of Orleans. By one of the strangest fatalities, which I am unable to explain, this young person, from the time she was fifteen, had been the object of her father's gloomy and violent dislike, and of her mother's aversion. She was beautiful as the Goddess of Love, and still more interesting by her kindness and native innocence, than by the lustre of her beauty ; she wept and lamented in this cruel and dismal situation, when her father suddenly formed the resolution of marrying her, by assigning, as a portion, his appointment of governor of the pages, which he yielded to his son-in-law. This husband, to whom he presented her, was also a gentleman of ancient family, whose whole fortune consisted of a little estate in Normandy. But, besides being poor, M. de Seran was ugly, and had something disgusting in his ugliness ; red-haired, ill-made, with only one eye, in which there was a cataract ; but, with all these defects, the worthiest and the best of men. When he was presented to our fair Adelaide, she grew pale with horror, and her heart revolted against him with disgust and repugnance. The presence of her parents led her, as much as possible, to conceal this first impression, but M. de Seran perceived it. He asked a few moments of private conversation with her ; and when they were alone, he said, " Mademoiselle, you think me very ugly, and you shrink from me. I see this ; you have no occasion to conceal it. If you believe this repugnance to be invincible, speak to me as your friend ; the secret shall be kept ; I will take the rupture upon myself ; neither your father nor mother shall know anything of the acknowledgment you have made. Nevertheless, were it possible to make you endure in a husband these injuries of Nature, and, for this purpose, were the attentions and complaisance of a kind and tender friendship sufficient, you might confidently expect these from a man whose soul is honourable, and who, through his whole life, would feel grateful for your not having rejected him. Consult your own mind, and answer me; you are at perfect liberty."

Adelaide was so unhappy; this worthy man had evidently so sincere a desire of procuring her a milder fate, that she was in hopes of being able to summon courage sufficient to accept him. "Sir," said she, "the speech I have heard, the stamp of goodness and uprightness which this language bears, inspires me with the most sincere esteem for you. Give me twenty-four hours to think of it, and come back to-morrow."

The most urgent counsels of reason and misfortune were necessary to determine her; but, at last, the esteem which she felt for M. de Seran triumphed over all her disgust. "Sir," said she, when he returned, "I am convinced that ugliness, as well as beauty, is soon forgotten; and that the only qualities whose impression is not weakened by habit, and whose value, on the contrary, is every day better felt, are the qualities of the mind. These I find in you, and that is enough; and I trust to your honour for making me happy. It is my wish to make you the same."

In this manner was Mademoiselle de Bulioud married before she was quite fifteen; and M. de Seran was everything to her that he had promised to be. I do not say that this union had the charms of love; but it was made agreeable by peace, by friendship, by the tenderest esteem. The husband felt no anxiety in seeing his wife surrounded with adorers; and the wife, by her steady and proper conduct, justified in the eyes of the public this confidence of her husband.

Nevertheless, as it was impossible to see, to hear,

and, above all, to be acquainted with her, without wishing her to be in more prosperous circumstances, her
friends interested themselves in the advancement of her
fortune; and at the marriage of the Duke de Chartres,
they formed the design of procuring her an honourable
situation with the young Princess. But for that purpose, an ancient and pure nobility was not sufficient,
unless she had been presented to the King: such was
the etiquette at the Court of Orleans. This, however,
was bestowed only on those who could trace their
nobility four hundred years back. Upon this footing
she was entitled to the honour, and it was granted. But
the King, after listening more attentively to the praises
of her beauty than to the proofs of her nobility, gave
his consent, only on condition that after being presented, she should go and thank him; an article which
was concealed from M. de Seran, and which was not
expected even by his wife; for in real good earnest, she
aimed only at the place which was promised her in the
Duke of Orleans' Court; and when she was required
to go alone to the rendezvous, which the King gave her
in his private apartments, and to thank him in person,
I know that she trembled exceedingly. Nevertheless,
she went; and I arrived at Madame de Filleul's just as
they were waiting her return. There it was that I
learned what I have mentioned; and I saw well that
her friends had considered the place at the Court of
Orleans as only a specious pretext, and considered the
present rendezvous as the important object.

I had the pleasure of seeing ambition raise its
castles in the air: the young countess was to be omnipotent, the King and the Court were to be at her feet,
while all her friends would be loaded with favours, and
I, myself, honoured with the confidence of the mistress,
might, through her, make the King do all the good I
wished: nothing could be so fine. The company expected the young sovereign, they counted every minute,

they died with impatience to see her arrive; and yet
they were glad at her being so long of arriving.

At last she does arrive, and gives us an account of
all that has passed. A page of the bed-chamber waited
for her at the gate of the chapel; it was quite dark;
she went up by a concealed staircase into the private
apartments. She had not long to wait for the King.
He had accosted her with an agreeable air, had taken
her hands, had pressed them respectfully, and, on seeing
her apprehensive, had encouraged her by gentle words
and a look full of kindness. He then made her sit down
opposite to him, congratulated her upon the success of
the appearance she had made, and said that everyone
agreed nothing so handsome had ever appeared in his
Court. "'Then,' said she, 'it must be true, sire, that
happiness makes us beautiful; and in that case, I should
be still handsomer now.', 'Accordingly you are so,'
said he, taking my hands and gently squeezing them
in his, which were then trembling. After a moment's
silence, in which his looks alone spoke, he asked me
what place at Court I should be ambitious to obtain. I
answered, 'The place of the Princess d'Armagnac.' (She
was an old friend of the King, who was lately dead.)
'Ah!' said he, 'you are very young to supply the
place of a friend who was present at my birth, who
held me upon her knees, and whom I have loved from
my cradle. Time, madam, is necessary to obtain my
confidence. I have been so often deceived.' 'Oh!'
said I, 'I will not deceive you; and if time only is
necessary to deserve the exalted title of your friend, I
have that to give you.' This language, from a person
only twenty, surprised, but did not displease him.
Changing the subject, he asked me if I thought his
private apartments furnished with taste. 'No,' said
I; 'I should like them blue.' As blue is his favourite
colour, he was flattered by this reply. I added that in
every other respect, they appeared to me charming.

' If you like them,' said he, ' I hope you will sometimes be so good as to come every Sunday, for instance,
at the same hour as now.' I assured him that I would
avail myself of every opportunity of paying my court to
him. Upon which he left me, and went to sup with his
children. He made an appointment for this day se'n-
night, at the same hour. I give you all warning, therefore, that I shall be the King's friend, and that I will
never be anything more."

As this resolution was formed, not only by her head,
but by her heart, she adhered to it ; of this I had full
proof. At the second meeting she found the drawing-
room furniture blue, according to her desire—a very
delicate piece of attention. She went there every
Sunday ; and through Janel, the postmaster - general,
she often, in the interval between these meetings, received letters, written by the King himself. In these
letters, however, which I have seen, he never went
beyond the bounds of a respectful gallantry ; and the
answers she wrote, full of wit, grace and delicacy, were
flattering to his vanity, but never to his love. Madame
de Seran had, in an infinite degree, that easy wit which,
being quite natural and agreeable, delights those who
have much wit and pleases those who have little. The
King's self-love, however difficult to satisfy, had been
soon at ease with her. After their second meeting, the
moments which preceded the royal supper appeared to
him so short, that he begged her to be so good as to wait
and allow a little supper to be served up to her, promising
to abridge his own as much as possible, in order to return
and be a few moments longer with her. As he had a
small library in his apartments, she one evening asked
for some agreeable book to amuse her in his absence ;
and the King desiring her to make a choice, she was so
kind and attentive to me as to name " Belisarius." " I
have it not," replied the King ; "it is the only one of
Marmontel's works which he has not given me." " Then,

sire," said she, "choose yourself a book which may amuse
and interest me." " I hope," said he, " that this will,"
and he gave her a collection of poems, written upon the
subject of his recovery. This furnished her, after supper,
with a rich and ample fund of praise ; the more flattering,
because genius was there employed to express feeling.
Had the King been young, and animated by that fire
which inspires boldness and makes it be forgiven, I
would not have sworn that the young countess, however
well-disposed, would never have found any danger in these
private interviews. But the feeble and timid desire of a
man who was worn out by pleasures more than by years,
stood in need of encouragement ; and it received none
from her air of decency, of reserve, and of modesty. Of
this, the young lady was quite sensible. " Accordingly,"
said she, " I am certain he will never dare to be anything more than my friend, and I am quite satisfied."

Yet she one day talked to him of his mistresses, and
asked if he had ever been really in love. He replied that
he had, with Madame de Chateauroux. " And with
Madame de Pompadour ? " " No," said he ; " I never
felt any love for her." " Yet you retained her as long
as she lived." " Yes ; because, had I dismissed her, it
would have killed her." There was nothing very seducing
in this frankness ; nor did Madame de Seran ever feel any
temptation to succeed a woman whom the King had retained only out of pity.

She was on this footing with him when she and I left
all to accompany our sick and dying friend to Aix-la-
Chapelle.

Madame de Seran regularly, by every post, received
a letter from the King, through the good offices of Janel.
She communicated to me both these letters and her
answers, and continued to do so as long as their correspondence lasted ; so that I am an ocular witness to the
purity of this connection. The letters of the King were
full of expressions which left no room for doubt. " You

are only too respectable. Allow me to kiss your hands. Allow me, in absence, at least, to embrace you." He spoke to her of the death of the Dauphin, whom he called "our sacred hero," and said to her that her absence deprived him of consolations which he much wanted on so cruel a loss. Such was his language ; and he would not have been so complaisant as to disguise in this manner the style of a happy lover. I shall have occasion to speak again of these letters of the King, and of the impression which they produced upon a mind less easily convinced than mine. Meanwhile, I may observe that the King, at his age, was not sorry to have an opportunity of tasting the charms of a sentimental union—the more flattering and agreeable that it was new, and that it sensibly affected him without endangering his vanity.

Though the noise which "Belisarius" made, and the celebrity which the "Moral Tales" possessed in the north of Europe, had already given me sufficient distinction among the crowd of those with whom I lived, a very honourable adventure made me the object of new attention. One morning, as we were passing before the great hotel where the Ridotto was held, I heard myself called by name. I looked up, and saw, at the window whence the voice came, a man, who immediately cried out, " It is he ! " and disappeared. I had not recognised him ; but he instantly came out from the hotel, ran up, and took me in his arms, exclaiming, " What a happy meeting ! " It was the Prince of Brunswick. " Come," continued he, " let me introduce you to my wife ; this will make her very happy." We then went in, and he said, " Madam, you were so desirous to be acquainted with the author of ' Belisarius ' and the ' Moral Tales '—here he is ; I introduce him to you." Her Royal Highness, sister to the Queen of England, received me with the same joy and cordiality with which the Prince introduced me. At this very time the magistrates of the city were waiting for them at the fountain, to cause it to be opened in their

presence, that they might see the concretion of pure
sulphur that was formed in stalactites under the stone of
the reservoir ; a species of honour that was shown only
to persons of the first distinction. " Go there by yourself," said the Prince to his wife ; " I will spend these
moments more agreeably with Marmontel." I wished to
decline this favour ; but was obliged to continue with
him at least a quarter of an hour, which he employed in
talking with enthusiasm of the literary men whom he had
met at Paris, and of the happy hours he had spent in
their company. He then told me that the afflicting idea
which our society had left in his mind, was the necessity
of renouncing all hope of prevailing upon us to leave our
country ; for that no sovereign in Europe was so rich, or
so powerful, as to make us any compensation for the
happiness of living together.

I found at last that the only means of prevailing
upon him to go to the fountain, was to express a desire
of seeing it opened myself; and I had the honour of
attending him.

As they were to set out next day, the Princess was
so good as to ask me to spend the evening with them at
the Ridotto. The moment I arrived, she gave over dancing, of which she was passionately fond, that she might
come and talk with me. Till one o'clock next morning,
she, the lady who accompanied her (Miss Stuart), and I,
remained in a corner, conversing upon everything which
this amiable Princess chose to enquire into. It is possible that her kindness might produce a deception upon
me, but her conversation appeared to me agreeable and
full of wit. " How then," said I, " have you been educated, in order to retain this adorable simplicity of
character ? How little you resemble the persons of your
rank whom I have hitherto seen ! " " Because," replied
Miss Stuart, " at your Court princes are taught to reign,
whereas at ours they are taught to please."

The Princess, before leaving me, was so kind as to

ask my promise to take a journey to England, at the
time she was to be there. " I will do you the honours of
that country," said she (these are her words); "and I
will, myself, present you to the King my brother." I
promised that, unless some unsurmountable obstacle
intervened, I would pay my court to her at London; and
I took leave of her and her worthy husband, sincerely
affected by the marks of kindness which I had received
from both. I did not feel any increase of pride; but in
the Ridotto circle, I thought I could perceive an increase
of respect towards me. There may seem, my children,
to be a degree of vanity in relating these particulars to
you; but it is of importance for you to know that a little
talent, joined to a plain and honourable conduct, makes a
man universally esteemed.

Though Madame de Seran and Madame de Marigny
were not ill, this did not prevent them from taking often
the pleasure of bathing; and I heard them talk of the
young girl who attended their bath as a model whom
sculptors would have gladly employed for the statue of
Atalanta, of Diana, or even of Venus. Having a taste
for the arts, I was curious to know this model that was
so much extolled. I went to see the young bathing
attendant. I found her really handsome, and almost as
virtuous as she was handsome. We formed an acquaintance. One of her friends, who soon became mine, was so
good as to allow us sometimes to go and take an evening
repast in her little garden. This humble society, by
bringing me nearer to simple nature, restored me philosophy enough to preserve my mind in peace beside my
two young ladies; a situation which otherwise could not
but have been painful. After all, these entertainments
were not ruinous; the whole expense consisted in a few
little cakes, with a bottle of Moselle wine; and Madame
Filleul, whom I had made my confidante, secretly supplied
me with little flasks of Malaga wine, which her attendant and I drank to her health. Alas! that health, which

in spite of all her intemperance, continued still improving through the wonderful virtue of the baths, soon experienced a fatal revolution.

M. de Marigny returned from his journey to Holland ; he meant to carry his wife back with him to Paris. But Madame Filleul having expressed how agreeable it would be if he would leave her daughter till the end of the watering season which was not far distant, he yielded with apparent willingness to this desire of a sick mother ; and, as he wished to visit Spa on his way, our young ladies resolved to accompany him. They all urged me to take this little journey. A kind of secret presentiment made me very urgent to keep Madame Filleul company ; but she herself, obstinately insisting upon being left alone, obliged me to depart. Bad omens preceded this unfortunate journey. The Messrs. Regewski, two Polish gentlemen, who were acquainted with our ladies, thought it would be a proper piece of gallantry to attend them on horseback. M. de Marigny no sooner saw them scampering by the side of the carriage, than he fell into a bad humour ; and from that moment the storm which rose in his mind continued to swell and become more tempestuous.

Yet, on our arrival at Spa, he came with us to the Ridotto ; but the more brilliant it appeared, the more struck he was with the kind of emotion produced by the appearance of our young ladies, the darker grew his chagrin. Yet he would not demean himself so far as to appear jealous. He covered his ill-humour under a more vague pretence.

At supper, as he was sitting gloomy and silent, Madame de Seran and his wife having urged him to declare the cause of his sadness, he at last answered that he saw too well that his presence was burdensome; that, after all he had done to gain his wife's affection, he was not beloved ; that he was hated, detested ; that the request of Madame Filleul was made in concert

with his wife ; that her object had been merely to get
rid of him ; that she had accompanied him to Spa
merely for her own amusement ; that he was not the
dupe of this pretty behaviour, and knew very well how
much she longed for his departure. She began to tell
him that he was behaving unjustly ; that if he had
expressed the slightest unwillingness to leave her with
her mother, neither of them would have wished to
abuse his complaisance ; that even now, though she
had left her trunks at Aix-la-Chapelle, she was resolved
to set out with him. " No, madam," said he ; "remain ;
it is too late ; I wish for no sacrifices." " Certainly,"
replied she, " it is a sacrifice to leave my mother in
her present situation ; but there is none which I am
not ready to make on your account." " I won't have
any," repeated he, rising from table. Madame de Seran
was attempting to soothe him. " As for you, madam,"
said he, " I am not speaking to you. I should then
have too much to say. I only beg you won't interfere
in anything which passes between me and my wife."
He went out abruptly, and left us all three in consternation. After having consulted for a moment, we
were of opinion that his wife should go to him. She
was pale, and all in tears. In this condition she would
have melted the heart of a tiger ; but he, afraid of being
softened by her presence, had given directions that she
should not be admitted, and had ordered that post-horses
should be put to his carriage by daybreak. Of all
masters, he was the most punctually obeyed. His *valet-
de-chambre* represented that if he allowed his mistress to
enter, he would be dismissed instantly ; and that his
master, in a fit of passion, would be capable of the
most extreme violence. We hoped that sleep might
calm him a little, and I only desired to be informed
the moment he awaked.

I had not slept, I was not even undressed when
his servant came and told me he was rising. I entered

his room, and, in the most affecting terms, represented
to him the condition in which he left his wife. " It is
all hypocrisy," said he; "you do not understand the
female character. I know it to my cost." The presence
of his servants forced me to be silent; and when he was
going to set out, "Adieu, my friend," said he, squeezing
my hand; " pity the most unfortunate of men. Adieu."
And with the same air with which he would have
mounted the scaffold, he went into his carriage and
drove off.

The grief of Madame de Marigny was then changed
into indignation. " He throws me off," said she; " he
wishes to alienate my heart from him; he will succeed.
Heaven is my witness how much I was disposed to love
him; it would have been my delight and my pride to have
made him happy; but he will not be happy; he has
sworn that he will force me to hate him."

We spent three days at Spa; the young ladies in dis-
persing the sadness with which their minds were affected,
and in reflecting upon the distressing consequences which
this journey might produce. I did not yet foresee the still
more cruel affliction which it was soon to occasion.

In proportion as the blood was purified in the veins
of our patient, an eruption came out upon the skin over
her whole body, which dried of itself and fell off in dust.
It was this which had produced her recovery; and the
moment that this impure part of the blood had begun to
make its appearance outwardly, the physician had considered her as restored to life. But she was disgusted with
this eruption, and thinking the cure too slow, wished to
accelerate it. Taking advantage, with that view, of the
period of our absence, she had covered her whole body
with cerate. Immediately the transpiration of the humour
had ceased, and we found the patient in a more desperate
state than ever. She wished to return to Paris, but was
with difficulty conducted thither, and continued ever after
in a languishing condition.

That she might have time to rest on the road, we travelled by short stages. At Liège, where we had slept, a citizen, of very good appearance, called on me in the morning, and said, "Sir, I learned yesterday evening that you were here. I lie under great obligations to you, and have come to thank you. My name is Bassompierre. I am a bookseller and printer in this city; I print your works, for which I have a great sale over all Germany. I have already published four large editions of your 'Moral Tales;' I am busy with the third edition of 'Belisarius.'" "What! sir," said I, interrupting him, "you first rob me of the fruit of my labour, and then you come and boast of it to myself!" "Softly," replied he; "your privileges do not extend to us. Liège is a free town. We have a right to print every work we think fit ; this is our trade. Provided you are not pirated in France, where your works have a privilege, you will be still abundantly rich. Do me the favour, then, to come and breakfast with me. You will see one of the finest printing-offices in Europe, and you will be satisfied with the manner in which your works are executed." I went to Bassompierre's house, in order to see this execution. The breakfast that awaited me was composed of cold meat and fish. My Liège friends entertained me in the best manner they could. I was at table between Bassompierre's two daughters, who said to me, as they poured out Rhenish wine, " M. Marmontel, why should you go to Paris, where you are persecuted ? Stay here ; live with our father ; we have a handsome room to give you. We will take care of you. You shall compose at perfect ease ; and what you have written in the evening shall be printed next day." I was almost tempted to accept the proposal. Bassompierre, by way of compensation for his piracies, presented me with the little edition of Molière, which you read—it cost me 10,000 crowns.

At Brussels, I was curious to see a rich collection of pictures. The amateur who had formed it was, I believe, a Chevalier Verule, a melancholy and vapourish man,

who firmly believed that a breath of air would be mortal
to him, and kept himself shut up at home as in a box.
His cabinet was open only to persons of rank, or famous
connoisseurs.   I was neither ; but after having formed
some idea of his character, I was in hopes of obtaining a
good reception.   I got myself introduced to him.   "Do
not wonder, sir," said I, " that a man of letters, who at
Paris is intimate with the most celebrated artists and
the amateurs of the fine arts, should wish to have it in
his power to give them accounts of a man for whom
they all entertain the most distinguished esteem.   They
will understand that I have passed through Brussels, and
would never forgive me had I omitted to call upon you
and enquire about the state of your health."   "Ah! sir,"
said he, " my health is very poor " ; and he began a long
catalogue of his nervous complaints, of his vapours, of
the excessive weakness of his organs.   I listened ; and
after exhorting him to take care of himself, was about
to take my leave.   "What! sir," said he, "will you go
without casting your eyes over my pictures ? "   " I am
not a judge of their merit," said I ; " I do not deserve
the trouble it would cost you to show them."   However,
I allowed myself to be led on ; and the first picture he
pointed out was a very fine landscape by Berghem.
"Ah!" exclaimed I, " I took that picture at first for a
window through which I saw the country, and these
beautiful flocks."   "This," said he, with transport, "is
the finest praise ever given to that picture."   I expressed
the same surprise and the same illusion on approaching
a glass cabinet, which contained a picture by Rubens,
representing his three wives painted as large as life ;
and as he thus showed me in succession his most remarkable pictures, I pretended always to receive the impression
of reality.   He was never tired of renewing my surprise.
I allowed him to enjoy it as much as he chose, so that
he at last told me that my instinct was a better judge of
his pictures than the skill of many others, who assumed

the character of connoisseurs, and who examined everything, but felt nothing.

At Valenciennes, a curiosity of another kind was
like to have cost me dear. As we had arrived early in
that place, I thought I might spend the rest of the evening in walking on the rampart, and taking a view of the
fortifications. While I was surveying them, an officer
on guard, at the head of his company, came up, and
abruptly asked me what I was doing. " I am walking,"
said I, " and looking at these fine fortifications." " Then
you do not know that you are prohibited to walk upon
these ramparts, and to examine these works ? " " I
certainly did not know this." " Where do you come
from ? " " From Paris." " Who are you ? " " A
literary man, who had never seen a fortified place,
except in books, and was curious to see one in reality."
" Where do you lodge ? " I named the inn, and the
three ladies whom I accompanied ; I told also my name.
He at last said, " What you say has the appearance
of truth ; withdraw." I gave him no occasion to repeat
the order.

As I was relating my adventure to the ladies, we
saw the commandant of the place arrive, who, proving
luckily to have been formerly patronised by Madame de
Pompadour, came to pay his respects to the sister-in-law
of his benefactress. He appeared to know what had
happened, and told me I was lucky in not having been
sent to prison. But he offered to be my guide himself
next morning, and to show me all the outworks of the
place. I accepted his offer with gratitude, and had the
pleasure of walking round the city at leisure and with
safety.

Shortly after our arrival at Paris, we had the
affliction of losing Madame Filleul. Never was death
more courageous and tranquil. She was a woman of a
very singular character, full of wit, and of a wit whose
penetration, vivacity and delicacy resembled a glance

from the eye of the lynx ; she had nothing bordering
either on stratagem or artifice. I never discovered in
her either the follies or vanities of her sex ; she had the
usual tastes, but plain, natural, and without caprice.
Her soul was lively, but peaceful ; she had enough of
feeling to be affectionate and beneficent, but not enough
to be the sport of her passions. Her inclinations were
mild, peaceful and steady ; she yielded to them without
weakness, and was never enslaved to them ; she viewed
the things of life and of the world as a game which she
was diverted with seeing played, and at which she was
occasionally obliged to play herself, " but without," as
she said, " being either a knave or a dupe." [1] Thus it
was that she acted with little attention to her own interest, but more to that of her friends. No event surprised her ; and in every situation she had the advantage
of coolness and prudence. She it was, I have no doubt,
who put Madame de Seran on the road to fortune ; but
she only smiled at the ingenuousness of this young lady
when she heard her say that " even in a king, were he
king of the world, she would not have a lover whom she
did not love." " You shall have kings made for you,"
said Madame Filleul, " with whom you may be in love,
and a fortune which you will only have to enjoy." " Indeed," said the young woman, " you would all be glad if
my power were absolute, that you might only have to ask
for whatever you wished ; but while you were diverting
yourselves here, I should die of *ennui* above-stairs, like
Madame de Pompadour." " Come, child, let us be
poor," said Madame Filleul ; " were I in your place, I
should be as foolish as yourself " ; and, in the evening,
we gaily ate our leg of mutton, and laughed at human

---

1 Probably in allusion to the following excellent lines of
Madame Deshoulieres :

> " On commence par être dupe,
> On finit par être fripon."

greatness. Thus, without being affected by the approach
of death, she took leave of her friends with a smile, and
her departure was only a gentle swoon.

On my return from Aix-la-Chapelle, I found the censure of the Sorbonne fixed on the door of the Academy,
and on that of Madame Geoffrin. But the Swiss porters
of the Louvre seemed to have unanimously agreed in
wiping their brooms upon this placard. The censure and
the mandate of the archbishop were read in the parish
churches throughout Paris, and they were scouted in
every company. Neither the Court nor the Parliament
had interfered in this business. I was only desired to
keep quiet, and "Belisarius" continued to be printed
and sold with the royal privilege. But a more afflicting
event than the decrees of the Sorbonne was awaiting me
at Maisons, and, on arriving there, I found all my
courage was necessary.

I mentioned a young niece of Madame Gaulard, and
the agreeable habit which I had formed of spending the
summer with them, and sometimes even the winter.
This habit of living together had produced an attachment between the niece and myself. Neither of us was
rich; but, through the interest of our friend Bouret,
nothing was easier than to procure me, either at Paris or
in the country, an appointment which would be sufficient
to place us in easy circumstances. We had made no
one the confidant of our desires and our hopes. But the
freedom with which we were left together, the tranquil
confidence with which Madame Gaulard herself viewed
our intimacy left us no doubt that she would be favourable to our wishes. Bouret, in particular, seemed to
take so much pleasure in seeing our good understanding
that I thought myself sure of him. I hoped, too, to be
able to bring back his friend in good health, and then
made no doubt of prevailing on him to interest himself
in my fortune and in my marriage.

But Madame Gaulard had a cousin whom she

tenderly loved, and whose fortune was made. This cousin, who bore the same relation to the young niece, fell in love with her, asked her in marriage during my absence, and without difficulty obtained her. Being too young and too timid to declare another inclination, she engaged herself so far that I arrived only in time to be present at the marriage. The dispensation from Rome alone was waited for, before going to the altar; and I, in the character of an intimate friend of the family, was to be witness and confidant of the whole. My situation was painful; that of the young lady was almost equally so; and, however good an appearance we had resolved to maintain, I can hardly conceive how our sadness was not betrayed to the eyes of the aunt and the future husband. Luckily, the freedom of the country allowed us to exchange a few words of consolation, and to inspire each other with the courage which we so much wanted. In such circumstances, hopeless love takes refuge in the arms of friendship; and to this we had recourse. We promised, therefore, to be at least friends for life; and so long as our two hearts were thus allowed to comfort each other, we were not unhappy. But till the fatal dispensation arrived, it was proper that I should absent myself, and a proper opportunity soon presented itself.

BOOK IX

M. DE MARIGNY, having become reconciled to his wife, shortened his journey to Fontainebleau, and went with her to Menars. He expressed a desire that I should accompany him in this journey; and his wife urged me still more earnestly. Being in the secret of their quarrel, I hoped to be able to confirm their reconciliation; and out of gratitude to him, as well as friendship for her, I agreed to accompany them. He wrote me from Fontainebleau on the 12th of October, 1767, "You cannot believe, sir, what pleasure you afford me by coming to Menars. I might, perhaps, be a little jealous of that which Madame de Marigny has expressed."

My presence was not useless during this journey. More than one cloud arose between them, which it was necessary to disperse. Even on the road, M. de Marigny, while praising his wife, wished to impute the faults, which she had committed, to the Countess de Seran. But the young lady, who had a great deal of spirit, refused to avail herself of this excuse. "There has been nothing to blame," said she, "in my conduct towards you, and you are accusing me unjustly; but you are still more unjust when you suppose that my friend is to blame." And when some expressions too rash and full of acrimony escaped him respecting this absent friend, "Sir," said his wife, "you ought to respect her both on your own account, and on mine; and I must say that you will never offend her without wounding my heart."

The truth is, that in the intimate conversation of these two ladies, Madame de Seran took the greatest care to inspire her friend with mildness, with complaisance, and, if possible, with love for a man who, she told her, possessed amiable qualities, and who, if his violence and ill-humour were a little softened, might make a very good husband.

A little energy and pride was necessary with a man who, himself possessing frankness and courage, esteemed a character which resembled his own. We therefore assumed with him a tone of reasoning which was mild, but firm ; and I fulfilled so well my office of mediator that I left them in perfect harmony together. But what I had seen, and, above all, what I had confidentially heard from the young lady, gave me reason to think that this married couple, though they might esteem, would never love each other.

The following spring, I again took a journey with them into Touraine. I had then the pleasure of seeing M. de Marigny fully reconciled to Madame de Seran ; except a few moments of jealous irritation on account of the great intimacy of the two ladies, he was very agreeable to them. With respect to me, he was so pleased at having me as his mediator, that he offered to present me for life with a pretty country-house near Menars. Nothing could be more captivating than its little grove, its garden, its brook of the clearest water, and its delicious retreat upon the banks of the Loire ; but this gift was a chain which I would not consent to wear.

On my return I went to Maisons. This retreat had charms for me ; I loved all its inhabitants, and had reason to hope that I was beloved. I could not have been more at ease in my own house. When any of my friends wished to see me, they came to Maisons, and were kindly received. The Count de Creutz was the man who took most pleasure and was most liked in the society; because, with the rarest mental endowments, he united simplicity and goodness.

A little grove near Alport was the resting-place during our walks. There his soul laid itself open before me. The sentiments which filled it, the images which the observation and study of Nature had engraved on his memory, and of which his imagination formed, as it were, a rich and splendid gallery; the lofty ideas with which meditation had inspired him, and which his mind poured copiously into mine, whether he spoke of politics or morals, of men or of things, of the arts or sciences, kept me for whole hours attentive and in a manner enchanted. His country and his king, Sweden and Gustavus, the objects of his idolatry, were the two subjects on which he conversed most eloquently and with the greatest delight. The enthusiasm with which he extolled them took such full possession of my mind and senses, that I would willingly have followed him beyond the Baltic.

One of his most passionate inclinations was the love of music; and beneficence was the soul of all his other virtues. One day he came and besought me, as I valued our friendship, to extend my aid to a young man who, he said, was in despair, and on the eve of drowning himself, unless I saved him. " He is a musician," continued he, "with a great deal of talent, and who only requires a pretty opera to make his fortune at Paris. He has just come from Italy; he has made some attempts at Geneva. He came with an opera written upon the subject of one of your tales—' Les Mariages Samnites.' The directors of the opera have heard and refused it. The poor young man has no resource; I have advanced him a few louis, but I can do no more; and, as a last favour, he begged me to recommend him to you."

I had hitherto composed nothing which came near the idea I had formed of a French poem suited to the Italian music; I did not even think myself qualified for it;

but, in order to please the Count de Creutz, I would have
undertaken impossibilities.

I had, just then, on my table one of Voltaire's tales—
" L'Ingenu." I thought it might furnish me with the
groundwork of a little comic opera. "I will go," said I to
the Count de Creutz, " and see if I can introduce it upon
the stage, and extract from it sentiments and descriptions
which may be favourable to song. Return in eight days,
and bring me the young man."

The half of my poem was written when they arrived.
Gretry, transported with joy, went and began his work,
while I was finishing mine. *The Huron* was completely
successful; and Gretry, more modest and more grateful
than he afterwards was, thinking his reputation not yet
sufficiently established, besought me not to abandon him.
Then it was that I wrote *Lucile*.

In consequence of the still greater success which this
met with, I perceived that the public was disposed to
relish a drama of a character suited to that of my tales.
Seeing, therefore, that with a musician and actors who
were capable of answering my intentions, faithful and
interesting representations might be formed, I was myself seized with a very keen relish for this kind of
creation; for I may say that, by raising the character,
I created a new species of comic opera. After *Lucile*, I
wrote *Sylvain;* after *Sylvain*, *L'Ami de la Maison*, and
Zemire et Azor; and our mutual success continued always
to increase. No labour ever afforded me purer enjoyment. My favourite actors, Clairval, Caillot, and
Madame la Ruette, were the managers of their own
theatre. Madame la Ruette invited us to dinner. There
I read my poem, and Gretry sang his music. Both
being approved in this little council, all due preparations
were made for introducing the work upon the stage, and
after two or three rehearsals, it was represented.

Our actors were perfectly sincere in their endeavours
to perform the opera in the best manner : both in acting

and singing, they understood what was proper ; and they had a presentiment of the effects still more infallible than ours. For my own part, I never hesitated in paying the greatest deference to their opinion ; nay, they sometimes accused me of being too ready to follow it. For instance, in the interval between *Lucile* and *Sylvain*, I had written an opera in three acts, upon that tale of my own which is entitled "The Connoisseur." I read it to the little committee. Gretry was charmed, Madame la Ruette and Clairval applauded, but Caillot was cold and silent. I took him aside. "You are not satisfied," said I, "speak freely ; what is your opinion of what you have just heard ? " "My opinion is," said he, "that it is only the *Metromanie* [1] on a small scale; that a satire upon false taste is not lively enough for a theatre like ours, and that this work might fail of success." I then returned to the fire-place where our company was sitting. "Madam," said I, "and you, gentlemen, we are all fools; Caillot alone is in the right," and I threw the manuscript into the fire. They exclaimed that Caillot had made me commit a piece of folly. Gretry shed tears of grief ; and when he went out with me, appeared in such despair, that I was really sorry for what I had done.

Impatience to relieve him from this condition having hindered me from sleeping, the plan and the first scenes of *Sylvain* were the first fruit of this watching. I was writing in the morning when I saw Gretry come in. "I have not shut my eyes to-night," said he. "No more have I ; sit down and listen." I read him my plan, and two scenes. "As to this work," continued I, "I am perfectly secure ; I assure you of its success." He got hold of the first two airs, and went away quite relieved.

Such was the employment of my leisure ; and the produce of this easy labour annually augmented my little fortune. But it was not so considerable as that Madame

---

1 Alluding to the celebrated comedy of that name by Piron.

Gaulard would consider as a suitable establishment for
her niece; she, therefore, as formerly mentioned, gave her
another husband; and this society, which I had so carefully cultivated, was soon broken up.   Another event
threw me into a new set of acquaintances.

It was natural that the fate of " Belisarius " should
have cooled Madame Geoffrin a little towards me.   Being
now more of a declared devotee, she felt some uneasiness
at lodging in her house an author whom the Church had
censured.   The moment I perceived this, I pretended
a desire to be lodged more commodiously.   " I regret
much," said she, " that I have nothing better to offer
you; but I hope that, though you no longer lodge in my
house, you will not the less continue to be one of my
friends, and to attend the dinners at which they meet."
After taking leave in this manner, I made my preparations for leaving her house, and a suitable lodging was
offered me by the Countess de Seran, in an hotel that the
King had given her.   This leads me to resume the thread
of her story.

On her return from Aix-la-Chapelle, the King had
received her better than ever, without being more daring.
However, the mystery of their private meetings had not
escaped the watchful eyes of the Court; and the Duke
de Choiseul, who was determined to keep at a distance
from the King every woman who was not devoted to
himself, had indulged in some hasty and satirical observations against her.   As soon as she learned this, she
was resolved to impose silence upon him.   She was
intimately acquainted with La Borde, the Court banker,
a man devoted to the Duke de Choiseul, to whom he
owed his fortune.   At his house, and in his presence, she
had an interview with the minister.   " My lord duke,"
said she, " I have a favour to ask you, but I must first
compel you to do me justice.   You, I understand, speak
very slightingly of me; you believe me to be one of those
women who aim at possessing the King's heart, and at

acquiring an influence over his mind, which gives you umbrage. I might have punished you for the liberty that you have taken; but I choose rather to undeceive you. The King expressed a desire to see me, which I did not refuse to gratify; we have had private conversations, and have carried on a constant correspondence. You know all this; but the letters of the King will soon inform you of something which you do not know. Read them; you will see an extreme kindness, but as much respect as tenderness, and nothing at which I have cause to blush. I love the King," continued she, " as a father. I would give my life for him; but, King as he is, he will never prevail upon me to deceive him, nor to lower myself by granting what my heart neither will nor can bestow."

The Duke de Choiseul, after reading the letters which she had given him, was about to throw himself at her feet. " Forgive me, madam," said he; " I own myself guilty of having trusted too much to appearances. The King is, indeed, in the right; you are but too admirable. Now, tell me what you ask, and what service can be rendered you by the new friend whom you have attached for life." " I am just about," said she, " to marry my sister to a respectable officer in the army. Neither my relations nor myself are able to give her a marriage portion."

" Well, madam," said he, the King must undertake to provide for the marriage of your sister; and I will procure for her an order on the Treasury for £8,000." " No, my lord duke, no; neither my sister nor I wish money for which we neither have done nor will do anything. What we ask is an appointment which is due to the services of M. de la Barthe; and the only favour we solicit for him is to obtain it in preference to other military men who might have an equal claim to it." This favour was easily granted. But all that the King could prevail upon her to accept for her own use was a present

of the little hotel in which she offered to accommodate me.

Just as I was going to settle there, I found myself
under the necessity of preferring another; and this necessity was produced by the following cause.

My old friend Mademoiselle Clairon having left the
theatre, and taken a pretty large house near the Pont-
Royal, was desirous of having me for an inmate. She
knew me to be engaged with Madame de Seran ; but
knowing that lady to be kind and feeling, she went and
called upon her without my knowledge. She related,
with her theatrical eloquence, the indignity she had
suffered from the gentlemen of the bed-chamber, and the
brutal ingratitude which she had experienced from the
public, in return for her services and her talents. In
this solitary retreat, her sweetest consolation would have
been the company of her old friend. She could let me a
commodious apartment, and was very sure I should accept
it, if not engaged to occupy that which the countess had
kindly offered me. She begged her to be so generous as
to break this engagement herself, and to insist upon my
going to lodge with her. "You are surrounded, madam,"
said she, "with every kind of happiness ; while I have
none remaining but that which I can derive from the
constant and intimate society of a real friend. Do not
in pity deprive me of this."

Madame de Seran was affected by her prayer. She
suspected me of having given my consent. I assured
her of the contrary. In fact, the lodging she was fitting
up for me would have been more agreeable. I should
have been more at liberty, and only a few steps from
the Academy. This last circumstance alone would have
been of inestimable value to me in bad weather, during
which I should have the Pont-Royal to cross if I lodged
with Mademoiselle Clairon. I had, therefore, no difficulty
in convincing Madame de Seran, that in every respect
this was a sacrifice which I was called upon to make.

"Well," said she, "you must make it; Mademoiselle Clairon has a right to you, which I have not."

I went, therefore, to lodge with my old friend, but perceived from the first day that, with the exception of a little room behind my apartment, it was not habitable for a studious man, on account of the infernal noise of carriages and waggons mounting the bridge, which was close at my ear. Most of the stone and wood which is brought into Paris passes this way. Day and night, therefore, without ceasing, the steep pavement resounded under the wheels of these waggons, and under the feet of the wretched horses which laboriously dragged them up, while the tremendous cries of the waggoners, and the still more piercing sound of their whips, realized to me what Virgil says of Tartarus:

> "Hinc exaudiri gemitus, et sæva sonare,
> Verbera; tum stridor ferri, tractæque catenæ."[1]

But however afflicting this inconvenience was, I said nothing of it to my dear neighbour; and every possible compensation was afforded by the pleasures of the most agreeable and best selected society which I enjoyed during the whole time that she and I dwelt in this house.

She often visited the Duchess of Villeroy, the Duke d'Aumont's daughter, who, at the time her father was persecuting me, had often expressed strongly to me her regret at his injustice, though she could not prevail upon him to mitigate his severity. One evening, when she had just quitted my neighbour, I was surprised when the latter began to say, "Well, Marmontel, you would never name the author of the parody of 'Cinna'; I have at last found it out;" and she named Cury. (Cury, his mother, and his son were by that that time dead.) "And who told you so?" inquired I, with surprise. "A person who knows it well—the Duchess of Villeroy. She has just

---

1 " Hence are heard groanings and the sound of the cruel lash; then the clank of iron and dragging chains."

gone out, and her visit was on your account. Her father wishes to see you." "Me! her father! the Duke d'Aumont!" "He wishes to consult with you about the entertainments which he is desired to give the Court on the occasion of the Dauphin's marriage; 'But my father,' said she, 'would wish Marmontel not to speak to him of what has passed.' 'Certainly,' replied I, 'Marmontel will say nothing. But, madam, has he no regret to express to Marmontel on account of having treated him with such cruel injustice? for I can assure you that he really did so.' 'I know it well,' said she; 'and my father himself is perfectly sensible of it. The parody of "Cinna" was by Cury; La Ferté, who heard him read it, told us so; but so long as the poor man lived, he would not betray him.'"

I was obliged to admit what La Ferté had said; and being curious to see the behaviour of a man condemned by his own conscience, I agreed to the interview, and went to his house.

I found him with this very La Ferté, the intendant of the *Menus Plaisirs*, examining on a table the plan of an artificial firework. As soon as he saw me come in, he dismissed La Ferté, and concealing his agitation under an appearance of vivacity, he led me into his room. There, with a trembling hand, he drew forward a chair, and with a hurried look invited me to sit down. The Duchess of Villeroy had told Mademoiselle Clairon that her father was embarrassed about entertainments for the Court. This expression came into my mind, and, in order to begin the conversation, I said, "Well, my lord duke, so you are very much embarrassed——" At this introduction I saw him turn pale, but luckily I added, "about your Court entertainments." He then recovered from the shock given him by my equivocal expression. "Yes," said he, "very much embarrassed; and I should be obliged to you if you would assist in relieving me." He talked a great deal of the difficulties of such a charge;

we looked over the theatrical repositories; he appeared
to relish my advice; and at length asked me if I had not
any new work in my own portfolio. He had heard
Zemire et Azor talked of; he begged me to read it, which
I agreed to do, but only in his own presence. This gave
occasion to a second private interview; but as his erudi-
tion extended to the "Fairy Tales," he discovered my
subject to be the same as "Beauty and the Beast."
"It is impossible," said he, "to give this drama at the
Dauphin's marriage; it would be thought I meant to
apply it to him." The application was of his own
making, and I kept the secret. It is remarkable that,
in neither of our conversations, had this weak and vain
man the magnanimity to express regret at the injustice
he had done me, and a desire, at least, of finding some
opportunity of repairing it.

At this time, the Prince Royal of Sweden made a
journey to Paris; he had already conceived a very warm
affection for the author of "Belisarius," and had been so
good as to enter into a correspondence with me. He expressed a desire to see me often, and in private. I paid
my court to him; and when he learned the death of his
royal father I was the only stranger whom he admitted
to see him in the first moments of his grief. In him I
really saw the singular instance of a young man who was
wise enough to feel sincere and deep affliction at becoming
a king. "What a misfortune," said he, "at my age, to
be loaded with a crown, and an immense duty which I
am incapable of fulfilling. I was travelling to acquire
the knowledge of which I stood in need; and now I
am interrupted in my travels, obliged to return without
having had time to acquire information, to see and to
know men with whom henceforth I can no longer hold
any intimate society, any steady or faithful intercourse.
I must bid an eternal adieu to friendship and truth."
"No, sire," said I; "Truth shuns only those kings who
repel and will not listen to her. Since you love her,

she will follow you; the sensibility of your heart, the frankness of your character, render you worthy of having friends, and they will be found." "Men," replied he, "have few friends; kings have none." "There is one," said I, pointing to the Count de Creutz, who was reading some despatches in a corner; "there is one who will never fail." "Yes," said he, "he is one upon whom I depend; but he will not be with me; my affairs oblige me to leave him here."

This little dialogue may give an idea of my conversations with this young Prince, with whom I was more delighted every day. After having heard a few readings of "The Incas," he desired his minister to ask me for a manuscript copy; and afterwards, when the work was printed, he allowed me to dedicate it to him.

The same year I took a journey to Croix-Fontaine, which was very agreeable at the time, but which, in the end, proved very unfortunate. There raged in this quarter, all along the Seine, a putrid and very dangerously malignant fever. Many persons had died at St. Port and at St. Assise; and it had attacked a great many of the domestics at Croix-Fontaine. Those who were not affected attended their companions; mine did not spare himself, and I myself went pretty often to visit the sick, an act of humanity which was at least perfectly useless. Yet I thought myself still in perfect health, when I received a letter from Paris, desiring me to come to a meeting of the Academy, which was to be held for the reception of the Archbishop of Toulouse, and which the King of Sweden meant to honour with his presence.

The day after my arrival at Paris, I felt as if I had received a blow on the head. Yet I attended the meeting of the Academy; I even read some passages from my work of "The Incas"; but my voice was weak, faint, and devoid of expression. I met with success, but my languor was observed with anxiety by my friends. In the evening the fever attacked me. My servant was struck at the

same time ; and both of us were forty days suspended
between life and death. This was the first illness of
which Bouvard cured me. He paid me all the attentions
of a tender friend. And Mademoiselle Clairon, during
my recovery, treated me with the most affecting attention ; she was my reader ; the reveries of the " Arabian
Nights " were the only study of which my weak brain
was capable.

Shortly after, the Academy lost Duclos ; and at his
death, the place of historiographer of France was given
to me without any solicitation. The manner in which I
received this favour was as follows :

Whilst I continued to lodge with Madame Geoffrin,
Garville, an acquaintance of Mademoiselle Clairon, with
whose frank and honourable character I was well
acquainted, called upon me, and said, " During the
journeys which I took into Brittany, at the time the
Duke d'Aiguillon commanded there, I saw and had
occasion to know him. I am certainly assured that
the action which is raised against him is a mere party
business ; but however good his cause is, the interest of
the States and Parliament of Brittany makes it impossible for him to find an advocate at Paris ; the only
one who has dared to undertake his defence is a poor
young man with no money, whose capacity is not yet
mature, but who is trying his fortune. His name is
Linguet. He has composed a memorial, with which
the Duke is very much dissatisfied. It is a piece of
empty declamation, a shapeless mass of ridiculous metaphors, and there is no possibility of publishing such an
awkward composition. The Duke talked to me of his
distress. I advised him to have recourse to some man
of letters. ' Men of letters,' said he, ' are all prepossessed against me ; they are my enemies.' I replied to
him, that I knew one who was the enemy only of injustice and falsehood ; and I named you. He embraced
me, saying that I would do him the greatest service if I

could prevail upon you to undertake his memoir. I come from him to beg, to beseech that you will do him this service." "Sir," replied I to Garville, "my pen will never decline the defence of a good cause. If that of the Duke d'Aiguillon be such as you describe it, you may depend upon me. Let him send me his papers. After reading them, I will say more positively what I can do. But tell him that the zeal which I will employ in defending him would be equally employed in defending the meanest of the populace, who, in such circumstances, should have recourse to me; and to the acquittal of this duty, I attach two conditions: one, that secrecy shall be observed; the other, that there shall be no thanks, no gratitude between us; I do not wish even to see him."

Garville gave him a faithful report of this answer; and next day he brought me the memorial with the papers. In these papers, it did really appear to me that the action which was raised against him was a mere persecution excited by personal animosity. Finding that the memorial, too, quite answered Garville's description, I moulded it anew. I preserved all that was tolerably well, only arranging it with more order and clearness. I rooted out the incoherent metaphors with which the style was loaded, and I substituted natural and simple expressions instead of this extravagant language. These little corrections alone produced a happy change; for it was chiefly in point of style that this memorial was absurd and ridiculous. However, I added a few passages of my own, such as the introduction—for Linguet had in his indulged an impertinent degree of arrogance—and the conclusion, in which he had neglected to bring into one view the strength of his proof and his arguments.

When the Duke d'Aiguillon saw what I had done, he was very well satisfied. He sent for Linguet, and said, "I have read your memorial, and have made a few alterations, which I beg you will adopt." Linguet read, and then said, foaming with rage, "No, my lord duke, no; it is not you; it is a man of the profession whose hand has been at this work. You have done me a mortal injury; you are attempting to dishonour me. But I am no man's scholar; no man has a right to correct me. I will sign only my own work, which this no longer is. Find out an advocate who will undertake your cause, for I will not." And he was just going, but the Duke d'Aiguillon desired him to stay. He saw himself at his mercy; for no other advocate would sign his memorial. He therefore allowed him to manage this as he thought fit. All the pages which I had written were expunged. Linguet himself wrote anew the introduction and conclusion, but he allowed my arrangement of all the rest to remain; he did not again introduce any of those absurdities which I had effaced from his style, so that he availed himself of my labour, even while he rejected it. However, he never rested till he had discovered who it was that had corrected his memorial; and on learning it, he became, I know not for what reason, my most cruel enemy. A journal, which he afterwards wrote, was deluged with the venom of rage which he poured out at the very mention of my name.

The Duke d'Aiguillon, in spite of his advocate, was extremely sensible of the improvement I had made in his memorial; and he urged Garville to bring me to his house that he might at least, as he said, have the satisfaction of thanking me in person. After having long declined his invitations, I at last yielded, and went once to dine with him. From that time I had not seen him till I received the following note in his own hand: "Sir, I have just asked the King to give you the place of historiographer of France, which is vacant by the death of M. Duclos. His Majesty has granted it, and I lose no time in giving you the information. Come and thank the King."

This mark of favour, the cause of which was unknown, imposed silence on my enemies at Court; and the Duke de Duras, not being so scrupulous as the Duke d'Aumont about " Beauty and the Beast," requested, in 1771, *Zemire et Azor*, for the entertainment at Fontainebleau. It met with unhoped-for success, but not without running the risk of being hissed. *L'Ami de la Maison*, which was presented the same year upon this stage, met with a very cold reception. As soon as I understood the reason, I applied the proper remedy ; and at Paris it met with the same success as *Zemire et Azor*. These are very little things ; but as they interested me, they will also have some degree of interest for my children.

When *Zemire et Azor* was announced at Fontaine-bleau, a report was spread that it was the story of " Beauty and the Beast " brought upon the stage, and that the principal character would creep on all fours. But I very quietly allowed them to say what they pleased. I had given very particular directions about the machinery and dresses; and made no doubt of my intentions having been fulfilled. Neither the tailor nor machinist, however, had taken the trouble to read my directions ; but had made their arrangements according to the tale of " Beauty and the Beast."

My friends were anxious about the success of my work ; Gretry looked dejected ; Clairval himself, who had acted so heartily all my other characters, expressed repugnance to appear in this. I asked him the reason. " How can you expect," said he, " that I can give any interest to a character in which I should be hideous?'" " Hideous !" said I, " you will not be at all hideous. The first glance of you will be frightful; but this ugliness will be united with dignity and grace." " Only look, then," said he, " at the beast's dress which is preparing, for I am told it is shocking." This was the evening before the representation, so that there was not a moment to lose. I asked them to show me Azor's dress ; it was with great difficulty I prevailed upon the

tailor to be so complaisant. He bade me be quite easy
and trust to him. But I insisted; and the Duke de
Duras, after ordering him to take me to the warehouse,
was so good as to accompany me. " Well," said the
tailor disdainfully to his servants, "show the gentleman
the beast's dress." What did I see! a pantaloon just
like the skin of a monkey with a long bare tail, a naked
back, enormous claws for each of the four hoofs, two
long horns in the head, and the most hideous mask,
with boar's teeth. I shrieked with horror, and declared
that my piece should not be acted under this ridiculous
and monstrous disguise. " Then what would you have
had? " asked the tailor, proudly. " I would have wished
you," replied I, " to read my directions, and you would
have seen that I asked a dress for a man, not for a
monkey." " A man's dress for a beast! " " And who
told you that Azor was a beast? " " The tale tells me
so." " The tale is not my work; and my work shall
not be acted till all this be changed." " It is too late."
" Then I will go and ask the King's permission not to
shock him with this hideous spectacle; and I will tell
him the reason." Our man then softened, and asked
what was to be done. " The simplest thing in the
world," replied I ; " tiger-coloured pantaloons, shoes
and gloves of the same, a dolman of purple satin, black
hair, waving and picturesquely disposed; an ugly, but
not deformed mask, nor at all resembling a snout." It
was with great difficulty that all this was found, for the
warehouse was empty; but, by dint of obstinacy, I
forced them to obey me; and I formed the mask myself, by putting together detached pieces cut out of
different masks.

Next morning I made Clairval try this dress; and
when he saw himself in the mirror, it appeared to him
dignified and commanding. " Now, my friend," said I,
" your success depends on the manner in which you
shall enter upon the theatre. If you appear confused,

timid, embarrassed, we are undone; but if you enter proudly, with a firm step, and showing yourself fully, you will command the audience; and after the first moment is over, I will answer for the rest."

I had been served by the machinist in the same negligent manner as by my impertinent tailor; and the magic picture, the most interesting moment of the piece, would have failed if I had not found a remedy for his awkwardness. With two ells of silver mohair to imitate a pier looking-glass, and two ells of clear and transparent gauze, I taught him to produce one of the most agreeable theatrical deceptions.

By these attentions I obtained the most brilliant success. Clairval acted his character to a wish. His proud and daring entrance produced only the suitable impression of astonishment; and from that time I felt no further apprehension. I was in a corner of the orchestra, and behind me was a seat full of Court ladies. When Azor on his knees, at the feet of Zemire, sang to her—

> " Du moment qu'on aime,
> L'on devient si doux,
> Et je suis moi-même
> Plus tremblant que vous." [1]

I heard these ladies say to each other, " He is not ugly now "; and immediately after, " He is handsome."

I must not deny that the charm of music had a wonderful influence in producing these effects. That of Gretry was then what it very seldom was after my time; and he was not sufficiently sensible of the care which I took in marking out the character and the design of an easy and agreeable song. In general, the folly of musicians consists in thinking that they owe nothing to their poet; and Gretry, with all his talents, had this folly in the most sovereign degree.

---

[1] " The moment one loves, one becomes so mild; and I am myself more trembling than you."

As for *L'Ami de la Maison*, my complaisance for
Madame la Ruette, my heroine, was the cause of the
little success which this work met with at Court. My
original plan was to give the character of l'Ami de la
Maison to Caillot, for whom, indeed, I had written it,
and who, I am certain, would have acted it in a superior
manner; but he declined it for a singular reason. " The
situation," said he, " is too like that which we sometimes
get into; and the character, also, is too like that which
is imputed to us. Were I to act l'Ami de la Maison,
according to your intention and my own feeling, no
mother would ever after leave me with her daughter."
" What ! " said I, " would you not act Tartuffe ? "
" Tartuffe," said he, " does not come so close to us;
no one is afraid of our being Tartuffes." Nothing could
overcome his repugnance for a character " which," he
said, " would injure him the more the better he played
it." However, I had observed that La Ruette had a
desire for it, and I perceived that his wife thought that,
next to Caillot, I could give it to no other; Gretry
thought the same, so that I yielded, but repented the
moment I saw the first rehearsal. This character required youth, liveliness, a clear and animated voice, and
delicacy in acting. Honest La Ruette, with his oldish
figure, his trembling and broken voice, was quite out of
place. He made it dull and dismal; not feeling at his
ease, he did not even give way to his natural animation;
he produced a failure in every scene.

Madame la Ruette, too, being a little of a prude,
imagined that the satirical penetration which I had
thrown into the character of Agatha was not becoming
in so young a person. She had thought it incumbent on
her to blunt the point of this pleasantry; and had substituted a severe and reserved air, which took away all
that was agreeable in the character.

Thus my whole work had been rendered unnatural.
Luckily, La Ruette was himself sensible that the cha-

racter of Cleon suited neither his acting nor his singing;
and I found on the same theatre an actor of the name of
Julian, who was less difficult than Caillot, and younger
than La Ruette, whose voice was brilliant, his action
lively, and his figure brisk. Gretry and I applied
ourselves to teach him his part, and he learned to sing
and act it very well.

Madame la Ruette had little inclination to listen to
what I had to say. However, I said, " Madam, we
should become cold if we attempted to be too wise ; be
so good as to give a natural representation of Agatha's
character. Her innocence is not that of Agnes, but still
it is innocence ; and as she employs her malicious penetration only in playing upon the scoundrel who is
attempting to seduce her, be assured it will be approved
of." Her character met with the greatest success ; and
the piece, being again called for at Versailles in 1772,
appeared so altered that it was not known. Yet I had
made no alteration whatever.

It was not till three years after that I gave *La Fausse
Magie;* and though the success was not at first so
brilliant as that of the two others, it has been no less
durable. For more than twenty years past it has frequently appeared on the stage, and yet the public has
never tired. It is true, indeed, that these little works
have lost a good deal of their lustre and grace by losing
the actors for whom I had composed them.

In the same year (1772), I had a prospect of success
at Court of another kind, which I felt much more sensibly ; it was the influence which my poem to the King
upon the burning of the Hôtel-Dieu produced, or seemed
to produce. The gratification of my vanity was nothing ;
but the strong and deep impression which it had made
promised, I was told, to improve the lot of those unfortunate persons whose groans and lamentations I had
brought to the royal ear ; and for the first time in my
life, I hoped to see myself the benefactor of humanity.

I was proud; I would have given my life that the event
had crowned my efforts; but I did not enjoy that happiness.

The ode in praise of Voltaire is nearly of the same
date. It was written on the following occasion. The
society of Mademoiselle Clairon was more numerous and
more brilliant than ever. The conversation was lively,
particularly on the subject of poetry; and a man of
letters could there exchange his ideas with men of the
world who possessed exquisite taste and highly cultivated
understandings. In one of these conversations, I said,
talking of lyric poets, that " the ode could not, among
us, possess that character of truth and dignity which it
had possessed in Greece: for this reason, that poets had
no longer the same ministry to fulfil; that the bards alone
among the Gauls had borne this high character, because
they, by their profession, were bound to celebrate the
glory of heroes."

" And what," said they, " should hinder the poet of
the present day from assuming this ancient character,
and devoting himself to this public ministry?" I replied
that " if there were, as formerly, feasts and public solemnities in which the poet was listened to, the pomp of these
great spectacles would exalt his soul and his genius." As
an instance, I supposed the apotheosis of Voltaire, and
Mademoiselle Clairon upon a large stage, standing at the
foot of his statue and reciting a poem in praise of that
illustrious man. " Do you think," said I, " that in the
ode destined for this solemn occasion the mind and soul
of the poet would not assume a tone of higher truth and
animation than in one which he coolly composes in his
closet?" I saw that this idea made a strong impression,
and Mademoiselle Clairon in particular appeared deeply
affected. This suggested to me the design of composing,
by way of essay, that ode which you will find in the collection of my poetry.

Mademoiselle Clairon, while reading it, felt that her

art could supply what was wanting in mine, and willingly agreed to lend to my verses the charm of that illusion which she was so well able to spread over them.

One evening, when the company were assembled in her drawing-room, a message was sent desiring them to wait for her. Then, while we are talking of Voltaire, a curtain is suddenly raised, and Mademoiselle Clairon appears, standing by the bust of that great man, and dressed as a priestess of Apollo, with a crown of laurel in her hand. She then begins to recite this ode with the look of inspiration and the tone of enthusiasm. This little solemnity had afterwards the merit of giving rise to a more pompous one, of which Voltaire was witness.

Shortly afterwards the Count de Valbelle, Mademoiselle Clairon's lover, having succeeded to an estate by the death of his eldest brother, and gone to enjoy his fortune in the city of Aix in Provence, and the Prince of Anspach having been seized with a passion for our theatrical princess, she was obliged to take a larger and more commodious house than that in which we lodged together. Then it was that I went to the house of the Countess de Seran, and occupied the apartments which she had reserved for me, and where M. Odde came and spent a year with me.

I should have wished to retire with him to Bort; and had in view a small property very near the village, where I would have got a cottage built for myself. Luckily, the price was raised so high as to be beyond my resources, and I was under the necessity of renouncing my scheme. I therefore allowed myself still to be carried along by the society of Paris, and particularly by that of women, though determined to shun every connection that would disturb my repose.

I paid my court to the Countess de Seran as constantly as possible, without being troublesome to her. She was so kind as to invite me to spend the spring with her in Normandy, in her little château of La Tour, which

she was embellishing.   I accompanied her.   What would
I not have quitted for her ?   With her I experienced
every charm which can be found in the friendship and
most intimate society of a woman, without love.   Certainly, had it been possible to be in love without hope, it
would have been with Madame de Seran; but she marked
out so skilfully the boundary within which my sentiments
for her, and hers for me, were to be confined, that not
even my wishes ever went beyond it.

I had formed, also, a connection of pure friendship
with women, who, in the decline of their age, still continued agreeable, and of whom Fontenelle would have
said, " You see well that love has been there."   I did not
feel that veneration which is reserved for virtue alone; but
they inspired me with a sentiment of benevolence which
attached me almost as much, and which was more flattering to them.   I was affected to see the sadness of
declining beauty, as it stood before the glass where its
charms could no longer be discovered.   Of all my female
friends, none were so much afflicted at this irreparable loss
as Madame de L. P.   Her melancholy reminded me of
the following words of a celebrated Grecian beauty, as she
suspended her mirror in the temple of her divinity :

> " Je le donne à Venus puis qu'elle est toujours belle ;
>   Il redouble trop mes ennuis.
>   Je ne sourais me voir dans ce miroir fidelle,
>   Ni telle que je fus, ni telle que je suis." [1]

No heart could be more feeling, more delicate, more
affectionate than that of Madame de L. P.   Though I

---

1 " I give it to Venus since she is always beautiful; it irritates
my chagrin too much.   I cannot view myself in this faithful mirror,
either such as I was or such as I am."
        Thus versified by Prior :
> " Venus take my votive glass,
>   Since I am not what I was ;
>   What from this time I shall be,
>   Venus, let me never see."

could not pretend to make her any compensation for that
of which years had deprived her, I endeavoured to console her by all the attentions of a rational and tender
friend; and, like an obedient patient, she accepted all the
consolations which my reason presented. She had even
previously adopted my advice, by attempting to divert
her sorrows with study, which formed the charm of our
leisure hours.

During the early lustre of her beauty, no one had
suspected her of possessing so much understanding as
Nature had really bestowed upon her. She did not know
it herself. Quite occupied with her other charms, and
thinking only of pleasure, her indolence and effeminacy
left slumbering, as it were, in the bottom of her mind, a
multitude of just and delicate perceptions, which, if I
may so speak, were lodged there without her knowledge,
but which, when the dismal leisure to which she was
now left forced her to attend to them, seemed to unfold
themselves spontaneously. In our conversations I saw
these ideas spring up and disclose themselves with much
grace and facility. Out of complaisance, she followed
my studies and employments; she assisted me in my
researches; but while her mind was occupied, her heart
was empty, and this was her torment. All her sensibility was directed towards our mutual friendship, which,
being confined within the limits prescribed by her age
and mine, became on that account only the more ardent.
Whether at Paris or in the country, I was as constant as
possible in my attendance upon her. Frequently I quitted
on her account companies in which I should have found
greater pleasure, and did for friendship what I had
seldom done for love. But no person in the world loved
me so much as Madame de L. P.; and when I had
said to myself, " Everyone else can endure my absence
without regret," I no longer hesitated to sacrifice everything for her. My literary and philosophical societies
alone inspired her with no jealousy, but every other

amusement afflicted her; and the reproach was the more sensible, that it was cautious, timid and mild.

At this time my employments were divided between history and the "Encyclopædia." I had made it a point of honour and delicacy to fulfil well my functions of historiographer, by carefully compiling memoirs for future historians. I applied to the most considerable characters of the time, with the view of drawing from their papers information respecting the reign of Louis XV., with which I intended to begin; and I was really astonished at the degree of confidence which they showed. The Count de Maillebois gave me all his own papers, and those of his father. The Marquis de Castries threw open his cabinet, which contained the memoirs of the Marshal de Belle-Isle; the Count de Broglio initiated me into the mysteries of his secret negotiations; the Marshal de Contades drew with his own hand the plan of his campaign, and of the disaster of Minden. I stood in need of the confidence of the Marshal de Richelieu; but, like all the literary men in the Academy, I was in disgrace with him. Chance brought about a reconciliation; and this, too, is one of the occasions in which I was met half-way by a favourable opportunity.

A lady, who was a particular friend of Marshal Richelieu, meeting me at a house in the country, said it was very strange that a man of Richelieu's importance should experience disagreeable and disgusting treatment from the French Academy. "Certainly, madam," said I; "nothing can be more strange; but who is the cause?" She named d'Alembert, who, she said, had taken a dislike to the marshal. I replied that the enemy of the marshal in the Academy was not d'Alembert, but he who sought to sour him against d'Alembert, and against all literary men.

"Do you know, madam," continued I, "what sort of men those are who embitter against the Academy a man whose personal qualities should make him honoured

and beloved ?   They are academicians who are enraged
against the body to which they belong on account of the
little consideration which they themselves enjoy.   There
is the advocate-general Seguier, the public accuser of
men of letters to the Parliament; there is Paulmi, and
some other intruders, who, displeased with a body where
they find themselves out of place, would wish, by joining
with our enemy Seguier, to compose a formidable party.
Such are the men who attempt to alienate from us the
mind of the marshal, with the view of having him at their
head and injuring us by his credit.   How glorious is it
for him to become subservient to their pitiful vanity and
hatred !   You see what is the consequence.   He prevails
upon the King to refuse his approbation to the election
of two men of irreproachable character.   The Academy
remonstrates against this refusal ; and the King, being
undeceived, agrees that these two men should be elected
to the two first places which shall become vacant.   This
is what really may be called ' fighting against the air.'
No, madam, the true party for a Richelieu in the Academy, the only party worthy of my lord marshal, is the
party of men of letters.''

She thought me in the right ; and some days after,
the marshal having come to the same country-house,
she wished me to talk with him.   I repeated nearly the
same things, though in milder language ; and with regard
to d'Alembert, I said, '' My lord marshal, d'Alembert
believes you the enemy of men of letters, and the friend
of their accuser, Seguier ; this is the reason why he does
not love you.   But d'Alembert is a good man, and the
sentiment of hatred never took root in his heart.   He
has wedded the Academy.   Love his *wife* in the same
way that you love so many others, and come sometimes
to see her ; he will be pleased, and will give you a good
reception, as so many other husbands do.''

The marshal was pleased with what I said ; and
when two other academicians were to be elected instead

of the Abbé Delille and Suard, who had been rejected by
the King, I was invited to dine with him on the day of
the election.   At this dinner I met Seguier, Paulmi, and
Bissy, the Bishop of Senlis.   Their party was not
numerous ; and though they should have had some
clandestine votes, ours was combined and united together in such a manner as to be sure of prevailing.
I took no notice, therefore, as if I supposed us to be
assembled about academical elections ; but, as if it had
been a dinner of gaiety and pleasure, as soon as the
soup appeared, I introduced those subjects which were
most agreeable to the marshal.   I led him to talk of
the old style of gallantry, of the pretty women of his
time, of the manners of the Regency—in short, of the
theatre, and, above all, the actresses ; so that dinner
was over before a single word was said of the Academy.
It was not till we were leaving table that the Bishop
of Senlis, taking me aside, asked whom we intended
to choose.   I frankly replied that I believed all votes
united in favour of Brequigny and Beauzee.   The
marshal, who had come up to us, enquired about the
literary merit of these gentlemen ; and after having
heard me, he said, " Well, they seem both worthy men ;
we must join in their favour."   " Since such is your
intention," said I, " my lord marshal, will you allow
me to go and give the information to the Academy.
These are words of peace, to which that assembly will
listen with pleasure."   " Go," said he, " and take one
of my carriages which are in the court ; we will not
be long in following."

" My friends," said I to d'Alembert, " they are
coming to join with us ; the marshal, with a good
grace, makes the first advances ; with a good grace
we must receive him accordingly."   He was, in fact,
well received ; the election was unanimous ; and from
that day to his death, he treated me with the greatest
kindness.   His portfolios, therefore, were at my disposal.

At the same time, the original manuscript of the memoirs of Saint-Simon, which I had been allowed to take out of the Office for Foreign Affairs, and from which I made copious extracts, supplied me with information respecting the affairs of the Regency. But the making of these extracts and the searching of the despatches and memorials with which I was abundantly supplied, would have been soon equally tiresome and fatiguing to me, had I not in the interval possessed some literary occupation, which was less laborious and more suited to my taste. The scheme of a supplement to the " Encyclopædia," in four folio volumes, supplied me with this relaxation.

You must know that after the publication of the seventh volume of the " Encyclopædia " the continuation had been interrupted by a decree of Parliament; and nothing had been done, except secretly, by a small number of writers, of whom I was not one. A laborious compiler, the Chevalier de Jaucourt, had undertaken the literary part, and had performed it in his own way, which was very different from mine. When, therefore, by dint of constant solicitation, permission was obtained to publish the whole work, and when the plan of a supplement had been formed, Robinet, one of those concerned, called on me and proposed that I should resume my labour where I had left it off. " You began," said he, " only at the third volume ; you left off at the seventh ; all the rest is by another hand. ' Pendent opera interrupta.' [1] We come to beg you will complete your work."

Being busy with history, I answered that it was impossible to engage in another employment. " At least," said he, " allow us to announce that you will give a few articles in the supplement." " I will do it," said I, " if I have time ; I can promise no more." Soon after he returned to the charge, and with him Panckoucke the book-

[1] " The works are broken off and suspended."

seller. They told me that in order to make the necessary arrangements for their enterprise it was necessary to know how the work would be divided among the different men of letters, and that they came to know what I wished for my share. " What can I ask," said I, " since I promise nothing?" "You will do whatever you please," said Panckoucke; "only promise to give us a few articles, and allow us to insert this promise in our prospectus; for this we will give you one hundred and sixty guineas and a copy of the supplement." They were pretty sure that I would make a point of justifying their confidence. I justified it so fully that they afterwards acknowledged I had exceeded their expectation. But let us resume the thread of the events of my life, which was varied by a thousand accidents.

The death of the King had produced a considerable change at Court, in the ministry, and particularly in the fortune of my friends.

M. Bouret had ruined himself by building and embellishing, for the King's use, the pavilion of Croix-Fontaine; and the King thought him sufficiently rewarded by being honoured, once a year, with his presence at a hunting party—an honour, too, which cost the unhappy man dear, being obliged, on that day, to give the whole party a dinner, in which nothing was spared. I had more than once lamented his profusion; but the most liberal, the most improvident of men, would never listen to the advice of his real friends upon the subject of expense. Meanwhile, he had completed the destruction of his credit by building, at great expense, five or six houses upon the Elysian fields, when the King died, without having so much as thought of saving himself from ruin; and this event, leaving him drowned in debt, destitute alike of resource and hope, he formed, I believe, the resolution of putting an end to his life. He was found dead in his bed. He was, to his own cost, in the highest degree imprudent; but he never was guilty of anything dishonourable.

Madame de Seran was more prudent. As, after the King's death, she had no prospect of favour and protection, she made a substantial use of the only benefit of which she had accepted, and sold her house at a suitable price to the Count d'Angiviller, the new director of buildings. Both of us were thus dislodged in 1776, three years after she had admitted me to this happy residence under her roof.

The accession of the new King to the throne was followed by his coronation in the cathedral at Rheims. As historiographer of France, I was enjoined to be present at this august ceremony. I shall not repeat here what I said in a letter, printed without my knowledge, and which I have since inserted in the collection of my works. It is a feeble representation of the effect produced by this grand spectacle upon fifty thousand spectators whom I saw assembled. With regard to myself, I never was so much affected by anything.

In other respects I enjoyed, during this journey, every accommodation which my place could procure ; and for this I had reason to think myself indebted to the honourable manner in which the Marshal Beauveau, captain of the guards on duty, and joint member of the French Academy, was so kind as to treat me.

Of all the women whom I ever knew, the lady of Marshal Beauveau is the one whose politeness is most natural and charming. She, as well as her husband, paid a delicate and marked attention to set the example to others, of the courteous manner in which they wished me to be treated ; and this example was followed. I was sensible of their kindness, which I have since carefully cultivated. The character of the marshal was not so engaging as that of his wife. Nevertheless, the cold dignity with which he was reproached never put me to a moment's constraint with him. I was convinced that, however different his rank might have been, his air and manner would have been the same ; and reconciling my-

self to what seemed in him to be nature, I found him
honourable and worthy, and even disposed to do a service without ostentation.   With regard to his wife, who
is now his widow, I do not believe that there is under
heaven a more amiable or more accomplished character.
She may truly, and without irony, be called " the woman
who is always in the right."   But the correctness and
unalterable clearness of her understanding is accompanied with so much mildness, simplicity, modesty and
grace, that we cannot but love the very superiority she
enjoys over us.   She seems to communicate to us her
understanding, to associate our ideas with hers, and to
enable us to share the advantage which she always
enjoys, of thinking so justly and so well.   Her great art,
and the object of her most constant attention, was to
make her husband be honoured and respected, to withdraw herself in order to put him in her place, and to
resign in his favour the interest and consideration of
which she was the object.   According to her, everything
which was praised in herself ought to be referred to M.
de Beauveau.   Observe, my children, that she lost nothing by this ; that she was only the more respected, and
that this borrowed lustre which she threw over her husband's character only rendered her own more brilliant and
conspicuous.   No one ever felt more fully the dignity of
her conjugal duties, or fulfilled them in a nobler manner.

My letter upon the ceremony of the coronation
being published and distributed at Court by the intendant of Champagne, had produced the effect of recalling to
the eyes of the King and Queen a day of glory and
happiness.   This made them begin to view me with
kindness.   The Queen shortly after expressed some
favour for me.   In a small theatre, fitted up in her own
palace, she was so good as to desire *Sylvain* and *L'Ami
de la Maison* to be acted.   This little entertainment gave a
sensible pleasure, and the Queen, as she passed by me,
said, with the most agreeable air, " Marmontel, that is

delightful." But these promises of favour were soon to be disappointed, in consequence of what happened in a musical dispute.

Under the deceased King, the Count de Caraccioli, ambassador from Naples, had persuaded the Court to send to Italy for an able musician, who might support the French opera-house, which had long been sinking, and which was supported, with difficulty, at the expense of the public treasury. The new mistress, Madame du Barri, had adopted this idea, and our ambassador at the Court of Naples, the Baron de Breteuil, had been instructed to engage Piccini to come and settle in France, with an annual pension of £250, on condition of giving us French operas.

Scarce had he arrived, when my friend the Marquis de Caraccioli, ambassador from Naples, came and recommended him to me, and begged that I would do for him, as he said, in the great opera-house, what I had done for Gretry in the *opéra-comique*.

At this very time the musician Gluck had arrived from Germany, as strongly recommended to the young Queen by her brother, the Emperor Joseph, as if the success of German music had been an important affair of State. There had been written at Vienna, upon the plan of a ballad, by Noverre, a French opera called *Iphigenia in Aulis*. Gluck had composed the music; and this opera, with which he began in France, had met with the greatest success. The young Queen had declared in favour of Gluck; and Piccini, on his arrival, found him established in the public opinion, both at Court and in the city. He not only found nobody to favour himself, but appeared at Court under the odious character of a musician protected by the mistress of the late King; while in the city he was regarded with enmity by all the French musicians, who found the German music more easily imitated than the Italian, the style and accent of which they despaired of attaining.

6—2

Had I been at all a politician, I would have taken the side on which Court favour lay ; but the favoured music, with its Teutonic accents, was no more like what I had heard by Pergolese, by Leo, by Burancello, &c., than the style of Crebillon is like that of Racine ; and to prefer the Crebillon to the Racine of music would have been an effort of dissimulation to which I could not have been equal.

Besides, I had taken it into my head to transport the Italian music to our two opera-houses ; and you have seen that in the comic opera I had made a very good beginning. Not that the music of Gretry was Italian music in high perfection ; it was as yet far from reaching that complete harmony which transports us in the music of the great masters. But he could make a good song ; his expression was natural ; his airs and duos agreeably composed ; sometimes, even, he used his instruments happily in the orchestra ; his taste and understanding were sufficient to supply what was deficient in point of art and genius ; and if his music had not all the charm and all the richness of that of Piccini, of Sacchini, of Paisiello, it had the same rhythm, accent and prosody. I had thus demonstrated that, in the comic department at least, the French language might possess a music of the same style as the Italian.

I had still the same trial to make in the tragic department, and chance supplied me with an opportunity. The problem was more difficult to solve, and that for other reasons than were commonly supposed.

Dignified language is less favourable to music ; first, because its turns are not so lively, so strongly accented, or so suited to the expression of song as comic language ; secondly, because it has less extent, copiousness, and freedom in the choice of expression. But a much greater difficulty arose to me from the idea I had formed of lyric poetry, and from the theatrical form I had designed to give it. In conjunction with Gretry, I had made the fruitless attempt in the opera of *Cephalus and Procris*. By dividing the action into three scenes, of which one was voluptuous and brilliant—the palace of Aurora, her waking, her loves, the pleasures of her celestial court; the second, gloomy and terrible—where jealousy pours her poison into the soul of Procris; the third, affecting, passionate, tragic—the error of Cephalus, and the death of his wife, pierced by his arrows and expiring in his arms. This seemed to answer my idea of an interesting representation; but as I did not succeed in this first attempt, and ascribed the disgrace in part to myself, my distrust of my own powers amounted to fear.

The sense of my own weakness, and the good opinion I had of the celebrated composer whom I had met with in Piccini, induced me, therefore, to think of taking the fine operas of Quinault; of retrenching the episodes and the superfluous details, and thus leaving only their beauties. I might also add airs, duos, monologues, in recitative; choruses in dialogue and in contrast. I might thus accommodate them to the Italian music, and might form a species of lyric poem, more varied, more animated, more simple, less detached in its action, and infinitely more rapid than the Italian opera.

Even Metastasio, whom I studied and admired as a model of the art of adapting words to singing, appeared to me insupportably languid and tedious. I was shocked at his double intrigues, his amorous episodes, the multitude of his detached scenes, and his airs, which were almost always lost like a vignette at the end of the scenes. I wished a full and closely united action, in which the incidents, well joined together, should be themselves the subject of the song, so that the song should be only a more lively expression of the sentiments that were diffused over the scene; while the airs, duos and choruses were interwoven in the recitative.

I wished, besides, that the French opera, while it acquired these advantages, should preserve its pomp, its wonders, its illusions; so that, though enriched with all the beauties of Italian music, it might still be that spectacle—

> " Où les beaux vers, la danse, la musique,
>   L'art de tromper les yeux par les couleurs,
>   L'art plus heureux de seduire les cœurs,
>   De cent plaisirs fait un plaisir unique." [1]—VOLTAIRE.

In this spirit it was that the opera of *Roland* was newly modelled. When I had brought that poem into the condition I desired, my joy was as great as if I had written it myself. I saw the work of Quinault in its native and simple beauty; I saw the idea which I had formed of a French lyric poem almost, if not wholly, realised by an able musician. This musician did not understand two words of French; I undertook to instruct him. "When," said he, "shall I be able to begin this work?" "To-morrow morning," said I; and next day I went to his house.

You may conceive how laborious I found it to instruct him; it was necessary to explain line by line, and almost word by word; and when he had become master of the meaning of a passage, I recited it to him, marking distinctly the accents, the prosody, the cadence of the lines, the pauses and semi-pauses; he listened with avidity, and I had the pleasure of seeing that what he had heard was faithfully noted down; the accent and quantity of the language struck so correctly his excellent ear that it seldom happened, in his music, that either the one or the other was mistaken. So quick was his sensibility in marking the most delicate inflexions of the voice, that he could express the very finest shades of sentiment.

It was inexpressibly delightful to me to see an art,

---

[1] " Where fine poetry, dancing, music, the art of spreading illusions of colouring before the eyes, the still happier art of captivating the heart, unite a thousand pleasure in one."

or rather a genius, displaying itself before my eyes, of
which, till then, I had not the least idea. His harmony
was in his mind. His orchestra, and all the effects
which it would produce, were full in his thoughts. He
wrote his song with a stroke of the pen ; and when
the plan was sketched out, he filled up all the parts,
whether performed by instruments or by the voice, and
distributed the strokes of melody and harmony as an
able painter would have disposed his shades and colours
upon canvas. Having completed this labour, he opened
his harpsichord, which till then he had been using as a
table ; and I heard an air, a duo, a chorus, complete
in every part, while my ear and soul were transported
by the truth, the intelligence of its expression and the
magic of its numbers.

Then it was that I found myself in possession of
the man whom I sought, the man who was master
of his art and disposed of it at pleasure ; and in this
manner the music of *Roland* was composed, which,
in spite of faction, met with the most splendid success.

Meanwhile, as the work proceeded, the zealous
admirers of good music, at the head of whom were the
Neapolitan and Swedish ambassadors, rallied round the
harpsichord of Piccini, with the view of hearing every
day some new scene ; and their enjoyment every day
formed a compensation for my trouble.

Among these admirers of music, none were more
distinguished than the MM. Morellet, my personal
friends, and the most useful whom Piccini had found
in France. By them, on his arrival, he had been received, had been lodged, and furnished with the first
necessaries of life. They spared nothing upon him,
and their house was his own. I took pleasure in thinking that the view of our connection was an additional
cause of the interest they felt in him ; and this object of
common affection furnished a new aliment to my friendship for them.

The Abbé Morellet and myself had, during twenty years, lived constantly in the same societies. We had often differed in opinion, but had always agreed in principles and sentiments, and in mutual esteem for each other. In our warmest disputes, no tendency towards bitterness or asperity had ever mingled; though we did not flatter, we loved each other.

His brother, having lately arrived from Italy, was quite a new friend to me, and had gained my heart by his probity and frankness. They lived together; and their sister, the widow of M. Leyrin de Montigny, was coming from Lyons with her young daughter to embellish their society.

The abbé, who had informed me of the happiness they had a prospect of enjoying, by being united into one family, wrote to me one day : " My friend, the ladies arrive to-morrow ; come, I beseech you, and assist us in giving them a good reception."

My destiny was now about to assume a new aspect ; and this note forms the era of that virtuous and unalterable happiness which awaited me in my old age, and which, for twenty years, I have uninterruptedly enjoyed.

BOOK X

So long as heaven had, in Madame Odde, left me
a sister whom I tenderly loved, and who loved me rather
with a filial than a sisterly affection, there was always a
place where I could go and spend my old age in peace. I
was sure of finding in her worthy and virtuous husband
a real friend, whose house and whose children would have
been my own. The esteem and the confidence which
Odde had acquired, the excellent reputation which he enjoyed in his profession, rendered his promotion easy and
certain ; and had he only retained his employment at Saumur, my little fortune, added to his, might have enabled
us to live genteelly and comfortably. When, therefore, the
world and I should have been tired of each other, there
remained an honourable and agreeable retreat for my old
age. In this happy assurance, I allowed myself, as you
have seen, to be carried along by the current of life, and
without anxiety saw myself approaching its decline.

But when I had lost my sister and her children,
when Odde's affliction prompted him to abandon a city
in which he saw nothing but tombs, and when, throwing
up his employment, he retired to his native place, my
future prospects, hitherto so serene, were darkened, and I
saw nothing for me except the dangers of marriage, or
the solitude of a dismal celibacy and a deserted old age.
I was afraid of finding in marriage domestic troubles, of
which I saw a thousand examples, and which I could
never have survived. But a still more dreadful condition
would be that of an old man forced either to drag himself
into company, infirm, tiresome, and an object of general

contempt, or to remain by himself, abandoned to the mercy of his servants, to their rude insolence and servile dominion.

In this painful situation, I had more than once attempted to find a companion, and to adopt a family which might supply the place of that which death had mown down around me. But, by a happy fatality, none of my plans had succeeded when the sister and the niece of my friends the Morellets arrived in Paris. It was a gift from heaven.

Both certainly appeared to me extremely agreeable ; the mother, from her frankness, cordiality and kindness ; the daughter, from an air of candour and modesty ; and both from a style of conversation which I easily perceived to be equally full of judgment and wit. But I did not conceive that now, when I was more than fifty years old, I could be a proper husband for a young person who was little more than eighteen. Her youth, the lustre of her beauty, those charms of which Nature had just completed the formation, while they dazzled me, tended also to banish hope, and with hope the desire of possessing her.

My expectations, therefore, from this agreeable adventure were confined to the advantage of a new and charming society.

Whether Madame de Montigny was prepossessed in my favour, or whether my plain good-humour pleased her at first sight, she soon treated the friend of her brothers like an old friend of her own whom she had met with anew. We supped together. This supper was animated by the joy which they all felt at meeting. I shared it, as if I had been one of themselves. I was invited to dinner next day, and gradually formed the habit of visiting them almost daily.

The more I talked with the mother, and the more I heard the daughter converse, the more did I discover in both that amiable character which has always charmed me. But once again, my age, and the narrowness of my

fortune, allowed me little pretensions to the happiness
which I foresaw would attend the husband of Mademoiselle de Montigny; and more than two months had
elapsed before the idea of aspiring to this happiness had
once occurred to me.

One morning, the Abbé Maury, a friend of mine and
of the Morellets, called upon me, and said, " Shall I tell
you a piece of news ?   Mademoiselle de Montigny is
going to be married."   " Married ! to whom ? "   " To
you."   " To me ? "   " Yes, to yourself."   " You are
either mad or dreaming."   " I am neither; it is a very
sensible thing, of which none of your friends entertain
the least doubt."

" Listen," said I, " and believe me, for I speak
seriously.   Mademoiselle de Montigny is charming ; she
is, I believe, accomplished ; and for that very reason I
never entertained the foolish thought of pretending to the
happiness of being her husband."   " Well, without pretending to it, you will be her husband."   " At my age ? "
" At your age, indeed ! you are young still, and in
perfect health."   He then begins and employs his whole
eloquence in proving that nothing could be more suitable ;
that I should be beloved ; that we should be very happy
together ; and, with a prophetic tone, he foretold that we
should have handsome children.

After this sally he left me to my own reflections ; and
while saying to myself that he was a fool, I began soon to
be no wiser than he.

My fifty-four years no longer appeared so formidable
an obstacle ; health, at this age, might supply the place of
youth.   I began to think that I might inspire, not love
indeed, but a kind and tender friendship ; and I recollected what wise men had said, that more happy mar-
riages are made by friendship than by love.

I thought I observed this young and handsome
person take pleasure in seeing and in listening to me ;
her fine eyes seemed to view me with an expression of

interest and kindness. I went even so far as to think that
the attentions with which her mother honoured me, and
the pleasure which her smiles expressed at seeing me a
constant visitor, might perhaps be mingled with some disposition favourable to the wish which I dared not form.
I was not rich, but about £5,500, securely lent out, were
the fruit of my economy. In short, since to a sincere
friend like the Abbé Maury this union appeared not only
reasonable, but desirable on both sides, why should I
myself think it so unsuitable ?

I had engaged this day to dine with the Morellets. I
went with an emotion which was new to me. I even
think I remember bestowing a little more care on my
dress ; and from that time I bestowed a serious attention
upon what began strongly to interest me. Not a word—
not a look was neglected : I made delicate and imperceptible advances, slight trials of their mind and disposition.
The abbé did not seem to pay any attention to this ; but
his sister, his brother and his niece appeared to me
pleased with everything which I did or said.

About this time the abbé took a voyage to Brienne,
in Champagne, to visit the unhappy Lomenies, with
whom he had been acquainted from his youth, and during his absence our society became more familiar and
more intimate.

I knew well that these appearances might be flattering, and that the charm of a first connection might be
deceitful; I knew the deception which might be produced
by the union of grace and beauty. Two or three months'
acquaintance were very little to ascertain the character of
a young person. I had seen more than one in the world
who had been taught only to feign and dissemble ; but I
had heard such a favourable account of Mademoiselle de
Montigny's character, and it appeared to me so pure and
so genuine, so remote from every kind of dissimulation ;
kindness, innocence, tender modesty, were so clearly expressed in her countenance and language, that I felt an

invincible inclination to believe her such as she appeared ; and if I was not satisfied with such strong probabilities, I could no longer trust to anything.

A walk to the gardens of Sceaux finally determined me. Never did this place appear so beautiful; never had I breathed the air of the country with so much delight; everything was embellished by the presence of Mademoiselle de Montigny ; her looks spread around her a new kind of enchantment. I did not experience that delirium of the senses which is called love ; but a tranquil pleasure, such as that of pure spirits is represented. Nay, it appears to me that then, for the first time, I knew the real feeling of love.

Till then, the pleasure of the senses had been the only allurement which had seduced me. Here I was transported beyond myself by more invincible charms ; these were candour, innocence, mild sensibility, timid modesty, propriety, like a veil, thrown over grace and beauty ; it was virtue crowned with the flowers of youth, which transported my soul still more than my eyes; a kind of enchantment a thousand times superior to all those of the Armidas whom I had met with in the world.

My emotion was the stronger from its being suppressed. I was ardently desirous of making the confession ; but to whom could it be addressed, and how would it be received ? The worthy mother gave me an opportunity. In the alley where we were walking, she was at a few steps' distance with her brother. " I must," said she, smiling, " have a great deal of confidence in you to allow you thus to carry on a private conversation with my daughter." " Madam," said I, " it is proper that I should justify this confidence by telling you the subject upon which we were conversing. Mademoiselle was describing to me the happiness which you experience from being all four together in the same family, and the account she gave appeared to me so enviable that I was going to ask you whether a fifth, like myself for instance,

would spoil your society?"   "I do not believe it,"
replied she; "but you should rather ask my brother."
"For my part," said the brother, frankly, "I should
think it a very good plan."   "And you, mademoiselle?"
"For my part," said she, "I hope my uncle the abbé
will be of mamma's opinion; but, till his return, allow
me to keep silence."

They had no doubt of his opinion being the same,
so that, my intention being once declared, and the
mother, the daughter, and the uncle having agreed, I
had no longer any occasion to dissemble.   I seemed even
to perceive that a sentiment with which my mind was
constantly filled did not find the heart of its object
altogether inaccessible.

The abbé's absence was long, but he arrived at last;
and, though the whole had been arranged without him,
he gave his consent.   Next day the contract was signed.
He appointed his niece his heiress after his own death and
that of his sister; and in this deed, drawn up by their
notary, my only care was that of leaving my wife a
handsome jointure, independent of her children.

Never was marriage concluded under happier au-
spices.   As mutual and perfect confidence was established
between Mademoiselle de Montigny and myself, and as
we were both perfectly satisfied with the vow which we
were about to pronounce at the altar, we pronounced
it without uneasiness and without anxiety.

On our return from church, where Chastellux and
Thomas had held over us the nuptial veil, they were
so attentive as to leave us a few moments alone; and
these moments were spent in assurances of mutual desire
to render each other happy.   This first effusion of two
hearts, which are for ever united by sincerity on one
side, by innocence on the other, and on both by the
most tender friendship, is perhaps the most delicious
moment of our lives.   The dinner, after dressing, was
animated with a gaiety of the good old times.   The

guests were d'Alembert, Chastellux, Thomas, Saint-Lambert, a cousin of the Morellets, and some other common friends. All were occupied with the young bride; and like me they were so charmed, so delighted, that anyone seeing them would have supposed that each was her husband.

On leaving table, we went into a drawing-room in the form of a gallery, which was adorned by the rich library of the Abbé Morellet. There a harpsichord and desks certainly gave a promise of music; but what new and delightful music were we to hear? The opera of *Roland*, the first French opera to which Italian music had been adapted, was executed by the finest voices and the most select performers of the opera.

The emotion excited by this novelty had all the charms of surprise. Piccini was at his harpsichord; he animated the orchestra and the actors with the fire of his genius and of his song. The Swedish and Neapolitan ambassadors were present at this concert, and were delighted. The Marshal de Beauveau was also there. This kind of enchantment lasted till supper, to which the singers and performers were invited.

Thus passed this happy day — the era and the presage of that happiness which has been diffused over the rest of my life, amid all the adversities which have often troubled but have never been able to poison it.

It was settled that the two uncles, the mother, and we, should live together, and should each pay a fifth of the household expense. This arrangement suited me in every respect; and it united the advantage of a set of friends completely formed, whom we had only to enjoy.

I have made you acquainted with part of those whom we could call our friends, but there are others whom I have hitherto mentioned only slightly, and upon whom my memory dwells with pleasure.

You, my children, have a thousand times heard your mother and her family say how agreeable it was

to us to live with M. de Saint-Lambert and his friend
the Countess d'Houdetot; and how charming a society
was that in which wit, taste, the love of literature, all
the most essential and most desirable qualities of the
heart, attracted us sometimes towards the wise d'Eau-
bonne, and sometimes into the agreeable retreat of La
Sévigné de Sanois. Never were two souls and two
minds united in more perfect union. But they particularly resembled each other in an amiable solicitude
to make their house agreeable to their friends. It was
a politeness at once easy, attentive, full of exquisite
taste, such as comes from the heart—and reaches it—
and which is known only to feeling souls.

Saint-Lambert and I had been members together
of the societies of the Baron d'Holbach, of Helvetius
and of Madame Geoffrin; we were constant members,
also, of that of Madame Necker; but, in the latter, I
dated farther back than he—I was almost the first
member.

It was at a citizen's ball, a singular enough circumstance, that I had become acquainted with Madame
Necker. She was still young, handsome enough, had
a brilliant complexion, and danced ill, but with spirit.

Scarce had she heard my name, than she came up to
me with a genuine expression of pleasure. "On my
arrival at Paris," said she, "one of my wishes was to
become acquainted with the author of the 'Moral
Tales.' I did not expect to make so fortunate a meeting
at a ball. I hope it will not be a passing acquaintance.
Necker," said she to her husband, calling to him, "come
and unite with me in inviting M. Marmontel, the author
of the 'Moral Tales,' to do us the honour of being
our visitor." M. Necker was very civil in his invitation. I went. Thomas was the only literary man whom
they knew before me. But in the fine hotel in which
they settled, Madame Necker soon selected and formed
her society after the model of that of Madame Geoffrin.

Madame Necker, unacquainted with the manners of Paris, had none of the charms of a young Frenchwoman. Neither her manners nor her language were those of a woman educated in the school of the arts and formed in the school of the world. There was no taste in her dress, no ease in her demeanour, no charm in her politeness. Her mind, as well as her countenance, was too carefully adjusted to possess grace.

But a charm more worthy of herself was that of decency, of candour, of kindness. A virtuous education and solitary studies had given her soul every improvement which excellent talents and dispositions can derive from cultivation. Feeling, in her, was perfect ; but her thought was often confused and vague. Meditation, instead of clearing, troubled her ideas ; by exaggerating, she expected to ennoble them ; in endeavouring to extend them, she lost herself in abstraction and hyperbole. She seemed to see certain objects only across a mist, which magnified them in her eyes ; and her expression then became pompous to a degree which would have been laughable had we not known her to be in earnest.

Taste, in her, was less a sentiment than a result of opinions collected and written out in her commonplace-book. Without hearing her authorities quoted, it was easy to know upon whose judgment she had formed her own. In the art of writing she esteemed only elevation, majesty and pomp. Gradations, shades, varieties of colouring and tone, affected her but faintly. She had heard men praise the simplicity of La Fontaine, the ease of Sevigné ; she spoke of them by hearsay, but scarcely felt them. The graces of negligent and careless ease were quite unknown to her. She disliked the language of familiarity even in conversation. I was sometimes amused to observe how far she carried this delicacy. One day I quoted some familiar expressions, saying that I thought they might be received into the lofty style.

She rejected them as unworthy of it. " Racine," said I, " was less difficult than you, for he has employed them all." Of this I showed her instances ; but her opinion, once formed, was invariable ; and the authority of Thomas, or that of Buffon, was received by her as an article of faith.

She seemed to possess rectitude and correctness only in the regulation of her duties. There, everything was precise, and strictly according to rule ; there was a reason, a method even in the amusements which she seemed desirous of procuring. She was evidently quite occupied in rendering herself agreeable to her company, solicitous to entertain those whom she had invited, and attentive in saying to everyone what was likely to be most agreeable ; but this was all premeditated—nothing flowed spontaneously, nothing excited any high degree of interest.

It was neither for us nor for herself that she took all these pains ; it was for her husband. To bring us acquainted with him, to make him be viewed with favour and talked of with praise in the world, and thus to lay the foundation of his renown, was her powerful motive in founding her literary society. But it was requisite also that her drawing-room, her dinner, should be an exhibition amusing to her husband ; for, in fact, he was only a cold and silent spectator. Except some acute observations which he threw out here and there, he was quite a mute, and left to his wife the care of keeping up the conversation. She did everything in her power, but there was nothing in her mind suited to table - talk. No sally, nothing quick, nothing which could keep us alive, ever escaped her. The moment she saw the scene and the dialogue languish, she became anxious and uneasy, and looked round, as if enquiring the cause. Sometimes, even, she had the simplicity to complain to me of it. "What would you have, madam?" said I ; " a man has not wit at command, nor is he always in a disposition to be agreeable. Is even M. Necker himself every day an amusing companion ? "

Madame Necker's attentions, and all her desire of pleasing, would have been insufficient to overcome the disgust of being invited to dinner only to amuse her husband. But at these dinners, as at many others, the society, enjoying each other, freed the landlord from any obligation to be agreeable, provided he freed them from any obligation to attend to him.

When Necker was minister, those who knew him only in his private life imputed his silence, his gravity, his reserve, to the arrogance inspired by his new situation. But I can bear witness that, even before his rise in life, when he was a mere partner of Thelluson the banker, he had the same look, the same grave and silent character, and that he was neither more amusing nor more familiar with us. He received his company civilly; but he treated none of us with that flattering cordiality which makes politeness assume the appearance of friendship.

His daughter has said of him that "he knew how to keep people at a distance." If such had been the intention of her father, she, in disclosing it, would have very rashly betrayed the secret of a pride which was at best ridiculous. But the plain truth was that a man accustomed from his youth to the mysterious operations of a bank, and plunged in commercial calculations—little acquainted with the world or with men, very little even with books, and whose information upon every subject not relating to his profession, was vague and superficial— such a man was called upon, by a prudent attention to his own reputation, to be reserved, that he might not betray the poverty of his own ideas ; accordingly, he spoke freely and copiously upon subjects which he knew well, but with great moderation upon every other. He was not arrogant, therefore, but skilful and prudent. His charming daughter must not always be trusted to.

7—2

With respect to Madame Necker, she had friends amongst us whom she particularly distinguished ; and I was always one of these. Not that our tastes or opinions agreed very well, for I even affected to oppose my plain and vulgar ideas to her lofty conceptions; and she was under the necessity of descending from these inaccessible heights before she could hold any communication with me. But though I could not be prevailed upon to follow her into the region of her ideas, and was more under the dominion of the senses than she could have wished, she did not love me the less.

Her society was most precious to me in one respect—from its including the Neapolitan and Swedish ambassadors, two of the men whose absence and loss I have most regretted. The one, by his good-humour and his cordiality, as well as his taste and understanding, rendered his intercourse more desirable every day. The other, by his tender friendship, his mild philosophy, by a certain sweetness of modest and genuine virtue, by something melancholy and interesting in his language and character, attached me still more intimately. I saw them at my house, at their own, and at the houses of our friends as often as possible, but never so often as I should have wished.

Thus happy in my society, and still more in my domestic circle, I was expecting after eighteen months of marriage the birth of my first child, as the event which would crown all my wishes. Alas! how cruelly was I deceived in my hopes; this child, so ardently wished for, died at its entrance into the world. Its mother, astonished and anxious at not hearing its cries, asked to see it; while I, motionless and trembling, was still in the neighbouring drawing-room waiting her delivery, when my mother-in-law came to me and said, " Come, embrace your wife and save her from despair; your child is dead." At these words, I felt my heart struck as with a mortal blow. Pale, cold, scarce able to stand, I dragged myself to the bed of my wife, where, making an effort to subdue my feelings, I said, " My amiable friend, now is the time to prove that you live for me alone. Our child is no more, he died before ever he saw the light." The poor girl raised a cry which pierced my heart, and fainted in my arms. As she will read these Memoirs, let me not dwell on such cruel moments, lest I should open again that wound which bled too long.

When she had her second child, I saw her determined to suckle it. Thinking her still too weak, I opposed this resolution. The nurse whom we had chosen seemed to be the best possible ; she had the look of health, a fresh complexion, a rosy mouth, fine teeth, the most beautiful bosom—everything except milk. This bosom was marble ; the child wasted away. He was at St. Cloud ; and the *curé*[1] of the village had promised that till its mother should be able to go and see it, he would pay attention to the child. He sent us accounts, but was so cruel as to deceive us. On our arrival at the nurse's house we were grievously undeceived. "My child is ill," said his mother ; " see how his hands are withered, and how he looks at me with eyes that implore my pity. I wish this woman to bring him to Paris, that my physician may see her." She came; he was sent for and examined her bosom, but found no milk. He went immediately and found for us another nurse; and as soon as the child was put to this new bosom, where he found an abundant supply, the milk appeared to him so good that he could not be satisfied.

How great was our joy to see him visibly recover, and revive like a dry and perishing plant when it is watered. This dear child was Albert, and we seemed to have a pleasing presentiment of the consolations which he now affords us.

---

1 Rector or pastor.

My wife, that she might keep the nurse at home, and make the child breathe a pure air, expressed a wish to have a country-house, and a friend of the Morellets lent us his at St. Brice.

This village contained two very respectable men, who were very intimate with each other, and with whom I myself soon became acquainted. One was the *curé*, the eldest brother of the Abbé Maury, a man of sound understanding and excellent character; the other was an old bookseller, Latour, a mild, peaceful man, of scrupulous fidelity, and as obliging to me as he was charitable towards the poor in the village. His library was mine.

I was employed on the "Encyclopædia." I rose with the sun; and after spending eight or ten hours of the morning in writing down upon paper the observations which I had made in the course of my studies, I spent the rest of the day with my wife and my child. Already he formed our delight.

In proportion as the good milk of our young Burgundian girl made health flow through his veins, we saw the flesh over his little body and his delicate limbs grow round and firm; we saw his eyes become animated; we saw his countenance acquire colour and beauty. We thought, also, we saw his little soul and understanding unfold themselves. Already he seemed to hear, and began to know us; his smile and his voice answered to the smile and voice of his mother; I saw him also take delight in my caresses. His tongue soon tried the first words of Nature, those sweet names, which, when they come from the lips of a child, make their way directly to the heart of the parents.

I shall never forget the moment when, in our little garden, my child, who had never till then dared to walk without leading-strings, seeing me on my knees at a few steps from him and holding out my hands, left the arms of his nurse, and with a tottering but determined step, came and threw himself into mine. I know well that the emotion which I then experienced is a pleasure which beneficent Nature has rendered common. But woe to those sophisticated hearts which cannot be affected but by rare and artificial impressions! A lady, a friend of ours, said of me, humorously enough, " He thinks there is not another father in the world but himself." No, I pretend not that paternal love has any charm peculiar to me ; but though this common happiness were granted to me alone, I should not feel it more sensibly. My wife felt no less the first delights of maternal affection ; and you may suppose that neither of us had a desire for any other sight, any other society, than that of our child.

Our family, however, and some of our friends, came and visited us on holidays. The Abbé Maury was among the number, and I wish you had heard how he boasted of having prophesied my happiness.

Sometimes, too, we saw our neighbours, the *curé* of St. Brice, the worthy Latour, and his worthy wife, who loved mine.

We took pretty often solitary walks, and the termination of these was commonly that chesnut wood at Montmorency to which Rousseau has given celebrity.

" Here," said I to my wife, " he composed that romance of ' Eloise ' in which he has employed so much art and eloquence in throwing over vice the colouring and the dignity of virtue."

My wife was partial to Rousseau ; she thought herself infinitely obliged to him for having persuaded women to nurse their children, and for the care he had taken to render this first period of life happy. " We must," said she, " forgive something to the man who has taught us to be mothers."

But I, in the conduct and writings of Rousseau, had seen a perpetual contrast of beautiful language with despicable morality ; I had seen him assume the character of an apostle and martyr of truth, yet sport with it incessantly by artful sophistry ; free himself by calumny from

the burden of gratitude ; paint his friends in the blackest
and falsest colours which his ferocious disposition and his
gloomy imagination could inspire ; defame those men of
letters whom he had most cause to praise, that he alone
might become celebrated, and might efface them all.   I
made my wife sensible, by the very good which Rousseau
had done, of all the mischief he might have ab-
stained from doing, if, instead of employing his art in
gratifying his passions — in giving a colour to his hatred,
his vengeance, his cruel ingratitude — in clothing his
calumnies under specious appearances, he had exerted
himself to subdue his own pride, his irascible humour,
his gloomy mistrust, his dismal animosities, and to become
again what Nature had formed him, full of innocent feeling, just and good.

My wife listened to me with sadness.   One day she
said to me, " My friend, I am sorry to hear you often
speak ill of Rousseau.   You will be accused of being
actuated by some personal enmity against him, and
perhaps by a little envy."

" With regard to personal feelings," said I, " they
would be very unjust, for he never injured nor offended
me.   Envy would be more possible, for my admiration
of his writings is sufficient to inspire me with that
passion ; and I should accuse myself of it if I surprised
myself slandering him.   But on the contrary, when I
speak of the maladies of his soul, I experience the same
deep sadness which you feel in listening to me."   " Why,
then," replied she, " should you, in your writings, your
conversation, treat him with such severity ?   Why dwell
upon his vices ?   Is there no impiety in disturbing the
ashes of the dead ? "   " Yes," said I, " the ashes of the
dead who have left no example, no recollection, which
can be pernicious to the living.   But ought poisons,
rendered palatable by the writings of an eloquent sophist,
and of a seducing corrupter ; ought the fatal impressions
which his specious calumnies have made on men's minds

—in short, ought all the contagion which his genius and celebrity have left behind them, to go down and be transmitted from age to age under favour of the respect which is due to the dead ? I shall certainly employ every means in my power, either to guard against or to counteract the evil; and were it only to clear the memory of my friends from the stains with which he has sullied it, I shall, if possible, leave his remaining proselytes and enthusiastic admirers no choice but either to think that Rousseau was a bad man, or that he was a fool. They will accuse me of envying him. But the many illustrious men to whom I have rendered the purest and the justest homage, will bear witness that in my writings justice and truth were never darkened by envy. I spared Rousseau as long as he lived, because he had need of men's kindness, and I did not wish to injure him. He is no more; nor is it my duty to spare the reputation of a man who never spared that of any, and who in his memoirs has defamed the men who loved him best.

With respect to " Eloise," my wife allowed that it was dangerous reading; nor was any apology necessary for what I have said in an " Essay on Romances." Yet, had I myself always censured as severely the artful manner in which Rousseau has given an interest to the crime of St. Preux and that of Julia, one seducing his scholar, and the other abusing the sincerity and probity of Wolmar ? I must acknowledge the contrary ; my moral feelings were affected by my new situation, and by the influence which personal interest has over our opinions and sentiments.

In consequence of living in a world where the public morals are corrupted, it is difficult not to contract, at least, indulgence for fashionable vices. Opinion, example, the seductions of vanity, and, above all, the allurements of pleasure, efface in young minds the original sense of right and wrong : the air and tone of levity with which old libertines laugh at the precepts of virtue and ridicule the rules of delicate propriety, make us become accustomed to these errors, and cease to attach any importance to them. This pliability of conscience was particularly cured by my new situation.

Shall I say it? a man must be a husband, he must be a father, in order to judge soundly of those contagious vices which attack morality in its very source; of those agreeable and treacherous vices which spread trouble, shame and despair through a family.

An unmarried man, insensible to those afflictions which he never experienced, thinks neither of the tears which he will make others shed nor of the fury and vengeance which he will kindle in their breasts. Busy, like the spider, in spreading his nets, and in watching the favourable moment for securing his prey, he either expunges from his moral system all respect for the most sacred ties, or, if they sometimes force themselves to his recollection, he regards them as laws that are now become obsolete. What so many others allow themselves to do, or boast of having done, appears to him, if not lawful, at least very excusable. Since licentiousness reigns, he thinks he may fairly avail himself of it.

But when he himself has been placed in the number of those whom an artful seducer may render unhappy for life, and sees that, when the artifices, the flattering and winning language of a young coxcomb have surprised either the innocence of a young girl or the weakness of a married woman, it is sufficient to drive to despair the most virtuous man, and one day, perhaps, himself; then, warned by his personal interest, he feels how inviolable in the eyes of a husband and of a father ought to be the sacredness of conjugal and domestic duties. Then it is that he views with an eye of severity the guilt and shame of dissolute behaviour, notwithstanding the embellish- ments of eloquence and the outward appearance of decency and propriety under which it may be disguised by the art of an industrious writer.

I blamed Rousseau, therefore; but, while blaming him, I grieved that malignant passions, gloomy pride and vainglory had spoiled a character originally so excellent.

Had I felt any passion for celebrity, two great examples would have cured me—that of Voltaire and that of Rousseau; examples different, and in many respects opposite, but agreeing in this, that the same thirst for praise and for renown had been the torment of their days.

Voltaire, who had lately died, had sought glory by every path which lies open to genius, and had deserved it by immense labours and by the splendour of his talents. But in every one of these paths he had met envy, and all the furies which follow in her train. Never was a man of letters exposed to so many attacks, with no crime except great talents and the ardent desire of displaying them. Those who appeared as his enemies, believed they would rank as his rivals; those whom he carelessly trampled under foot continued still to insult him in the mire. His whole life was a contest, which he carried on with indefatigable eagerness. The combat was not always worthy of him; he had oftener insects to crush than serpents to stifle. But though he did not provoke, he never could overlook an offence; the meanest of his aggressors was chastised with his own hand; ridicule was the instrument of his vengeance, and he made cruel and dreadful use of it. But to repose, the greatest of blessings, he was always a stranger. Envy, it is true, seemed at length weary of persecuting him, and spared him at least on the brink of the tomb. On the journey to Paris, which, after a long exile, he was allowed to take, he enjoyed his renown, and the enthusiastic gratitude of a whole people, for the pleasures which they owed him. The last and feeble effort which he made to please them, *Irene*, was applauded as much as *Zara* had been; and this representation, in which he was crowned, afforded him the most splendid triumph. But what a moment was that in which he obtained this consolation! Next day, I saw him in bed. "Well," said I, "are you at length satiated with glory?" "Ah! my friend," cried he, "you talk to me of glory, and I am on the rack; I am dying amid frightful sufferings."

Thus closed the career of a man, the most illustrious in literature, the most agreeable in society. He was susceptible of resentment, but he was also warmly alive to friendship. That with which he honoured my youth was unaltered till his death; and one of the last proofs of it which he gave me was the kind and graceful manner in which he received my wife when I introduced her to him. His house at this time was never empty of persons who came to call upon him, and we were witnesses of the trouble which he took to give each a suitable answer. His strength was exhausted by this continual attention; and to his true friends the spectacle was painful. But we often supped with him, and there we enjoyed the last faint lights of that mind which was soon to be extinguished.

Rousseau was unhappy as well as he, and through the same passion. But you may see by the letters of Voltaire that in his ambition there was modesty at bottom; whereas the writings of Rousseau prove his to be swollen with pride.

I had seen him in the society of the most distinguished literary men: this was not enough for him; he was offended by their celebrity; he thought them jealous of his. Their kindness was viewed by him with mistrust. He first suspected, and then slandered them. He had friends in spite of himself, who heaped benefits upon him; their kindness was burdensome to him. He received their benefits; but he accused them of having wished to degrade him; and their benevolence was rewarded with the most odious defamation.

He was always spoken of in company with a particular interest. Censure, even when it touched him, was full of respect, and tempered with praise; it was on that account, he said, only the more artful and treacherous. In the most peaceful repose he always chose either to believe or to say that he was persecuted. His malady consisted in imagining that the most common and accidental occurrences were contrived with some intention of injuring him, as if the whole world had fixed upon him eyes of envy. If the Duke de Choiseul had undertaken the conquest of Corsica, it had been in order to deprive him of the glory of being its legislator. If the same duke went to Montmorency, to sup with the lady of Marshal Luxembourg, it was in order to usurp the place which he usually held at her table. Hume, according to him, had felt envy at the reception which he had received from the Prince of Conti. He never forgave Grimm for some preference which he had obtained over him from Madame d'Epinay; and you may see in his memoirs how severely his vanity revenged this offence.

Thus Voltaire's life and his had been perpetually, but differently, agitated. To the one it had brought often very severe uneasiness, but at other times very lively enjoyments; to the other there had been nothing but floods of bitterness, with hardly any mixture of joy and sweetness. Nothing assuredly could have tempted me to put myself in the condition of Rousseau; he himself had not been able to endure it; and after having embittered his own days, I do not wonder that he should voluntarily have abridged their sad period.

With regard to Voltaire, I own his glory appeared to me too dearly purchased by all the tribulations to which it had exposed him; and I again say, "Less splendour, and more repose."

Limited in my ambition, first by the necessity of suiting my flight to the feebleness of my wings, and then by the love of that ease of mind which accompanies peaceful labour, and which appeared to me the share of humble mediocrity, I should have been satisfied with this happy condition. Early, therefore, renouncing all pre-sumptuous attempts, I had in a manner capitulated with envy, and had confined myself to modes of writing in which success could be easily forgiven. I was not on that account spared, and I experienced that, in little minds, little things can excite an envious malignity.

But I had laid down two principles—one, never to provoke hostility by anything offensive in my writings; the other, to despise its attack, and never to answer. I continued for thirty years immovable in this resolution, and all the rage of the Frerons, the Auberts and others of the same stamp had not been able to rouse me against them.

Why, then, had I been less passive on occasion of the musical quarrel? Because I was not the only person insulted by my adversaries; and because I had to avenge the cause of an artist inhumanly attacked in his dearest interests.

Piccini was the father of a numerous family, which subsisted by the fruits of his industry; his mild and peaceful character rendered him still more interesting. I saw him alone, devoid of intrigue, labouring with all his might to please a new nation; and I, at the same time, saw a merciless junto furiously attacking him like a swarm of wasps. I expressed my indignation; the junto was enraged, and the wasps turned all their stings upon me.

The leaders of the party had a press at command to print their witticisms, and a journal to give them circu-lation. Here I was insulted every day. I had not the same advantage for defending myself; and though I had, I should not have liked this pitiful warfare. However, I wished to laugh in my turn; since to be angry would have been making a very foolish figure.

I conceived the idea of putting their intrigue into action, and painting them to the life; indeed, to make them ridiculous, I had only to put their own words into rhyme. They printed their prose, I repeated my verses; and every day we tried who could raise the heartiest laugh.

Thus was composed my poem upon music, in defence of Piccini. Perhaps it would have been better had I allowed *Roland*, *Atys*, *Didon*, &c., to speak for themselves; but I have not always done what was best; and, on this occasion, I own his injury and mine did not appear sufficiently avenged by a contemptuous silence. After all, if, out of a dispute so frivolous and ephemeral, I have composed a poem in twelve cantos, these are the incidents which insensibly led me on. I might certainly have spent my time better, but my habitual labour required relaxation, and the moments which I bestowed on Polyhymnia were only those of amusement.

The period of my residence at St. Brice was marked by an event of more serious interest. This was the retreat of M. Necker from the ministry of finance. I have already said that his character was not at all seducing. He had never given me any reason to think him my friend; nor did I consider myself as his. But as he expressed for me as much esteem and benevolence as I could expect from a man so coldly polite, and as I had a high opinion of his talents, his understanding, his ambition to distinguish himself in office by doing good to the nation, I was afflicted at his retreat.

I had, besides, the most sincere veneration for Madame Necker, for I had seen nothing in her but kindness, wisdom and virtue; and the particular affection with which she honoured me, made it highly incumbent on me to feel an interest in an event which, I had no doubt, would affect her very much.

When I learned it at St. Brice, thinking them already retired to their country-house at St. Ouen, I went there immediately. They were not yet arrived, and I went on to meet them at Paris. I met them on the road.

"You were coming to see us?" said Necker; "get into our carriage and come to St. Ouen." I accompanied them thither. We were alone the whole evening with Germani, Necker's brother; and neither the husband nor wife made any secret of their deep sadness. I attempted to lighten it by talking of the regret which the public would feel, and the just respect which would follow them into their retirement—in which I was not flattering them. "I regret," said Necker, "only the good which I had to do, and which I might have done had time been allowed me."

For my part, I then saw in his situation only an honourable retreat, an independent fortune, repose, liberty, freedom in the choice of his occupations, a society which was not affected by the vicissitudes of Court honour, while his domestic life united every pleasure which a wise man could desire. But I own that I spoke according to my own tastes, rather than according to his; for I was fully sensible that he could not be satisfied without the occupation of public business and the influence which it bestows. His wife appeared grateful for the care which I took to weaken the impression of the blow which had struck him. My connection with them, therefore, far from being loosened by this event, became only the closer.

My wife, out of love for me, received gracefully their attentions and invitations. But she had an insurmountable aversion for M. Necker. She had brought from Lyons a conviction that M. Necker was the cause of the disgrace of M. Turgot, the benefactor of her family. Nor did she find in Madame Necker that winning air which she herself had with her friends.

Very different and much more agreeable was another Genevese lady, the fair Vermenoux, the most intimate friend of M. and Madame Necker. Since meeting her at their house, whose union she had promoted, I had always cultivated her acquaintance. But her friendship for my wife had, since our marriage, formed a new tie between us.

Madame de Vermenoux, at first sight, was the
image of Minerva ; but this commanding countenance
was soon enlivened by an air of kindness, of serenity, by
that decent and unaffected gaiety which adorns wisdom
and renders it agreeable. The mutual inclination which
she and my wife felt for each other was sympathy, if by
that word we understand the perfect harmony of mind,
taste and character ; and though habitually retired, and
naturally reserved, with what pleasure did she see us
arrive at her country-house at Sèves ! In the little
suppers which we took with her in Paris, how joyfully
and how frankly did her soul yield itself to the pleasures
of intimacy ! Death carried her off while she was still
young enough to taste the charms of life. But, though I
regretted her, I have since discovered that her life, had it
continued longer, would have been filled with nothing but
sadness and bitterness. In a short time she would have
lived too long.

I returned to St. Brice, where my wife and I had
an object of tender interest ; it was her new pregnancy.
Good air, exercise, a regular country life, had been in her
favour ; and at Paris, to which the winter recalled us,
she brought into the world the most handsome of our
children. To us, therefore, everything seemed still prosperous, and as yet nothing could be more agreeable than
the life which we led.

Atys, in spite of envy, met with the same success as
Roland. The fine airs of these two operas, sung to the
harpsichord, were the delight of our society, in the concerts of the Countess d'Houdetot, and of her sister-in-
law, Madame de la Briche.

The latter, who was a good musician and sang with
taste, though with a weak voice, was so singularly modest
as to bring to her house talents which eclipsed her
own ; and, far from showing the least jealousy, she was
the first to draw them forth. She was a perfect model
of propriety without any affectation ; easy and polite in

her conversation; frank in her gaiety. She talked well; she told a story well; she was simple, yet naturally agreeable. Her language and her style were pure, and even elegant; but, though she had feeling enough to be capable of friendship, no passion interrupted her mildness and equanimity. She was not the woman whom you would have wished for in order to be inspired with any violent emotion; but she it was whom you would have selected in order to taste a tranquil happiness.

Talking of my old acquaintances, I mentioned having seen M. Turgot; but whether there was anything unsuitable in our manners and character, or that my connection with M. Necker displeased him still more, he had treated me with uniform coldness. Nevertheless, as the old friend of the Abbé Morellet, he had taken an interest in my marriage; and I was indebted to my wife for some marks of his kindness, which I accepted with the more respect because he was in disgrace.

Meanwhile, I was successively losing my old friends. The Swedish ambassador, recalled by the King to be his confidential minister, was taken away from me for ever. The Neapolitan ambassador left us on being appointed Viceroy of Sicily. My separation from both was the more grievous, as being likely to prove eternal. The letters of Caraccioli were full of his regret. He was constantly inviting me to come with my family to Sicily, offering to send a vessel to Marseilles which might transport us to Palermo.

I have mentioned the friendship which for forty years I had cherished for d'Alembert, as well as how valuable his was to me. Since the death of Mademoiselle l'Espinasse, he was consumed with languor and sadness. Still, however, he sometimes allowed this consoling friendship to pour a few drops of its balm into the deep wound of his heart. With my wife, in particular, he took pleasure in withdrawing himself from his sorrow. She regarded him with the tenderest interest. He and Thomas, the two men of letters whose talents and understanding seemed most likely to strike her with awe, were those with whom she felt herself most at her ease. There was no amusement which she preferred to their conversation.

Thomas appeared still likely to live long to glory and friendship.

But d'Alembert began to feel the agonies of the stone; and he soon existed only to linger and die slowly amid the most cruel sufferings.

In the eulogy of him which I have feebly attempted, I have endeavoured to paint the mild equality of his character, always genuine, always simple, because it was natural, remote from every kind of falsehood and ostentation, *compounded of strength and weakness; but whose strength was virtue, and whose weakness, benevolence.*

While I wept for him, I was far from any thought of succeeding him in the office of perpetual secretary to the French Academy. I was myself on the point of following him to the tomb, being struck with a malignant fever similar to that from which Bouvard had already saved me, and of which he cured me again. How ought I to bless the memory of a man to whom I have twice owed my life, and who, till his mind and strength failed, never ceased to pay my children the most tender attention.

Scarce was I recovered, when I found it necessary to go to Fontainebleau, in order to present the new opera which I had composed with Piccini. This opera was *Didon*. As it was wholly my own, I had written it according to my taste; and that our new music might be fowarded another step, I had taken advantage of the moment when Piccini had newly obtained a mark of favour which rekindled his genius. It happened in the following manner :

This year (1783), the Marshal de Duras, gentleman of the bed-chamber in waiting, asked me if I had not written anything new? and expressed a desire of being able to present the Queen, at Fontainebleau, with the

novelty of a fine opera. "But," said he, "I wish it
to be your own work. We are not satisfied with your
vamping up the old operas of Quinault." This was such
language as I should have expected from my brother-
member of the Academy, and from the kindness with
which he had long treated me.

"My lord marshal," said I, "I can promise nothing
so long as Piccini, my musician, shall continue in disgrace. You know the rage with which the success
of *Roland* and *Atys* has been disputed against him;
they have both succeeded, and hitherto real talent has
triumphed over faction; but the *Iphigenia in Tauris* has
failed.

"De Vismes, the manager of the opera, in order
to swell his profits by the rivalship of the two parties,
has determined to make Gluck and Piccini try their
strength upon the same subject; he has supplied them
with two poems upon the subject of *Iphigenia in Tauris*.
In the barbarous poem which has fallen to the share
of Gluck, he has found horrors suited to the energy of
his style, and has strongly expressed them. The poem
given to Piccini, however ill composed, was found
susceptible of a milder interest; and by means of the
corrections which the author made under my eyes, he
has been able to produce an affecting music. But after
the strong impression which the ferocious opera of Gluck
had made upon men's eyes and ears, that produced by
the opera of Piccini appeared slight and feeble. The
Iphigenia of Gluck has remained upon the theatre of
which it had got possession; that of Piccini could not
support itself. He is in consternation; you alone, my
lord marshal, can rouse him from his dejection." "What
must be done for that purpose?" enquired he. "A
thing," said I, "which is very easy and very just. To
change into a pension the annual gratification which
was promised him when he was desired to come to
France." "Very willingly," said the marshal. "I will

ask the Queen to bestow upon him this favour, and hope to obtain it."

He asked and obtained it; and when Piccini went with me to thank him, he said, "You must prove your gratitude to Her Majesty by composing, this year, a fine opera for her."

"I ask no better," said Piccini, as he went away; "but what opera shall we compose?" "We must compose," said I, "the opera of *Didon*. I have long been revolving the plan of it. But I forewarn you that I mean to unfold my ideas at length; that you will have long scenes to set to music; and that in these scenes I shall require a recitative as natural as simple repetition. Your Italian cadences are monotonous; the accents of our language are more various and better supported, and I beseech you to mark it down in the same manner as I repeat it." "Well," said he, "we shall see." In this manner we formed the design of bestowing on recitative that ease, that truth of expression, which was so favourable to the performance of the celebrated actress for whom the character of Didon was destined.

The time was short: I wrote the poem with great rapidity, and, in order to withdraw Piccini from the distractions of Paris, I invited him to come and compose with me in my country-house—for I had got a very agreeable one, where we lived as a family during the summer months. On his arrival there, he began to work; and when he had completed it, Saint-Huberti, the actress who was to perform the part of Didon, was invited to come and dine with us. She sang her part at night, from one end to the other, and expressed it so well that I thought I saw her on the stage.

She was going to take a journey into Provence: she wished to carry her part there in order to study it by the way; and, during her absence, we were busy with the rehearsals. It was at this time that I ex-

perienced the illness which brought me to the brink of
the tomb. When the moment came for going to Fontainebleau, my health was not yet completely restored,
and my wife, anxious about my recovery, wished to
accompany me.

While there, we dined one day with Madame de
Beauveau, and heard for the first time that my friends
had in view for me the place of secretary to the
Academy, which, after d'Alembert, it was so difficult
to fill.

This difficulty, which might have intimidated the
vainest man, was not the one that withheld me. The
place required a constant attendance, of which I thought
myself incapable. With great sincerity, therefore, I
declined the honour which they wished to procure for
me. But motives were urged, to which I thought it my
duty to yield; and it was determined that I should be
one of the candidates for this place. I only insisted that
there should be no solicitation on my part.

Circumstances were favourable for procuring the
votes of the Court. The success of *Didon* was complete;
and with the panegyrics that were bestowed on the music
of Piccini, some words of praise to the author of the
poem were also mingled. "It is the only opera," said
the King, "in which I have felt any interest." He asked
to see it twice.

This success gave me great pleasure; my wife enjoyed it, and it was this which interested me most. The
excursion was agreeable to her beyond expression. We
had walks in the forest, hunting-parties, horse-races,
parties of pleasure at Tomeri, where we were entertained
with sumptuous dinners of fish, and excellent grapes.
Whenever the theatre was open, we had places in the
box of Madame d'Angiviller, whose house was ours, and
who, as well as her husband, bestowed a pleasing attention in directing towards us the notice of the numerous
and excellent company of which her house was always

full. My wife, in short, enjoyed all the pleasures which could be assembled by a youthful and magnificent Court, and everything which could prove how much she herself was esteemed and loved by this elegant society; so that both for her and for me, the abode of Fontainebleau was a continual enchantment.

Two incidents occasioned us a little uneasiness; the first was my being threatened with a relapse of the fever which I had experienced at the beginning of my journey. The Court physicians would have made it a serious illness if my wife would have listened to them. But she, without any of their remedies, restored me to health by making me breakfast every day on a basket of ripe grapes. The other incident was the small-pox of Albert, whom we had brought along with us. But the eruption not having appeared till towards the end of the journey, we set out immediately; and Albert was put into the hands of our friend Bouvard, who took the same care of him as if he had been his own child.

BOOK XI

ON our return to Paris, the French Academy having assembled for the election of its perpetual secretary, I had eighteen votes out of the twenty-four. My two competitors were Beauzee and Suard.

Didon had met with the same success at Paris as at Court ; and this opera supplied us with amusement during the winter, as *Roland* and *Atys* had done when new.

M. de la Borde, the old Court banker, joined his concerts with those of the Countess d'Houdetot and of Madame de la Briche ; this gave occasion to my acquaintance with him.

He had two daughters upon whom Nature had bestowed every charm of countenance and voice. They were scholars of Piccini, and rendered the expression of his song still more mild and affecting.

Pleased with the politeness of M. de la Borde, I went to see him ; I went sometimes and dined with him ; he appeared to me honourable but plain, enjoying his prosperity without pride or ostentation, and with an equanimity the more to be esteemed when we consider how difficult it is for a man to possess so large a fortune without having his head a little turned. With how many favours had heaven loaded him ! Great affluence, a universal reputation for honour and uprightness, an unbounded credit throughout Europe; while his family consisted of six amiable children, and a wife of a mild, judicious, and agreeable character, in whose propriety and modesty there was nothing affected. She was an excellent wife, an excellent mother—a woman, in short, who appeared blameless in the eyes of envy itself.

" Che non trova l'invidia ove l'emende."—ARIOSTO.

What was wanting to the wishes of a man so completely happy? He perished on a scaffold, for no other crime besides his wealth, among that multitude of virtuous men whom an abominable wretch had consigned to death. We were not yet threatened with this dreadful calamity, and I thought myself happy in my humble mediocrity. My country-house, during the summer, was still more agreeable to me than the city. A select society, chosen by my wife, gave variety to our leisure hours, and enjoyed with us that rural abundance supplied by our espaliers, our orchard, our vine-arbours, the fruits and vegetables of every season—cheap blessings with which Nature covered a frugal table and which converted a moderate dinner into a delicious feast.

There reigned an innocent joy, a perfect confidence, a freedom of thought, whose limits were known and were never transgressed.

Shall I name all the guests who were assembled by friendship? Raynal, the most affectionate, the liveliest of old men; Silesia, a Genoese philosopher, who resembled Vauvenargue; Barthelemi, our walks with whom resembled those of Plato with his disciples; Bréquigny, who had much also of this ancient mildness and wisdom; Carbury, a man who, from the rich variety of his talents and knowledge, seemed to belong to every age and to every country; Boismont, a complete Frenchman in his manners, but whose agreeable conversation formed a singular contrast to his eloquence in the pulpit; Maury, who was prouder of diverting us with an amusing story than of raising our admiration by a stroke of eloquence, and who in company made us forget his learning and regard him only as an agreeable man; Godard, who had also a flow

of lively wit ; De Seze, who soon came and rendered our
conversations still more animated and charming.

"We are too happy," said my wife; "some misfortune will happen to us." She was, indeed, in the
right. Learn, my children, how closely grief follows joy
in every situation of life.

This kind and feeling mother had nursed the third of
her children. He was handsome and in perfect health ;
we thought we had only to see him grow up and become
still more handsome, when he was suddenly struck with a
mortal stupor. Bouvard hastened to him ; he employed,
he exhausted, all the aids of art without being able to
awaken him from this fatal slumber. The child's eyes
were open, but Bouvard perceived that the pupil was
dilated : he drew a light over it ; the eyes and the eyelid
remained immovable. " Ah ! " said he, " the organ of
sight is paralysed ; the brain is affected ; there is no
remedy." The good old man wept as he said these
words ; he felt the blow with which he had struck the
heart of a father.

At this cruel moment, I would have wished to remove the mother ; but she was on her knees by the
child's bedside, her eyes full of tears, her arms raised
to heaven, while sobs choked her utterance. " Allow
me," said she, " ah ! allow me, at least, to receive his
last sigh." But how did her sobs, her cries and her
tears redouble when she saw him expire ? I do not
speak of my own grief, I can think only of hers. It
was so deep, that for several years she was not able to
hear its object named. If she spoke of it herself, it
was only in ambiguous terms: "Since my misfortune,"
she would say—not being able to say, "Since the death
of my child."

In the melancholy condition of my soul, what employment could I undertake which had not some relation
to maternal love and conjugal tenderness ? While my
heart was yet full of the sentiments of which I had before

me the most affecting model, I formed the design of the opera of *Penelope*. This subject took possession of my fancy; the more I thought of it, the more capable it appeared of producing great effects in music and theatrical representation.

I wrote with warmth, with all the illusion which a pathetic subject can excite in him who paints it. But it was this illusion by which I was deceived. I first persuaded myself, that the fidelity of conjugal affection would, in the lyrical drama, be equally interesting with the intoxication and despair of Didon's love; I persuaded myself, also, that in a subject which was wholly composed of interesting situations, of descriptions, of theatrical incidents, everything would be executed according to my design, and that the probability and dignity of the action would be observed, according to the directions which I had given out to bad machinists and awkward performers. The contrary happened; in the most interesting moments all illusion was destroyed. Accordingly, the fine music of Piccini failed of producing almost any effect. Saint-Huberti, indeed, was as admirable in the character of Penelope as she had been in that of Didon. But though she was applauded every time she appeared on the stage, she was so ill seconded, that neither at Court, nor at Paris, did this opera meet with the success which I had hoped; and the fault was my own. I ought to have known better the foolish personages upon whom I made the success of such a work depend; what I have said of *Zemire et Azor* ought to have shown me how little they were to be trusted.

I had not been happier in choosing the subject of a comic opera, which I had composed with Piccini, for the Italian theatre; and I can hardly conceive what seduced me in the subject of the *Dormeur Eveillé*, which might be entertaining in the "Arabian Nights," but in which there was nothing comic. For the truly comic consists in laughing at a ridiculous character, which that of Assan was not.

In general, after any success, we must expect to find the public more difficult and severe. I did not consider this sufficiently. I became more confident when I ought to have been more timid; and my vanity was punished by theatrical failures.

More indulgence was granted me in the public assemblies of the French Academy. There I made no demand for applause; I spoke only to fulfil the functions of my office, or to supply the place of those who were absent. If sometimes, in my turn, I paid the tribute due to a man of letters, it was without ostentation. The little essays which I read aimed at nothing brilliant. They were the fruit of my studies and reflections upon taste, upon language, upon style, upon the caprices of fashion, which were all subjects suited to the spirit of an academical audience, and habitually treated amongst us. Accordingly, this audience was willing to be pleased, and I felt as if surrounded by a circle of friends.

The favour which I enjoyed in our public assemblies, joined to the strict discipline of which, without any partiality, I enforced the observance in our private sittings, gave me some degree of weight and interest. The clergy thought themselves obliged to me for the attention with which they were treated; the high nobility were not less satisfied with those customary respects which were paid them, after my example; and with respect to men of letters, they knew me to be so jealous of academical equality, that they might trust to me for reminding of its rights anyone who should have forgotten them. Many even, convinced that in our elections I sought only to make the best possible choice, consulted me, and joined their votes with mine. I possessed influence, therefore, without intrigue, and I employed it, as was just, in overcoming the obstacles which some persons attempted to raise against the election of one of my friends.

The Abbé Maury in his youth had, with great success, pronounced at the Louvre the panegyric of St. Louis, in presence of the French Academy, and afterwards that of St. Augustine, before the assembly of the French clergy; he had soon become celebrated in the pulpits of Paris, and was called to preach before the King at Versailles during Christmas and Advent. He had thus acquired undoubted rights to the French Academy; and he did not deny that such was the object of his ambition.

Then it was that the rumours of calumny were raised against him; and as these reports were intended for the ears of the Academy, care was taken to address them directly to its secretary. I listened to all the ill which they chose to say of him; and when I had heard the whole, I took him aside: "You are attacked," said I, "and it is I who must defend you; but you must furnish me with arms to refute your enemies." I then explained to him successively, every article of the charges which were brought against him.

He listened without emotion, and with astonishing facility refuted these accusations, demonstrating some to be false, and with respect to the others, putting me in the way of ascertaining the whole myself.

The only charge which at first he could only disprove in a vague manner, because its nature was vague, was that brought against him by an academician, who accused him of treachery and slander. The accuser was La Harpe, with whom he had been extremely intimate.

"Since it is he who accuses me of treachery," said the Abbé Maury, "I am entitled to demand proof. I dispense with it, however, and I undertake to prove that he calumniates me, provided always that he will explain himself and specify the facts. Let me be confronted with him."

I proposed this interview to the accuser, and he accepted it. But I did not choose to be the sole witness and judge; and while I invited them both to dinner, I asked permission to admit also two of the most upright and most judicious of the academicians, M. Thomas and M. Gaillard.

The dinner went on quietly and politely. But on rising from table we all withdrew into a closet, and I said to our two arbiters: "Gentlemen, M. de La Harpe thinks he has reason to complain of the Abbé Maury. The latter asserts that the complaint is without foundation. We shall hear them. Speak, M. de La Harpe, you shall be listened to in silence; and after you, the Abbé Maury shall, in like manner, be heard in silence."

The charge was serious. It related to a satire which the Abbé Maury was said to have advised a Russian, a friend of La Harpe, to write against him, during the time that all the three were intimately acquainted.

The Count de Schouvalof, the only witness whom La Harpe could have produced, had returned to Russia, and as he could not be heard, there was no means of refutation.

The Abbé Maury, therefore, in defending himself, was reduced to the necessity of discussing the accusation by itself, and of bringing forward circumstances which demonstrated its falsehood. This he did with such order, precision and clearness, with so wonderful a degree of recollection and presence of mind, that we were confounded. In short, during this discussion, he pressed his adversary so closely, and so powerfully, that the latter remained mute. The unanimous opinion, therefore, of the three witnesses was that La Harpe had no reason to complain of the Abbé Maury; and, in our presence, an apparent reconciliation took place between them.

" I am not the less convinced," said La Harpe to me, "of what my friend Schouvalof has declared." " You may believe it," said I, "but, as an honest man, you have no longer right to say it; and without mentioning my own opinion, that of two men so just, so impartial

as Thomas and Gaillard ought to shut your mouth. For
my part, you must expect that, should I hear your complaints repeated in company, you must not be offended
if I give an account of what has just passed at my
house."

I employed equal attention in clearing up all the
other misdeeds imputed to the Abbé Maury. I found
them all imaginary, and destitute, not only of truth, but
even of probability. From that time it was in vain for
anyone to continue obstinately speaking ill of him; I
replied that "groundless praise, as well as groundless
satire, would be employed only by a mean flatterer, or a
malicious slanderer." I defied even his greatest enemies
to specify a fact of which I could not prove the falsehood;
and I employed my whole interest in urging my brethren
to console an able man under a severe persecution by
admitting him into the Academy. He was admitted, and
from that time nothing could be more intimate than our
mutual friendship.

There was in the character of the Abbé Maury an
excessive energy and vehemence which he could with
difficulty restrain, but which he allowed me to moderate.
When I found it necessary to check his violent emotions,
I censured him with a frankness which sometimes displeased, but never irritated him. He was at once violent
and mild, and his justice atoned for the quickness of his
feelings. One day he hastily said that I made too much
use of the ascendency which I had assumed over him.
" I neither have," said I, " nor wish to have any ascendency over you, except that of reason, inspired by friendship; and, if I employ it, it is only to prevent you from
hurting yourself. I know the goodness, the uprightness
of your heart; but your head is still too youthful and
ardent. Your understanding is not mature, those spirits
in which its strength consists require to be tempered.
You know the pleasure with which I praise whatever is
laudable in you; with the same sincerity I will blame

whatever is reprehensible ; and when a harsh truth shall appear necessary, I esteem you too much to think myself under the necessity of softening it.   In short, such is the condition on which I intend to be your friend.   If you do not like it, you have only to speak ; I would then be your friend no longer."   He replied only by embracing me.

"This is not all," replied I ; "I think it my duty to exercise this severity towards you, and you ought to exercise it towards me ; you have the faults which are natural to a strong mind, while I have those of a weak one.   The temper of your soul may communicate tone and vigour to mine, and I require of you not to overlook anything which marks feebleness or timidity.   On proper occasions, therefore, I may give you counsels of prudence and moderation, while you may give me those of resolution and courageous firmness."   This mutual convention dispersed those clouds which might have been raised between us by vanity and self-love.

During the same year that my friend was received into the Academy we lost Thomas, one of our most illustrious members, and highly admirable for the integrity of his manners and the excellence of his writings.

A life uniformly upright and irreproachable !   This, my children, is a rare panegyric ; yet who has deserved it better than Thomas ?   Part, indeed, was due to Nature. He was born virtuous, and had the virtues suited to every age of life.   Temperate and chaste, none of the vices of effeminacy, of luxury, of voluptuousness, found access to his soul.   No violent passions disturbed his repose ; he knew nothing of sensual pleasure beyond what was innocent; and even of this he tasted with extreme moderation. All his powers of thought and feeling were centred in one point—the love of truth, justice and honour, and the passion for glory.   This was the spring, the active principle of his soul, the fountain of his eloquence.

He lived in the world without ever yielding to its

frivolous tastes and vain amusements; he made allow-
ance for all weaknesses, but had none himself. He was
capable of friendship, and carefully cultivated it, but
he wished it to be moderate; he loved it as a tie, but
would have dreaded its chain; it filled up the intervals
of his labours and studies, but did not draw him from
them; solitude and silence had charms for him which
he often preferred to the conversation of his friends.
He allowed himself to be loved as much as you pleased,
but he kept his own love within bounds.

In common society he appeared timid, but was only
indifferent. Conversation seldom fixed his attention.
With a friend, or in a small circle, when he was allowed
to speak on any of the subjects which he had revolved
in his mind, he inspired admiration by the loftiness and
abundance of his ideas, and by the majesty and dignity of
his language. But in a crowd he was eclipsed, and his
soul then seemed to withdraw within itself. Lively and
humorous sallies made him sometimes smile, but never
laugh. He viewed women only as a cool observer, as a
botanist views the flowers of a plant, but never as an
amateur of grace and beauty. Accordingly, women said
that they were less flattered by his praises than by the
vehement and passionate abuse of Rousseau.

Thomas was by disposition and by principle a stoic,
whose virtue would have stood in time of great trials.
He would, I think, have been a Rutilius in exile, a
Thrasea or a Seranus under Tiberius, better than a
Seneca under Nero, a Marcus Aurelius on the throne.
But, placed in a period of tranquility, and under mild
reigns, Fortune withheld from him both her high favours
and her extreme severities. His worth and modesty had
some of the seductions of prosperity to guard against; his
fortitude was not proved by any adversity. Free from
those anxieties to which he who becomes a husband and
a father is exposed, he was not tried by any of the great
interests of Nature. He was as completely insulated as

a mere individual can be in the social state, and had not even an enemy who was worthy of his anger.

It is only by his writings, therefore, that we can form a high idea of his character. There it is that we find everywhere the stamp of an upright heart—of an exalted soul ; there courageous truth, the love of justice, the eloquence of virtue display themselves.

The French Academy laid the foundation of the reputation of Thomas by proposing prizes for the most eloquent eulogies of our great men. No person could outstrip, or even equal him in this career, and in the eulogy on Marcus Aurelius he surpassed himself. Elevation and depth formed the character of his ideas. Never did orator better embrace or penetrate deeper into his subjects. Before entering upon a eulogy, he began by studying the profession in which his hero had distinguished himself; he thus praised Maurice of Saxony like a well-informed soldier ; Duguay-Trouin, like a seaman ; Descartes, like a natural philosopher ; d'Aguesseau, like a lawyer ; Sully, like a financier ; Marcus Aurelius, like a moral philosopher who was equal in wisdom to Appollonius or Marcus Aurelius himself. In like manner, while he meant only to write a preface to these eulogies, he composed, under the title of essays, the most beautiful and most learned treatise of historical morality, on the subject of the praises given in every age, with various degrees of justice and truth, according to the manners of the time and the genius of the orators—a work which has not met with the celebrity it deserves.

You may suppose that a continual tension and monotonous loftiness must be the fault of Thomas's writings. His eloquence wanted that which forms the charm of Fénélon and Massillon in prose, of Virgil and Racine in verse—the effusion of a feeling heart, and the interest which it bestows. His style was grave, commanding, but not agreeable. We admired all the characters of manly beauty ; women would have desired some features of theirs. He had copiousness and magnificence, but he never had ease and facility, never the pliancy of the Graces; and the same style which made him admirable for a few moments, became at length fatiguing. He was particularly blamed for exhausting his subjects, and leaving nothing to the imagination of his reader—which might, indeed, imply a want of taste and address, but which yet arose from a very singular excess of abundance.

At a time when I myself so much needed a sincere and rigid censor, Thomas, being much younger, had taken me for his. I praised him with frankness, and often even with transport; but I did not conceal my wish that his style had been more flexible and less monotonous. "You touch only one string," said I; "its sounds are indeed exquisite, but are they sufficiently varied?" He listened with a modest and attentive air, and perhaps owned to himself that my censure was just. But the austerity of his morals had been transferred to his eloquence; in attempting to render it more pliant, he would have been afraid of weakening it.

It was not my fault if he did not employ more usefully the years which he bestowed on his poem of "The Czar." I allowed him clearly, that the story of this poem would be destitute of unity and interest; and I set before his eyes all the models of the epic. "Homer," said I, "has, in the 'Iliad,' sung the anger of Achilles, and in the 'Odyssey,' the return of Ulysses to Ithaca; Virgil has sung the foundation of the Roman Empire; Tasso, the deliverance of the Holy City; Milton, the fall of the first man; Voltaire, the conquest of France by Henry de Bourbon, the heir of Valois. But what are you to sing? To what event, to what principal action will your narrative relate? You will describe the travels of the Czar, his wars with Charles XII., the disobedience and death of his son, the factions which he destroyed in his dominions, the military discipline which

he established in his armies, the arts and sciences which
he transplanted into his empire, the city of St. Petersburg
which he founded on the shores of the Baltic ; and these
certainly furnish materials for an historical poem, for an
eloquent eulogy ; but I do not see the single and simple
subject of an epic poem." He allowed that there was no
answering my objection ; but said that " if he had no
room for a dramatic plot, he had a very great character
to paint in the Czar." Before consulting me, he had
already composed four cantos upon the travels of the
Czar into Holland, into England, into France, into
Italy. This magnificent portico contained great beauties, and he hoped to find means to complete the edifice.
He was at length sensible that he was attempting an
impossibility, and at the end of nine years he expressed
his regret at not having followed my advice to abandon
his enterprise.

A design, which I knew him to have formed, and
which he would have executed in a most superior manner,
was that of writing discourses on the history of France,
of the same kind with those of Bossuet upon universal
history. He would not, like Bossuet, have had the
advantage of linking his events by a mysterious chain
in the order of providence. But, without looking beyond
the political and moral order, he would have drawn from
it important lessons and valuable inferences.

Thomas left behind him a high character, rather than
a splendid renown ; and he ought to be numbered among
illustrious, rather than celebrated writers. Women con-
tribute essentially to celebrity, and their votes were not
in his favour.

The same year that Thomas died, I had the consolation of seeing the Abbé Morellet admitted into the
Academy with claims less brilliant, but not less solid, than
the Abbé Maury. His understanding was steady and
enlightened, full of sound knowledge, particularly upon
subjects of public utility, and he had distinguished him-

self by writings which displayed a correct and pure style, a severe judgment, and a systematic arrangement. In another department, he was known to be the author of some excellent works of humour, full of taste, lively and agreeable. Lucian, Rabelais and Swift had taught him to handle irony and ridicule, and their disciple had become their rival. Thus my dearest friends came and sat down by me, filling up in the Academy the places of those I yearly lost.

While I saw this multitude of literary men mingled in succession with the dust, I considered that I might soon follow them, and that it was time to think of my literary testament, and of selecting what I wished to remain behind me. With this view, I collected the edition of my works. I have said enough on this subject in my prefaces, and have only to point out the occasion and the design of some of my writings.

At the time when d'Alembert was secretary to the French Academy, he had it very much at heart to give an interest in our public assemblies, and to those of our private sittings at which sovereigns were present. No one contributed to this so much as himself. Nevertheless, his resources sometimes failed, and he was seriously vexed to see himself abandoned by the rest. He had then recourse to me, complaining of the negligence of so many literary men who composed the Academy, and beseeching me to assist him in supporting the honour of the body.

On these august occasions, I composed pieces of poetry adapted to circumstances, such as the three poetical discourses upon eloquence, upon history, and upon the hope of surviving ourselves. This last, which was read at the reception of Ducis, the successor of Voltaire, had the merit of being suited to the occasion, and made a deep impression on the assembly. Among the prose writings which I read, that with which the public seemed most pleased was the eulogy of Colardeau, at the reception of La Harpe. But the success which gratified myself most was that obtained by my sketch of d'Alembert's eulogy, and by the little poem on the self-devotion[1] of Leopold of Brunswick. With regard to this last, I think it necessary to enter into some detail, in order to give a clear view of my conduct.

The humane and heroic self-devotion displayed by Prince Leopold of Brunswick having deeply affected the young Count d'Artois, that Prince had proposed to the French Academy a prize of a thousand crowns for the poem in which this noble action should be most worthily celebrated.

I was then perpetual secretary of the Academy, and my character of judge rendered it improper for me to enter the lists; but as it happened pretty often that the prize for poetry was not granted, even when we allowed the poets to choose their own subject, I felt some anxiety lest nothing should appear which was worthy of the present; and how shameful and humiliating would this have been to French literature, and how distressing to the Academy to acknowledge in the eyes of Europe that so fine a subject had failed!

As I was full of the subject, and deeply affected, I could not resist the desire of treating it myself, being fully resolved that my work should not appear till after it was determined that no other should receive the prize.

I allowed, therefore, all the poems that were presented to pass before the Academy, but they were all rejected. At last, seeing them vexed that this most virtuous heroism should not be duly praised, I laid before the Academy the attempt which I had made without aiming at the prize. They were pleased to express their approbation, and the Count d'Artois, to whom they were obliged to state the bad success of the offered prize, was at the same time informed of what

---

1 See note (1) at the end.

one of the members of the Academy had done to supply it. The Prince ordered the same prize to be offered for the following year; but he wished my work to be secretly shown to him, and allowed me to send it to the reigning Prince of Brunswick.

A few days after, the Count d'Artois desired me to be informed by M. de Vaudreuil that he had ordered for me a very rich box of gold. I replied that, on any other occasion, I would receive with respect a present from His Royal Highness, but that at present I could accept nothing which might lead to a suspicion of my having acted with a view to reward; that this rich box would be but a prize in disguise; that if the Prince would have the goodness to give me a paper box with his own portrait upon it, I would receive it as a very precious gift, but that I wished no other. M. de Vaudreuil insisted: but he saw me so firm in my resolution, that he gave up all hope of shaking it, and carried back the above answer to the Count d'Artois.

"Marmontel," said the Prince, "feels these scruples only on his own account; but it would be improper in me to make him a mean present"; and, after thinking a moment, he said, "Well, I will give him my portrait at full length." The Bailli de Crussol, his gentleman of the bed-chamber, was instructed to get a fine copy made, and the frame was embellished with emblems in the highest degree honourable to me.

The reigning Prince of Brunswick received my homage no less favourably; he wrote with his own hand a very kind answer, accompanied by two gold medals which had been struck to the memory of his virtuous brother.

About this period, my wife being with child for the fourth time, she and I agreed upon the necessity of taking up house. But as the separation was made with the full consent of her uncles and mother, we went to as short a distance as possible. My wife was not insensible

to the pleasure of being mistress of her own house. For
my part, I must own it had been most agreeable to me
to live with the Abbé Morellet in perfect independence ;
and he himself felt much more at his ease with me. He
had brought to his house another niece, young, agreeable,
full of wit and talents, who is now Madame Cheron, and
to her my wife yielded her apartment. The whole affair
was thus managed in the most amicable manner.

What rendered our new situation still more agreeable was the comfort we derived from an increase of
fortune. Without mentioning the very considerable
profits which I derived from my works, the office of
secretary to the French Academy, joined to that of
historiographer of buildings, which my friend M. d'Angiviller had obtained for me on the death of Thomas,
produced £125. My constant attendance at the Academy
doubled my fees. On the death of Thomas I had succeeded to half the pension of eighty guineas which he
had enjoyed, and which was divided between Gaillard
and myself, as that of Batteux had been. My apartments
at Versailles, as secretary to the Louvre and historiographer of France, were let for seventy guineas. I had
a pension of £125 on the *Mercury*. I had some of my
funds advantageously employed in the enterprise of *l'Isle
des Cygnes;* those which I had lodged in the Customs of
the city of Lyons yielded me legal interest, as well as
those which lay in other hands. I saw myself, therefore,
in a situation of living agreeably, both at Paris and in the
country ; and from that time I took upon myself all the
expense of Grignon. My wife's mother, her cousin, and
her uncles had their apartments when they chose to come;
but it was to my house that they came.

I indulged myself in a carriage, which thrice a week
conveyed me, in an hour and a half, from my country-
house to the Louvre, and brought me back after the
sitting of the Academy from the Louvre to my country-
house.

From that time till the era of the Revolution I cannot express the delight which I found in life and society. My wife had been happily delivered of her fourth child; M. and Madame d'Angiviller had stood godfather and godmother: they had made it a kind of holiday, and had given us, on this occasion, the warmest and most tender proofs of friendship. Charles, their godson, became as dear to them as if he had been their own child.

Soon after we were happy enough to acquire another society of friends in M. and Madame de Seze. In that lady my wife found everything which can be attractive in an amiable character : accordingly they soon felt that inclination which arises from the congeniality of two amiable and virtuous hearts. With respect to M. de Seze, I do not believe there is a man in the world whose company is more desirable. An unaffected, lively, amusing gaiety; a natural eloquence, which, even in the most familiar conversation, flowed copiously and spontaneously; a readiness, a correctness of thought and expression, which resembled inspiration ; and, better than all, an open heart, full of rectitude, sensibility, goodness and candour—such was the man whose friendship the Abbé Maury had long taught me to desire, and whom the vicinity of our country-houses soon made my friend.

From Brevane, where, in summer, De Seze spent his leisure hours—from Brevane, I say, to Grignon, we had only to pass the Seine and the plain which it waters ; our two rising grounds faced each other. A young man whom we loved, and who loved us both, acquainted us with the mutual desire which each felt to become acquainted with the other. As soon as we met, the immediate effect was to make us fond of one another, and desirous of meeting again ; and distant as we now are, this attachment continues the same. On my side, at least, nothing during my solitude has more occupied or interested my mind. De Seze is one of those singular

men of whom we may say, "You must love him if you
did not love him before ; if you love him once, you must
love him always." ("Cras amet, qui nunquam amavit ;
quique amavit, cras amet." [1]—*Catul.*)

The young man who had taken care to make us
acquainted was Laborie, who, from the age of nineteen,
has made himself known by writings which might readily
be ascribed to the maturity of understanding and taste :
a new friend, who, prompted by spontaneous inclination,
had offered himself to me, and whom I had soon taught
to esteem and love me.

In this amiable and happy character, the desire of
becoming useful is an habitual and ruling passion. Full
of ardour for everything which wears the appearance of
virtue, the rapidity of his action equals that of his
thoughts. I never knew anyone so economical of time ;
he divides it by minutes, and every instant is employed
usefully, either for himself, or still oftener for his friends.

The change of ministers was likewise attended with
some improvement of my fortune.

The appointment of historiographer of France, which
had formerly been a thousand crowns, had, by some sort
of wretched economy, been reduced to about seventy
guineas. D'Ormesson, the comptroller-general, thought
proper to replace it on its ancient footing.

It is well known that M. de Calonne, on coming to
this office, declared his contempt for mean parsimony.
He particularly wished that the labours of literary men
should be honourably rewarded. In my character of
perpetual secretary to the French Academy, he begged
me to call on him. He expressed his intention of treating the Academy well, and asked if there were any
pensions attached to it, as to the academies of sciences
and *belles lettres*. I replied that there were none. He

---

1 "Let him who has never loved, love to-morrow ; and let him
who has loved, love to-morrow."

asked me what the daily fees might amount to in the
case of those who gave the most constant attendance.
I assured him that they could not exceed £35 or £40
a year, being only two shillings each. He promised to
double the amount. He wished to know what was the
salary of the secretary; I replied that it was £50. He
thought it too little. He therefore prevailed upon the
King to raise the fee to two shillings and sixpence, and
the secretary's salary to £125. My revenue from the
Academy might thus amount to about £200 a year.

I obtained also a new degree of favour, and new
hopes, under the ministry of M. de Lamoignon, the
keeper of the seals. The occasion was as follows:

One of the objects of this minister was to reform
the institutions for public instruction, and to render them
flourishing.   But as he himself did not possess the
knowledge requisite for forming a plan of study which
might fulfil his intentions, he consulted the Abbé Maury,
for whom he entertained much friendship and esteem.
The latter, not thinking himself sufficiently acquainted
with the subjects to which he had not specially attended,
advised him to apply to me, and the minister begged
that he would ask me to call upon him. In the conversations which we had together, I saw that, upon the
whole, he had conceived his design like a statesman,
and had taken a full view of its extent. But he was
not sufficiently acquainted with the difficulties and
details.   That we might both be assured if I had
perfectly understood his plan, I begged that he would
allow me to explain it in a memorial which I should
lay before him ; but I observed to him that nothing
appeared to me more to be dreaded in all reforms than
the ambition of destroying and changing everything ;
that I felt much respect for ancient institutions ; that I
paid a willing deference to the lessons of experience ;
and that I viewed past errors and abuses as weeds
which mix with the wheat, but which must be extir-

pated with a light and careful hand, lest we should injure the harvest.

My memorial was divided into eight principal articles: the distribution of the schools, and the subjects of instruction, which were to be adapted either to general or to local objects; the establishments to be made with a view to both of these objects; the discipline; the method; the gradations, and the exact correspondence of the remote schools to their central points of superintendence; the mode of encouragement; the means of knowing and employing those men who should be formed by this mode of instruction.

In the general aspect, and in the details of this vast composition, my model had been the institutions of the Jesuits, in which all were subjected to a single rule, superintended and governed by a central authority, and moved by a common principle of action. But we wanted that bond of union which subsists in a religious society, as well as the spirit which animates it; and the great difficulty was to find a principle of interest and emulation which might dispose men to yield a willing obedience. For this institution ought to rest upon the morals and discipline to be established among the masters, as well as among the scholars. It was necessary, therefore, that the places should be desirable, not only in their present state, but in the prospects and hopes which they held out; and, in order that exclusion or dismissal might be a punishment, I required that perseverance in these honourable functions should be attended with progressive and certain advantages.

The keeper of the seals approved of my plan in all its parts; and with regard to the necessity of rewards, he assured me that they should not be spared. "No, professor," said he, "no man of merit shall grow old in obscurity; no scholar who has distinguished himself in his course of study shall remained unemployed. You engage to let me know of the best talents which are to be found from one extremity of the kingdom to another, and I undertake to find situations for them. I see," continued he, squeezing my hand, "that we understand each other ; we shall agree together. I depend upon you, Marmontel ; and you, in like manner, may depend upon me for life."

As the Abbé Maury had assured me that the keeper of the seals was a frank and upright man, I made no difficulty in entering into the engagement which he proposed, and thought that, by completing and extending his plan, I should be labouring for his glory.

I had formed an acquaintance in the country which assisted me greatly in this employment.

Louis, the fifth of my children, was newly born, and his mother was nursing him. Albert, the eldest of the three who remained, was in his ninth year ; Charles had just completed his fourth, when I formed the resolution of educating them at home ; and in consequence of the reputation of the College of St. Barbe, I applied to it for a preceptor who had been inured to the manners and discipline of the house, which was as much celebrated for its laborious and frugal manner of living as for the superior manner in which studies were carried on in this school.

Charpentier, the excellent young man whom I received, and of whom death has deprived me, was constantly praising St. Barbe, for this house was singularly noted for the tender affection with which it was always regarded by those who had left it. He never spoke without enthusiasm of the manners, the discipline and the studies of St. Barbe. He always expressed a profound esteem for the superiors of the house and for the professors who still continued there. They were his friends ; he expressed a desire to make them mine. I allowed him to introduce them, and received them with a cordiality which made them find my country-house agreeable.

A branch of the school of St. Barbe had been established at Gentilly, a village in the vicinity of Grignon. The superiors, the professors of both houses, sometimes came together and dined with me. They took an interest in the studies of my children. On the days when the young school of Gentilly had public exercises, my children were invited, and were admitted to the examination. This supplied them with a good example and a subject of emulation. But to me it was a source of observation and instruction, for I naturally enquired into the cause of the easy and natural manner in which the studies of this school were carried on, and the cause could be no other than a good and steady arrangement.

I made most particular enquiries upon this subject, and by means of these conferences I thought myself in a capacity of putting the last hand to my plan of national instruction when, all of a sudden, by one of those changes which were constantly taking place in the ministry, M. de Lamoignon was removed and exiled to Baville.

Interest and anxiety about public affairs and about the fate of the nation soon took full possession of my mind ; my private life changed its aspect, and assumed a colouring which will necessarily be diffused over the rest of my Memoirs.

BOOK XII

I AM not writing the history of the Revolution. "Quæ contentio divina et humana cuncta permiscuit, eoque vecordiæ processit, uti studiis civilibus bellum finem faceret."[1] (*Sallust. Jug.*) But if the life of man is a journey, can I relate mine without describing the dreadful accidents, the torrents, the abysses, the regions haunted by tigers and serpents, through which I have passed? For thus it is that I remember the ten years of our misfortunes, almost doubting if it is not a wild and terrible dream.

This dreadful calamity will be everywhere described in characters of blood ; its recollections are such as it will be but too impossible to efface. But we cannot too carefully investigate its causes ; for, in the diseases of the body politic, as in those of the human body, we must ascend to their source before we can judge with probability how they will terminate or how they might have been avoided ; and the past may thus throw light upon the future.

Though for a long time the situation of public affairs and the fermentation of men's minds, through all ranks of the State, appeared to threaten the approach of some great crisis, it is nevertheless true that it happened only through the imprudence of those who obstinately persisted in thinking it impossible.

---

[1] "This struggle has thrown all things divine and human into confusion, and has reached such a height of frenzy that war was the end of civil discord."

The nation, always faithful to its laws, to its King, to its ancient constitution, instinctively content with that portion of freedom, of prosperity and of glory which it enjoyed, was never weary of hoping for some salutary amendment of the vices and errors of the old administration.

This hope had been particularly enlivened by the accession of Louis XVI. to the throne. And then, indeed, if the wishes of a young King, full of candour and uprightness, had been seconded as they ought to have been, the whole might have been repaired without any convulsion.

Louis XVI. came to the throne at the age of twenty, full of a sentiment which is most valuable so long as it is moderate, but very dangerous when it becomes excessive —distrust of himself. The fault of his education had been directly the reverse of that for which the education of princes is usually blamed—he had been too much intimidated; and as long as his elder brother, the Duke of Normandy, lived, he had been made too sensible of the superiority which that Prince, whose capacity was certainly premature, possessed over him in point of understanding.

The Dauphin was thus in the anxious and perplexed situation of a man who feels his destiny and his duty, but who dares not hope to be capable of fulfilling them, when he saw himself suddenly burdened with the government of an empire. His first feeling on finding himself a king at twenty, was fear; the first thing he did was to seek a man whose wisdom and ability might enlighten and guide him. Such men are always rare; and the young King asked the advice of his family with respect to a choice, which was then, perhaps, more difficult than ever. Nothing could be more important, both for the nation and himself, than the step which should be the result of this deliberation. His political education was to be begun, his views to be directed, his mind to be

formed, and Nature had completely disposed him to
receive good impressions. His understanding was solid,
his soul uncorrupted, ingenuous and feeling, free from
vice, full of contempt for pomp and luxury, of hatred for
falsehood and flattery, of love for justice and truth. His
manners, indeed, might be a little blunt and rude, but he
possessed that rectitude and moral goodness which is the
basis of virtue. In a word, this king of twenty, superior
to all selfish considerations, was disposed to adopt every
measure that was just and good ; and around him was a
kingdom, every part of which called for reform. The
greatest good was to be done, and the greatest evil to be
repaired : such was the prospect which awaited the man
whom Louis XVI. should choose for his confidant and
guide. He chose the Count de Maurepas, May, 1774.

Maurepas, after a ministry of thirty years, and a
long exile, had suffered a still longer period of disgrace
under the deceased King, for a very slight fault, at which
the royal family had never felt any displeasure. In his
retreat he had acquired that respect which is granted to
age and to unmerited misfortune supported with dignity.
His former ministry had been distinguished only by the
ruin of the navy ; but as the timid policy of Cardinal
Fleury had palsied this part of our forces, the negligence
of Maurepas might have been a matter of necessity ; and
in a subordinate place, where he was under no necessity
of being a statesman, he had only to display his natural
qualities, the agreeable manners of a man of the world,
and the talents of a courtier.

He was superficial and incapable of any profound
and serious application, but endowed with that quickness
of perception which instantly penetrates into the most
complicated part of business. In council, his habitual
dexterity supplied the want of study and meditation. As
courteous, as mild, as his father had been harsh and
blunt ; his mind was pliant, flexible, full of stratagems
to attack, of address to defend himself, of subterfuges to

elude, of quick turns to shift a subject at will, of witticisms whose pleasantry might disconcert the serious, of expedients to extricate himself from a slippery and difficult position; his eye instantaneously seized whatever was weak and ridiculous in men; with imperceptible art he drew them into his snare, or led them on to his purpose; with an art still more formidable he could throw ridicule on everything, even on merit itself, when he wished to undervalue it. All these arts, joined to that of enlivening, of simplifying the labour of the cabinet, rendered Maurepas the most seducing of ministers. Had nothing more been wanting than to teach the young King how to handle affairs lightly and skilfully, to laugh at men and things, and to turn the duty of reigning into an amusement, Maurepas would have been, beyond all comparison, the man to be chosen. Hopes had been perhaps entertained that age and misfortune might have rendered his character more firm, more steady and more energetic. But he was naturally feeble, indolent, selfish; loved his own comfort and repose; wished his old age to be respected, but peaceful; shunned whatever could make his suppers dull, or his sleep restless; he hardly believed in the reality of difficult virtues, and regarded a pure attachment to the public good as mere ostentation or hypocrisy; cared little for rendering his ministry splendid, and made the art of government consist in managing everything quietly, by adopting always temporary expedients rather than adhering to fixed principles. Maurepas, therefore, was in old age what he had been in his youth—an agreeable man, quite taken up with himself, and uniting the characters of minister and courtier.

A watchful attention to preserve his ascendency over the mind of the King, and his predominance in the councils, made him easily become jealous, even of those whom he himself had chosen; and this uneasiness was the only active passion of his soul. In other respects there was no spring, no vigour, either for doing good or evil; but weakness without kindness, malice without atrocity, resentment without anger, carelessness for a future with which he would have nothing to do. He might, perhaps, be sincerely desirous of the public good, when he could bring it about with perfect security to himself; but this desire was cooled the moment he saw either his credit or his repose in danger. Such was always the character of this old man who had been given to the young King as his guide and adviser.

As it was easy for him to see that frankness and kindness formed the ground-work of the character of this Prince, he studied, in the first place, to appear kind and frank. The King made no secret to him of that excessive timidity which had been left by the first impressions of childhood. He perceived, therefore, that the surest mode of gaining his kindness was to make those duties which now terrified him appear easy. He employed his talent of simplifying affairs in order to render their burden lighter. But, whether it was that he regarded inveterate evils as now past remedy, whether his indolence and levity prevented him from discovering them, or whether he neglected them as maladies arising from an excess of strength and health, and, perhaps, as constitutional vices inherent in the body politic, he did not allow the young King to trouble his mind with them, but assured him that all things would go on well, provided they were wisely and moderately directed. The excuse of Cardinal Fleury for his pusillanimous anxiety was, that an edifice which had lasted more than thirteen hundred years must bend to its fall, and that while we propped it up there was a danger of shaking it; on the contrary, the pretence of Maurepas for his indolent security was, that a kingdom so vigorously constituted would be easily restored by its natural strength, and that it might, therefore, be allowed to subsist with its faults and abuses.

But the bad state of the finances is not an evil which can be long palliated or dissembled; want of money and loss of credit soon bear witness against the minister who conceals and neglects them; and so long as the true remedy has not been found, it grows always worse instead of better.

The Abbé Terrai had been given to Louis XV. as an able minister. Twenty years spent in a court of law, amid a multitude of discontented clients, had hardened him against complaint; he was not much less hardened against censure, and thought himself bound by his profession to be the object of public hatred. Maurepas removed him, and appointed in his place Turgot, a man alike distinguished for understanding and virtue.

The latter was deeply sensible that a reduction of expense, economy in collecting the revenue, the abolition of privileges burdensome to commerce and agriculture, and a more equal distribution of taxes through the different classes of the people, were the true remedies which must be applied to the great malady of the State, and of this he found it easy to convince a King who breathed nothing but justice and love for his people. But Maurepas, now seeing that this esteem and confidence of the young King for his new minister was going too far, became jealous of his own work, and hastened to destroy it.

In a country where so many persons live by abuses and disorders, a man who introduced regularity and economy into the finances, a man whom no credit could bend or favour corrupt, must necessarily have as enemies all those whose requests he either refused or was ever likely to refuse. Turgot was too proud and too candid to descend to Court intrigues. His demeanour was severe, and he was said to want address; and when ridicule, which with us sinks the value of everything, had once seized upon him, Maurepas perceived that his ruin would be easily accomplished. He began with listening, with

encouraging by a smile the ill-natured remarks of the
courtiers. His next step was to own that the views of
Turgot were rather those of a theoretical reasoner than
of a real man of business ; that the public opinion had
been mistaken with respect to the ability of this pretended sage ; that his head was full of nothing but
philosophical reveries and speculations, without any experience of business, any knowledge of men, any capacity
for the management of finance, or any inventive powers
for supplying the pressing exigencies of the State: he had
a system of perfection which did not belong to this world,
and was to be found only in books ; a minute search
after that ideal excellence which is never to be found ;
instead of the means of providing for present exigencies,
vague and fantastical schemes for a distant futurity ; a
number of ideas, but these confused ; great extent of
knowledge, but foreign to the purpose of his ministry ;
the pride of Lucifer ; and, along with his presumption,
the most inflexible obstinacy.

These confidential observations of the old man,
which were spread from mouth to mouth that they might
reach the King's ear, were the more successful from not
being absolutely devoid of plausibility. Turgot was
surrounded by studious men, who had devoted themselves to economical science, and formed a kind of sect,
the object of whose labours was doubtless valuable, but
whose confident language, sententious tone, and sometimes chimerical notions, wrapped in an odd and obscure
style, gave scope for raillery. Turgot associated with
them, and expressed an esteem of which they themselves
boasted too loudly, representing it as greater than it really
was. It was not difficult, therefore, for his enemies to
represent him as the head of the sect, and the ridicule
attached to the name of economist fell upon him.

Besides, there is no doubt that Turgot, proud of
the uprightness of his intentions, valued himself more on
being dexterous in business than on being pliant and

engaging in his intercourse with the Court; his address was mild and polite, but cold. You were sure of finding him just, but inflexible in his principles; and interest and favour could not brook the immovable tranquility with which he rejected their applications.

Though, in the course of two years, by means of economy and reduction of expenditure, he had considerably diminished the load of debt which pressed upon the treasury, he was still thought to treat the ruin of the finances and of public credit too much as a chronic malady. The wisdom of his arrangements, his prospects of improvement, the encouragement and the relief which he afforded to agriculture, the liberty which he restored to commerce and industry, offered only slow success and distant resources, whilst there were urgent wants which it was necessary to supply.

In his system of free trade, he admitted of no restriction and no limits. Now, in the case of necessaries of life, even though this liberty should be attended only with momentary dangers, the risk of leaving a whole people in want of the means of subsistence was not one which could be incurred without uneasiness. The obstinacy of Turgot in withdrawing every kind of superintendence from the corn trade, appeared to be too headstrong. This gave a mortal blow to his influence over the mind of the King.

During a popular disturbance which was excited in 1775 by the dearness of bread, the King, who still retained for Turgot that esteem of which Maurepas was jealous, placed his whole confidence in him, and left the affair entirely to his management. Turgot was not so prudent as to require that Maurepas should be called to the secret council in which the King committed to him this sacred charge; and he was besides so imprudent as loudly to undertake to prove that the riot was prompted by high authority. Le Noir, the minister of police, was dismissed on suspicion of having acted in concert with the authors of this plot. Certain it is that the plunder of the bakers' shops had been carried on without opposition. The riot went on also in a systematic manner, which seemed to indicate a plan ; nor would I venture to say that Turgot was mistaken in the person to whom he ascribed it. The Prince of Conti, a spendthrift who was always in want, and full of the old spirit of the Fronde, bustled in the Parliament only that he might be dreaded at Court ; and being accustomed to a timid compliance with all his demands, could not but be offended by an unbending respect like that of Turgot. Possibly, therefore, he might wish, by a commotion among the people in the country and city, to spread a report of famine, to raise alarm, and thus destroy the King's favour for that troublesome minister, from whom he had nothing to expect. But whatever probability there might be in this cause of the disturbance, Turgot could not produce the proof which he had promised ; this rash step determined his fall.

Maurepas gave the King to understand that this story of a pretended plot was only the pitiful excuse of a vain man, who would neither acknowledge nor correct his error ; and that a systematic and obstinate head, which must have everything its own way, was not suited to a place where everything should be carefully calculated and a judicious and conciliatory plan of conduct followed.

Turgot was dismissed in May, 1776, and the finances given to Clugny, who appeared to have come only to make spoil with his jovial companions and his opera-girls, and who died in the ministry, after four or five months of impudent plunder, of which the King alone was ignorant. His place was supplied by Taboreau, who, being an honest man, soon owned himself incapable of filling it. He acknowledged the superiority of a man who had been given him as a second, under the title of director of the royal treasure. His retreat was dignified by modesty, and Necker succeeded him under the character of director-general of the finances.

This Genevese, who has since been the sport of opinion, and celebrated in such a variety of ways, was then one of the most distinguished bankers of Europe. In this profession he enjoyed the public confidence and a very extensive credit. He had produced proof of his talents, and his writings upon subjects connected with the ministry of finance had displayed a judicious and reflecting mind ; but another merit which he had, with Maurepas, was his hatred of Turgot. The cause of this hatred was as follows :

Turgot could not endure that commerce, industry and agriculture should be subjected to the restrictive system of Colbert. He considered it as a right inherent in property that every man should be at liberty to dispose as he pleased of his property and his talents ; he wished that a man should be allowed to follow his private interest, being convinced that he would best promote it, and that from the reciprocal operation of private interests the general good would result. Necker was more timid, and thought that in almost every man this individual interest stood in need of being guided and restrained ; that, till it had received the lessons of experience, it would be advisable to supply the place of these by judicious regulations ; that the care of the public good ought not to be entrusted to the care of private interest ; that if, with a view to the safety and tranquility of a whole nation, civil and moral liberty ought to be restrained and subjected to laws, it was just also that the liberty of commerce should be moderated, and even suspended, whenever the common safety was concerned ; that the property of the necessaries of life did not so completely belong to individuals as to give one part of the nation a right to let the other die of want ; and that, while it would be unjust to keep down these articles at a low price, it would be equally so to allow them to rise to an excessive value—in short, that to allow the rich miser to impose too imperiously upon the poor the severe law of necessity, would be placing the many at the mercy of the few, and that it was the wisdom and the duty of administration to hold the balance between them.

"Avarice," said Turgot, "will not be dreaded where liberty reigns; and the means of securing abundance is to allow commodities a free circulation. The corn will be sometimes dear, but labour will be dear also, and everything will find its level."

"When the price of corn rises gradually," said Necker, "doubtless it will regulate the price of industry, and no person will suffer; but when it rises suddenly to an excessive height, the people will have long to suffer before everything finds its level."

Upon this system of superintendence and moderate liberty Necker had composed the eulogy of Colbert, and this eulogy had met with success. It was a double crime, which Turgot could not forgive. This zealot for the freedom of commerce and industry thought his opinion infallible; and viewing it always as self-evident, he considered the man who did not yield to it as insincere.

Till then, however, the principles of Necker had not been made public; but, when Turgot issued his edict allowing the free exportation of corn, not only from province to province, but to foreign parts, and at all times, Necker could not forbear saying that it appeared to him somewhat dangerous, and that he would have a few observations to communicate to him upon this branch of commerce, which might, perhaps, deserve his attention. These words rekindled the antipathy of Turgot against the system of restrictive laws. He replied that his opinion upon that subject was unalterable; but that everyone, notwithstanding, was at liberty to express and publish his opinion.

Necker replied that such had not been his intention; but that, since permission was given to him, he

might, perhaps, make use of it.   Some time after appeared
his book upon the laws concerning the corn trade ; and
immediately upon the publication of this book, the riot
which I have mentioned took place.   Turgot had no doubt
that the one had contributed to the other, although he
might have known that the populace when they pillage
bakers' shops do not apply to books for advice.

The friends of Turgot, more incensed than himself,
proposed that he should punish Necker by banishing him
to Geneva ; he had it in his power, for he was still in full
possession of the King's confidence.   His uprightness
and justice saved him from this shame ; but he preserved
till death his hatred against a man who had injured
him only by accepting his challenge and combating his
opinion.

The moment that Necker took the administration of
finance into his hands, his first care and employment was
to unravel the chaos in which it was plunged.   Clugny
had left an annual deficit of £1,000,000 sterling, which
appeared then enormous; yet it was necessary that it
should be supplied.   Necker found means of doing this.
These means consisted, on one side, in regulating the
collection of the public money, and clearing the channel
through which it flowed ; on the other, in discovering
the manner in which it was misapplied, and in reforming
abuses.

Nothing prevented the King from being as economical as his minister, except his too kind and easy
disposition.   It was with a view, therefore, of guarding
against perpetual seductions that Necker prevailed upon
him to suspend, till the end of each year, the confirmation of the favours which he should incline to bestow, in
order that he might see the whole amount before dis-
tributing it.

Thus Necker, by means of economy alone, was
about to secure a surplus which would have enabled him
to relieve the public treasury, when the signal of war

informed him that he would need more copious resources
to form, immediately, a respectable navy, as well as to
arm and equip it. These urgent expenses would amount
annually to upwards of £6,000,000 sterling. It was by
credit alone that he could look them in the face, and
credit was gone. The bad faith of administration had
ruined it during a period of peace ; yet he must either
restore it or sink, for even the most burdensome taxes
cannot supply the exigencies of an expensive war, and
England, our enemy, was then able to borrow two or
three hundred millions,[1] at a moderate interest. Necker
has since been censured for his loans, but this censure
ought to have been directed against the war which
rendered them indispensable, and which might itself
have been dispensed with.

Necker's art of raising and supporting public credit
was to afford ground of confidence by stating the resources secured by his economy, and thereby showing a
solid and sure foundation for the loans which he was to
open. The same economical plan, which he had marked
out during peace, was sufficient to procure those funds
which the war required. It was well known that he
had constantly under his eye complete and precise statements of the situation of the finances, and that in every
operation, if the expression may be used, he had scales in
his hands, so as never to make his engagements exceed
his resources. By means of this spirit of order, after
finding credit destroyed at the end of fifteen years' peace,
he was able to restore it amid a war which demanded
the greatest efforts. Notwithstanding the deficit of 1776,
notwithstanding the expenses of this war, and loans
to the amount of £17,000,000 sterling, which had been
made for its support, he was able, in the account which
he delivered to the King in 1781, to state that the ordinary revenues then exceeded, by £400,000, the annual

---

1 Francs.

and ordinary expenses.   The English were thus warned
that, without any new tax, and even without any new
retrenchment, France would still have funds sufficient
for two campaigns, since a free revenue of £400,000
was sufficient to pay the interest of £8,000,000.   This
information was very capable of producing a good peace ;
yet Necker was not the less accused of vanity in publishing the account.

In an able minister, this manner of openly disclosing his operations and the state of affairs, is doubtless
attended with many advantages, and its success is infallible with a nation which is capable of thought and
application.   But with a thoughtless people, who, without examination, judge men and things upon mere report,
this method had its dangers, and Necker ought to have
foreseen them.   There is no safety in taking such a
public for your judge, except when the subjects which
are placed under their eyes possess the most palpable
certainty ; now, to the multitude, financial statements
will never attain this degree of evidence.   No one in our
gay circles chooses to grow pale over calculations.   It is
very easy, therefore, to shake the public opinion of the
exactness of an account ; and, as soon as the doubt
arises, it is a cloud which malignity never fails to swell.
Necker, while he did a thing exemplary to future ministers, satisfactory to the King, imposing towards England,
encouraging to the nation, animating to public credit—
did a thing which was very bold and very dangerous to
himself.

Every article which this account contained was
confirmed and supported by vouchers.   Public opinion
seemed even to dispense with their production, and its
first burst was completely in his favour.

But as soon as a man was found bold enough to
attack him, this aggressor met with a cordial reception
from envy and malignity.   In a memorial, he asserted that
Necker's account was incorrect, and this memorial went

from hand to hand, the more eagerly sought after from its being in manuscript. An economical minister is never in want of enemies : Necker had multitudes, and some of these were powerful. Maurepas, without declaring himself, rallied them round him ; and here we have an instance of one of those wretched interests of vanity to which the destiny of States is so often attached.

Maurepas was president of the council of finance. Now in the account in which Necker laid open the situation of the finances with so much honour to himself, Maurepas was not named. This silence appeared injurious to the old minister ; he said nothing, but did not forgive it.

Another grievance was the disgrace of a minister, the creature of Maurepas, or rather of his wife. His dismissal was procured by Necker. Maurepas, who never had any excuse for allowing himself to be governed by women, was yet in subjection to his own wife. That continual complaisance which is the adulation of every instant, and which is so particularly agreeable in old age and adversity, had subdued him, as love would have done. He had formed a habit of loving and hating whatever was loved or hated by the companion of his disgrace ; and Sartines was one of the men for whom the Countess de Maurepas had the greatest affection.

Sartines, formerly lieutenant of police, possessed circumspection, pliancy, discretion—all the little talents which belong to mediocrity ; but, between the obscure detail of the police of Paris and the ministry of marine amid the dangers of a naval war, the distance was tremendous. Sartines had never acquired the least of the knowledge which was requisite for this great office ; so that if there was a man who could be opposed to the English Admiralty in the midst of this war, which embraced both worlds, most certainly it was not he. The ill-success of our operations corresponded to the total incapacity of the person who directed them ; there was no plan, no union, no concert; enormous expenses, disastrous defeats; fleets issuing from our harbours only to become the prey of the enemy; our commerce and colonies abandoned, our convoys taken, our squadrons destroyed; and, without mentioning the irreparable loss of our sailors, and the ruin of our dockyards, upwards of £4,200,000 of extraordinary expenses were thrown every year into the sea, from which we saw ourselves shamefully driven, notwithstanding the devoted bravery of our sailors: such were the rights of Sartines to be supported by Maurepas.

Necker, who was grieved at the deplorable use that was made of so much treasure, and at seeing the fortune and glory of a great nation thrown into such hands, did not the less redouble his efforts to supply the necessities of the war, and to support its weight. He had agreed with Sartines that, beside the sums which he annually drew from the royal treasure, the latter, on urgent occasions, might borrow from the treasurer of the navy to the extent of £200,000 or £250,000; and he trusted that the minister was keeping strictly within these limits, when he learned from the treasurer himself, that, in obedience to his order, he had advanced to the amount of £1,000,000, payable at three months. This was like a thunderbolt to the director of finance; for, as he had taken no steps to provide for an engagement of which he had been kept ignorant, the term of payment was at hand without his knowing how to answer it. He provided for the emergency; but, whether the conduct of Sartines arose from bad intention, or only from imprudence, Necker thought it no longer safe to be connected with such a man; he complained to the King, and positively demanded either his own dismissal or that of Sartines.

Maurepas was detained at Paris by the gout. The King, before forming any resolution, wrote and asked his advice. " When he received the King's letter," said the Duke de Nivernois to me, " his wife and I were sitting by his bedside. He read it to us. The determination was long delayed ; but at length he himself, forming his resolution, said, ' We must sacrifice Sartines ; we cannot do without Necker.' "

The King, on dismissing Sartines, consulted Necker with regard to his successor ; and Necker mentioned the Marshal de Castries. It is well known how much reason the management and final issue of the war gave to applaud this choice. The old minister became only the more jealous, and his closet was thenceforth a kind of centre of action to the party that was hostile to Necker. That party thought themselves also protected by the royal brothers.

However cautious the conduct of Necker towards those princes was, they had been suspected of considering it as too rigid ; but, what was still more true, its strictness was displeasing to their creatures ; and exchanges, cessions, sales, all the affairs which men in power were accustomed to transact with the King, had to fear, in this director of the finances, a severe and clear-sighted censor, from whom they all longed to be free.

There were no more snares to be laid for the easy disposition of the King, no more favours secretly and skilfully snatched ; in particular, there was no longer a possibility of concealing in the corners, as it were, of the ministerial portfolio, the secret articles of a lease, of a contract, or of a privilege ; nor did the obscure windings of the financial labyrinth afford the means of securing clandestine profits. The man who struck at the root of so many abuses could not but be hated. The memorial, therefore, which accused him of imposing upon the King, was warmly supported.

Far be it from me to throw upon the royal brothers the slightest suspicion of having wished to favour the calumny ; but falsehood, in their eyes, could assume the colouring of truth, in the same manner as the most contemptible interests had assumed the colouring of zeal.

Bourboulon, the author of the memorial, and treasurer to the Count d'Artois, had made himself agreeable
to that Prince. Proud, therefore, of his protection, he
raised his head; and owning himself the accuser of
Necker, he defied him to answer. So much assurance
had an air of truth, which imposed upon the public.
Many persons could with difficulty believe that Necker
had so suddenly and so wonderfully changed the situation of the finances; and without treating the specious
account which he had given as a crime, they thought
that this account had been artfully drawn up with a
view to support public credit, and to hold forth the means
of continuing the war and rendering peace more easy
to be obtained. Maurepas listened to this opinion with a
significant look, which seemed to applaud the penetration
of those who could guess so well.

But Necker thought it his duty not to be satisfied
with such an apology, and, being incapable of com-
pounding with public opinion on the subject of his
honour, he asked the King to allow him to lay before
him, in presence of his ministers, the memorial of Bourboulon, and to answer to each separate article. The
King consented; and Maurepas, Miromesnil and Vergennes, three enemies of Necker, were present at this
examination. The memorial was read, and its falsehood
proved from one end to the other by papers which
ascertained the situation of the finances, and of which
the account presented to the King was only a dis-
closure.

In answer to these incontestable proofs, the three
ministers could not produce the shadow of a doubt; but
when the King asked confidentially of Maurepas what he
thought of these calculations, and of this financial account, "Sire," replied the old courtier, "it appears to me
as full of truth as of modesty."

After this examination it followed, of course, either
that the false accusation must be punished or that

Necker must be suspected of having failed in defending himself. He had despised the injurious libels which attacked only his person; but ought he to neglect in like manner that which decried his administration? The more the King's justice was acknowledged, the more impossible it must be believed that Bourboulon should continue to be endured in the Prince's household if he were convicted of lying and calumny. Now, after this conviction, he remained in his office, and appeared everywhere, even at royal suppers.

In this crisis, upon which I dwell on account of the fatal consequences which were about to follow from the resolution of Necker, he had three parts to act; one was to trust more to his own reputation, to overlook and endure everything till the death of Maurepas, which was not far distant; another, to defend himself by merely getting printed upon two columns the memorial of Bourboulon and the statements which gave the lie to this calumnious memorial; lastly, to demand from the King that his accuser, as being convicted of calumny, should be punished. The first would have been the advice given him by the most judicious. "Why did he not wait?" said the Duke de Nivernois to me after the death of Maurepas; "patience for six months would have saved us. Peace would have come, and the restoration of the finances by a good economist under the best of kings would have enabled us to enjoy long his reign and his virtues." The second, too, would have been a rational line of conduct; for when the public had the proofs under their eyes, the truth would have been evident, and the detractor confounded. But pretended friends of Necker thought it unworthy of him to enter the lists with such an antagonist. He ought, in my opinion, either to have despised or encountered him. He demanded his punishment. It is true that he was every day threatened with libels still more atrocious and more infamous, and if an example should not be made of

Bourboulon, it was impossible that Necker, abandoned by the hatred of the old minister to the insolence and rage of a faction supported by authority, should not lose at least a part of that respect on which his credit rested. It was for the support of this credit, this powerful opinion, without which he could do nothing, that he demanded as the sole punishment the dismissal of his detractor from the household of the Count d'Artois. The reply of Maurepas was that he asked what was impossible. "Then," urged Necker, "the King himself must bear witness to the truth by some mark of the confidence with which he honours me," and he demanded admission into the council of State. He thought it, indeed, a great evil, that in this council, where subjects most connected with the situation of the finances were canvassed, the minister of finance should not have full right of admittance. But Maurepas viewed, or pretended to view, this demand as arising only from a preposterous vanity. "What!" said he, "you admitted to the council, who do not go to mass!" "My lord," replied Necker, "this reason does not hold good. Sully did not go to mass, yet Sully was admitted to the council." In this reply Maurepas noticed only the foolish vanity of comparing himself to Sully; and, instead of the council, offered to ask his admission into the cabinet.[1] Necker openly treated this offer as a mockery, and asked leave to resign.

This was a thing expected with the most eager impatience in the drawing-room of Maurepas, and of which his niece, the Marchioness of Flamarens, made no secret. But he, pretending not to consent to what he desired most, refused to lay Necker's resignation before the King, and said to him, at last, that it must be put into the Queen's hands, if he was finally determined to give it in.

---

1 See note (2) at the end.

The Queen, who listened to him with favour, and expressed esteem for him, was sensible of the loss which the King was about to suffer; and seeing that Necker persisted in his resolution, she required him to take at least twenty-four hours to reflect maturely upon it.

Necker consulted his own mind, recollected the good which he had done, thought of that which he might still do, anticipated the bitter regret which he might feel after renouncing it. Thinking it impossible that an old man, on the brink of the tomb, should be obstinately unjust towards him, he resolved to see him once more.

" Sir," said he, " if the King really wishes to express his satisfaction with my services, he may give me a proof which will only supply me with new means of serving him—I mean the direction of the contracts for the army and navy." " What you ask," said Maurepas, " would offend the two ministers." " I do not think so," replied Necker; " yet, after all, so much the worse for the minister, who, in examining expenses which it is impossible for him to estimate himself, should envy me a labour which he leaves to his clerks." The last words of the one were, that the thing could not be mentioned; the last resolution of the other was to go and entreat the Queen to get his resignation accepted. The Queen received it, and the King gave his consent. Such is the source whence all our misfortunes have flowed. We shall soon see them swell and overflow in torrents, till they plunge us into the deepest ruin.

It may appear not very probable that the King should so readily deprive himself of an able man, who had served him so well. But his favourable opinion of him was impaired by artful and treacherous insinuations. Necker was represented to him as a man full of pride —of inexorable pride. His enemies said they had attempted to make him sensible that, even supposing errors of calculation in the memorial of Bourboulon, these errors were not crimes; that there was no sufficient ground for requiring that a prince, a brother of the King, should disgrace, by dismissal, a man who belonged to him, because he had displeased a minister of finance; but nothing could appease him. They had offered to demand for him, and to obtain from His Majesty a privilege which was considered as honourable by the highest nobility—admission into the cabinet; but he had treated it with disdain. Thinking himself necessary, he pretended to give law; he compared himself to Sully, and asked nothing else than to rule in the councils, to superintend all the ministers—in a word, to sit on the throne by the side of His Majesty.

The disinterestedness with which Necker had chosen to serve the State, contributed also to make him be considered as a stern Republican, who wished to oblige without lying under any obligations; and if I may be allowed to express my own opinion, Necker, when refusing as he did the emoluments of his office, might have expected malignant comments to be made upon a pride which was mortifying to all those who had not, and could not have it.

In short, that the King might feel no regret on account of the dismissal of Necker, they had found means to convince him that, if it was an evil, it was one that could not be avoided.

One of Necker's schemes is well known to have been the establishment of provincial assemblies throughout the kingdom. Now, in order to make the King sensible of the advantage of these assemblies, Necker, in a memorial which he had read when they were together, and which was intended for the King alone, had shown, on one side, the inconveniences of the arbitrary power entrusted to intendants, and the manner in which it was abused by their subaltern agents; on the other, the advantage which the King would derive from a more immediate intercourse with his people, so as to depend less on the mediation of parliaments. This memorial having been secretly obtained and published at the same time that Bourboulon was circulating his, displeased the magistracy, and gave them such a dislike to Necker as enabled the old minister to persuade the King that Necker had entirely lost the confidence of the parliaments; that bodies of men never forgive; that he, who had once offended them, would find them ever after quite unmanageable; that this misunderstanding was a hydra which must be incessantly combated; that Necker himself was sensible of it, and that, while he retired upon other pretences, he was sensible that his place was no longer tenable.

A remarkable circumstance, which would be alone sufficient to show the thoughtlessness of Maurepas, is, that when he returned into his drawing-room, quite happy at the departure of Necker, his friends having asked whom he would appoint in his place, he owned that he had never thought on the subject. I was told by my niece that the Cardinal de Rohan happening to be there by chance, mentioned Fleury; and Fleury was named.

This old counsellor of State, an acute, pliant and insinuating character, was recommended by his connections and alliances in the magistracy; this, in the eyes of Maurepas, was a considerable advantage; for as he considered the finances only as a war to be carried on between the Court and the Parliament, the ablest comptroller-general for him would be the man who could most readily prevail upon them to pass the edicts.[1] He had made it a grand object to acquire the favour of the parliaments, and he wished that, after his example, a minister of finance should treat them with that address which obtains, by gentle means, what authority could with difficulty command.

Fleury, in this respect, answered his expectation

---

1 See note (3) at the end.

very well. He obtained, without obstacle, the passing
of £2,100,000 of taxes. Necker had left them upwards
of £8,000,000 in the royal coffers. This was more than
necessary to place an able and respected minister in easy
circumstances ; but even with these aids, Fleury got into
difficulties, for want of that credit which public esteem
grants only to integrity.

Six months after the death of Maurepas, Fleury was
dismissed ; and the King, that he might at least have
an honest man at the head of the finances, appointed
d'Ormesson.

The latter, unhappily, had nothing but honesty. He
had no talents, no knowledge of finance, and no invention. Assailed by want, urged by men in power, and
reduced to the alternative of either withdrawing or
maintaining himself by unworthy complaisance, he
wavered not in his choice, and chose, rather than
degrade himself, to descend from the ministry with his
integrity unimpaired.

A post so slippery, from which every man fell,
might, one would think, have intimidated the ambition
of candidates ; yet this passion became only the more
ardent ; nor was there a man of intrigue in any of the
avenues of favour, who, if he possessed the slightest
knowledge of business, did not aspire to filling the place
of him who had fallen.

Amid this crowd, a man of ingenuity and talents
distinguished himself—it was Calonne. He had resorted
to means of success, the more singular from their
simplicity. Far from concealing his ambition, he had
published it ; and instead of the austerity with which
some of his predecessors had armed themselves, he had
employed every means of making himself agreeable,
especially to women ; he was known by them as the most
obliging of men, and when he confided his views to such
as were in power, he was lavish of every hope which
could gain him their votes. Accordingly, they never

ceased to extol his information, his ability, his genius.
His manner towards men was little less engaging, in
consequence of an easy and natural politeness which
marked distinctions without making them offensive, and
by an air of good-will which seemed favourable to every
man's ambition. At every new change he was called
upon by the unanimous voice of the higher circles. At
last he was named, and on his arrival at Fontainebleau,
where the Court was, you would have said that he held
in his hand the horn of abundance—it was a kind of
triumph (November 3rd, 1783).

At first, thinking himself at a fountain of inexhaustible wealth, and never calculating either the wants or
the expenses which awaited him, but intoxicated with
his prosperity, in which he expected soon to see that of
the State, he despised all foresight, and neglected all
economy as unworthy of one possessing such power.
Convinced that the first art of a man of power was the
art of pleasing, he trusted to favour for his fortune, and
studied only to render himself agreeable to those who
sought to become formidable in order to sell their favour.
He thus saw himself suddenly surrounded with praise
and vainglory. People talked of nothing but the graces
of his address and the charms of his language. It was in
order to paint his character that the expression of "elegant forms" was borrowed from the Arts, and *l'obligeance*,
a new word, seemed invented for him. The ministry of
finance was said never to have been filled with so much
gaiety, ease and dignity. The readiness with which he
despatched business astonished every person, and the
gaiety with which he treated the most serious matters
made him admired as a man of prodigious capacity.
Even those, in short, who ventured to doubt if he was
the best of ministers, were forced to acknowledge that he
was the most delightful. It was published that he did
business with the King in such a manner as to make it a
mere amusement : there was nothing thorny, nothing

laborious, no difficulty for the present, no anxiety for
the future.   The King was at ease, and everyone was
satisfied—till, at the end of three years and a few months
of this brilliant and smiling administration, the fatal
secret was disclosed that the State was ruined.

Then it was that invention and courage were found
in Calonne.   After having exhausted every means of
giving new life to expiring credit, he saw that his only
hope lay in some brilliant stroke, which might make the
edicts appear like a restoration of public affairs, and in
order to display them invested with a commanding authority, he asked of the King an assembly of Notables, in
which he might lay open the situation of the finances,
and might consult with them upon the means of filling
up the deficiency which, according to his own account,
he had found on coming into office, and which the war
in both the Indies had naturally augmented.

This assembly was opened at Versailles on the 22nd
of February, 1787.   The proposal which Calonne presented was vast and daring.   Perhaps it deserved more
favour than it obtained, for it brought forward that equal
distribution of taxes which would both increase their
amount and, at the same time, alleviate their burden.
But the Notables were among the number of those who
would be affected by the new impositions, and to this,
most unhappily for themselves and for the State, they
had never been able to consent.   Of the projects of
Calonne some were judged confused and subtle, others
full of difficulties, which rendered them impracticable ;
others, in short, bad, even though they could have been
executed.   Such was the result of the observations of the
Notables upon the part of his proposal which underwent
their examination, for it was not even discussed to the
end.

His fundamental principle was a territorial impost,
the advantage of which would have consisted in following the progressive rise in the value of land.   If, how-

ever, the collection had been found too difficult he would
have changed its mode, provided it had been equally
derived from all kinds of property. But they would not
even enter into a composition with him ; and, with
regard both to matter and form, the Notables determined
that this was inadmissible, and they at the same time
expressly refused to deliberate upon any species of tax,
unless detailed statements were laid before them of the
receipts and expenditure, by which they might see how
the deficit had been incurred ; that if, after an examination of the accounts, a new supply was indispensable,
they would consent to have the imposition equally laid
upon every sort of property.

The reply of the King was such as had been foreseen.
They were forbidden to insist upon this examination ; but
the explanation which Calonne refused had been provoked by himself when he entered into a contest with
Necker respecting the origin of the deficit. The following is the manner in which he had got into this dangerous defile.

In 1787, at the opening of the assembly, the deficit,
by Calonne's own acknowledgment, was £4,750,000 ;
and as it was desirable for him to believe that a considerable part of this deficit existed before his time, he
actually did believe and assert it in the assembly of the
Notables.

Necker, on being informed that in this assembly
Calonne meant to dispute, as incorrect, all the accounts
given in before his administration, wrote to him that,
having bestowed the most scrupulous attention on the
account which he had given in 1781, he considered it
as perfectly correct; and, continued he, " As I have
vouchers for all the articles which admitted of such
proof, I, luckily, find myself able to give full evidence of
the truth. Surely, then, sir, I have a right to demand
either that you will not impair, in any degree, the confidence due to the correctness of this account, or that

you will communicate to me an explanation of your doubts."

Calonne, with a very slight promise not to attack this account, shunned the explanation. Necker insisted, and in reply to the most urgent letter, he received a note politely ironical, with a copy of the discourse which Calonne had just pronounced in the assembly of Notables, and in which he had asserted that in 1781 there was a considerable deficit in the ordinary revenues. Necker was at the same time informed that in the great committee of the Notables, which was held at the house of Monsieur, Calonne had expressly said that this sum was considerably above £2,300,000. Necker then complained to the King that the comptroller-general of finance had accused, without consenting to hear him. "Sire," said he in his letter, "I should of all men in the world be the most deserving of contempt if there was the least foundation for such a charge; I must repel it at the risk of my repose and my happiness, and I come humbly to entreat that Your Majesty will have the goodness to allow me to appear before my public accuser, either in the assembly of Notables, or in the great committee of that assembly, always, however, in Your Majesty's presence." No answer was given to this letter; but Necker did not think himself obliged to understand this silence of the King as Calonne wished it to be understood. "The King," said he, in the memorial which he published, "has not thought fit to grant my demand; but, satisfied with the extent of his kindness and justice, I submit with confidence to the obligation which is imposed upon me by honour and truth."

In this memorial he admitted that in 1776 Cluny had left in the finances a void of £1,000,000; he allowed, also, that from the death of Cluny, in October, 1776, to the month of May, 1781, the era at which he himself had retired from the finances, the increase of expenditure had amounted to nearly £1,875,000; but he at the same time showed how he had filled up this void, both by economy and by improvements in the national revenue. The Notables pretended that Calonne was obliged to discuss and refute these calculations; and it must be owned that he himself had too hastily undertaken it.

Necker had rendered his calculations as clear as possible, and they derived great additional weight from his acknowledged veracity. The book which he had just published upon the finances had strengthened his personal reputation; his manners, his talents, his information, had secured to him a degree of public esteem, which Calonne should never, without strong and powerful means, have attempted to shake.

Necker was banished for having dared to defend himself. This was another injurious part of Calonne's conduct; he ought either to have heard before attacking him, or given him full permission to repel the attack. He imputed to him his ill success in the assembly of the Notables; but he should have known that in this assembly a much more real enemy was seeking his ruin.

The King felt repugnance to separate from Calonne. He liked his manner of doing business, he was convinced of the goodness of his schemes; but foreseeing that they would be rejected by the Parliament, as they had been by the Notables, he did violence to himself and dismissed him. He knew that Miromenil, the keeper of the seals, was Calonne's enemy, and had thwarted his operations to the utmost of his power; he dismissed him at the same time, as if sacrificing the one to the other—Calonne on the 8th April, Miromenil on the 9th. Fourqueux was called to the ministry of finance; the seals were given to the president de Lamoignon.

It was not possible that Fourqueux should continue long in this situation: but he had been pointed out to the King by persons who wished to have time for destroying his prejudices against a man whom they wished to give him as his confidential minister, and from whom they expected the salvation of the State.

The situation of the King's mind at this moment is expressed to the life in details which I shall now transcribe.

"When the King entrusted me with his letter to M. de Fourqueux," says the Count de Montmorin, in notes which he put into my hands, "I thought it my duty to represent to him that the powers of this worthy magistrate appeared to me unequal to the burden of the finances. The King seemed sensible that my uneasiness was well founded. 'But whom, then, can we take?' said he. I replied that it was impossible not to be astonished at this question while there existed a man who united in himself all the wishes of the public; that at all times it was necessary not to thwart public opinion in the choice of a minister of finance; but that, in the critical circumstances in which he now was, it was not enough to forbear thwarting, it was indispensably necessary to follow it. I added that, so long as M. Necker existed, it was impossible for him to have another minister of finance, because the public could never, without irritation and chagrin, see this place filled by another. The King admitted the talents of M. Necker, but he objected to the faults of his character; and I easily recognised the unfavourable impressions which he had originally received from Maurepas, and which Vergennes, Calonne, Miromenil and Breteuil had engraved more deeply. I did not know M. Necker personally; I could oppose only doubts to what the King told me of his character, of his haughtiness and spirit of dominion. It is not unlikely that if I had known him I should have accomplished his recall. I ought, perhaps, to have insisted farther, even though I did not know him. From how many evils should I have saved France, and how many afflictions should I have saved the King!" (What would M. de Montmorin have said had he foreseen that, in consequence of missing this favourable moment for changing the course of our fatal destinies, he himself would be massacred by an infuriate people, and that three months after his death the King would perish on a scaffold ?) " I was obliged," continued he, "to give to M. Fourqueux the letter addressed to him, and even to overcome his resistance ; my orders were positive. Nevertheless, it is certain that the place had been offered to M. de la Milliere. The Queen had sent for him ; the King had gone to her apartment at the hour appointed, and both urged him very much to accept ; but he had good sense enough not to yield to their urgency. M. de Fourqueux made difficulty enough at first, but at length he agreed. Scarce was he in office when the modest opinion which he entertained of himself was but too fully confirmed.

" Meanwhile," continued M. de Montmorin, " affairs were in a state of complete stagnation ; public credit was every day more completely destroyed ; the factitious and ruinous resources which M. de Calonne had employed for the supply of the treasury suddenly failed, and produced a daily and considerable fall in the funds ; the royal treasury was empty ; a stoppage of all payments seemed approaching, nor could any resource be thought of except a loan, which it was impossible to attempt at a period of such desperate poverty. Ill-humour prevailed more and more in the assembly of Notables, their disposition became unfriendly, and low murmurs began to be heard of the States-General. In these circumstances it was necessary to have a man who could command public opinion. M. de Lamoignon and myself communicated our ideas to each other, and we agreed that the only man on whom any hope could be founded was Necker. But I mentioned to him the obstacles which I had discovered arising from the disposition of the King, and warned him that they would become still more unsurmountable from the presence of the Baron de Breteuil. We had a con-

ference with the latter, and attempted, but in vain, to
convert him. At last, after a long sitting, we determined
upon going up to the King; and when we had all three
entered upon the subject of the change which was necessary in the ministry of finance, I spoke forcibly upon the
necessity of having recourse to the man who was called
for by the wishes of the public. The King replied (with
a look indeed of the deepest affliction), 'Well, we have
nothing for it but to recall him.' But the Baron de
Breteuil then rose, and, with the greatest warmth, opposed this half-extorted resolution; he represented the
inconsistency there would be in recalling and placing at
the head of administration a man who had scarcely
reached the place appointed for his exile: how great
would be the weakness of such a conduct: what power
would it put in the hands of him, who, being raised
to his office by public opinion, would think himself indebted to it alone. He enlarged forcibly and at great
length on the abuse which M. Necker would not fail to
make of such circumstances. He painted his character
in the colours most likely to make an impression on a
King naturally jealous of his authority, but who had a
confused idea of an attempt being made to wrest it from
him, and wished to retain what he still thought himself
in full possession of. There was something very specious
in the arguments urged by the Baron de Breteuil; but
though they had been less so, they would still have produced the same effect upon the King, who had yielded to
my opinion with the utmost reluctance, and, perhaps,
only because he thought us all three of one mind. The
Archbishop of Toulouse was then proposed, and accepted
without opposition. The King said to us, however, that
he was supposed to have a restless and ambitious
character, and that we might, perhaps, repent of having
suggested this choice to him. But he added that he
had reason to think that the faults of this prelate had
been exaggerated; that for some time past the prejudices

which he had entertained against him had been weakened, and that he had been satisfied with several memorials which he had transmitted to him on the subject of administration."

I have omitted none of these particulars, both because they will lay open the King's character—a little too easy, perhaps, but natural and good; and because they will show how the principal link was forged in the chain of our misfortunes.

BOOK XIII

BRIENNE had distinguished himself in the States of
Languedoc. He had there shown the abilities suited to
his office, and, within a small sphere of administration,
had rendered it possible to believe him an able man.
Like Calonne, he had that quick, hasty, determined
character which imposes on the multitude. He had
something, too, of the address of Maurepas. But he
had neither the pliancy and agreeable manners of the
one, nor the look of good-humour and affability of the
other. Naturally artful, subtle, penetrating, he neither
could conceal these qualities, nor wished to do so. His
look, while it observed, looked through you ; even in his
gaiety there was something which prevented you from
being at ease ; and his expression had something too
sly, which disposed you to mistrust. In his intellectual
character there was a sagacity which resembled cun-
ning ; his ideas were clear, and extended tolerably far,
but only over the surface ; he had some information,
but quite scattered ; glimpses rather than views ; a
mind, if I may so speak, glittering like a cut diamond
from a number of little surfaces. In great subjects he
could easily make himself master of the minute details,
but was quite incapable of comprehending the whole.
His moral character displayed the most keen priestly
selfishness, and the eagerness of avarice united in the
highest degree with that of ambition. In a world which
merely skims over the surface, Brienne knew how to
employ a sort of political small-talk, concise, rapid, interrupted with those intervals of mysterious silence, by

which a man seems to intimate that, had he chosen, he could have said a great deal more, and which leaves something vague and unlimited in the opinion formed of his capacity. This manner of bringing himself forward while he pretended to conceal himself, this apparent ability which was mere reserve and discretion, this alternate use of half-words and of studied silence, with sometimes a slight and disdainful censure of anything that was not done by himself, wondering that nobody saw how it might have been done better—in this really consisted the whole art and secret of Brienne. He showed only patterns of himself, and even these were often not of his own stuff. Nevertheless, in almost every circle where political reputation was determined, no one doubted that when he became minister his head would be replete with grand views, and his portfolio filled with the most luminous projects. He became minister, and his portfolio and his head were found equally empty.

In the shipwreck of Calonne he appeared merely to have collected all that could be saved; he presented nothing to the Parliament but his predecessor's edicts of the stamp-duty and land-tax. He might have supported himself by the authority of the Notables, and, by laying before them the two fatal alternatives of the States-General and of bankruptcy, have had powerful means of bringing them to acknowledge the necessity of taxes. All he could do was to dismiss them. Nothing was determined in this assembly.

He heard the nation loudly demanding the recall of Necker; and, by soliciting the King to comply with this demand, he might have raised his character and strengthened himself in the eminent post which he occupied. Thus, too, he might have eased himself of the burden of the finances, might have secured his tranquility, made his elevation be viewed as a blessing, and thrown a veil of dignity over the indecent magnitude of his own for-

tune. His lazy incapacity might thus have been concealed—in a word, he might have acted like an able and
an honest man ; but he never had that magnanimity.   A
fatal dread of being supplanted, of having the first place
occupied by another, prevailed in his mind.   In vain did
his friends urge him to call to his aid the man named by
the public voice. He answered, " The King and the
Queen do not wish it."   " It is in your power," said
Montmorin, " to persuade the Queen that Necker is
necessary, and I myself undertake to persuade the King."
Brienne, when pressed so closely, replied, " I can do
without him."   Thus it is that empires fall.

Tired of hearing the public calling eagerly for
Necker, he took pleasure in seeing him lashed by hungry
writers, whom he is asserted to have paid for calum-
niating him.   Meanwhile he saw himself lost in the void
of his own ideas.   In less than five months he tried two
comptrollers-general, Villedeuil and Lambert ; the incapacity of both was soon evident.   A new council of
finance, a deliberative committee, everything was acceptable except Necker, and yet everything was equally
useless.   In the very last extremity he still attempted to
employ temporary expedients ; but nothing succeeded.
Having lost his way, sailing without a compass, he no
longer knew what impulse to give to the helm of the
State.   In his conduct and character he was always in
contradiction with himself, for, with all his temerity, he
was irresolute—with all his boldness, pusillanimous.
There was nothing which he would not venture upon,
or which, after venturing, he did not give up almost
immediately ; so that he never ceased to endanger and
to weaken the royal authority, making himself at once
odious by despotism, and contemptible by thoughtlessness and want of stability.

With the view of gaining the public favour, he
began with endeavouring to establish provincial assemblies ; and, by rendering them elective and dependent

upon the people, he rashly and thoughtlessly granted what would have demanded the greatest reflection. Despotic as he was, he would have wished to appear popular, and to be accounted a Republican; but this character was very ill supported.

After having dismissed the Notables, he sent to the Parliament his two edicts of the stamp-duty and land-tax, as if they could have been passed without any difficulty and on their first appearance. But then it was that young and hot heads had begun to pass those respectable boundaries, and to agitate those critical and delicate questions of public right which were soon debated with such warmth and temerity. Yet he gave himself no uneasiness: in the sittings and debates of Parliament he appeared even to have forgotten his favourite talent—address and insinuation. There was no negotiation, no conference, no way left open for accommodation; he wished to overpower them and to carry everything by main force. The magistracy were disgusted by seeing him so arrogant and inflexible, and all the parliaments of the kingdom formed at once a determination of rejecting the new edicts even before they were sent. All that Brienne did against this insurrection, which threatened the royal authority, was to reject every mode of conciliation and to abandon public affairs to the hazard of events.

The Parliament of Paris asked him to lay before them his financial accounts: this demand was well founded, for it was impossible that the Parliament should suit the amount and duration of the taxes to the real exigencies of the State unless they knew what those exigencies were. The right of remonstrance involved that of examination; nor could he, without exacting a slavish obedience, refuse to enlighten them upon their duty. This was what Brienne would never listen to. He did not see that it was more necessary than ever to have the taxes formally debated upon and accepted in the name of the people, and that, if the

right of the Parliament to verify and confirm the edicts
were disputed in any way whatever, the nation would
find representatives who would be less easily dealt with.
This was what the minister and the Parliament together
ought to have foreseen and prevented.

In order to cut short the difficulty, Brienne made
the King hold a Bed of Justice[1] at Versailles, in which,
by his express order, the edict of the stamp-duty and
land-tax were registered. Next day, the Parliament
having declared null and illegal the engrossing of the
two edicts on their registers, the expedient proposed by
Brienne was to send the Parliament into exile, and to
disperse all its members.

Lamoignon,[2] keeper of the seals, a man of a frank
and steady character, joined to great prudence, victo-
riously opposed in the council this opinion of Brienne ;
he showed that dispersed magistrates would be quite
inaccessible to negotiation, and he concluded by telling
the King that though the translation of the sovereign
courts might sometimes be useful, the individual exile
of the magistrates would be always imprudent.

Brienne, to whom this idea of translation appeared
quite new, presently adopted it, and made the King
sign letters patent which transferred the Parliament from
Paris to Troyes. The keeper of the seals asked a short
delay, but he was not listened to. Brienne said to him,
in the presence of the King, " Your ideas are excellent,
but you are too slow in your determinations." Scarce
was the Parliament arrived at Troyes, when Brienne,
in a conference with the keeper of the seals, recollected,
as it were by chance, that the presence of this court
would be necessary for his loans in the month of November. " Had I thought of that sooner," exclaimed he,
" I would not have sent them into exile—they must be

1 See note (4) at the end.
2 See note (5) at the end.

instantly recalled," and presently his emissaries were
set in motion. (These particulars I heard from the
keeper of the seals.)

Lamoignon, who had been a member of the Parliament before being keeper of the seals, had intimated the
views he had formed for the reformation of our laws; he
was known to be contriving means for simplifying the
mode of procedure, and rendering it less tedious and
expensive. This, in the eyes of that ancient body, was
a kind of hostility which made him feared and hated.
Brienne having learnt this aversion of the Parliament for
the keeper of the seals, took it into his head to promise
the dismissal of that minister if they would become tract-
able. "My letter is sent off," said he to Lamoignon, after
having written. "What letter?" asked Lamoignon.
"That," replied Brienne, "in which I have promised
your disgrace if they will act reasonably; but do not you
be at all anxious."

The letter arrived at Troyes; on its appearance a
sudden change was wrought in every mind. They
became persuaded that their exile, the authoritative
and despotic measures of the ministry, were the actions
of him who had long meditated the ruin of the magistracy. "Brienne, left to himself, would have been more
weak and more timid; this character of vigour which
they saw him constantly first assume and then lay aside,
was not his own; he borrowed it from Lamoignon; that
was the man who must be destroyed; nothing should be
spared to destroy the common enemy." On this condition
it was that the edict of the twentieths passed; for as to
those of the land-tax and stamp-duty, Brienne had found
himself under the necessity of withdrawing them. But
he reckoned upon a considerable loan, and thought he
had gained a kind of triumph in having abused and
recalled the Parliament. I must not omit that, in order
to acquire more weight and dignity in his negotiation, he
had attempted to prevail upon the King to name him

Prime Minister, and that the issue of this attempt, which at first was very ill received, had been to declare him Principal Minister.

The Parliament came to Versailles; the reconciliation seemed complete, and Brienne, on the same day, said to the keeper of the seals, " You see how well I have managed; had I not promised those people your dismissal, both you and I were in danger of not continuing here long." But while Brienne fancied himself deceiving the Parliament, it was himself who was deceived.

From the terms of the edict which was about to be passed, he reckoned that the two twentieths would be levied exactly upon all property without exception, in proportion to the actual revenue. The Parliament, on the contrary, pretended that this edict should change nothing in the ancient mode of collection; that it gave no authority for any new enquiry or examination; and all the parliaments united in declaring, that if a fiscal inquisition were practised upon their property, they would oppose it to the utmost. They were supported in this opposition by a considerable party of the privileged bodies; and to intimidate the ministry, they raised the cry for the States-General. Miserable avarice, that was the ruin of them all.

As the vices of the private character are sometimes united with public spirit, it is possible that there might be, among the Clergy and Nobility, men of warm minds, who were so much struck by the inveterate abuses of arbitrary authority as to sincerely wish for the meeting of the States-General, as the sole and indispensable remedy; but, taking the mass of men together, this appeal to the nation could be nothing more than a dissembled threat, or an impulse of blind passion. They must have known well that, to privileged bodies, to favoured classes, the people were the most formidable of all tribunals; that the latter, overloaded with taxes, would never be dis-

posed to grant to the former an exemption that did not
extend to themselves ; and as these bodies had everything to fear from the discussion of their privileges, it
was not at all probable that they should prefer entrusting
them to the debates of a popular assembly to treating
with a reasonable and conciliating minister. Brienne,
instead of showing the Parliament how dangerous their
demands were, thought only of evading them, and made
a proposal that the provinces should compound for the
twentieth. Many consented ; others, encouraged by the
resistance of the parliaments, would not listen to any
composition.

The battle was begun ; the parliaments were about
to issue the prohibitory decrees, which formed their *corps
de reserve*, and threatened to prosecute every man as an
exactor and extortioner, who, in estimating or collecting
the twentieth, should conform to the royal edicts ; the
whole kingdom was like to be in flames from one end
to the other—when the minister, suddenly affecting a
different kind of assurance, caused a decree of council
to be passed, by which the King declared the condition
of his finances to be so good as to make any new extension of the twentieths unnecessary. At the same time,
he prepared a decree for a loan of £2,500,000 at ten per
cent. on annuities ; and it was determined that the King
in person should go to the Parliament and cause this
edict to be registered.

Two days previous to the royal sitting, the keeper
of the seals having come to Paris, was visited by a
man whose turbulent and daring character had brought
him into distinguished notice among the young magistrates, and rendered him their orator. It was Duval
d'Espremenil, a judge in the Court of Inquiry. He told
Lamoignon that a loan of £2,500,000 would be quite
insufficient ; that he must open one of £20,000,000, to
be paid by instalments in the course of five years ; that
this time and these funds might be employed in restoring

order to the finances, and that then the States-General might be assembled.

Brienne, on receiving the letter in which Lamoignon transmitted to him this advice, leaped for joy, and not doubting that the message came to him from the Court of Inquiry, replied that he made no hesitation in availing himself of this overture. " By that means," said he, " I shall have nothing to do with the Parliament for five years." Immediately he ordered an edict to be prepared for loans amounting to £20,000,000, which should be successively paid in the course of five years, at the end of which he promised to assemble the States-General. Meanwhile he promised a saving of above £2,000,000, both by the reduction of expenses and the improvement of the revenue, which would provide for the interest of the loan. But, as if in the sitting which he was to make the King hold, his object had been to revolt instead of tranquilize men's minds, he made the King and the keeper of the seals assume the most severe tone; the Parliament were reminded of their maxims respecting the absolute power and complete independence of kings; of the words written in their own decrees, that to the King alone belonged the sovereign power in the kingdom; that he was accountable to God alone for the exercise of the supreme power; that the legislative power resided in the person of the sovereign, independent and undivided; and as for the States-General, they stood on the defensive, saying, that to the King alone belonged the right of assembling them; that he alone was the proper judge whether this measure was useful and necessary; that the three orders assembled would, with regard to him, be only a more numerous council, and that he would be always the supreme arbiter of their statements and grievances. Nothing could, in the present circumstances, be more idle than this haughty language. The effervescence of men's minds became only the more violent, their passions were inflamed, and the sitting became tumultuous. The King, in the mere expectation of receiving advice and information, had permitted them to give their opinions aloud; many made an indecent abuse of this liberty; and the bitter and violent censure which was mixed with their opinions showed the King too clearly that they thought themselves entitled to examine, not his edicts only, but his conduct and his reign. He kept silence during the space of seven hours, which this sitting occupied; and though deeply affected by the licentious tone which was assumed, he did not allow the least symptom of impatience to escape him. From this time, therefore, began the trial of that patience, of which afterwards he stood so much in need.

However, the great bulk of the opinions concluded with demanding the assemblage of the States-General for the month of May, in the following year; and d'Espremenil said to the King: " I see this wished-for word about to escape your lips; let Your Majesty pronounce it, and your Parliament subscribes your edicts." Had the King yielded, there is no doubt that the edicts would have been passed. But Brienne had exhorted him not to listen to any condition, but to adhere to the principle that wherever the King was present his will was law.

After all, notwithstanding the silence of the King, and the refusal expressed by it, many have supposed that, had he allowed the votes to have been collected, the majority would still have been in favour of accepting the edicts. But he, punctually exact in observing what had been prescribed by his minister, ordered the edicts to be engrossed without any collection of votes; and, at the same time, a declaration to be registered, by which all the parliaments in the kingdom were prorogued. The Duke of Orleans, who was beginning by that time to act his part, protested, in the King's presence, against this act of authority; and as soon as the King went out, the assembly, in which the peers still continued, adhered by a decree to the Prince's protest.

Next day the great deputation of the Parliament was ordered to Versailles. The King cancelled the decree of the preceding evening, prohibited any new deliberation upon the same subject, exiled the Duke of Orleans to Villers-Cotterets, and two judges in the High Court, Freteau and Sabatier—one to the castle of Ham, and the other to Mount St. Michael.

From that time a general league was formed by the Parliament against the ministry ; and Brienne, despairing of being able to subdue, resolved to annihilate them. With this daring plan, which he proposed to the council, he combined that of a permanent *cour pleniere* for registering the laws.

At this meeting of council Lamoignon opposed, but in vain, the plan of the *cour pleniere*. He was more successful in opposing the destruction of the high magistracy ; a measure which, he said, was too violent, and which Maupeou had brought into discredit. In its stead he proposed a plan to weaken the influence and force of resistance of the Parliament of Paris, by erecting, within its jurisdiction, considerable bailiwicks, the powers entrusted to which would extinguish the greater number of law-suits, and would supersede the necessity of the Court of Inquiry—a tumultuous and noisy meeting, from which it would be a desirable object to free themselves. This simple and certain mode of weakening the Parliament by the augmentation of bailiwicks was likely to be agreeable to the people ; it shortened the mode of procedure, saved clients from the expense of long journeys, and from being plundered by their lawyers in the course of a tedious appeal ; and with regard to a jurisdiction so vast as that of Paris, this project carried in itself the proof of its excellence. Brienne resolved to extend it to all the parliaments of the kingdom ; and, without calculating the mass of resistance which he would thus have to overcome, he directed the keeper of the seals to draw up the plan and to prepare the edict. At the same time, he traced out a form for the *cour plenieve*, which he thought so commanding as to secure respect and obedience to the laws. This great operation was the secret concealed under the Bed of Justice, which assembled in May, 1788. But the silence which was observed about what was then to be done, the order given to the governors of provinces to repair to their stations, the despatches sent to the commanders of those cities in which the parliaments resided, and, perhaps, also, some treachery on the part of the printers, betrayed the design of attacking the magistracy, and put that body on their guard. On the 5th of May, therefore, three days previous to the Bed of Justice, the Parliament met and protested against whatever should be done at that meeting. They entered also into a promise, confirmed by the most solemn oath, not to resume their functions, except in the same place, and with their whole body assembled, without suffering any one of its members to be separated or excluded.

As soon as the Court was informed of the resolution into which the Parliament had entered, and of d'Espremenil being its mover, Brienne obtained an order from the King to arrest that dangerous man; and d'Espremenil having, just as they came to arrest him, taken refuge in the High Court, which was then sitting, was there taken, and led prisoner to the Island of Sainte-Marguerite.

The Bed of Justice which was held at Versailles on the 8th of May, was held on the same day by the governors of provinces in all the parliaments of the kingdom; and the laws which were promulgated, though almost all conformable to the wishes of the nation, met everywhere with equal resistance. The administration of justice was to be better distributed through the provinces, the tribunals less remote, the appeals not so frequent, great causes reserved for the superior courts, while the smaller would be brought to a determination with less time and expense. A reform in criminal law was promised, and already begun, by which a month was to elapse between the condemnation of the criminal and his execution; torture was to be abolished; a compensation granted by the law to the man against whom a groundless prosecution had been raised; and an obligation imposed upon the judge that, while inflicting the punishment, he should specify the crime. All this seemed desirable, and, besides, it was promised that there should be a meeting of the States-General before the end of five years, and the King's word was given to render their meetings periodical; all the new taxes were to be accepted by the nation itself, and the other laws registered by a tribunal for that express purpose, in which causes of forfeiture alone should be judged: in all this there was nothing which, with a view to the future, seemed at all alarming. But, in the first place, till the time arrived for assembling the States-General, the ruin of the parliaments seemed to overthrow the only barrier that could be opposed to the despotism of ministers; in the second place, this *cour pleniere*, the very name of which would have given disgust, suggested the idea of an oligarchical tribunal, the more formidable as it would be invested with all the national force and with all the ceremonial of law.

This tribunal, which was to be composed of officers of the Crown, of commanders of armies, of the peers and grandees of the kingdom, of magistrates chosen by the King, and of that High Court of Parliament which had at all times been faithful and submissive to the sovereign authority, seemed likely to be too powerful a counterpoise to the Assembly of the States.

This Bed of Justice, therefore, was viewed by the nation as no more than despotism disguised under a specious appearance of public advantage. The course of justice, which was suspended throughout the whole kingdom, excited a universal murmur; and, in Paris, the avenues to the hall where the Parliament sat were inundated. The citizens were tranquil; they knew that the quarrel between the Parliament and the Court arose from the refusal of the latter to consent to the equal imposition of the twentieths; and this refusal did not dispose them to unite with the privileged class. But Paris contains a great mass of persons who observe, with an envious eye, the pleasures which surround them, and impatiently endure the labour and poverty which falls to their share. These, from a vague hope of some fortunate change in their condition, crowd hastily at the first signal of disorder, and rally round any factious man who promises them a milder lot. This multitude, surrounding the court in which the Parliament was held, strengthened the party of its defenders. The magistrates applied to the populace for protection; and, under the eyes of the police, all the excesses of the coarsest licentiousness were committed with impunity: a pernicious example, which was afterwards but too well imitated. The Parliament, therefore, were the first to provoke insurrection in the mob. The goodness of the King led him always to shun the adoption of rigorous measures. He ordered that guards should be stationed at the avenues to the hall of Parliament, but that they should employ their arms only in securing the life and tranquility of the citizens. Thus it was that the tumult was restrained and suppressed without violence. Nevertheless, whether through the inaction of a feeble and timid police, or through the impulse of those, who, while they excited disturbance among the Parisian populace, assured them of impunity, the seditious movements continued always to increase.

In the provinces, the despotism which was exercised by each of the parliaments in its own jurisdiction, the security which their members enjoyed amid the vexations which they practised upon their neighbours, their arrogance, their pride, were not calculated to render their cause interesting; but, in consequence of their connections with the privileged class, they formed, when combined with it, a numerous and powerful party. Even the people had allowed themselves to be convinced that the cause of the parliaments was their own. In Brittany, and in other provinces, they were led to believe that new and odious taxes were in agitation; and the magistrates themselves stooped so low as to circulate these falsehoods.

In the midst of these agitations, Brienne learned that the nobility of Brittany were sending twelve deputies to remonstrate with the King upon the iniquity of his Bed of Justice. Presently the minister of the King's household, the Baron de Breteuil, was ordered to go in advance of the deputies to Senlis, to wait for them there, and to force them to return. The order was badly executed; the deputies passed; but scarce were they arrived, when they were sent to the Bastille. Immediately the Breton nobility, instead of twelve deputies sent fifty-four. These last were admitted to the King's presence, and the other twelve set at liberty. The Baron de Breteuil, when accused by Brienne of not having properly followed his directions, made no secret of his repugnance to do what he did not approve, and asked permission to retire. At this very time the province of Dauphiny raised the standard of liberty, by assuming to itself that constitution which was boasted as a model, and had afterwards so much influence. In the new form which Dauphiny gave to its states, the Tiers Etat had the half of the votes. Brienne, with his natural rashness, sanctioned this arrangement, never looking to anything beyond the present moment. At last his own weakness and the general insurrection of the parliaments forced him to yield, and he agreed to what he had refused with the greatest obstinacy. By a decree of council of the 8th of August, he pledged the King's promise to assemble the States-General in the month of May following— a resolution which was formed too late, and which

only announced the termination of his ministerial
career.

The finances were ruined, the coffers of the King
empty; there was no new tax, no new loan, no hope
of credit, but on all sides the most pressing necessities;
the annuities on the city, the pay of the troops, were
all likely to fail at once. Nothing less could have
forced upon Brienne the conviction of his own incapacity, or, at least, of the impossibility of his extri-
cating the State out of this abyss of misery. He
resolved to consummate his dishonour, and by a decree
of council, on the 16th of August, he declared that
two-fifths of the payments from the royal treasury
should be made in government paper. The male-
dictions of the public poured upon him like a deluge;
then, at last, he resolved to ask the recall of Necker.
But Necker refused to become his associate. He replied that if he had still any hope of being useful to
the State, this hope was founded on the confidence
with which the nation honoured him, and that, in order
to preserve any credit for himself, there was one obvious condition which he must attach to his return.
"This reply is my doom," said Brienne to the keeper
of the seals, "I must yield my place"; and he gave
in his resignation on the 23rd of August, 1788.

He did not leave in the royal treasury above £17,000,
either in money or in effects; yet, the evening before
his departure, he sent and drew his £800 of monthly
salary, though that month was not yet expired — an
exactness the more remarkable as, without mentioning
the emoluments of his office and a pension of £250
attached to his blue riband, he possessed property to
the amount of £28,000 a year; and he had recently
cut down wood on one of his estates which had produced £42,000.

The respect which Necker had enjoyed was augmented during his disgrace; but the greater encourage-

ment he derived from public esteem, the more anxiety
must he have felt on account of the situation of the
kingdom.

Around the capital sixty square leagues of the
richest territory were completely laid waste by a storm
of hail on the eve of harvest; the crop was bad through
all the rest of the kingdom, the price of corn was raised
still higher by the dread of famine, while there were no
funds and no credit to supply the urgent necessity of
importing it; the funds discredited and bearing scarcely
any value, while every mode of raising loans and taxes
was at a standstill. On one side, the produce of the
taxes was necessarily diminished, while on the other the
expense was as necessarily augmented. Instead of the
contributions to which the inhabitants of the country
are usually subjected, it was necessary that immediate
aid should be given to those places which had been
ruined by the hail. The tribunals were inactive, licentiousness was everywhere left unpunished, the police
was intimidated; even the discipline of the troops was
shaken, and the principle of obedience and fidelity, upon
which it rests, was undermined. All the ancient public
law was discussed and doubted, and all classes and ranks
in the State, though they could not agree with each other
or with themselves about what the States-General ought
to be, agreed in calling out for them with the utmost
eagerness, and in the meantime would not hear of any
supply. Such was the tremendous crisis in which
Necker found the kingdom.

His first care was the restoration of order: the in-
terdict upon the parliaments was withdrawn, justice
resumed its course, and the police was again put in
motion. The treasury, which had been empty at
Necker's arrival, seemed to be filled at once; the payments were renewed; and if the decree of the 16th of
August, which had spread such consternation, was not
immediately revoked, at least it was never acted upon;

everything was paid in specie, and some weeks after, a
new decree of council completely wiped off the shame of
Brienne's bankruptcy.

While this disgraced minister was allowed to sink
into contempt, the public hatred had fallen on Lamoignon, who was viewed as his accomplice ; it became
necessary to sacrifice him.   Nevertheless, as I owe more
to truth than to public opinion, I will venture to say
that in Lamoignon the King lost a good minister and
the State a good citizen.   Deceived by the reputation
which Brienne had usurped, Lamoignon had at first
thought that he could do nothing better than unite
with him, under the reciprocal promise of acting in
concert.   He was not long in discovering the emptiness
and levity of his head ; but when he saw him involved
in difficulties, he often warned, sometimes stopped, but
never abandoned him.   The fault, or the misfortune,
of Lamoignon consisted in having united himself with
such an associate.   He was ardently desirous of doing
good, and tenderly loved the King : he told me himself
that he did not know a better or worthier man ; and
full of that old spirit of integrity, which descended to
him from his ancestors, he seemed to have taken courage and loyalty for his characteristic virtues.   Even the
hatred of the parliaments redounded to his praise.   The
esteem and the secret confidence of the King had followed him to his retreat at Baville.   But either the
vexation of exile, or some domestic affliction, brought
on his death, on the 18th of May, 1789, and saved him
from seeing objects which would have killed him with
grief.

Necker had assumed an ascendency in the council,
which will be easily conceived when we consider what
his return to the ministry produced.   A winter as severe
and longer than that of 1709 made the efforts of this
minister appear still more astonishing.   Without any
new tax, or any new loan that was known of, by means

only of a little delay which excited no complaint, the
annuities, the pensions, the debts, as they became due,
were regularly discharged.   Corn, pouring into our
harbours from all the countries of the world, saved
us from famine; aid was granted to the unfortunate
labourers, relief to the sick, to the old, to the children
abandoned in the hospitals; immense sums were ex-
pended in securing and in accelerating the arrival of
subsistence.   Such were the services which Necker
rendered to the State; and it is probable that, had he
continued in the ministry without interruption, and been
allowed to avail himself of the advantages of peace, he
would have brought the kingdom into such a prosperous
condition that no one would have thought of the States-
General; no one, at least, would have proposed them.

But when the King had once promised to assemble
them in the month of May, it was not easy for Necker
to make him break that engagement without alienating
the minds of the nation.   Besides (he made no secret
of it), he wished from the bottom of his heart the
meeting of the States.   " I thought," said he, talking
of his conduct at this period, " I thought that by maintaining tranquility in the kingdom, by propping up the
sinking edifice of the finances, by relieving the want
of subsistence, and by thus paving the way for the
greatest and most desirable of events, I should have
sufficiently fulfilled my task — I should have acquitted
my duty as a public man, as a good citizen, and as the
faithful servant of a King who wished the public good."
As for the motives by which he was animated, he has
explained them himself.   " I knew," said he, " better
than anyone, the unstable and transitory nature of that
good which could be done under a government where
the principles of administration changed with every
minister, and ministers with every intrigue.   I had
observed that, amid the constant changes of administration, no general idea had time to be established, no

benefit could become permanent." He remembered
that cabinet of Maurepas, to which he himself never
went without fear and melancholy when it became
necessary to speak of reform and economy to a minister
grown old amid the pomp and expensive habits of the
Court. The opposition and disgust which he had often
experienced, and the contests in which he was under the
necessity of engaging, had made so deep an impression
upon him that he viewed the States-General as a har-
bour of safety for the nation.

But, notwithstanding the advantages of that assembly, it had also its dangers; and the form, in particular, which it should assume would be of the last
importance.

Necker appeared at first unwilling to take upon
himself the risk of this primary operation. He advised
the King to call the assembly of the Notables, whose
zeal he had experienced, and to consult with them.

The examples of former times with regard to the
formation of the States - General were various and
changeable. But the greater number of these examples
were favourable to the privileged class; and if that of
1614 was followed, as the Parliament demanded and
expected to obtain, the Orders of Nobility and Clergy
would be secure of preponderance. Their rights, their
privileges would be preserved; and the Parliament, in
return for the service which it should have rendered,
might expect, in the interval of these assemblies, to
be established as their perpetual representative. But,
among the body of the people, the public mind had
assumed a character which no longer suited with the
pretensions of the parliamentary and feudal class. The
labourer in the fields, the artisan in the city, the honest
citizen employed in his business, sought only for relief,
and if left to themselves would have chosen only peace-
able characters to represent them. But in the cities,
and, above all, in Paris, there is a class of men who,

13—2

though distinguished from the people by education, are attached to it by birth, and when its rights are in agitation make its cause their own, afford it the assistance of their information, and inspire it with their passions. In this class a spirit of daring innovation had long been forming, which was every day acquiring more force and influence.

The recent example of North America, which had asserted its independence by its own courage and by the aid of our arms, was extolled without ceasing. The vicinity of the English, the more frequent habit of travelling into their country, the study of their language, the fashion of reading their books, the constant perusal of their public papers, the eager curiosity about what was said and done in their Parliament, the warmth of the praises which were given to their orators, the interest which was taken in their debates ; in short, the very affectation of their tastes and manners—all these things announced an approaching disposition to assimilate with them ; and really the view of this public liberty and perfect security, this worthy and noble use of the right of property in the free acceptance and equal division of the taxes required for the exigencies of the State, might justly excite in us a sentiment of emulation. After such examples, well-informed, restless and daring men everywhere warned the people not to forget their rights, and called upon the minister to attend to them.

The minister sought only to support the rights of the people ; for the league between the Parliaments, the Nobility and the Clergy against the royal authority had forced him to consider the people as a refuge for the King. But he felt himself too weak against so great a mass of power and influence, and had need of being strongly supported.

This support he was not very sure of obtaining from the assembly of Notables. An assembly composed chiefly of the Church, the Army, and the Law, and in which the representatives from the cities would not even have a third of the votes, was not likely to be very favourable to the Commons.

But, whatever might be the result of the deliberations, men's minds would be put in motion throughout the whole kingdom, and the great political interests which were agitated within this assembly would be agitated still more warmly without. From that quarter, in particular, the minister expected his strength to come; and perhaps this pomp of consultation was only a mode of rousing the national opinion, or a signal for its display. The King had encouraged it by a decree of council previous to the dismissal of Brienne. It was probable, therefore, that the public opinion would command the Notables. Already, during their first assembly in 1787, they had not only agreed, but had themselves demanded, that in the provincial assemblies proposed by Calonne, the number of members from the Tiers Etat should be equal to that from the Nobility and Clergy united. The question seemed, therefore, to be judged by themselves, and Necker merely allowed them the honour of confirming the decision. The some disposition in the states of Dauphiny had been loudly praised and extolled as a model. From all quarters, therefore, the Notables were admonished to be favourable to the people; and there was no likelihood that, after they had once been so, they should either wish or dare to be otherwise. In the assurance of this, the same assembly of 1787 was convoked anew on the 5th of October, 1788, and met at Versailles on the 3rd of November in the same year.

But when they came to deliberate upon the formation of this national council, of this supreme tribunal, in which their rights, their privileges, and all the greatest interests of their rank and fortune were to be discussed, each of the Orders thought only of the dangers it was about to incur.

The subjects upon which they were to deliberate were proposed in questions, the principal of which were : What should be the respective number of deputies from each Order ?   What had been, and what should be, the form of deliberation ?   What should be the necessary qualifications for being electors, and for being eligible, in the Order of the Clergy, and in that of the Tiers Etat, whether in the country or in the cities ?   Should these two qualities be determined by the amount of real property, or only by a quota of contribution ; and what should that quota be ?

The assembly was divided into six chambers, in each of which a prince presided ; and the King required that, after the departments had each formed the final wish with respect to each of the questions proposed, these opinions, with the grounds on which they rested, explained at sufficient length, should all be transmitted to him, with the state of the votes upon each opinion.

In the department where Monsieur presided, the opinions were divided with respect to the number of deputies which each Order should send ; and by a majority of thirteen against twelve it was determined that each deputation should be composed of four deputies, one from the Church, one from the Nobility, and two from the Tiers Etat.

The other five departments, some unanimously, and others by a great majority of votes, petitioned that the number of representatives should be equal in each of the three Orders, and that the King should be besought not to violate this equality of votes, which they regarded as the safeguard of the State, as the surest support of the constitution, of civil and political liberty.   They all conceived that no legal deliberation could be entered into without the concurrence of the three Orders, that two should have no right to bind the third, and that thus the vote of a single Order should be sufficient to secure its liberty.   But this very principle established the right of equality with respect to each other. "Such," said they, "is with us the balance of public strength. The Tiers Etat does not enjoy an unjust ascendency over the two other Orders, but it is entitled to the same degree of power; it is not authorised to give law, but neither can it be domineered over. Now, the double deputation, were it granted, would destroy this equal and independent relation; it would lead to the form of individual suffrage; it would make men think of, and contrive the means of bringing about, this mode of voting; and who could calculate the pernicious consequences? The first deliberation of the States would be directed to this subject, and the effect would be to produce the most dangerous fermentation."

Upon the second question, which respected the form of deliberation, there was no difference of opinion, and, with the exception of the department of Monsieur, which referred the choice to the States, all demanded that the Orders should give their opinions separately.

The reasons urged by the minority for granting a double representation to the Tiers Etat were, that, supposing the opinions to be given by the Orders separately, it was just and natural that, in an assembly where laws, arts, industry, commerce, agriculture and the finances would be constant subjects of deliberation, the class which was professionally informed upon all these subjects should possess, at least, an equal strength with the classes which paid no attention to them; that it must often happen that the subject of deliberation might be of such a nature as to require individual suffrage; then, in particular, the right of the Tiers Etat to oppose two votes to the other two united was as incontestable as the right which they possessed of not being eternally ruled over.

"No one," continued they, "can dispute the right which the States-General have to regulate their interior arrangements and to determine the manner in which the votes shall be given and received. With regard to taxes,

for instance, it would be impossible, without manifest injustice, to take the votes by individual suffrage, if out of
three votes the Tiers Etat should have only one; for the
interests of the Nobility and the Clergy upon this article
being inseparable, their opinions would always coincide,
and there would only be two parties, one of which would
be double that of the other.

With respect to the elections, all the departments,
seduced by this principle, that confidence alone ought
to determine the choice, rendered the qualifications for
electing and being elected as slight as possible : no regard was paid to property, and, by means of a moderate
contribution, every householder, within his bailiwick, was
to have the right of being an elector and of being eligible.
In the same manner every ecclesiastic, whose living and
private property equalled the revenue of a village rector,
might both elect and be elected.

Meanwhile the same questions were agitated out of
the assembly; they were seized upon by the public; and
in conversation, as well as in writing, the cause of the
people was supported with warmth and vehemence.

Upon the opening of the assembly of the Notables,
in the committee where Monsieur presided, the Prince of
Conti had remonstrated against those writings with
which France was inundated. " Be so good, sir," said
he, " as to represent to the King how important it is
for the stability of his throne, for laws and for good
order, that all the new plans should be proscribed for
ever, and that the constitution and its ancient forms
should be maintained entire." Had Necker possessed
this requisite degree of foresight, he would not have
made the King answer that "this was not one of the
subjects for which he had assembled the Notables."

All the cities in the kingdom took an interest in the
subject of the deputations, and urged, in favour of the
Tiers Etat, not only the circumstance of their composing nine-tenths of the nation and paying the two

twentieths, but the still more incontestable political right
which this laborious class derived from the importance
of its labours. Brave and obedient in the armies, indefatigable in cultivating the fields, industrious in the
cities : security, riches, abundance, strength, information,
enjoyment of every kind, were all furnished by them.
Yet this class, the source and the preserver of all property,
found a small number of men, for the most part rich and
idle, disputing their right of equal deputation into the
national council ; and who, with the view of holding
them in subjection, would have arrogated over them the
ascendency of an eternal majority. Thus it was that the
popular associations animated each other to defend their
rights; and this rising spirit of liberty, which it was
alike necessary and difficult to suppress, took possession
of every mind. The moment at last came when, after
having heard the opinions of the assembly of Notables,
and the demands from the cities and provinces of the
kingdom, it became necessary for the King to form his
final resolution. This was the object of the Council of
State, which was held on the 27th of December, 1788.
Necker there reported the opinions of the departments
upon the most important subjects, and particularly upon
the number of deputies from each of the three Orders ;
and after having weighed together the reasons and
authorities on both sides, he gave his own opinion.
" I think," said he, " that the King may, and ought to,
call to the States-General a number of deputies from
the Tiers Etat equal to that of the deputies from the
two other Orders united ; not, as might be feared,
with the view of forcing individual suffrage, but of
satisfying the general and reasonable wish of the Commons of his kingdom." The advice of Necker was
adopted by the council, and the King determined that
the letters which were to summon the assembly should
be written in conformity to it. Upon this essential
article, therefore, Necker appeared to have consulted

the Notables, only in order to obtain the sanction of their opinion, if it should be favourable to the people, or to reject it if otherwise, and give the provinces time to make a public declaration of their sentiments.

Necker made no secret of his wish to establish a proper and durable relation between the revenue and expense of the State, a prudent use of public credit, an equal distribution of taxes, a general plan of beneficence, an enlightened system of legislation ; above all, a constitutional guarantee of civil and political liberty : and all these advantages could be hoped for from the States-General, only in so far as the just remonstrances of the Commons were respected. The veto of one of the three Orders, if they should give their opinions separately, appeared to him a perpetual and invincible obstacle to the best resolutions. He wished, therefore, individual suffrage to be adopted, which would be equitable only in so far as the number of the Commons should equal that of the Clergy and Nobility. It was the union of of these two Orders with the parliaments which had produced the resistance to the collection of the twentieth ; and it was with a view of breaking this union that recourse was had to the Commons. Then, too, the language of the Commons was expressive of the most proper sentiments, both for the royal authority and for the person of the King ; and the minister was deceived by this language.

You have seen that the Notables, by making the right of election and of eligibility to depend upon a moderate contribution, had rendered it independent of all real property, at the risk of allowing the introduction of a great number of men indifferent to the fortune of the State. Necker, unfortunately deceived as to the attention which he expected the people would pay to make a proper choice of deputies, and as to the character of wisdom and probity which a sacred respect for their functions would impress upon the popular deputies, thought, like the Notables, that he ought to lay as little restraint as possible upon the freedom of election, and to fix at the very lowest the quota of taxation which was to qualify for being elected. This was one of his errors. When he allowed the Tiers Etat to be equal in number to the other two Orders, he should have well foreseen that a part of the Clergy would join the people; and yet he gave this popular Clergy every means of strengthening themselves in the first elections: all the curates were admitted, whilst he allowed the collegiates only a representative for each Chapter. The curates, therefore, were likely to be elected in great numbers, and to augment that party in the States to which they were attached by the ties of blood, by their habits of life, and, above all, by the inveterate hatred which they cherished against the dignified Clergy.

As this advantage, however, was too evident in case of individual suffrage being determined upon, the minister left the first Orders at liberty to vote thus only with their own consent, a source of dissensions in which the weakest would infallibly be overwhelmed.

Here was the critical moment when the conduct of this minister ceases to be blameless and stands in need of apology. No man was ever farther than he from the base treachery of which the misfortunes of the time have made him be accused. But it is too true that nothing can excuse the blind confidence which he placed in a people with whom the League and the Fronde should have made him sufficiently acquainted.

Doubtless, in order to fulfil the duties of a private individual, of a citizen, and of the servant of a young and virtuous monarch, it was necessary, as he says himself, to enlighten his justice, to direct his inclinations, and to make him enjoy the first privilege of a throne in the happiness of his people and in their affecting benedictions. But he ought to have enlightened his wisdom as well as his justice; while conducting him, he should have warned him of the dangers he was about to incur, and instead of covering with flowers the brink of the precipice, should have carefully guarded him against it; he should have taken care that he was not exposing him to deadly insult instead of blessings. The King trusted wholly to the prudence of his minister; this imposed on the latter a sacred obligation to be cautious, timid and distrustful. Here Necker was deficient. There were great evils to be feared, but he could foresee only good. His mind was solitary, abstracted, withdrawn into itself, and naturally lofty; he conversed little with men, and few men felt any temptation to converse with him; he observed them only by glimpses, which were either too detached or too vague: hence those delusive ideas respecting the character of the populace. The continual struggle which he had to maintain against all the factions which were set in motion by private interest had led him to form an unfavourable judgment of the Court and of the higher circles; and this judgment was sound. But he had formed a fantastical and an infinitely too flattering opinion of the great mass of the nation. He had heard this populace praising and blessing him; he had enjoyed their confidence, their affection and their regret; they had avenged him under the weight of calumny which he had endured; their voice had recalled him from exile to the ministry, and still continued to support him. He was bound, not by gratitude only, but by his own benefits; and being obliged by his personal feelings to believe the people feeling and just, he was convinced that they would continue always the same. His own, therefore, made him forget other examples which would have warned him of the inconstancy of this people, of their levity, of the readiness with which they pass from one extreme to another, and allow themselves to be corrupted, led astray, and worked up to frenzy and the most brutal fury.

In a class immediately above the people, but attached

to their party, he did not consider how many passions, now obscure and timid, wanted only a common point of union to kindle and disclose themselves. Vanity, pride, envy, the ambition of governing, or, at least, of humbling those whom with a jealous eye they saw above themselves; meaner interests, and views still meaner, the speculations of avarice, the calculations of venality—all these eternal sources of faction and discord were elements which Necker seemed not to have perceived. The abstract and seducing idea of a mild, amiable and generous nation wholly engrossed his mind.

In this species of intoxication, he thought it impossible to grant too much favour to the popular party. After securing them a constant plurality of votes, he was going to add the advantage of place to that of number. The security, the liberty, the tranquility of deliberation essentially required a place inaccessible to the insults of the populace, and easily secured from every kind of tumult; while his first thought was to place the States-General in Paris, amid a people of all others the most numerous, most easily moved to insurrection, and whose insurrections were the most formidable, it was only out of deference to the advice of the council that he was satisfied with fixing them at Versailles, *statio male fida carinis*.

The hall, which was destined for the general assemblies, and in which the highest interests of the State were to be canvassed between the three Orders, was surrounded by galleries, as if for the express purpose of inviting the populace to interfere in the deliberations by supporting their own party while they threatened and insulted the other, and thus to change the House of Assembly into a theatre, in which the actors were to be animated by their applause. I mention these particulars because they became of the most serious importance. But M. Necker could never consider the assembly of the States as anything but a peaceful, commanding and august spectacle,

which the people would have to enjoy.   His hopes could
not fail to be mingled with anxiety ; but, as he ascribed
great power to moral ideas, he hoped that the surest
means of preventing the disturbances which might arise
from the dissension of the Orders was to animate them all
with that enthusiasm for the public good by which the
greatest sacrifice, both of party and of private interest,
is rendered easy and agreeable.   He tried this first by
the publication of his report to the Council of State of
the 27th of December, 1788, and hoped, by the example
of the King himself, to excite from that time the general
emulation.   After alluding to the confession which the
King had made to him, that for some years past he had
enjoyed only moments of happiness : " Sire," said he,
" you will recover this happiness, and will enjoy it.   You
rule over a nation who know what it is to love.   Political
novelties, of which they have not yet had sufficient experience, were able for a time to pervert their natural
character ; but, attached as they will soon be, by your
benefits, and confirmed in their confidence by the purity
of your intentions, they will think only of enjoying the
steady and happy order which they will owe to you.
This grateful nation does not yet know all that you intend to do for its happiness.   You have told it, sire, to
those ministers who are honoured with your confidence :
you not only intend to fulfil the promise you have made,
not to impose any new tax without the consent of the
States but you do not even intend to continue any tax
without this condition.   You intend, besides, to secure
the renewal of the States-General, and to consult them
as to the interval which should elapse between their
meetings, and as to the means of giving a lasting
stability to these arrangements.   In order to form a
strong tie between the private administration of each
province and the general legislation, you wish the deputies from each department of the kingdom to concert
together the most proper plan, to which Your Majesty

will then be disposed to give your consent. Your
Majesty wishes also to prevent, in the most efficacious
manner, the disorder which the bad conduct or incapacity of your ministers might introduce into the
finances ; and, among the expenses which you wish to
be limited to a fixed amount, you do not except even
those which more particularly concern your own person.
It is the intention of Your Majesty to anticipate the
lawful wish of your subjects by inviting the States-
General themselves to examine the great question concerning *lettres-de-cachet*. You, sire, desire only the maintenance of order, and wish to leave to the law everything
which it is capable of executing. Upon the same principle, Your Majesty is impatient to receive the advice
of the States-General respecting the degree of liberty
which ought to be granted to the Press, and to the
publication of works relating to the administration. In
short, sire, you prefer, with reason, the durable deliberations of the States-General of the kingdom, to the transient advice of your ministers ; and when you shall have
experienced their wisdom, you will not be afraid to give
them a stability which may produce confidence and secure
them from any variation in the sentiments of your royal
successors."

This discourse of the minister being printed, published and circulated throughout the whole kingdom, as
the solemn expression of the King's sentiments, gave him
a lawful right to the confidence of the nation ; and if, in
pursuance of these dispositions, the States had chosen to
establish themselves as the supreme council of a King
who desired everything that was just, and nothing that
was otherwise ; of a King who, uniting himself with the
nation, was determined to place upon an immovable basis
his own limited power, the pillar of liberty and of public
happiness—then the French monarchy, without changing
its nature, would have become the mildest, most moderate and steadiest government that ever existed. The

King, in this legislative council of the nation, was to preside, like a father consulting with his children, to settle their rights as a friend rather than an arbiter, and, in conjunction with them, to form into laws the means of rendering them happy. In this spirit it was that the minister thought he was making every preparation for bestowing upon the nation, and for preserving to the Crown, that character of greatness, of power, and of majesty which they ought mutually to possess, and which the one cannot possess fully without the other (for such was the language of the King).

But in a nation full of petulance and levity, which wishes to be suddenly free without having learned what liberty is, it is but too natural that the first violence should carry men beyond the proper limits; and when these limits are once overstepped, full scope is given to passion, to error and to guilt.

BOOK XIV

ALTHOUGH Paris was, as it were, the common centre of the fermentation excited throughout the kingdom, the primary assemblies there were sufficiently quiet, and appeared solely occupied with the choice of good electors, in order to have good deputies.

I was one of the electors named by the section *des Feuillans;* I was also one of the commissaries appointed to draw up the statement of their demands, and, I may say, that these demands contained nothing but what was useful and just. The spirit of this section, therefore, was reasonable and moderate.

It was otherwise with the electoral assembly ; the greater part were sound when they arrived, but we saw them assailed by a crowd of intriguing men, who came and breathed among us the contagious air which they had inhaled in their conferences with Duport, one of the factious members of the Parliament.

Whether Duport was sincere in his dangerous fanaticism, or whether, having calculated better than the rest of his body those dangers which it was about to incur, he wished to acquire a political existence of his own, it was well known that the winter before he had opened at his house a kind of school of Republicanism, to which his friends took care to draw those minds which were most heated, or most likely to become so.

I observed this band of noisy and restless men contending with each other for the privilege of speech, impatient to display themselves, and aspiring to be

registered among the list of orators. I was not long
in seeing how great their influence would be, and, raising
my thoughts from a particular example to a general observation, I became sensible that in every division there
would be such quibbling lawyers, who, being all accustomed to speak in public, would be ready as fit instruments
of faction.

It is a well-known truth that no people can govern
itself; that the opinion, the will of an assembled multitude
is seldom or never anything more than an impulse which
it receives from a small number of men, and sometimes
from a single man who moves at pleasure their thoughts
and inclinations. The people have passions, but these
passions, slumbering, as it were, wait till a voice comes to
rouse and inflame them. They have been compared to
the sails of a ship, which would remain loose and motionless if the wind did not swell them.

Now, it is well known that to move the passions of
the people was always the aim of eloquence in a public
assembly ; and with us the only school for this eloquence
was the Bar. Even those who by the habit of pleading
had acquired nothing but boldness and clamour, possessed
a very great advantage over other men. A cool judgment,
a steady and thoughtful mind, if deficient when necessary
of a copious and ready elocution, could not keep its guard
against the vehemence of a practised declaimer.

The surest method of propagating revolutionary doctrines throughout the kingdom had therefore been, to
engage the body of advocates on their side, than which
nothing had been easier. They were naturally Republican,
proud, and jealous of their liberty, fond of dominion from
the habit of holding the fate of their clients in their hands,
dispersed throughout the kingdom, possessed of the public
esteem and confidence, holding a continual intercourse
with all classes of society, and skilled in the art of rousing
and commanding men's minds. The profession of advocates, therefore, were likely to possess an irresistible

ascendency over the multitude, some by the force of true eloquence, others by that noise and torrent of words which dazzles and imposes upon weak minds. In short, they could not fail to hold the first place in the popular assemblies, and to govern the public opinion; above all, when they held themselves forth as the avengers of the people's injuries and the defenders of their rights.

This body itself had an obvious interest in seeing the reform changed into a revolution, the monarchy into a republic; their object was to organise a perpetual aristocracy. They were successively destined to be the movers of the Republican faction, and nothing was more agreeable to ambitious men, who, possessing everywhere the authority of understanding and talents, would by turns be called to public functions, and would be almost the sole legislators of France—first its chief magistrates, and soon its real sovereigns.

The same prospect was opened not only to men of the law, but to all the classes of well-informed citizens, each of whom had sufficient confidence in his own talents as to entertain the same hope and the same ambition.

I do not deny that this ambition had an honourable and a laudable pretext. In human institutions it is impossible for everything to be well; it is even infinitely rare that it unites the greatest good or the least ill that is possible. A government is always a machine more or less subject to frequent derangements. It is necessary, therefore, at least at intervals, either to regulate its movements or to repair its springs; and when we examine the form of any State, whether monarchical or republican, there is none whose condition does not appear dreadful, when we see accumulated in the same description all the vices, all the abuses, and all the crimes of a former period. Thus it was that the reign of Louis XVI. was calumniated. Whatever were the errors and the faults which he himself had not been able to avoid, he sought only to obliterate every trace of them, and no one was more

14—2

earnestly desirous than he of this salutary reform ; but
under the vague and deceitful name of reform, a revolution was disguised ; and this error explains the almost
universal success of a plan which, as in various points of
view it seemed useful and just, suited itself to every
character and consolidated the general wish.

The best citizens thought the wishes and intentions
of the most wicked the very same with their own ; whether
men's minds were animated with the love of the public
good, or with the desire of glory and dominion, or with
a base envy, or with an infamous rage for plunder, all
followed the same impulse, and the result of these different movements was the same—the subversion of the
State. This appears to me to present an apology for a
great number of men who have been supposed to have
been depraved, but who were only led astray.

It is conceivable, indeed, that some men with the
propensities of tigers, might have planned the Revolution
such as it was executed ; but no one, I think, can dare to
maintain that the French nation, that the very lowest
populace, without any previous seduction, should have
consented to this inhuman and impious conspiracy. It is
false, therefore, that the crimes of the Revolution were the
crimes of the nation ; and I am far from supposing that
any of my colleagues in the electoral assembly could
have so much as foreseen them.

A band of lawyers came to us, animated, I believe,
with a blind enthusiasm for the public good. They were
supported by a train of ambitious Republicans, who
aspired, like them, to become celebrated in the assemblies
of a free people. Target, a man distinguished at the Bar,
and who, in other respects, had a very good character
among us, acted the foremost part.

The Government had sent us the minister of police as
our president. This was a false step, for it was one which
could not be supported. An assembly cannot be fundamentally free without having a president from its own

body and of its own choosing. This magistrate supported his office well; he compelled us to admire his
firmness and his wisdom, but in vain. The cause was
pleaded against him by the advocate Target; and the
latter, as a reward for having defended the rights of the
assembly, was proclaimed president.

Target was a champion long inured to the struggles
of the Bar, full of boldness and assurance, devoured with
ambition, and escorted by a band of friends who loudly
applauded him on every occasion. He began with insinuating himself into men's minds as a conciliating and
pacific man. But when he had got the command over
this assembly of citizens, who were yet new to the
functions of public men, he raised his head and loudly
proclaimed what he was. He did not content himself, as
the duty of his place required, with giving a faithful
statement of the questions subjected to the assembly's
examination; he dictated their opinion, instead of collecting and declaring it.

Our functions were not confined to the election of
deputies; we had also, in giving them their instructions,
to make up an account of our grievances, and each of
these grievances gave occasion to new declamations.
The indefinite words of equality, of liberty, of the sovereignty of the people resounded in our ears; every man
heard them, and made his own application. The regulations of police, the financial edicts, the gradations of
authority, upon which the public order and tranquility
rested, were thought to bear a character of tyranny. A
ridiculous importance was attached to the most minute
circumstances, of which I shall mention only one
example.

A discussion had taken place about the wall and
the gates with which Paris was enclosed, which were
denounced as suited only for enclosing deer, but injurious to men.

" What, citizens !" said one of the Orders, "what

do you think I saw engraved on one of the pillars at the gate of St. Victor? I saw the head of an enormous lion, with its mouth open and vomiting chains, with which it threatened the passengers. Is it possible to conceive a more frightful emblem of despotism and slavery?" The orator himself imitated the roaring of the lion. The whole audience was moved; and I, who passed so often the gate of St. Victor, was astonished at never having been struck with this horrible image. That day, therefore, I paid particular attention to it; and I saw, by way of ornament upon the pilaster, a buckler suspended by a slender chain, which the sculptor had attached to a small lion's muzzle, such as we see at the knocker of a door, or the well of a fountain.

Intrigue had also its secret committees, which threw off all respect for those principles and objects that had been held most sacred. Neither morality nor religious worship was spared. It was proved, according to the doctrine of Mirabeau, that civil policy was incompatible with morality, the religious spirit with patriotism, and old prejudices with new virtues. Royalty and tyranny, obedience and slavery, power and oppression, were represented as inseparable under the government of a single man.

On the contrary, the most absurdly extravagant hopes and promises were held out, of what was to happen when the people should be restored to their equal and independent rights. It appeared that we were to be governed by men of the age of gold. This free, wise and just people were to be always in unison with themselves, always enlightened in the choice of their councils and of their ministers, moderate in the use of their power, never erring, never deceived, never governed by those to whom their authority was entrusted. Their will was to be law, and these laws were all to conduce to their happiness. Though I was left almost alone, and though my party in the electoral assembly grew weaker and weaker every

day, I never ceased representing to everyone who would
listen to me that this art of imposing upon the assembly
by impudent declamation appeared to me quite stupid
and easy. My principles were well known—I made no
secret of them; and care was taken to whisper about
that I was the friend of ministers, and was loaded with
favours from the King. The elections were made, and I
was not chosen; the Abbé Sieyes was preferred. I
thanked heaven for my exclusion, for I thought I foresaw
what was to happen in the National Assembly, with
which, soon after, I was better acquainted.

We had in the French Academy one of the fiercest
partisans of the Republican faction; it was Chamfort, an
acute and penetrating genius, endowed with a very agreeable wit when he amused himself with the vices and the
follies of society, but severe and keenly satirical against
the superiority of rank and fortune, which wounded his
jealous pride. Of all the envious men who were dispersed through the world, Chamfort was the man who
could least forgive the rich and great for the opulence of
their houses and the pleasures of their tables, which he
himself was very glad to enjoy. In their own presence,
in private, he courted, flattered, and was ingenious in
pleasing them; there were even some whom he appeared
to love and esteem, and upon whom he pronounced pompous panegyrics; always understanding, however, that
if he was so complaisant as to be their inmate, and to
lodge in their house, they, by their credit, must obtain for
him from the Court literary rewards; nor did he think
them absolved by the pensions which he enjoyed to the
amount of some thousand crowns—this was too little
for him. "These people," said he to Florian, "should
get me £800 a year; I deserve no less." With this
view he had favourites among the great, whom he ex-
cepted from his satires. But, with regard to the caste
in general, he lashed them without mercy; and when he
thought their fortune and grandeur on the point of being

overthrown, he no longer cared for any, threw them all off, and took the side of the people.

In our companies we were sometimes amused with the sallies of his humour ; and, though I did not love him, yet I treated him with precaution and respect, not wishing to make him my enemy.

One day, therefore, when we were left alone at the Louvre, after the sitting of the Academy, he said, " Well, you are not a deputy." " No," replied I, "and I comfort myself like the fox about the grapes which he could not reach—they are too green." " Really," replied he, " I do not think them ripe enough for you. Your soul is of too mild and flexible a cast for the trial to which it would have been exposed. They judged well in reserving you for another legislature. You are excellent for building, but can do little in the way of destroying."

Knowing that Chamfort was the friend and confidant of Mirabeau, one of the leaders of the faction, I thought myself at the fountain-head of information ; and in order to get him to explain himself, I pretended not to understand him. " You make me tremble," said I, " when you talk of destroying ; I thought our object had been only to repair."

" Ay," said he, " but reparation often occasions ruin. When you attack an old wall, you cannot be assured that it will not crumble under the hammer ; and the edifice here is really so decayed that I should not be surprised if it were necessary to demolish it from top to bottom." " From top to bottom ! " exclaimed I. " Why not ? " replied Chamfort, " and build it anew, upon a less Gothic and more regular plan. Would it, for instance, be so great an evil, though there were fewer stories, and though all were on one floor ? Would you be in despair though you no longer heard of eminence, of highness, of titles, of heraldry, of nobles, of plebeians, of high and low clergy?" I observed, that " equality had always been the chimera of republics, and the

lure which ambition presented to vanity. But this
levelling system is particularly impossible in a vast
monarchy; and it appears to me," added I, "that in attempting to abolish everything, you go further than the
nation intends and requires." "Very good," replied he;
"do the nation know what they wish? We will make
them wish and say what they never thought of; and if
they hesitate, we will answer as Crispin, in the comedy of
the *Legataire*—'It is all owing to your lethargy.' The
nation is a great flock, which thinks only of feeding, and
which the shepherds, with good dogs, may guide at
pleasure. After all, we wish to do good to them without
their knowledge; for, my friend, neither your old regimen,
nor your religious worship, nor your morals, nor all your
antiquated prejudices deserve to be spared. All this can
excite only shame and pity in an age such as ours; and
those who are forming a new plan have every reason for
wishing to make the ground clear."

"The ground clear!" urged I, "but the throne—the
altar!" "Well," said he, "the throne and the altar will
fall together: they are two arches which rest upon each
other; and, whenever one of the two is broken, the other
must bend."

I concealed the impression which his confidence
made upon me, and with the view of drawing him farther
on, said, "In the enterprise which you announce, the
difficulties appear to me to be greater than the resources."

"Trust me," said he, "the difficulties are foreseen,
and the resources are calculated." He then explained
himself, and I learned that the calculations of faction
rested upon the character of the King, who was so averse
to every kind of violence that he was believed pusillanimous: upon the actual condition of the Clergy, which,
he said, contained now only some virtuous men destitute
of ability, and some able men degraded and dishonoured
by vices: lastly, upon the condition of the high Nobility
themselves, who were said to be degenerated, and among

whom few great characters supported the lustre of a great
name.   But it was particularly in themselves that the
Tiers Etat had reason to place confidence.   This Order,
long worn out with an arbitrary authority, the oppression
of which descended to its lowest ramifications, was
superior to the other two Orders, not only in numbers,
but also in union, in courage, and in a daring determination to brave everything.   " In short," said Chamfort,
" you see this impatience and indignation, which has long
been brooding, confirmed into a storm, and that storm
ready to burst ; confederation and insurrection everywhere declared, and, upon the signal being given by the
province of Dauphiny, the whole kingdom ready to
answer with acclamation that they are determined to
be free ; you see the provinces linked together, a correspondence established between them ; while from Paris,
as from their common centre, the Republican spirit
diffuses far and wide its warmth and lustre.   Such is the
state of things—are these castles in the air ?"

I allowed that, in speculation, all this was very fine ;
but, I added, that the best part of the nation would not
go beyond the bounds of a desirable reform, nor would
allow any breach to be made in the laws of their country
and in the fundamental principles of the monarchy.

He admitted that, at their firesides, and in their
workshops, many of these domestic citizens might, perhaps, think there was too much boldness in plans which
threatened to interrupt their repose and enjoyment.
" But their disapprobation," said he, " will be timid and
silent, and we can easily overawe them by that determined class who think that in a change they have nothing to lose and everything to gain.   We have the most
powerful instruments for raising commotions—famine,
money, alarming reports, and the delirium of rage and
fear with which men's minds can be struck.   You have
heard only elegant speakers among the citizens.   Know
that all our assembly orators are nothing in comparison

to the Demostheneses, at half-a-crown a-head, who get
up in the taverns, the public places, in the gardens, and
on the quays, and tell of ravages, of fires, of villages
plundered and deluged with blood, of plots for besieging
Paris! Now these are what I call eloquent men. Above
all things, money and the hope of pillage are omnipotent
among the populace. We have just made the attempt in
the suburb of St. Antoine; and you cannot believe how
little it has cost the Duke of Orleans to make them
plunder the manufactory of honest Reveillon, who gave
subsistence to a hundred families of this very people.
Mirabeau humorously maintains that with a thousand
louis one may make a very nice sedition."

"So," said I, "your experiments are crimes, and
your militia consists of robbers?" "It must be so,"
replied he coolly. "What would you make of all this
people if they were muzzled with your principles of
honesty and justice? Virtuous men are weak, timid, and
careful of themselves; knaves only are determined. The
best thing for the people, in a revolution, is to have no
morality. How is it possible to resist men to whom all
means are good? Mirabeau is in the right: there is not
one of our old virtues which can be of any use to us; the
people have no occasion for any, at least of the same
stamp. The great principle is that everything necessary, everything useful to the Revolution, is just."

"Such," said I, "is, perhaps, the principle of the
Duke of Orleans; for it appears to me that when the
people rise he must be their leader, and I own to you I
have no very high opinion of his courage." "You are in
the right," said he; "and Mirabeau, who knows him
well, said that to reckon upon him would be building
upon clay. But he has shown a popular disposition, he
bears a commanding name, he has thousands to spend,
he detests the King, and the Queen still more; and if he
is deficient in courage, it will be found for him. Intrepid
leaders will be procured among the people themselves,

especially when they have once appeared in rebellion, and view themselves as criminals; for they cannot draw back when no retreat is left but the scaffold. Fear, without hope of safety, is to the people a sure source of courage. Our force will be immense, if we can involve an immense number in the guilt of conspiracy. But," continued he, " I see that my hopes make you melancholy; you do not wish a liberty which will cost a great deal of money and blood. Would you have us make revolutions with rose-water ? "

Such was the end of the conversation, and we separated; he, doubtless, full of contempt for my silly scruples, and I not at all satisfied with his daring immorality. The poor man afterwards punished himself by putting an end to his own life when he became sensible of his errors.

I communicated this conversation to the Abbé Maury that very evening. " It is but too true," said he, " that they are little mistaken in their speculations, and that the faction have chosen the time when they will find fewest obstacles. I have watched the two parties. My resolution is formed to perish upon the breach ; but I do not the less feel a sad assurance that they will take the place by storm, and that it will be given up to plunder.

" If so," said I, " what madness is it, then, in the Clergy and Nobility to allow the King to engage in this war ! " " What would you have them do ? " " What is done during a fire. I wish them to assist in extinguishing it ; to supply the deficit by charging themselves with the public debt ; to set the vessel of the nation afloat—in short, to withdraw the King from amid the rocks upon which they have themselves driven him, and, whatever it may cost, to prevail upon him to send back the States-General before they are assembled. I wish them to be informed that they are undone if the States assemble, and that there is not a moment to lose

in order to dissipate the storm that is about to fall upon
them." Maury made objections, but I would listen to
none. " Well," said he, " since you require it, I will
take this step ; but I shall not be listened to."

Unfortunately he addressed himself to the Bishop
D——, an empty head, who treated my information as
chimerical. He replied that things were not so bad
as supposed, and that the Clergy, with a sword in one
hand and a crucifix in the other, would defend their
rights.

Released from my deputation at the electoral assembly, I went to my country-house in search of the repose
which I so much needed, and thereby lost a new society
which was forming at my house : it consisted of men
with whom I should have been happy to meet in more
peaceful times. There was the Abbé de Perigord, newly
created Bishop of Autun ; the Count de Narbonne, and
the Marquis de la Fayette. I had seen them in the
world as free from intrigues and cares as myself. The
character of the first was engaging, mild and judicious ;
the second had a gay, lively and brilliant wit ; the last
had a cordiality which was extremely graceful and captivating. The society of all the three was most agreeable.

But in their meetings at my house I saw their
humour darkened by a shade of politics, and some hints
which they dropped led me to suspect causes for this
alteration which did not accord with my principles. They
perceived, as well as myself, that my house was no longer
a proper rendezvous for their communications and their
conferences. We were separated by my retreat.

On the days of the week when I went to the
Academy I slept at Paris, and I very often spent the
evenings with M. Necker. Finding myself there, in
company with the ministers, I spoke to them openly of
what I had seen and learned. They appeared quite
astonished, like men who did not know where to turn
themselves. What was going on at Versailles had un-

deceived M. Necker, and I now saw him in consternation. He invited me to dine with him, along with the principal deputies of the Commons, and the cold air with which they received his attentions led me to suppose that they wished to have him for their steward, but not for their guide.

M. de Montmorin, whom I urged to prevail upon the King to withdraw into one of his strong places, and to the head of his armies, objected the want of money, bankruptcy, civil war.

" Then," continued he, " you think the danger very urgent, that you would have such speedy recourse to these extremities ? " " I think it so urgent," said I, " that a month hence I would no longer be answerable for the King's liberty, for his head, or for yours." Alas ! Chamfort had made me a prophet. But I was not listened to, or rather I was listened to by a weak minister who was not listened to himself.

Meanwhile, the deputies from the three Orders had come to Versailles, nearly in the number prescribed : three hundred of the Order of the Clergy, three hundred of the Order of the Nobility, and six hundred of the Order of the Tiers Etat, including the Parisian deputies who did not arrive for some days after.

The assembly was opened on the 5th of May. Never had the nation been so fully represented, never had such important interests been entrusted to its representatives; never, too, had so much talent and information been united in forwarding the great work of the public good; never, in short, had a better or more just King presented himself to promote it. What happiness has been destroyed by a blind system of revolution !

The King, in all the pomp of majesty, attended by the Queen and the two royal brothers, by the princes of the blood, by the peers of the kingdom, by the officers of the Crown, by the keeper of the seals, and by the minister of finance, entered the hall of the assembled States.

He appeared with simple dignity, equally free from pride and timidity, and bore in his countenance that character of goodness which was in his heart. He was sweetly affected by that sentiment with which the view of deputies from a faithful nation tends naturally to inspire their King.

Nothing could be more genuine than the look, the simple and feeling tone coming from the heart, with which he pronounced the discourse which I will now transcribe.

" Gentlemen,—The day to which my heart has long looked forward is at last arrived, and I see myself surrounded by the representatives of a nation which I am proud of commanding. A long interval has elapsed since the last meeting of the States-General; and, though the calling of these assemblies seems to have fallen into disuse, I make no hesitation in restoring a practice from which the kingdom might derive new strength, and which may open to the nation a new source of happiness.

" The national debt, which was already immense at my accession to the throne, has increased under my reign. This has been occasioned by an expensive though honourable war; the increase of taxes has been the necessary consequence, and has rendered their unequal division more sensible. A general restlessness, an immoderate desire for innovation, have taken possession of men's minds, and would, in the end, lead their opinions totally astray, did we not hasten to fix them by a union of sound and moderate judgments. In this assurance, gentlemen, I have called you together, and I see, with sensible pleasure, that my confidence has been already justified by the disposition which the two higher orders have shown to renounce their pecuniary interests. The hope which I have entertained of seeing all ranks unanimously concur with me in consulting the general good of the State will not be deceived.

"I have already directed considerable retrenchments to be made in the expenditure. I shall be happy
to receive any suggestions which you may make upon
this subject. But, notwithstanding the resources which
may be offered by the most rigid economy, I am afraid,
gentlemen, it will be impossible to relieve my subjects
so speedily as I could desire.

"I will cause the exact situation of the finances to
be laid before you; and I am already confident that,
when you have examined it, you will propose the most
effectual means for establishing a permanent order, and
for confirming public credit. You will diligently employ
yourselves in this great and salutary operation, which
will secure at once the internal happiness of the kingdom, and its respect among foreign nations.

"Men's minds are in a state of agitation; but an
assembly of national representatives will, doubtless,
listen only to the counsels of wisdom and prudence.
You yourselves, gentlemen, must have been sensible that
it has been overlooked on several recent occasions. But
the ruling spirit of your determinations will correspond
with the true sentiments of a generous nation, whose
distinguishing character has always been the love of its
Kings. I shall banish every other recollection.

"I know the authority and the power of a just King,
surrounded by a faithful people, who have at all times
been attached to the principles of monarchy. They have
formed the glory and the ornament of France; it is my
duty to be its support, and this duty I will always fulfil.
But you may, with confidence, expect from me everything
which can be inspired by the most tender interest in the
public welfare, or which can be demanded from a
sovereign who is the first friend of his people.

"Gentlemen, may a happy union reign in this assembly, and may this become ever memorable as the era
of national prosperity and happiness; it is the desire of
my heart—it is the most ardent of my wishes; in short,

it is the reward which I expect from the uprightness of my intentions and the love of my people."

These words of the King produced the most favourable impression on the assembly.

The keeper of the seals, according to custom, explained the intentions of the King; he observed that anciently the military service being at the expense of the Nobility, and the subsistence of widows, of orphans, and the poor, being drawn from the property of the Clergy, this kind of contribution absolved them towards the State; but that now, when the Clergy were possessed of considerable wealth, and when the Nobility obtained honourable and pecuniary rewards, the possessions of these two Orders ought to be subjected to the common rule. Among the subjects upon which the assembly should fix its attention, he mentioned the useful changes which might be required in civil legislation and in criminal procedure; and, while he acknowledged the necessity of rendering the administration of justice easier, of correcting its abuses, of limiting its expense, of putting a stop to those endless discussions by which families were ruined, and of enabling the accused to be brought speedily to trial, he paid a tacit homage to the principles of Lamoignon.

Lastly, by the King's express order, the director-general of the finances rose and laid open the situation in which they stood, and, without concealing the evil, pointed out the remedies. He threw an encouraging light over this object which, in the shade, appeared so terrible, and with the most afflicting statements mingled the consolations of a courageous hope. He showed that the object which was most urgent and difficult, the establishment of equality between the revenue and expenditure, did not require even the aid of a new tax; that this deficiency would be supplied by mere reductions and moderate savings. As for the resources which remained for the wants of the present year, for the extraordinary expenses of the two following, for successively paying off the old debts, for diminishing the amount of anticipations —in short, for discharging some urgent debts, whose payment might be immediately required : he pointed them out in the gradual extinction of life annuities, in the produce of savings and new improvements, in the increase which would arise from the more equal imposition and more regular levy of the subsidies. Lastly, thinking himself sure that time and national credit would form the only lawful means of lightening the public burdens, he wished no others to be resorted to, and rejected as unworthy of the royal and national magnanimity every violation of their engagements. " Let greater precaution," said he, " be taken for the future ; this is the King's desire and wish. But at so solemn an era, when the nation is called by their sovereign to assemble round him, not for a moment, but for ever—at an era when this nation is called to join, in some degree, in the thoughts and wishes of their King, they will, doubtless, second with the greatest eagerness those sentiments of honour and fidelity of which he is full. This protection granted to the national creditors, this long and constant fidelity will one day, gentlemen, be a noble monument of the moral character of His Majesty ; for the King, had he chosen to withdraw it, would have stood in need of no aid—and this, perhaps, is the first advice which modern Machiavels would have been sure to have given."

In addition to these maxims of justice and probity, Necker added the great interest of political power which rested upon these principles, and employed the same eloquence in pleading the cause of the annuitants as in pleading that of the national creditors. His honesty was applauded.

But when talking of certain conditional mandates, in which the engagements to be taken with regard to the finances were to be considered as a secondary object, which ought to be preceded by all the concessions and all the assurances which the nation should demand, the minister observed that the embarrassments of the finances were embarrassments of the public; that the expenses of the State concerned the nation no less than the monarch; that upon them depended its security, its repose, its defence, all the advantages of its public existence; and that the obligation which they imposed was too absolute to admit of being rendered conditional; lastly, when even on the supposition that the King had more interest than the nation in the restoration of order and credit, and in the discharge of the public debt, Necker dared to say to the deputies: " Know, gentlemen, —and it is proper that you should observe this, in order that you may love the more our august monarch—know it is not to the absolute necessity of a supply of money that the States-General are indebted for the precious advantage of being assembled by His Majesty"; and when he showed them, by stating one article after another, that the King, without committing any injustice, and by mere retrenchments which lay in his own power, might have had in his hands most of the resources for supplying the wants of the State and for filling up the deficit, those persons who, in pursuance of their system of dominion wished to subject the King to the law of necessity, were offended that his minister should show a wish to keep him free. They had been heard to say that "the nation ought to stone the man who should teach the King no longer to stand in need of new aid."

Necker, it is true, wished to convince the assembly that they had no right to refuse their assistance; but, while he made the King support the dignity of his crown, he left the nation in possession of every means of restraining his lawful authority within the bounds of equity.

And really, when by a common agreement between the monarch and the people, the expenditure was fixed, the taxes agreed to, the ministers accountable, the accounts of receipt and expenditure published and vouched before the eye of the nation; when the abuses, in short, were reformed and the administration subjected to the rules of the strictest economy—after all this, what did they wish more? And if the equal imposition of taxes was agreed upon, if fixed periods were appointed for the renewal of the States-General, if the Press was as free as it ought to be, if the *lettres-de-cachet* were abolished or entrusted to the wisdom of a tribunal, if liberty, the security of person and property, the equality of all the citizens in the eye of the law were rendered inviolable— if all these benefits were not only offered, but secured to the nation, what was wanting to the unheard-of success of this first assembly? Nothing but that character of independence and dominion which the fanatical partisans of an absolute and despotic democracy wished that their decrees should possess.

"When the proper time shall come," said M. Necker to them, "His Majesty will form a just estimate of the character of your deliberations, and if it be such as he hopes, and such as he has a right to expect,—if, in short, it be such as the soundest part of the nation wishes and demands, the King will second your inclinations; he will make it his glory to crown them ; and the spirit of the best of princes being mingled, if I may so say, with the spirit which will inspire the most faithful of nations, the greatest benefit, the most solid power, will be seen to arise from this union."

This expression of an authority, which retained in its own hands the power of examination and free consent, was what wounded the pride of the democratical party. They were jealous of seeing the sovereign choose to do, of his own accord, what they meant to command, and accused Necker of investing despotism with the forms of beneficence. They wished a king who should be a king no longer.

Meanwhile, in spite of Mirabeau, and in spite of the

violent libel which he published, the discourses of the King and of the minister obtained the approbation of every virtuous mind, both within and without the assembly.

An immense crowd of the inhabitants of Paris had thronged to Versailles, in order to enjoy the view of the opening of the States. And when the King, after the meeting, came with the national deputies to the church of St. Louis, the pomp, the order, the majesty of this august march, the respectful silence of a crowd of spectators arranged on each side, the appearance of the King in the midst of this national Court, full of a sweet joy, free from all mistrust, with his family around him happy in the same happiness—all these objects together made so deep and so lively an impression upon men's minds, that involuntary tears flowed from every eye. Hope seemed to precede the walk of the States-General, and prosperity to follow it. But amid this outward show of patriotism and concord, the hollow sound which precedes a storm began already to be heard.

BOOK XV

THE first contest which arose between the different Orders related, as had been foreseen, to the manner in which they should be formed. The first resolution of the Tiers Etat was, never to deliberate in separate chambers; while the first resolution of the Nobility and Clergy was, never to admit of individual suffrage: resolutions which would have broken up at once the assembly of the States if each of the parties had continued immovable. But the party of the higher Orders, which was already too weak, was rendered still weaker by the imprudent ground which they took. The Tiers Etat, with the view of engaging them to deliberate in common, began with demanding a scrutiny of the commissions; and they were evidently right in wishing that this examination should be made together and in common; for it was surely proper that they should recognise each other. By showing each other the authorities upon which they acted, they entered into no engagement; for would not each, after this examination, have been as free as before? The higher Orders refused this. Instead of waiting the favourable moment for taking a strong position, they thought it advisable to dispute every inch of ground; and they seriously injured themselves at the very first by taking a false position which they were unable to maintain.

This conduct of the two first Orders was prompted by their knowledge of the characters of many of their own confederates.

A very considerable number of the Nobility had their minds inflamed, some by a spirit of liberty and independence, others by views and calculations of ambition. These leaned towards the party of the people, among whom they hoped to be honoured, distinguished and raised to the first employments. Among the Clergy a still greater number, and, as I formerly mentioned, the whole mass of parochial clergy were attached to the Commons by ties of every kind. A parish priest, if he be virtuous, is the most popular of all men. But a sentiment less laudable, though equally natural, was their aversion, first to the bishops, whose severity they often found vexatious, and then for that middle class of abbés, whom they regarded with envy. This class, they said, was useless, and yet was alone favoured; it was idle, yet proud of its idleness; it disdained the ministerial office, while with the pride of an ostentatious opulence it insulted the humble mediocrity, and sometimes even the poverty which accompanied the laborious condition of a pastor. This particularly alienated the lower clergy and drove them towards an Order in which Nature had placed them, and which, besides, neglected not to promise them a milder lot.

Now, so long as each should be kept in his own body, under the restraint of example and shame, there was reason to think that he would remain attached to it; but if they once entered into a common deliberation with the Tiers Etat, and saw themselves encircled by the popular party, it was to be feared they might adhere to it; there was a wish to shun this first meeting. But the only means of preventing desertion would have been to render it shameful and dishonourable in the public opinion by assuming a character of frankness and generosity, which would deprive deserters of every cover for their meanness. Commissioners, for the purpose of conciliation, were named by the three Orders; but no effect resulted from their conferences.

A monarch who took a greater interest in himself than in the State, and who, jealous of his power, saw attempts being made to restrain and subject it, would have allowed the Orders to weary themselves out with their disputes, till discord disgusted and dissolved this dangerous assembly. But the King, who was sincerely desirous of the public good, and hoped to engage the Orders to unite with him in promoting it, was afraid of nothing so much as seeing them separate ; and, with the same sincerity which had led him to call them to his aid, he sought the means of bringing about an agreement, urging them out of love for him to give their consent.

The Clergy accepted the mediation of the King. The Nobility, distrustful of the minister, gave their consent only under restrictions which amounted to a refusal. The Tiers Etat declined accepting the offer of the King, urging that the modifications attached by the Nobility to their pretended acquiescence rendered it no longer a conciliatory measure. The Clergy felt their weakness ; the Nobility mistook their courage for strength ; the Tiers Etat felt their strength—they made use of it, and a bad use.

On the 10th of June they formed an almost unanimous decree to terminate useless delays, and to pass from expectation to action. They made, however, a last attempt, and urged again the Clergy and Nobility to be present at the scrutiny of the commissions, warning them that otherwise they would proceed in the absence of the privileged classes. They added that the Commons would lay before the King the motives of this great deliberation.

The name of Commons, which the Tiers Etat had assumed, and that of Classes, which they gave to the two first Orders, showed that they no longer chose any distinction of ranks between them, so that the Nobility and Clergy had no longer any middle way to take, or any delay to hope for. They ought either to have united with the Tiers Etat, as they did afterwards, or, after examining the commissions in common, each of the two Orders

ought to have withdrawn to its own side, and have
constituted itself an integral part of the States-General;
they ought themselves to have made the most generous
sacrifices to the public good, to have declared their
readiness to submit to the most exact equality of taxation, to have acknowledged their obligation to secure
the national debt, and to meet the exigencies of the
State; to have accounted personal servitude as abolished,
and allowed the commutation of all rights which were
burdensome to the people. They ought to have improved
the lot of the inferior clergy, to have consecrated by
law the principles of equality, security of person and
property, and religious toleration. They should have
professed an inviolable attachment to the fundamental
principles of the French monarchy; should have laid
at the foot of the throne, and signified to the Tiers
Etat their solemn engagements, and should have demanded upon every other subject the right of separate
deliberation, reserving to the King the inalienable right
of granting or refusing his sanction to the decrees of
the States. At the same time they ought to have protested against every act in which they were supposed
absent; should have declared null all those which should
bind them without the concurrence of their votes. These
resolutions they ought to have published; and if the
behaviour of the Commons allowed it, should have co-
operated with them; or, if the Tiers Etats declined this,
should have retired with the dignity which became men
who, of their own accord, had performed their duty.
Their conduct, when published through the provinces,
would have rendered the ambition of the Tiers Etat
odious—the more so, as courageous truth was not yet
banished from the pulpit, where it might have been
heard. This happy moment was lost.

The Nobility formed themselves, but stood on the
defensive. The Clergy thought they might observe a
pretended neutrality. " They waited," said Tolendal,

"till a conqueror should appear, whom they might make their ally."

Since the decree of the 10th, the Commons had been busily employed in examining their commissions. Having completed this operation, and thinking that the work of national restoration ought to be begun without delay by the deputies who were present, a decree was passed on the 15th of June for pursuing it without interruption, declaring, however, that if the absent deputies should present themselves during the course of the opening session, the assembly would receive them with joy, and, after examining their commissions, would lose no time in admitting them to a share in their labours. Care was taken to add that the national representation should be one and indivisible, and that representatives only, legally elected and duly recognised, should be allowed to concur in expressing the national wish.

The object now was to know what name the assembly should assume. That of National Assembly, the most ambitious of all, was preferred (17th June); and those who were of opinion that the Commons should not usurp the title of Nation, had their names written in a list, which was circulated through Paris— a form of accusation which afterwards gave a formal blow to the freedom of voting.

The second act of the omnipotence which the Commons assumed was to declare null all the contributions which had hitherto existed, and to lay it down as a principle that even former taxes could not have been lawful unless they had received, not merely the tacit, but the formal consent of the nation.

From this moment the ministry ought to have put the King on his guard against this usurpation of power. They should have advised him to dissolve this factious assembly, as exceeding the bounds of their functions and arrogating a power to which they had no title.

But the council, very far from being capable of forming such a resolution, had not even a plan formed for conducting its resistance. I was informed by Malouet, one of the men who had shown most courage, understanding and talents, that he one day asked Necker, in presence of two other ministers, if he had formed any plan for defending the throne against the attacks with which it was threatened; and Necker replied that he had none whatever.

By this time Necker was no longer the minister whom circumstances required. He had engaged the State in difficulties, out of which he had no power to extricate it.

However, he could not conceal from the King that the assembly assumed an exorbitant power; and, with the view of restraining it, on the 20th of the month a royal sitting was proclaimed for the 22nd. Till then the halls were ordered to be shut, and the States to suspend their meetings. This was but a weak mode of preventing the union which was apprehended of a part of the Clergy with the Commons.

The Court and council were full of agitation. The Nobility and the higher Clergy saw their ruin approaching if the King abandoned them, and they demanded his support. It was resolved, therefore, in council, that the King should go in person and point out to the deputies of the people the limits of their power; should engage them to union in consideration of the national safety, and manifest his own beneficent intention of seconding their efforts.

Much prudence was required in composing this declaration. Two opposite dangers were to be shunned: that of yielding to the Commons, and that of revolting them. Necker, to whom this task was entrusted, studied, according to his principles, to temper without weakening the language of authority; to make the King desire nothing which was not just and desirable, and to conciliate what belonged to the majesty of the monarch with what seemed due to the dignity of the national representatives. The discourse drawn out by him was, at first, adopted; but, in a council which was held at Marly, during his absence, some alterations were made which were said to be slight, but which he himself told me were such as to prevent the declaration from having any longer the effect intended.

Whatever the change might have been, which I have not been able to ascertain, it is certain that the speech wanted connection, and was ill-suited to its object.

On the 20th, the Order of the Nobility had obtained an audience from the King, in which their president, the Duke de Luxembourg, had said in their name, " Sire, the deputies of the Order of the Tiers Etat have boldly attempted to centre in themselves the authority of the States-General. Without waiting for the assembly of the other two Orders, and the sanction of Your Majesty, they have thought proper to convert their decrees into laws. They have ordered them to be printed and sent into the provinces; they have declared the contributions as they are now levied, null and illegal. They have agreed to them, in the name of the nation, only provisionally and for a limited period; they have, doubtless, thought they might claim the united rights of the King and the three Orders. We lay before Your Majesty our protest against such pretensions."

The Nobility added the strongest assurances of zeal, of fidelity, of courage, of devotion.

" I know," replied the King, " the rights attached to my birth; I shall find means to defend them—and to maintain, for the interest of all my subjects, the authority with which I am entrusted, and which I will never allow to be encroached upon. I depend upon your zeal for your country, upon your attachment to my person; and I am confident that your fidelity will lead you to adopt those schemes of conciliation with which I am occupied for the happiness of my people."

Both the harangue and the reply supposed measures and resources which ought to have been secured. The Court was too forgetful of the maxim that "authority is undone when it is in danger of showing its weakness."

During the interval that passed previous to the royal sitting, the Commons, having no decent place where they could assemble, took the first that offered. It was a tennis-court, rendered famous by the oath which they took—never to separate, and to assemble wherever circumstances might require till the constitution of the kingdom and the restoration of order should be established upon solid foundations. The other party were far from being on their guard against these acts of vigour. .

The sitting announced for Monday, the 22nd, having been delayed till next day, the assembly removed from the tennis-court to the church of St. Louis, in order, doubtless, that the sacredness of the place might give a character of greater importance to what should be there transacted.

Scarcely had they taken their seats, when the gates of the sanctuary opened, and the archbishops of Bordeaux and Vienne, and the bishops of Chartres and Rhodez, at the head of a hundred and forty-five deputies from the Clergy, came out and advanced into the middle of the assembly. The Commons received them with joy, as victims who were led to them; and the populace, with whom the church was filled, seemed desirous by their applause to blind them completely to the fate which awaited them. The body of the Commons, swelled by this reinforcement, redoubled their assurance and determination for next day's sitting.

Necker declined accompanying the King. Though I cannot approve, I must explain the motive of so strange a conduct. He had openly maintained in the

council that the union of the three chambers into
one was inevitable ; that it could not be delayed without
the greatest danger to the State ; that it was easy to see
how irrevocably determined the Commons were not to
admit of deliberation by Orders, and that the authority
of the King would be uselessly committed by an attempt
to compel them ; that if the same resistance were made
by the two first Orders, the States must either be held
without their concurrence, or must be dissolved ; that
the one alternative would lead to the ruin of the Nobility
and the Clergy, and the other to that of the kingdom ;
that in the exhausted state of every resource, the fatal
moment was approaching in which even the payments
which were most immediately required—those of the
royal treasury, those of the Hôtel de Ville, even the pay
of the troops, the subsistence of Paris—were all about
to fail ; that the kingdom was threatened with famine,
bankruptcy and, perhaps, with civil war, if the States
should dissolve, or should not come to an immediate
agreement ; and, after having struck the King and the
council with these alarming truths, he had made them
adopt a declaration in which he attempted to reconcile
the royal dignity with republican pride.

Now it was here, particularly, that the declaration
had been altered. In its present state it supposed incontestable those principles which were most likely to
be contested ; the King was made to adopt all the wishes
of the Nobility ; he was made to annul or prohibit everything that was contrary to their wishes. This was
supposing him to possess both the actual power and
the firm determination of instantly dissolving the assembly in case of their resisting his authority. Now
the one was in as tottering a condition as the other.
Bankruptcy and civil war were, as it were, two spectres
which struck the King with terror.

Necker having, therefore, learned that his work was
altered, and that the royal authority was set in opposition

to public liberty, thought it proper for him to avoid appearing at this sitting, where his presence would have
led to the belief that he adhered to what was done in
opposition to his advice.   From his conduct, some have
inferred that he wished to gain the favour of the people
for himself alone ; others, that he had given the signal
of rebellion ; and the most moderate, that, solely occupied
with his own reputation, he had sacrificed everything
to private interest.   The declaration was read to the
assembly in the King's presence ; and in it two incoherent characters were easily recognised.   It was divided
into two parts.   In the first, as I have said, the most
absolute power was displayed.   In the other, as a sequel
to these maxims of despotism which had already been
too rigorously applied in the Beds of Justice, came an
affecting statement of the good intentions of the King,
and of the measures which he meant to take for securing
the prosperity of the kingdom.   The King then, after
calling the States-General to join with him in canvassing
the great objects of public advantage, proposed that all
the laws which he should sanction during the present
meeting of the States, should never be changed without
the consent of the united Orders.   With regard to the
public force alone, which had been established for the
protection of public safety both within and without,
he expressly declared his determination to preserve
entire, without the least alteration, the management of
the army, as well as full authority over military arrangements and discipline, such as the French monarchs had
constantly enjoyed.

Had the States chosen to be indebted to the King
for a moderate and limited monarchy, the King was
willing to bestow it.   But they thought it beneath
their dignity to receive it from him ; and whatever the
new constitution might be, which they had not yet
considered, they meant it to be their own work and
not a favour from the King.   The whole attention of

men's minds was, therefore, directed towards that part
of the declaration which reminded them of arbitrary
power. The mild and feeling language which had
been added was considered as a lure to win them into
obedience, and as a vain and feeble palliative of those
acts of despotism which the King came to exercise.

The Commons were particularly wounded with the
following conclusion of the King. When addressing
them he said:

"Gentlemen, you have heard the result of my
disposition and my views. They are in conformity
with the strong desire which I feel of promoting the
public good; and if, in consequence of a fatality which
is far from my thoughts, you should abandon me in
so noble an enterprise, I alone will make my people
happy—I alone will consider myself as their true representative; and knowing, as I do, your instructions—
knowing the perfect harmony which exists between the
general wish of the nation and my beneficent intentions,
I shall feel all the confidence which so singular a harmony ought to inspire, and will advance towards the
desired object with proper courage and firmness. It
is I, from this time, who do everything for the happiness
of my people; and it is, perhaps, rare that the only
ambition of a sovereign should be that of prevailing
upon his subjects to listen and accept his benefits."

This authoritative tone, these words of "sovereign,"
"subjects," "benefits," appeared offensive to republican
ears; and when the King concluded with commanding the
three Orders to withdraw, each into their chamber, the
tacit resolution of the Commons was not to obey. The
good wishes of the King were thus thrown away, and
discord was increased by a sitting which was held with
the view of suppressing it.

At the end of the sitting, the Commons, in a respectful but gloomy silence, allowed the Order of the
Nobility to accompany the King, and remained in that

hall which, from this moment, became their own. In vain did the King send an order to them to leave it. Upon that very spot they determined to adhere to their preceding decrees, and this resolution was formed unanimously. It was at the same time resolved that the persons of the deputies should be inviolable; that none of them, either in the time of the session, or after it, should be prosecuted or arrested by the executive power on account of what he had said or done in the assembly; by this decree the authors and instigators of such deeds were declared infamous, and traitors towards their country. It was added, that during the session the persons of the deputies should be subject neither to criminal nor civil prosecution. The proposal was made by Mirabeau, who was more interested than any other person in raising a barrier between the laws and himself.

A numerous populace, who were sent from Paris to Versailles, had surrounded the hall of the States during the royal sitting. They still surrounded it, when news came that Necker was going to give in his resignation. This report was well founded.

The King, struck with astonishment at not having seen the minister of finance in his train, and still more surprised at not finding him in the palace at his return, had anxiously enquired of Montmorin if Necker meant to leave him; and Montmorin having given him to understand that he believed so, the King desired him to go and say that he wished to speak to him.

It was at seven in the evening, the time when Necker was shut up alone with the King, that the people deluged the courts and interior of the palace, crying out that the King was deceived, and that the voice of the people called for M. Necker.

The conversation of the King with his minister lasted a whole hour. The people waited the issue. At last they saw the King set out for Trianon without saluting him with that cry of " Vive le roi ! " which

he so well merited; and the instant after they saw
Necker come downstairs and get into his carriage.
Then it was that their prayers and blessings were
poured upon him. The minister has been reproached
with having wished to enjoy his triumph, and there
really would have been a degree of insolence had such
been his intention; but though Necker might, through
the galleries, have returned modestly to his own house
without appearing before the people, yet it would be
too rigorous, I think, to make a crime of his not having
paid the King this respectful attention.

Necker, overwhelmed by the gratitude and applause
of the people who attended him home, had so sooner
arrived there than he was visited not only by a deputation of the assembly, but by the whole of that body,
who, thronging around him, besought him, if he regarded his country, if he regarded the King himself
and the safety of the State, not to abandon him. This
was all a stage-trick to throw odium upon the Royalist
party; and the faction were not the less determined
to destroy the minister himself if he should not be devoted to the popular party.

Necker endeavoured to represent to them that,
being left alone, it was no longer in his power to do
any good. "We will assist you," exclaimed Target,
assuming the right of speaking in the name of all, "and
there are no efforts, no sacrifices, which we are not
ready to make for that purpose." "Sir," said Mirabeau, with a deceitful frankness, "I do not love you,
but I bow to virtue." "Remain, M. Necker," exclaimed the crowd; "we beseech you to remain."
The minister, sensibly affected, said, "Speak for me,
M. Target, for I cannot speak myself." Target then
cried, "Gentlemen, I remain: this is the reply of
M. Necker." It was afterwards known how deeply
the King was affected by this scene, and this, indeed,
formed part of the intention of its actors.

There was no hope of breaking the union of the Commons, or of conquering their resistance. Every day there arrived from the different cities of the kingdom congratulations, dictated by themselves, upon their courageous firmness. In these addresses it was said that, if snares were set before the National Assembly, they had only to look behind, where they would see twenty-five millions of Frenchmen, whose eyes were fixed upon their conduct, silently awaiting their own fate and that of their posterity. It was not to be expected that a party who had once declared themselves so strongly would go back one step.

The resolution of the other party was far from being so unanimous, or their resistance so firm. Division, as we have seen, had arisen among the Clergy. The Nobility could not place much greater reliance upon themselves; sixty deputies of that Order had already declared loudly in their chamber against the refusal which had been given to the King's mediation. With regard to the Clergy, on the day after the royal sitting a hundred and sixty parish priests had gone into the common hall. Two days after, two other bishops, those of Orange and of Autun, had followed. On the same day the humble and mild Archbishop of Paris had presented his credentials. Forty-seven of the Nobility, among whom were some men of distinction, had joined the Commons. The rest of the two first Orders could not avoid following this example; and, in the critical situation of affairs, every delay was dangerous. The King, in order to determine them, did what he ought to have done previous to the royal sitting. The letter which he wrote, by saving them the humiliation of yielding to the Commons, gave them an opportunity of acquiring the respectable appearance of acting from love to him and respect for his will. They yielded to him; and that day (the 27th of June) was distinguished by the union of the three Orders in the common hall of the States-General.

16—2

This solemn union was made, at first, in a profound silence; but, on its completion, this respectful silence was suddenly succeeded by an explosion of joy, which was communicated to those without.

The people, who were still capable of mild and worthy sentiments, were informed that their triumph was the King's work. Doubly happy to obtain it and to be indebted for it to him, they thronged towards that palace, to which, some days before, they had gone with such alarm. They made it resound with the sweetest wish of Frenchmen. They asked to see their good King, that they might show how much they loved him, and might make him a witness of the transports which he inspired.

The King appears on the balcony of his apartment, accompanied by the Queen; and both hear their names resound to heaven. Amid their embraces, delicious tears flow, and the Queen, by an emotion with which every heart is affected, strains in her arms the object of their gratitude. Then that populace, which afterwards displayed so much ferocity, but which was still good (I take pleasure in repeating it), seized this instant to reward the Queen for her conjugal affection by maternal happiness. They ask to see her son—they ask to see the Dauphin. This feeble and precious child, carried in his mother's arms, is presented by maternal love to national tenderness: happy in not living long enough to see how this favour was deceitful and changeable.

"After the good King, the good minister!" then exclaimed the multitude; and, by a common impulse, they flew towards the house of Necker, which they again made resound with vows and blessings.

During the night of this great day Versailles was illuminated, and presented everywhere only the image of public felicity.

Nothing could be more pleasing than the spectacle of a nation exalted by generous sentiments. But the enthusiasm of the populace is dangerous, even when it is most laudable; for they know no interval between two extremes, and allow themselves to be carried from one to the other by the passion of the moment. They felt then all the value of liberty. But this new liberty, with which they were in a manner intoxicated, was soon to pervert them, by causing to ferment the elements of every vice.

Already, under the specious name of public good, a spirit of licentiousness, of faction and anarchy, was diffused through the multitude. The independence and the perpetuity of a National Assembly in which the Commons should have the mastery, and, by means of this assembly, the sovereignty of the people concentrated in the will of their representatives under all the characters of the most frightful despotism—a constitution which would convert the kingdom into an armed democracy, under a shade, indeed, of monarchy, but governed in reality by an aristocratical body, periodically elected at the pleasure of the ruling party: such was the project formed by the Republican faction. Now they were well aware that obstacles would be found; and they foresaw that in the attacks which they were either to make or to sustain, there would be need of a people intoxicated with liberty and mad with rage. Then it was that I comprehended what Chamfort had foretold of the system which would be adopted by the factious in order to spread the fury of discord among the lower orders, and to keep them incessantly in convulsive movements of fear or of blind audacity.

In addition to the domestic distress arising from the dearness of bread and the dread of wanting it, and to that uneasiness which naturally arose from the difficulty of bringing in provisions—though this, too, was exaggerated—the people were, besides, inflamed by the blackest allegations of conspiracies said to be formed against them. Terror was struck into them in order to render them terrible, and mistrust became every day more fierce and gloomy.

The robbers known under the name of Marseillais were called to Paris to be the instruments of the Republican faction. These were men habituated to rapine and carnage, thirsting alike for blood and booty, who mingled among the people and inspired them with their own ferocity.

The presence of the tribunals was still a restraint upon them, and rendered their guilt less daring. But this feeble barrier seemed every moment likely to be overleaped, and the crowd of vagabonds who mingled with the leaders of faction, and were ready to serve them, increased every day; the harbours, the quays, were covered; the Hôtel de Ville was invested by them; they surrounded the palace, and seemed to insult the inactivity of justice disarmed—twelve thousand were kept uselessly employed in digging the hill of Montmartre, for which they were paid tenpence a-day. They had been posted as a rear guard, to be brought forward when necessary. At night a misled and threatening multitude assembled at the Palais Royal. Its porticos, its gardens were filled. A hundred groups were formed to listen to calumnious accusations and inflammatory motions. The most furious declaimers were best listened to. Men's minds were fed with a thousand pretended atrocities, which were invented and circulated. There it was that furious declamations were made against the royal authority, which was represented as the cause of the dearness of corn and of the national poverty. There it was that victims, devoted to death, were marked out to the votaries of sedition, intoxicated with foolish hopes or troubled with gloomy fears. No public men, not even the most upright and most respectable, could depend upon being spared. Thence issued in crowds men either themselves terrified, or bribed to sow alarm and sedition throughout Paris.

But, improbable as it may seem, at Versailles itself a class of men who depended upon the Court for their whole rank and fortune, showed themselves most infatuated with Republican maxims.

These men, whilst part of the Clergy were still deliberating upon the union of the Orders, had been seen insulting such of the priests as they had observed to be hostile to this measure, and, urged by false accusations, had attacked the worthy Archbishop of Paris, had thrown stones at him, and had pursued him into his carriage; the French Guards, far from restraining the mutineers, had been observed to encourage them by signs of intelligence; and it was well known that in Paris, these soldiers, caressed in the Palais Royal and treated in the coffee-houses, were accustomed to call themselves the friends of the people. It was natural, therefore, that the King, though he might have no anxiety about himself, should wish the people, both in Paris and Versailles, to be subjected to their accustomed police, to return to order, and peaceably give themselves up to their labours.

The King might conceive that a faction constantly present and threatening, would not allow the National Assembly to carry on their deliberations with that degree of freedom which was indispensable; that personal security was the foundation of this liberty; that the security ought to be equally inviolable to all, and that the sovereign ought to be its guardian. He might think that the hall of assembly, open like a theatre, ought not to be a focus of sedition. It appeared, therefore, at once just and wise to employ a respectful guard in protecting the freedom of opinion and personal security. At the same time, he ordered the soldiers of the French Guards, who were then wandering throughout Paris, to be again subjected to discipline, and punished if they deviated from it.

But neither the people nor their movers would submit to any restraint. The guard which surrounded the hall was forced, and the assembly sent a deputation to

the King, declaring that the States, assembled free, could
not act freely in the midst of the guards by which they
were surrounded.   The guard was taken off, and it
became necessary to leave the hall open to the concourse
of the public.

The King was sensible that the disorder would continue to increase if the people were left exempt from all
apprehensions; that it would then be no longer possible
to appease them unless by yielding; that, while he used
indulgence towards the votaries of faction, he ought, at
least, to show them that it was in his power to be
rigorous; and that, as he was not sure of being obeyed
by the French Guards, it was time to bring forward
some troops on which he could depend.   He sent for
them accordingly, but in a very small number at first,
and most sincerely with the sole intention of protecting
public order and the tranquility of the citizens.   Nobody
doubted this: but that very tranquility and order would
give a mortal blow to the revolution which they aimed
at producing.

The King had been heard replying to the Nobility,
that he knew the rights attached to his birth and how
to maintain them.   He had said to the States-General
that none of their plans, none of their deliberations,
could have the authority of a law without his special
approbation, and that all the Orders of the State might
trust to his impartial equity.   Now, before the King
brought forward this system of authority and of protecting power, in opposition to a popular faction which
regarded itself as the sole and supreme legislative body,
and as the depository of the national will—before holding this language he ought to have had arms in his
hands; and it was necessary that he should have had it
in his power, if circumstances should require it, to act
as he had spoken—as a good King, but as a real monarch.   This was precisely what the factious and revolutionary party would not endure.   Their strength resided

in that mass of people who blindly follow those that declare in their favour; and if Versailles were guarded, if Paris were calm, or kept in order by troops of the line, the votaries of faction would be left without resource and without hope.

They did not yet excite the people to crimes, nor were they insensible of the dangers of anarchy. But it was necessary to intimidate the King and the party of good men, though it should cost at first some mischief, and even some innocent blood; Republican freedom was of such high value that, to obtain it, small sacrifices might be allowed. Such were the politics and morals of the greater number, and these were the most moderate; others thought everything lawful which could be of service to them; and Mirabeau, at their head, loudly professed, under the title of modern virtue, a contempt for the most sacred rights and duties.

It was necessary, they said, to nourish the flame of patriotism; and the liberty which, in order to attain it, was granted to the Press, gave rise every day to calumnious libels, which devoted to public hatred and vengeance everyone who dared to dispute the power of universal oppression which the people assumed. If a nobleman defended, with any degree of warmth, the cause of the Nobles; if a Churchman, with any degree of eloquence, pleaded the cause of the Clergy, they were instantly accused in these writings as traitors to their country. Even in the Tiers Etat, a moderate opinion was accounted meanness, and exposed its author to suspicion. Thus, while the Commons surrounded the two first Orders with restraint and violence, they pretended to be repelling restraint and violence from themselves. Everything which could rouse and enrage the people was allowed and provoked; everything which could restrain or suppress their movements gave birth to the warmest remonstrances, even in the States. The name of liberty was given to the right of extinguishing all liberty. The meaning of these remonstrances was not doubtful. " We wish, by means of the people, to have everything in our power, and to allow nothing to be done without us."

But when the King assembled the States-General, did he mean to form a democracy, and to bestow on the Commons the threatening despotism which they pretended to exercise ? " What, sire," said the oppressed Orders to him, " what has become of that safety which you guaranteed to us ? What has become of that equality which the Commons demanded? Can a shadow of it be retained by two Orders who would hear themselves denounced and devoted to popular fury if they did not consent without remonstrance to whatever the Tiers Etat should desire ? " Doubtless this hall of the National Assembly ought not to have been surrounded by a military guard. But neither ought it to have been surrounded by bands of ruffians ready to stone us. That peaceful guard, which was said to be so injurious to the assembly of the States, was placed there only to secure the tranquility of debate and the freedom of voting. Did they wish all restraint to be banished ? then, at the same time that the troops were removed they should have removed also that populace who came into the very assembly encouraging their partisans, marking out their victims, and rendering the formidable trial of the *appel nominal* terrible to the weak.

The orators of the people extolled their goodness, their natural justice ; and this praise was undoubtedly due to a select class of citizens. But, looking beneath this class, did they not see those robbers who, in Paris, had not long ago plundered the house of a peaceful and good citizen ? those who spread calumny and revolt through the royal palace ? those who, at Versailles, had attempted to stone a charitable and pious archbishop ? those who rescued from punishment a son, the murderer of his father ? those who afterwards committed so many

atrocities in Paris, at the gates of the Hôtel de Ville, and
even in the royal palace at Versailles ? and those who
have applauded after exciting them, and have rejoiced
when they saw the heads of citizens, inhumanly massacred, carried about at the end of pikes ?

Then, said the two Orders who called out for the
common security, then, indeed, it was a cruel mockery
thus to confound the people who ought to be restrained
with those who ought to be protected. By a monstrous
abuse of words, the populace were represented as the
people, and this people as the nation, who were declared
to be sovereign.

At Paris the Commons demanded a guard of citizens.
But, till it was organised, what could be alarming in the
small number of regular troops which the King had sent
for ? Since their arrival everything was tranquil. But
this military police was not relished by the Commons.
Their emissaries never ceased to agitate the Palais Royal,
the infamous haunt of guilt—they invited thither the
guards, and kept them all night. The Duke de Chatelet,
their colonel, could not overlook this ; he caused two of
these vagabond soldiers to be taken up at an undue hour,
and they were conducted to the prison of the Abbaye.
This was the signal of an insurrection. The most common act of military authority was treated as an offence
against liberty ; and, in less than an hour, the prison of
the two soldiers, who were called friends of the people,
was besieged by twenty thousand men. The jailers
having attempted to resist, they took hatchets and levers,
broke open the doors, and allowed all the prisoners, even
the criminals, to escape during the night.

Next day, at the opening of the National Assembly,
the deputies of this mutinous crowd arrived at Versailles.
In their address, which was put into the hands of the
president, it was said that these two unhappy victims
of despotism had been delivered from their chains ; that
they had been led back amid the sound of acclamation

to the Palais Royal, where they were under the guard
of the people, who had become responsible for them.
" We expect your reply," said they, " to restore
tranquility to our fellow - citizens and liberty to our
brethren."

The reply of the president was, that the assembly,
while they besought the King to pardon the offenders,
would set an example of the respect due to the royal
authority, and that they besought the inhabitants of
Paris immediately to return to order. This reply,
though feeble, was at least sincere, and conformable
to the wish of the Commons ; for the assembly did
not know that the populace were set in motion by the
most distinguished and infamous ruffians, and that this
fury, with which they were inspired, was for the purpose
of making the Court dread a revolt. The assembly did
not know the springs by which they themselves were
moved : the people were raised in their name, and yet
it was the people who ruled over them. Such was the
mechanism of the revolution.

The King was therefore besought, in the name of
the assembly, to have the goodness to employ, for the
restoration of order, those infallible means of clemency
and kindness which were so natural to his heart. He
consented without difficulty ; but, before indulging in
the exercise of mercy, he wished order to be re-estab-
lished, which it was not in any respect. The people
neither re-committed the two soldiers to their prison,
nor discontinued their own nocturnal assemblages, but,
on the contrary, redoubled their tumult and violence,
demanded the promise of the King in a tone which
would brook no delay, and discipline and the royal
authority were under the necessity of bending to their
will.

Then it was that the resolutions of the council
seemed to assume some degree of energy ; but weakness never shakes off its character but by halves, and

after a trembling and fruitless effort, becomes more timid than ever.

The adventure of the guard-soldiers, the spirit of insubordination with which the populace inspired them, the daring tone which this populace had assumed, their manner of commanding while they seemed to entreat, their fiery impatience to obtain what they asked, and the merit which they claimed for becoming quiet after they had been obeyed—in short, that character of imperious and threatening liberty which they constantly displayed, had been eagerly laid hold of in the council to make the King understand that the greatest of evils, both for the State and for himself, would be to allow the authority which was in his hands to be despised, which would infallibly be the case if it was seen without arms ; that the appearance of weakness had already emboldened them to attack it, and that a formidable force alone could secure for it respect and obedience ; that the multitude must either tremble themselves, or make others tremble ; that it was not by laws alone that States, especially such vast States, were governed ; that justice had need of the sword and the buckler ; that wisdom and equity consisted in knowing how to use force without ever abusing it ; that it was thus good kings were distinguished from the weak or tyrannical. It were, doubtless, to be wished that the meeting of the States could have passed in perfect security, without being surrounded by any military retinue. It was so in countries where the people chose to rely upon the wisdom and fidelity of their representatives ; it would be the same in France after order and tranquility were reestablished ; but so long as the populace—and the most seditious and turbulent of the populace—should come and interrupt the deliberations of the States-General with insults and threats, the public force had a right to arm in order to restrain them.

" They suppose, sire," added those who demanded

the use of coercive authority, " they suppose it will be as easy to quiet the lower orders as it is to rouse them; after they have made them subservient to the design of a general subversion of the kingdom, they will wish again to confine the tiger in his cage, and to make him forget how terrible he can be when he chooses; but it will be too late—the wild beast will have learned his strength, and the weakness of his chains. Above all, how dreadful will he be if he has tasted blood! He will long, perhaps, make those tremble who have dared to unchain him. Let this people, then, be informed that justice is still in your hands, and that it is still to be feared.

" From the beginning of your reign, sire, you have been made to reduce and to weaken your military establishment; and, flattering yourself that you had to reign only over a virtuous and faithful people, in the uprightness of your heart you consented to this fatal reduction. But the discipline and obedience of your armies are not destroyed, and you have still sufficient forces remaining to oppose the daring attempts of the votaries of faction. To use these forces against the laws would be despotism; but when employed in maintaining order and law, they are the proper retinue of lawful authority, the safeguard of the State and the support of royalty.

" If, sire, all the members of the National Assembly were equally attached as you to the public good, they would unite in demanding that around the sanctuary of legislation there should be placed an impenetrable, and even an inaccessible barrier, for the troops on one side, and for the people on the other. Then all would be on an equal footing. But, no; they wish the troops to be removed, only that full license and impunity may be allowed to the populace. It is feared that they may be cooled or intimidated; the votaries of faction wish them to dare everything, and to have nothing to fear; through them they wish to reign. Have we not seen how, from the centre to the extremities of the kingdom, this name of liberty, which with the populace means only licen-

tiousness, has resounded like a signal of insurrection and
anarchy ?   The police among the populace, discipline in
the armies, order and law in every department, have been
branded as remnants of slavery.   Independence, and
contempt for every kind of authority, appear on the
very face of the kingdom ; and upon the ruins of the
monarchy, with its rubbish, they boast of erecting a
democratical empire.   A vile collection of vagabonds,
without morals, profession, or designation of any kind,
are called the sovereign people.   But the nation desires
and demands that the constitution of the kingdom should
be established upon a firm foundation, and the object is
to render it at once firmer and more regular.   It is
in this employment, sire, that the States are bound
to unite with you.   By the ancient and venerable constitution of our monarchy, you are King ; the supreme
authority, the executive power, has been placed in your
hands ; your ancestors, on whom the nation bestowed it,
have transmitted it to you as an inheritance.   The nation
neither wishes, nor intends, to depose its King.   And
what would a monarch be, if he were not the protector
of the rights and liberties of all.

"Be the protector, sire, of all Orders, and allow none
to be oppressed.   Protect the States themselves, and
especially protect those honest citizens, those peaceful
labourers in the city and country, who are threatened at
their firesides by an idle and vagrant populace, whom,
they dread with reason, it will soon be too late to place
under the restraint of laws.   No, sire, we speak to you
no longer in the name of the Clergy and Nobility, but in
the name of that virtuous people whose father you are ;
we beseech you not to abandon them to the most cruel
of tyrannies—to that of the populace and their perfidious
instigators."

The King was thus persuaded that, by displaying
a military power before the eyes of the people, he would
restrain one force by another, and would leave public
liberty between them, protected and free from danger.

BOOK XVI

THE King, therefore, ordered troops to advance; but those who prompted him to this vigorous resolution ought to have foreseen its consequences, to have calculated their own strength, and the resistance they would meet with, and to have determined previously the position they should assume upon every event. Nothing was calculated, nothing was provided for; no means were even taken to secure the troops from being corrupted by the Parisian populace. No arrangement was made to shelter the King and royal family from insult in case of revolt; and in the suburbs of Paris the only commanding position, the Bastille, was neither supplied with a sufficient garrison, nor with provisions to support the few soldiers whom it contained. Lastly, the very subsistence of the troops who were assembled, was so completely neglected, that their bread was made only of spoiled corn, while the women of the populace came and offered them some that was excellent, with plenty of wine and butchers' meat, not to mention their other means of corruption.

While the Court and council were sunk in this kind of stupor, the opposite party held a steady, systematic, and progressive conduct, advancing from post to post towards dominion, without ever losing a moment, or falling back one step. Being determined, therefore, that they would suffer no assemblage of troops to be formed, either around Versailles or Paris, they prepared an address to the King on the 8th of July, 1789. It was the work of Mirabeau, the leading orator of the Commons,

a man endowed by Nature with all the talents of a tri-
bune of the people; of an ardent character, but as pliant
in his conduct as he was fiery in his passions; skilful in
foreseeing the turns of public opinion, and, that he might
appear to conduct, careful to anticipate it. He was
cowardly, but headstrong, with all the intrepidity of
impudence. He was dissolute to the greatest degree,
and boasted of being so; from his youth he had been
dishonoured by the most shameful vices, but he set no
value upon honour. He thought himself assured that
a dangerous man could not be despised, even though
he should have rendered himself contemptible, and
was resolved to dispense with the esteem attached to
moral character, provided he obtained that which is
extorted by great talents when they become formidable.

The following is the address which he proposed to
send to the King—a masterpiece of artful and treacherous
eloquence, which, after being applauded, as might naturally be expected, was adopted with acclamation on the
9th of July:

"Sire, you have invited the National Assembly to
express to you their confidence; this was anticipating
the dearest of their wishes. We are now to declare to
Your Majesty the deep alarm which has seized us.
Were we aimed at, had we the weakness to fear for
ourselves, your goodness would still deign to assure us
of safety; and, even while you blamed the doubt we
had expressed of your intentions, you would remove
the cause, you would leave us in no uncertainty relative
to the situation of the National Assembly.

"But, sire, we do not implore your protection; this
would be offending your justice. We have conceived
apprehensions, which we will venture to say are founded
upon the purest patriotism, upon the interest of our
constituents, upon the public tranquility, upon the
happiness of that beloved monarch who, while he
smooths to us the path of happiness, fully deserves

that he should meet with no obstacle in his own."
(Detestable hypocrite.)

"The emotions of your heart, sire, are the true
safety of Frenchmen. When troops advance from all
quarters, when camps are formed around us, when the
capital is invested, we ask with astonishment, 'Has the
King doubted the fidelity of his people? Could he have
doubted it, would he not have poured his paternal
sorrows into our bosom? What is the meaning of these
threatening appearances? Where are the enemies of
the State and of the King, who are to be subdued?
Where are the conspirators who must be reduced to
obedience?' The unanimous reply of the capital, and
throughout the whole extent of the kingdom is: 'We
love our King; we bless heaven for having bestowed his
love upon us.'

"Sire, Your Majesty's regard for the good of your
people can be surprised only under the pretence of public
advantage. If those who gave our King this advice had
so much confidence in their own principles as to state
them before us, that moment would lead to the noblest
triumph of truth.

"The State has nothing to fear, except the bad
principles which dare to beset the throne itself, and do
not respect the crown of the most pure and virtuous of
princes. And what method do they take, sire, to make
you doubt the attachment and love of your subjects?

"Have you lavished their blood? Are you cruel—
implacable? Have you abused justice? Do the people
impute their misfortunes to you? Do they name you as
the author of their calamities? Was it possible for our
enemies to say that the people are impatient under your
yoke? No, no; they have not done so. Their calumny,
at least, is not absurd; they seek to throw a shade of
probability over its atrocities.

"Your Majesty has had a late opportunity of seeing
all the power which you possess over your people. Sub-

ordination has been established in the disturbed capital; the prisoners who were set at liberty by the people have voluntarily resumed their chains; and public order, which, if force had been employed, might perhaps have cost torrents of blood, has been restored by a word of your mouth. But this word was a word of peace; it was the expression of your heart, and your subjects place their glory in never resisting it. How noble is it to exercise this empire! It is the empire of Louis IX., of Louis XII. and of Henry IV., and the only one which is worthy of you. We should deceive you, sire, if, forced by circumstances, we did not add that this is the only empire which, in France, it is now possible to exercise. France will not suffer the best of Kings to be abused and led astray by sinister paths from the noble plan which he himself has traced. You call upon us to unite with you in fixing the constitution, and in effecting the regeneration of the kingdom. The National Assembly has solemnly declared that your wishes shall be fulfilled, that your promises shall not be in vain, that snares, difficulties and terror shall not retard their progress, nor damp their courage.

" 'Where, then, is the danger of troops?' will our enemies affect to say; 'and what is the meaning of their complaints, since nothing can discourage them?' The danger, sire, is urgent and universal; it is beyond all the calculations of human prudence.

" The danger is for the inhabitants of the provinces; if they once think our liberty in danger, we no longer know of any tie which can bind them. Distance of itself exaggerates everything, increases and rouses men's anxiety. The danger is for the capital. How will the people, sunk in indigence, and tormented with the most cruel anguish—how will they see the remnant of their subsistence disputed by a crowd of threatening soldiers? The presence of the troops will lead to riot, will produce a universal fermentation; and the first act of violence

exercised under pretence of maintaining the police, may
lead to a horrible train of misfortunes.

" The danger is for the troops.   French soldiers,
when they approach the centre of discussions, when they
share in the passions and in the interests of the people,
may forget the engagement which has made them soldiers,
and remember only that Nature has made them men.

" Danger, sire, threatens those employments which
are our first duty, and which will never be fully or permanently successful, unless in so far as the people shall consider them as entirely free.   There is, besides, a contagion
in all passionate emotions.   We are but men ; a distrust
of ourselves, a dread of appearing weak, may carry us
beyond our aim.   We shall be beset, besides, by violent
and unguarded counsels ; and calm reason, tranquil wisdom, do not deliver their oracles in the midst of tumult,
of disorder, and of faction.   The danger, sire, is still more
terrible ; and you may judge of its extent by the alarms
which bring us into your presence.   Great revolutions
have arisen from causes much less striking.   More than
one enterprise, fatal to the nations, has been announced
in a manner less threatening and less formidable.

" Do not believe those who speak to you with levity
of the nation, and who represent it only according to
their own particular views ; sometimes insolent, rebellious and seditious ; sometimes submissive, obedient
to the yoke, and ready to bend their neck in order to
receive it.   These two representations are equally false.
We are always ready to obey you, sire, because you
command in the name of the laws ; our fidelity is as
unbounded as it is unquestioned.   But we are prepared
to resist all the arbitrary commands of those who abuse
your name, because they are the enemies of the laws ;
our fidelity itself prescribes this resistance, and we shall
always be proud of deserving the reproaches which are
drawn upon us by our firmness.

" Sire, we beseech you, in the name of your coun-

try, in the name of your happiness and of your glory,
dismiss your soldiers to the quarters whence your
counsellors have drawn them ; dismiss this artillery,
which is destined to cover your frontiers ; dismiss, in
particular, foreign troops, these allies of the nation
whom we pay to defend us, and not to trouble our
domestic peace ; Your Majesty has no need of them.
And why should a King, adored by twenty millions of
Frenchmen—why should he, at great expense, surround
his throne with some thousands of strangers ? Sire, surrounded by your children, let their love be your guard.
The deputies of the nation are called upon to join with
you in consecrating the distinguishing privileges of
royalty, and in placing them upon the immovable basis
of the liberty of the people. But when they fulfil their
duty, when they yield to their judgment and their feelings, would you expose them to the suspicion of having
yielded only to fear ? Alas ! the only pure, the only immovable authority is that which is yielded to you by all
hearts ; it is the just return for your benefits, and the
immortal inheritance of the princes whose model you
are."

This insolently flattering harangue ; this eloquently
turned threat of a general insurrection, if the King, with
a view to the security of good men, and the terror of bad,
should keep a part of his armies with himself ; if he
should not give up his capital city to every excess of
robbery and licentiousness, and the National Assembly
to the insults and threats of an assembled mob ; this
affectation of including mutineers and revolted vagrants
in the praises of a virtuous people ; the arrogant warning
that it was incumbent on the King to yield, and the
formal declaration that this was the only empire which it
would be possible for him henceforth to exercise, did not
produce the expected effect upon the King's mind. Amid
these respectful threats and hypocritical alarms, he saw
too well that the time was come when he must either

abandon or maintain his lawful authority ; that they were exhorting him to allow himself to be disarmed, and to have ʼhis hands tied : he saw, in particular, that by slightly alluding to his good intentions, they avoided every mention of the facts which rendered the precautions he had taken just and necessary. It became requisite, therefore, to explain himself ; and he replied to this artificial language by reasons full of force and candour.

" No one," said he to the deputies, " is ignorant of the disorders and scandalous scenes which have been repeatedly acted at Paris and Versailles, under my eyes, and under those of the States-General. It is necessary for me to make use of those means which are in my power, to restore and to maintain order in the capital and in its neighbourhood. One of my principal duties is to watch over the public safety. This is the motive which has led me to assemble troops around Paris. You may assure the States-General that they are destined only to suppress, or rather to prevent such disorders, to maintain the exercise of the laws, to secure, and even to protect, that liberty which ought to reign in your deliberations. From them every kind of restraint, as well as of tumult and violence, ought to be removed. None but ill-designing people could have led my subjects into error respecting the true motives of the precautions which I take. I have constantly sought to do everything which could tend to their happiness, and I have always had reason to be assured of their love and fidelity.

" If, however, the necessary presence of troops in the neighbourhood of Paris should still give umbrage, I should be disposed, upon the demand of the assembly, to transfer the States-General to Noyon, or to Soissons, and I would repair to Compiègne."

He was very sure that they would not demand this. Nothing was more contrary to the plan which they had

formed, than to separate from the Parisian populace. It
was therefore more than useless to express this intention;
and if, in consequence of a new tumult, the King found
such a translation necessary, why did he not command
it ? Why did he not go to Compiègne with his household
and a respectable guard, declaring null, and contrary to
the freedom of voting, every deliberation which should
be formed amid the troubles with which Paris and Versailles were agitated.

The popular party took care not to leave their post.
They had need of being supported by the populace; it
was by agitating them that they rendered themselves
powerful and formidable. Accordingly they replied,
by the mouth of Mirabeau, that it was the troops who
ought to remove from the assembly, not the assembly
from the troops. "We petitioned," said they, "that the
army, not that we ourselves, should be translated."

From that time, at least, it was quite evident that
the Commons wished to act by means of the people;
and in that contest on which the two authorities were
about to enter, they wished to retain all their own
strength and to leave none to the King.

It was just, however, that the King should retain,
at least, a power of resistance. In the most limited
monarchies the King has the right of the veto; and
none had ever doubted the necessity of the royal sanction in order to bestow the form and the force of laws
on the decrees of the popular representatives. The
King, in fact, as being entrusted with the executive
power, had a right to examine laws the execution of
which he was to enforce; and in his character of first
national representative, he was constituted the super-
intendent of the rest. In the tumult and shock of
opposing passions and interests which might divide a
political assembly, it was often to be feared that a
tumultuous discussion might not lead to the wisest and
most useful resolution. Decrees might often pass which

were contrary to the public good.   A single voice above
numerical equality might convert an unjust and violent
decree into a law.   Every time that passionate eloquence
and sound reason should have to contend with each
other, there was little security for the most just and the
best side of the question.   The King, therefore, was
necessary for moderating and regulating the legislation;
the fulness of a legislative power ought to reside neither
in his will alone nor in that of the popular representatives, but in the union of these two wills; and the consent of the one to the resolutions of the other composed
this royal sanction.

Now, if the monarch was not allowed this right
of examining and sanctioning the laws, of giving his
consent, or opposing his veto; if he saw himself deprived
of his lawful authority; if he saw his throne shaken, his
crown degraded, the sceptre of his fathers about to be
broken in his hands, would it not be necessary that he
should arm to defend them ?   Would it not be just, even
in the eyes of the nation, that he should teach the Commons to keep within the bounds which were marked out
to them by their own deeds ?

These questions agitated in council struck the ministers with terror.

"Every act of rigour," said they, "would be a step
equally fatal, whether it was necessary to support or
abandon it ; it would be a hostility contrary to the sentiments of the King, capable of kindling the flames of civil
war between himself and his people.   If it succeeded it
would render him odious ; if it failed it would render him
contemptible."

Placed, themselves, in a strait between two rocks, in
which either the royal authority, or what was called public liberty, must perish, and with no credit or influence
sufficient to save both, they used with the King every
means of discussion which was afforded by his esteem and
their own zeal ; they showed him nothing but imprudence

and danger in forming this assemblage of discontented
and corruptible troops of whom he thought himself secure.
But, however firm might be their obedience, who could
be assured that their approach would be sufficient to
restore order and tranquility? And if they should miss
their aim of intimidating the people; if, instead of restraining them, they should encourage them still more,
what could be done to reduce—what to appease them?
They saw at the head of the popular party men of a perverse disposition; they saw also hypocrites endowed with
profound dissimulation; but they still judged well of the
national character; they numbered a great many virtuous
men among the Commons; and the example of the King,
his moderation, his frankness, his generous kindness,
might give prevalence to sentiments suited to his own.
Their hope was the same as that of Lally-Tolendal.
When talking to the Nobility of his district, he said to
them, " Noble citizens, those men deceive you who say
that the Tiers Etat have demanded justice only that
they might be unjust, and have wished to free themselves from oppression only that they might become
oppressors." This worthy young man was not long in
owning that he himself was deceived. But he sincerely hoped this; and Necker, Montmorin, La Luzerne
and Saint-Priest hoped it as well as he. Thus, faithful
alike to the State and to the King, they thought conciliatory measures alone practicable; for those of corruption were not to their taste, and the King would
have rejected them.

It may be conceived how great the perplexity of this
Prince must have been. But everything warned him that
it was time to act with firmness, and for this new line of
conduct new ministers were required. The dismissal of
those now in power was determined upon, on the 11th
of July.

On the morning of the 12th the intelligence was
known at Paris; but it was not divulged till the even-

ing, at the hour of the theatre. A gloomy indignation
took possession of every mind. It was no longer doubted
that a determination had been formed at Court, without
the King's knowledge, to act with open force, and that
they were determined violently to drag him into this
fatal design, by removing wise and moderate men from
his councils. The dismissal of Necker, in particular,
in the present critical state of the kingdom seemed to
be a proof that they were determined to ruin and starve
Paris. At every theatre the play was instantly interrupted. Men came in with a distracted air, and called
out to the actors, " Stop! withdraw! the kingdom is in
mourning. Paris is threatened—our enemies prevail.
Necker is no longer in power. He is dismissed—he is
gone, and all the ministers who loved the people are
dismissed along with him."

A sudden fear is spread through the halls, the actors
disappear, the audience withdraw in consternation ; and
already a resolution is formed throughout the whole city
of demanding that Necker, and all the good ministers who
think with him, shall be restored to the State.

In all the places where the people are accustomed to
assemble on holidays the fermentation was excessive.
The Palais Royal was filled with a multitude agitated
like the waves of the sea in a storm. First a long dismal
murmur, and then a more formidable sound was heard.
The populace put on the green cockade—leaves of trees
served their purpose ; and, having taken out of a shop
the busts in wax of Necker and the Duke of Orleans,
they carried them through Paris as a signal of insurrection.

Another mob collected in the square of Louis XV.,
and the tumult continued to increase. Some troops were
brought forward in order to disperse it. Their commandant, the Baron de Bezenval, had gone thither with
a grenadier company of the Swiss Guards. The Prince
de Lambesc came and joined him at the head of fifty

dragoons of the Royal German Regiment. The presence
of the troops completed the irritation of the populace.
They began to insult them. Their clamours were neglected ; but the dragoons being assaulted with stones,
which wounded some of them, lost patience, and Bezenval
ordered the Prince de Lambesc to make a movement
which would oblige the people to fall back into the
Tuileries. This movement was made with so much
moderation that not one of the people was overturned or
bruised. It was not till the dragoons were retreating
that the Prince, with his own hand, slightly wounded a
madman who was obstinately shutting against him the
Pont-Tournant.

Presently a report was spread through Paris of a
massacre of the citizens in the garden of the Tuileries,
into which, they said, the dragoons of Lambesc had
rushed on horseback, sword in hand, with the colonel at
their head, slaying the old men, trampling upon the
children, overthrowing the women with child, or making
them miscarry through fear. At the same time, upon a
false report that their regiment was insulted, the grena-
diers of the French Guards forced the Duke de Chatelet
their colonel, to allow them to leave the garden of the
Hôtel de Richelieu, where he kept them confined. From
that time the regiment of Guards was altogether devoted
to the people ; and this was what the seditious most
ardently desired.

Thus Paris, left without tribunals, guard or police,
to the mercy of a hundred thousand men, wandering
at midnight, and most of them wanting bread, seemed
to be on the point of being besieged without and plundered within. Twenty thousand troops were stationed
round its walls, at St. Denis, at Courbevoye, at Char-
enton, at Sèves, at La Muette, in the Champ du Mars;
and whilst they should blockade and cut off its provisions,
it was on the point of being the prey of a starving
people. Such was the terrible image which, on the

night between the 12th and 13th of July, was present to every mind.

But the insurgents themselves, struck with the common terror, made no plunder; they opened no shops but those of the armourers, and they carried off nothing but arms.

As soon as day appeared, the city was found full of a distracted populace, who, striking at every door, demanded, with loud cries, "Arms and bread!" Thinking that there was a magazine of muskets and swords in the apartments below the town hall, they went there with the view of procuring admittance. I stop here to explain who were the persons that at this moment occupied the Hôtel de Ville, and by what kind of tribunal its police was enforced.

On the 10th of May, after the elections of the Commons were finished, Target, the president of the assembly of the electors, persuaded them to hold a permanent sitting during the assemblage of the States-General. The resolution was formed with the full consent of the popular faction. Accordingly, at the end of June, after the royal sitting, when the electors found their hall at the archbishop's shut, they caused the Hôtel de Ville to be opened, and there stationed themselves as the agents of the National Assembly with the people of Paris.

I must bear them this testimony that, being invested with the care of public affairs in difficult and dangerous circumstances, they discharged their functions as became brave and worthy citizens.

To this assembly, then, the people, on the 13th of July, applied for arms, of which, they said, there was a collection in the cellars of the Hôtel de Ville. But as no such magazine was in existence, it was in vain that the people forced open the doors, the muskets belonging to the guards were alone found, and these were carried off.

Meanwhile, upon the sound of the alarm-bell, which was rung in every church, the districts assembled to consider the means of providing for the security of the city, both within and without; for there was an equally urgent necessity to defend it from the insurgents of which it was full, as from the troops by which it was surrounded. From that moment the citizens formed bands of volunteers, who voluntarily drew themselves up in the squares and public gardens. But arms were wanting; the people demanded them constantly at the Hôtel de Ville. The mayor was sent for, who was the unfortunate Flesselles; he makes his way through the crowd; he calls himself the father of the people, and he is applauded in that very place over which, next day, his bleeding body was dragged.

The electors name a permanent committee at the town hall, to which the people, tormented with fear, might have access day and night. Flesselles, who was at the head of the committee, imprudently announces that he expects immediately ten thousand muskets from Charleville, and thirty thousand soon after. Nay, it is said he carried his fatal rashness so far as to sport with the most impatient by sending them to different places where he made them believe they would find arms. They ran to these places, found they were deceived, and on their return publicly denounced him to the people as an impostor who at once betrayed and insulted them.

The committee of the electors, in order to quiet the apprehensions of the people, determined that a Parisian army should be immediately formed to the number of forty-eight thousand men. All the districts came that very day and offered to enlist in it. The green livery was thrown aside, and its place supplied by red and blue. (Green was the colour of a prince who was not a Republican.)

Meanwhile, the people had gone to the *garde-meuble*, and had carried off those precious arms that were kept there as curiosities, either for the beauty of the workmanship, or out of respect for their antiquity and for

the heroes whose glory they recalled.   The sword of
Henry IV. was the spoil of a vagabond !

This small number of arms, however, was a feeble
resource for so many thousands of men.   They returned
furiously to demand them from the town hall, declaring
that it contained some, and accusing the electors of acting
in concert with the enemies of the people, in order to
leave Paris defenceless.   Urged by these reproaches,
which were accompanied with threats, the committee gave
authority to all the districts to make pikes, and other
arms of that kind, with which the people were satisfied.

But a better expedient, to which the districts themselves had recourse, was to send that evening to *les Invalides*, and summon the governor, Sombreuil, to give up
to them the arms which they knew to be there deposited.
The commander-in-chief of the troops, who had a camp
in the neighbourhood, and to whom Sombreuil desired
them to apply, asked time to send to Versailles, in order to
ask the King's permission ; and this time was granted him.

The terror of the following night assumed a more
solemn and mournful appearance ; the gates of the city
were shut and guarded ; patrols, already formed, kept the
vagabonds in awe.   Fires kindled in the streets made the
horror more visible, struck terror into guilt, and showed
everywhere bands of the populace wandering like spectres.
This vast and dismal silence was interrupted only by the
stifled and terrible voices of those men who cried from
door to door, " Arms and bread ! "

In the suburb of St. Laurent, the house of the monks
of St. Lazare was set fire to and plundered.   They expected to find a magazine of corn there.

Meanwhile, the Palais Royal was full of those mer-
cenaries who were employed in fanning the flame of
sedition ; and the night was spent in accusations and
in atrocious proposals, not only against Flesselles, but
against the committee of electors, who were denounced
as traitors to their country.

The evening before, five thousand pounds of powder which were being carried out of Paris, had been seized at the gates and deposited in the Hôtel de Ville, beneath the apartment of the electors. At midnight the small number of superintendents who had remained in the hall were informed that fifteen thousand men, the trusty militia of the mutineers in the Palais Royal, were coming with a resolution of forcing the Hôtel de Ville. Among the superintendents was a citizen, Le Grand de Saint-Rene, a man of a weak and sickly temperament, but of firm and steady courage. " Let them come and attack us," said he, " we will be blown up together." Immediately he ordered the guards of the Hôtel to bring six barrels of powder into the neighbouring apartment. His resolution became known. The first barrel that was brought made the most courageous turn pale, and the people withdrew. The Hôtel de Ville was thus preserved by a single man. The kingdom would, in like manner, have been saved if the King had had such men at the head of his councils and his armies. But he himself exhorted them to spare the people, and never could consent to any act of rigour against them—a virtuous weakness which made his head fall under the axe of the executioner.

During this fearful night the citizens shut themselves up, each trembling for himself and for his family. But, on the morning of the 14th, these personal fears yielding to the public alarm, the whole city was completely united. Paris had an army ; this army, hastily and spontaneously assembled, was as yet ill-acquainted with the rules of discipline, but public spirit supplied its place. It alone, like an invisible power, arranged everything. What gave such a powerful influence to public spirit was the address which had been employed in captivating public opinion. The best citizens, considering the troops who came to protect Paris only as enemies who were introducing fire and sword within its walls, all

thought that they were fighting for their firesides, for
their wives and children.   Necessity, danger, the care of
defence and of common safety, the determination to
perish, or to save what was dearest to them in the world,
alone took possession of every mind.   Hence that surprising union of will and courage by which an immense
and violently-agitated city was converted into an army
obedient to the general intention, without receiving any
particular order ; so that, for once, every person was
willing to obey without anyone to command.

This army was still in want of firearms and powder ; and the committee of the city having declared anew
that none could be found even in the arsenal, the people
returned to *les Invalides*.   The order which Sombreuil expected from Versailles did not arrive.   The people were
about to employ force ; and such was the irresolution of
the Court, or such, rather, was the repugnance of the
King to every kind of violence, that in the Champ de
Mars, a few steps from the house which had been forced
open, the troops had received no order to defend it.
Without meaning to yield anything, they abandoned
everything, and thereby involved themselves both in
disgrace and ruin.

It was under the eyes, therefore, of six Swiss bat-
talions and eight hundred cavalry, both dragoons and
hussars, who all remained motionless in their camp, that
the Hôpital des Invalides was opened to the mob.   Here
we have a positive proof of what Bezenval has since
affirmed, that the troops were forbidden to fire upon the
citizens.   The great advantage of the populace was,
that the King would consent only to restrain them,
without allowing them to be treated either as enemies
or rebels.   The same order seemed to be observed in
Paris, at the barriers, at the boulevards, in the square
of Louis XV.   This, too, was what rendered the troops
in all the surrounding posts accessible to corruption,
by the ease with which the people were allowed to
converse with them.

The populace, both men and women, addressed the
soldiers, and, with the glass in their hand, held out to
them the allurement of joy and licentiousness. "What!"
said they, "are you coming to make war against us?
Are you coming to shed our blood? Could you be so
inhuman as draw your sword against your brethren
and friends? Are you not like us, Frenchmen and citizens? Are you not like us, the children of that people
who seek only to be free and to be delivered from
oppression? You serve the King, you love him, and
we, too, love this good King; we are ready to serve him.
He is not the enemy of his people, but he is deceived;
and you are commanded, in his name, to do what he
does not wish. You serve not him, but those unjust
nobles who disgrace you by treating you like slaves.
Come, brave soldiers, come and avenge yourselves of
those unworthy punishments by which you are degraded.
The King and liberty! Down with the aristocrats,
our oppressors and our tyrants!"

The soldiers, who are naturally friendly to the
people, were not deaf to this language. They saw only
a step to take from poverty to abundance, from restraint
to liberty. A great number deserted; and while they
were so near Paris, it was impossible that they should
not be corrupted.

The populace, in the presence of the troops of the
Champ de Mars, were left, therefore, at full liberty to ran-
sack the Hôpital des Invalides. They found in it twenty-
eight thousand muskets; and, dragging this booty and
the cannons of the esplanade in triumph into Paris, they
returned to the Hôtel de Ville. There they learned that
the Marquis de Launay, governor of the Bastille, on
being called upon in his turn to furnish arms and ammunition, replied that he had none. Instantly a general cry
was heard in the Place de Grève: "Let us go and attack
the Bastille."

BOOK XVII

Among the populace this resolution appeared sudden and unexpected; but it had been previously concerted in the councils of the revolutionary chiefs. The Bastille, as a State prison, was always odious in consequence of the unjust manner in which, under the preceding reigns, the despotism of ministers had often employed it; as a fortress, too, it was formidable, particularly to those populous and discontented suburbs which its walls commanded, and which, when they attempted to raise a riot, saw themselves under the cannon of its towers. The Republican faction, therefore, in order to move the people at pleasure and to make them act with boldness, wished to be freed from this troublesome neighbour. The most peaceful and enlightened men also wished the Bastille to be destroyed, from hatred to that despotism of which it was the bulwark; in which they paid more regard to their apparent than real security, for the despotism of license is a thousand times more formidable than that of authority, and an enraged mob is the most cruel of tyrants. The Bastille, therefore, ought not to have been destroyed; but its keys should have been placed in the sanctuary of the laws. The Court thought it impregnable; and so it would have been, or, at least, the attack would have cost much blood, if it had been defended. But the Marquis de Launay, to whom it had been entrusted, wanted the inclination, or the courage, or the skill, to employ the means which he had in his power of rendering the resistance destructive; and the populace, by whom he was so basely assassinated, ought to have returned him their thanks.

De Launay had been in hopes of striking the people with terror; but, it is evident that he wished to spare them. He had fifteen pieces of cannon upon the towers; and, whatever calumny may have said, in order to palliate the guilt of his assassination, not one of these cannons was fired. There were besides, within the castle, three cannons loaded with case-shot, pointed in front of the drawbridge. These would have done great execution at the moment when the mob came rushing in crowds into the outer court; he fired no more than one, and that but once. He was provided with firearms of every description: six hundred musketoons, twelve rampart guns that carried balls of a pound-and-a-half, and four hundred *biscaïens*. He had brought from the arsenal ammunition of every kind: bullets, fifteen thousand cartridges, and twenty thousand pounds of powder. Lastly, in order to crush the besiegers if they should advance to the foot of the walls, he had caused a heap of stones and broken iron to be laid upon the two towers of the drawbridge. But, amid all these preparations to maintain a siege, he had forgotten provisions; shut up in his castle, with eighty invalids, thirty-two Swiss soldiers, and his staff, all his provisions on the day of attack consisted of two sacks of flour and a little rice—a proof that the rest was merely for the sake of terror.

The small number of Swiss soldiers who had been sent to him were determined men, who were ready to defend themselves; the invalids he must have known to be otherwise; but he ought not, at least, to have exposed them to the fear of dying of hunger. Unequal to his situation, and full of that stupor into which a weak mind is thrown by the presence of danger, he viewed it with an eye fixed but troubled, rendered immovable by astonishment rather than by resolution. Unhappily, not a man in the council had that foresight which he wanted.

In order to intoxicate the people with their first success, the attack and taking of the Bastille has, as an

18—2

exploit, been extravagantly boasted of. The following is what I learned from the mouth of the very man who was proclaimed and carried in triumph as the hero and leader of the enterprise.

" The Bastille," said the brave Elie to me, " was not taken by main force. It surrendered even before it was attacked. It surrendered upon the promise which I gave as a French officer, and in the name of the people, that no injury should be done to anyone provided they surrendered." Such is the plain fact, as it was attested to me by Elie. He dictated to me the following details.

The outer courts of the Bastille had been abandoned. Some determined fellows having dared to break the chains of the drawbridge which enclosed the first, the populace entered in crowds. Then, deaf to the voice of the soldiers, who, standing on the tops of the towers, avoided firing, but called out to them to depart, they attempted to make their way towards the walls of the castle. Then it was that the garrison fired, and the populace took to flight and saved themselves under the walls of the outer court. One man dead, and a few wounded, struck terror as far as the Hôtel de Ville ; and an urgent application was made by the mob that the carnage should be stopped, and that deputations should be employed. Two arrived ; one by the arsenal, and the other by the suburb of St. Antoine. " Come forward," cried the invalids from the top of the towers, " we will not fire upon you—come forward with your flags. The governor is about to come down ; we are just going to lower the bridge of the castle in order to introduce you, and we will give hostages." Already the white flag was hoisted upon the towers, and the soldiers held their muskets inverted as a signal of peace. But neither deputation dared to advance as far as the last outer court. Meanwhile, the mob pressed towards the draw- bridge, firing on all sides. The besieged had, therefore, reason to believe, that these pretended deputations were

only a stratagem to surprise them ; and, after having in
vain called out to the people not to advance, they saw
themselves under the necessity of firing in their turn.

The people, a second time repulsed, and enraged at
seeing some of their number fall, took their usual vengeance. The barracks and shops of the outer court were
plundered; the governor's house was burned to the
ground. The firing of a single cannon and the discharge
of musketry, had dispersed that crowd of plunderers and
incendiaries, when Elie, advancing at the head of a dozen
brave citizens to the very brink of the ditch, called upon
them to surrender, and promised that no harm should be
done to anyone. He then saw a hand pass through an
opening of the drawbridge, and present him with a note.
This note was received by means of a plank laid over the
ditch ; it was couched in these terms : " We have twenty
thousand pounds of powder. We will blow up the castle
if you do not accept the capitulation. (Signed) DE
LAUNAY."

Elie, after reading the note, called out that he accepted; and all hostilities from the fort ceased. De
Launay, however, before surrendering to the people,
wished that the capitulation should be ratified and signed
at the town hall, and that, in order to secure his own
safety and that of his band, a strong guard should receive
and protect them. But the unhappy invalids, thinking to
hasten their deliverance, did violence to the governor, and
shouted to those in the court, "The Bastille surrenders!"

Then it was that De Launay, seizing the match of a
cannon, threatened, and perhaps determined, to set fire
to the powder. The sentinels who guarded it presented
their bayonets to him ; and he found himself under the
necessity of surrendering without any further precaution
or delay.

The small drawbridge of the fort being first
opened, Elie entered with his companions, who were
all brave men, and fully determined to keep their pro-

mise. As soon as the governor saw him, he embraced
him and presented him with his sword and the keys
of the Bastille.

"I refused the sword," said he, "and accepted
only the keys." The companions of Elie received the
staff, and the officers of the place with the same cordiality, swearing to guard and defend them. But they
swore in vain.

As soon as the great bridge was let down, and
nobody knew what hand had done it, the people rushed
into the court of the castle, and furiously seized upon
the company of invalids. The Swiss soldiers, being
dressed only in linen frocks, escaped amid the crowd;
all the rest were seized. Elie, and the honest fellows
who had first entered along with him, used their utmost
efforts to tear from the hands of the people the victims
who had been delivered up by themselves. But their
ferocity stuck obstinately to its prey. Many of these
soldiers, who had been promised their lives, were assassinated; others were dragged like slaves into Paris.
Twenty-two were led to the Grève, and after every
mortification and inhuman treatment, they had the
affliction of seeing two of their companions hanged.
On their being presented at the town hall, a madman
said, "You have fired upon your countrymen, you
deserve to be hanged, which you shall be immediately."
Luckily, the French Guards asked pardon for them,
and the people relented. But they had no pity for the
officers of the place. De Launay, torn from the arms
of those who wished to save him, had his head cut
off under the walls of the Hôtel de Ville. Amid these
assassins he defended his life with the courage of despair;
but he was overwhelmed by numbers. Delorme Salbray,
his major, was slain in the same manner. The assistant-
major, Mirai, had met with the same fate near the
Bastille. Pernon, an old lieutenant of invalids, was
assassinated on the wharf of St. Paul, as he was return-

ing to the hotel. Another lieutenant, Caron, was covered with wounds. The head of the Marquis de Launay was carried through Paris by that very populace whom, if destitute of pity, he might have destroyed.

Such were the exploits of those who have since been called the heroes and conquerors of the Bastille. On the 14th July, 1789, the people had assembled about eleven in the morning; at forty minutes after four it had surrendered. At half-past six the head of the governor was carried in triumph to the Palais Royal. The number of the conquerors has been estimated at eight hundred; but this calculation included men who had not even approached the place.

The populace, after this conquest, intoxicated with their power, but agitated with never-ceasing anxieties and suspicions, and rendered more fierce by the dangers which they still trembled at having encountered, now appeared only under the character of a cruel and jealous tyrant. It should have been considered that the dread of punishment was for them the only barrier against the most criminal licentiousness, and in a time of trouble and sedition the defence of the Bastille was an object of high importance to the public repose. We have seen the extreme degree in which it had been neglected. Not even Broglie, though both minister and general, nor the King's council, nor the party of the Nobles, nor any person whatever, had thought of enquiring if the garrison was sufficient, if it had bread and provisions, and if the governor was possessed of that cool and determined courage which was necessary to defend it. It had been supposed either useless or impregnable, or rather it had been altogether forgotten.

It is not the less true that if De Launay had employed his artillery he would have struck Paris with terror. He, doubtless, remembered that he served a good King; and everyone of the populace remembered it as well as he.

All Paris, at the moment of attack, had run to the Bastille. Persons of every age and sex crowded confusedly around these ramparts planted with cannon. What was it, then, which freed them from apprehension? *The King allows his servants to threaten, but the King does not wish his people to be destroyed.* What a fatal lesson has this example given to kings!

In the evening the mob, still more thirsty for blood, driven from crime to crime, demanded the head of Flesselles, who, in the morning, they said, had refused them arms, and who, in concert with the Court, had deceived, betrayed and mocked them with the utmost insolence; the Grève and the Hôtel de Ville resounded with these clamours. But the focus of the fermentation and popular fury was not the Grève, it was the district of St. Roch, in the division of the Palais Royal; there it was that Flesselles had been proscribed.

During the attack of the Bastille, the unhappy man had been at the committee in the Hôtel de Ville, when he was assaulted by a band of wretches, who loaded him with abuse and warned him of approaching death. After two hours of silent anguish, weary of life, and wishing rather to die than to endure so cruel an agony, he resolved to go from the hall of the committee into the great hall, and ask from the people to be heard and judged by the general assembly of the electors. In fact, to throw himself among this merciless rabble, was delivering himself to certain death. He went and took his seat in the circle of the electors. He saw himself aimed at from all quarters. But other incidents having diverted the fury of which he was the object, he took advantage of this respite, and leaning towards a clergyman who sat near him (it was the Abbé Fauchet), he held out his hand, and besought him, in a whisper, to hasten to the district of St. Roch. " My life is at stake," added he; "it is from that quarter that all the accusations against me are brought. Go and tell them that I ask only time

to justify myself." Fauchet, being moved with a sentiment of compassion towards him, went to implore this
favour, but implored it in vain. Their object was to
terrify those who, like Flesselles, thought themselves
attached by duty to the King's party; and, in order to
overcome probity by terror, victims were still necessary.
The people were not yet sufficiently inured to guilt, and
they wished to harden them by practice. The district
by which the insurrection was conducted was, therefore,
inexorable, and Flesselles never again saw the man from
whom he expected safety.

Here I must notice what sort of men those were who
were sent to the Hôtel de Ville to demand the head of
Flesselles. They were, according to the report of a
faithful witness, men armed like savages; they were men
such as one never remembers having seen in daylight.
Whence did they come? Who had drawn them from
their dark retreats?

At the head of the committee of electors, said the
same witness, Flesselles still showed some degree of confidence; even to the fatal moment he was seen listening
to every person with so natural an air of attention and
affability that he would have extricated himself had not
the resolution of destroying him been irrevocably formed.
He was witness to the ferocious joy displayed at the sight
of that lance on the point of which was the head of the
governor of the Bastille. He was witness to the efforts
which were made on this occasion, by some good citizens,
to rescue from the people some of their victims. He
heard the cries of those who demanded that he himself
should be given up to them. Nevertheless, amid so
many horrors, he made a desperate attempt to escape;
and thinking himself forgotten for a moment, he dared
to leave his place and mix among the crowd. He had
actually penetrated it. But those who had pursued him
out of this hall, and who, doubtless, had promised his
death, pursued him, still crying out, "To the Palais

Royal ! To the Palais Royal ! " " Let it be so," said he,
going out.   And the moment after, upon the stair of the
Hôtel de Ville, one of these wretches shot him through
the head with a pistol.   This head was also carried
through Paris in triumph, and the triumph was applauded.   The same applause was given to the murder
of the invalid soldiers, who were seen slaughtered in
the streets—so completely had the delirium of fury
stifled in their souls every sentiment of humanity.

   " I observed," continues my witness, making use of
an expression of Tacitus, " that if few of the people
then dared to commit crimes, many were pleased with
them, and nobody resisted them."   These ruffians who
were seen filling the town hall were not the nation.
Some were almost naked, others were strangely dressed
in habits of different colours, half frantic, and most of
them either wishing they knew not what, or demanding the death of those who were marked out to them,
and demanding it in a tone which, more than once, was
impossible to resist.

   If the National Assembly had chosen to foresee the
evils with which the kingdom was threatened by this
tremendous anarchy ; if they had foreseen how impossible it would be for them again to throw the
chains of lawful authority over this wild beast which
they had let loose ; if those who flattered it had reflected that one day, perhaps, they themselves might
be its prey, they would have shuddered with a salutary fear.   But, in order to acquire supreme authority
for themselves, they thought only of disarming that
authority which alone could produce general safety.

   The citizens of Paris, allowing themselves to be
blinded to their true interests, gave up their minds to
the transports of a senseless joy when it was determined
that the Bastille should be destroyed.   They had not
displayed more gladness when, under the reign of Louis
XI., the iron cages were broken.   Yet history will bear

this testimony to the memory of Louis XVI., that of seven prisoners who were then in the Bastille, not one had been sent there during his reign.

Whilst the city of Paris broke into insurrection against the royal authority, the stirrers-up of rebellion triumphed at Versailles, while they appeared to lament over the misfortunes and the crimes which they had commanded ; and in order to terrify the King they afflicted him with daily accounts of them. " You rend my heart more and more," said he at last, " by the account you give me of the misfortunes of Paris. It is not possible to believe that they can have been occasioned by the orders which I gave to the troops." No, they were not ; for these were only to maintain order and peace.

Meanwhile the assembly demanded from the King, with the most extreme urgency, the removal of the troops, the dismissal of the new, and the recall of the former ministers. He began by ordering the dismissal of the troops which were in the Champ de Mars. But the departure of the troops from the other encampments was not ordered ; and, in Paris, which always thought itself threatened with an assault, the night between the 14th and 15th of July was still terrible. The people, becoming always fiercer, trembled with fear and rage ; the motions made at the Palais Royal were only for lists of proscription. Next day, while the National Assembly was agitated by a multitude of opinions, the voice of the Baron de Marguerit was heard. "No discussion," said he, " ought to be carried on in such afflicting circumstances. Every superfluous word is a crime against humanity. I persist in the proposal which I yesterday made, to send new deputies immediately to the King, who will say : " Sire, blood flows, and the blood of your subjects. Every day, every instant, augments the frightful disorders which reign in the capital and throughout the whole kingdom. Sire, the evil is at its height. It is only by removing the troops from Paris and Versailles, and by instructing the representatives of the nation to carry in your name words of peace, that tranquility can be restored. Yes, sire, there is a means worthy of you, and especially of your private virtues. This means, founded on the unalterable love of Frenchmen for their King, is from this day to place your whole confidence in the representatives of your faithful nation. We beseech you, sire, to come without delay to the National Assembly, where you may hear truth, and may concert with the natural council of Your Majesty the speediest measures for restoring tranquility and union, and for securing the safety of the State."

This proposal was adopted by acclamation, and a new deputation was about to be sent to the King when the Duke de Liancourt arrived and informed them that the King was just coming, and that he was in the most favourable disposition that could be wished.

This news gave the assembly the most sensible pleasure, and all virtuous men showed it openly, when Mirabeau made haste to quench it. " The blood of our brethren," said Mirabeau, " is flowing at Paris. This good city has been thrown into convulsive agonies by its attempts to defend its own liberty and ours. Can we, then, abandon ourselves to any degree of joy before knowing whether tranquility, peace and happiness are to be restored ? Although all the evils of the people were to end, should we be insensible to those which they have already endured ? Let a mournful respect be the first reception given to the monarch by the representatives of an unfortunate people. The silence of the people is the best lesson for kings."

As if the blood shed, as if the crimes of the people, the crimes commanded by himself and by his accomplices, could be imputed to the King ! Nevertheless, notwithstanding this palpable and atrocious calumny, the vehemence of his discourse threw the assembly anew into a gloomy silence when the King appeared, and, standing in the midst of the deputies, who stood, like him, and listened, the King thus spoke:

"Gentlemen, I have assembled you in order to consult upon the most important affairs of the State. None is more urgent, or more sensibly affects my heart, than the terrible disorders which reign in the capital. The chief of the nation comes with confidence into the midst of its representatives, expresses to them his affliction, and invites them to discover the means of restoring order and tranquility. I know the unjust prejudices which have been inspired; some, I know, have dared to publish that your persons were not secure. Can it be necessary, then, to assure you of the falsity of these criminal reports, which my known character was already sufficient to disprove? Well, then, I now unite myself with my nation; I trust myself with you. In these circumstances, then, assist me to secure the safety of the State; I expect this from the National Assembly. The zeal of the representatives of my people combined for the common safety, inspires me with the fullest confidence; and, depending upon the fidelity and love of my subjects, I have given orders for the troops to remove from Paris and Versailles. I authorise, and even invite you, to make known my intentions to the capital."

After the reply of the president, which ended with requesting the King to allow the assembly always a free and immediate communication with his person, the King withdrew, when the whole assembly followed, and formed a procession behind him from the hall to the palace.

A majestic spectacle was, doubtless, formed by this national procession which accompanied the King through a crowd who made the air resound with vows and acclamations; whilst the Queen, who was on the balcony, upon the top of the castle, embraced the Dauphin, presented him to the people, and recommended him, as it

were, to the deputies of the nation.   But this was really
the triumph of the votaries of sedition, to whom the King
had delivered himself.   Few as yet were in the secret of
the revolution ; the rest were sincere.   But the hypocrites, laughing in the bottom of their heart at the noble
sincerity of the King, and the credulous simplicity of
the multitude, applauded each other on account of the
rapid strides which their power was making, and allowed
these sentiments of joy and mutual love to evaporate,
knowing that they would be able to suppress them in
due time.

The numerous deputation which set out for Paris
was received, in its passage from the barrier to the Hôtel
de Ville, by an army of a hundred thousand men,
variously armed with instruments of destruction.   This
was a scene evidently preconcerted, as if with a view of
displaying their power, of commanding obedience if the
King had not yielded ; and with this terrible display was
mingled the joy of conquerors, on account of that unbounded liberty which had produced only crimes, and
with which the best citizens still allowed themselves to
be intoxicated.   A blockade, a siege, a famine, a massacre, were the gloomy phantoms with which they had
been terrified ; and, on seeing the departure of the
troops, which, they believed, were instructed to commit
those crimes, Paris thought she had no longer anything
to fear.

The deputies, on their arrival at the Hôtel de Ville,
were applauded and crowned as the saviours and de-
liverers of a besieged city—a perpetual calumny which
the Marquis de la Fayette, in the discourse which he
pronounced, did not choose to contradict, not daring to
do homage to the King's intentions from the fear of
offending the people.

It would have been natural, it would have been just,
at this moment, to have reminded them of what the King
had so often said, that he had assembled troops only with

the view of maintaining order and tranquility in Paris,
and to secure the repose of good citizens. But this La
Fayette passed over in silence.

"Gentlemen," said he, "the moment most desired
by the National Assembly is now come. The King was
deceived, but he is deceived no longer. He has come
this day into the midst of us without arms, without
troops, without any of that parade which is useless to
good kings. He informs us that he has ordered the
troops to withdraw. *Let us forget our misfortunes*, or
rather let us remember them only that we may for ever
shun similar disasters."

The sincere and courageous Lally - Tolendal spoke
in his turn, and that my relation may be as genuine as
possible, I shall copy his own.

"In the hall where we were received, there were
citizens," says he, "of every class. An immense multitude was in the square, and I experienced how easily,
if everyone had agreed in wishing it, all their warmth
might have been directed towards order and justice.
They fell into raptures when they heard me speak of the
honour of the French name. When I said to them that
they should be free, that the King had given his promise,
that he had thrown himself into our arms, that he entrusted himself to them, that he dismissed his troops—
they interrupted me with cries of ' Vive le roi.' When I
said to them, ' We come from the King and the National
Assembly to present you with peace; you, on your side,
must present peace to the King, and to the National
Assembly,' they eagerly repeated, ' Peace, peace !' When
I added, ' You love your wives, your children, your
King, your country,' they all replied a thousand times,
' Yes !' Then, urging them farther, I ventured to say,
' You would not wish to destroy all that you love by a
sanguinary discord ; there will surely be no more proscrip-
tions. The law alone ought to pronounce them. There
will be no more bad citizens ; your example will render

them good citizens.' They again repeated, ' Peace, and no more proscriptions!' "

From that time, therefore, nothing was more easy than to restore order and to maintain the happiest intelligence between the monarch and his people.

The King wished nothing so much as to be beloved; he thought nothing a hardship which could obtain this reward. The city of Paris had just chosen Bailly as its mayor and La Fayette as the commander of its militia. The King, who alone ought to have made these appointments, agreed without difficulty to the choice which the city made. They had demanded the recall of Necker. Necker was recalled, as well as Montmorin, La Luzerne, and Saint-Priest, who had shared his disgrace; and the new ministers prevented their dismissal by giving in their resignation. Lastly, Paris, troubled anew by perfidious promoters of disturbance, expressed a desire that the King himself should come to the Hôtel de Ville in order to disperse their false alarms; and the King went, on the 17th of July, 1789, without any other guard than the armed citizens of Versailles and Paris, amid two thousand men, armed with scythes, with pickaxes, with muskets, and lances, and dragging cannons along with them.

On the arrival of the King, and during his passage, every acclamation in his favour was prohibited; and if, in addition to the cries of " Vive la nation!" some cried " Vive le roi!" silence was imposed upon them by villains stationed for that purpose. The King perceived this insult, and silently endured it. After having heard the harangue made at the barrier by Bailly the mayor, in which he told him that if Henry IV. had conquered his city, the city in its turn had how won its King, he received at the Hôtel de Ville the Republican cockade. He received it without repugnance; and as he himself was sincerely reconciled to his people, he showed so much candour and kindness that all hearts were at last moved. The congra-

tulation of the orators raised the emotion to enthusiasm ;
and when Lally-Tolendal began to speak, there was
nothing but bursts of sensibility, and transports of love.

"Well, citizens," said he, "are you satisfied? You
now see that King whom you loudly demanded, and
whose very name excited your transports when, two
days ago, we brought him into the midst of you. Enjoy
his presence and his benefits. Behold him who has
restored your national assemblies, and who wishes to
render them perpetual! Behold him who has been pleased
to establish your liberty, your property, upon an immovable foundation! Behold him who has offered, if we may
so speak, to admit you to a share of his authority, reserving only that which was necessary for your happiness,
that which ought for ever to belong to him, and which
you yourselves ought to entreat he would never relin-
quish. Ah! let him at length meet with consolation ; let
his noble and pure heart carry hence that peace which he
so well deserves ; and since he has surpassed his predecessors in virtue, since he has chosen to centre his power
and his grandeur in your love, to be obeyed, to be guarded
by it alone, let us be neither less feeling nor less generous
than our King; and let us prove that even in power, even
in grandeur, he has gained a thousand times more than
he has sacrificed.

"And you, sire, allow a subject, who in fidelity and
devotion is not inferior to all those who surround you, or
to any of those by whom you are obeyed—allow him to
raise his voice towards you, and to say : Behold that
people which idolises you, that people which is intoxicated by your very presence, and whose sentiments for
your sacred person can never be the object of a doubt.
View, sire, and console yourself with the view of all the
citizens in your capital ; their eyes, their voices, their
hearts fly to meet you. There not a single man here
who, for you and for your lawful authority, is not ready
to shed the last drop of his blood. No, sire, no such

misfortune is reserved for this generation of the French as that of giving the lie to fourteen centuries of loyalty. We will all perish, if necessary, to defend a throne which is as sacred to us as to you, and to the august family which we placed upon it eight hundred years ago. Believe, sire, believe, that we never wounded your heart without rending our own; that, amid the calamities which the nation feels, one is the necessity of afflicting you even with a complaint, by which it warns, by which it implores, but by which it never accuses you. At length, all afflictions are to disappear, all troubles are to be appeased. One word of your mouth has restored everything to tranquility. Our virtuous King has recalled our virtuous counsellors; woe to the public enemies who should again attempt to sow division between the nation and its chief! King, subjects, citizens, let us join our hearts, our wishes, our efforts, and let us display, before the eyes of the universe, the magnificent spectacle of one of the first of nations, free, happy, triumphing under a just King whom it reveres and loves, and who, as he owes nothing to force, will be wholly indebted to his virtues and our affection."

Tolendal was a thousand times interrupted with cries of "Vive le roi!" The people were delighted to be restored to their natural feelings; the King shared them; and his emotion expressed them more warmly than eloquence could have done. But if these sentiments had been lasting between him and his people, he would have been thought too powerful by those factious men who wished to reduce him to the mere phantom of a king.

BOOK XVIII

AMONG the Commons, as among the people, there were two characters: one, moderate, feeble and timid, which was that of the greater number; the other, fiery, outrageous and violent—this was the party of the votaries of faction. The latter, with the view of gaining the other, had at first displayed only reasonable and pacific views. One of their organs had been heard beseeching the Clergy, "in the name of a God of peace," to unite with the Order among whom their ruin was planning. We have just seen Mirabeau, in his harangue to the King, affect an hypocritical zeal and respect; but, after being secure of the determination and devoted attachment of the lower orders; of the feebleness, the carelessness, the timidity of the opulent and peaceful class, this party saw itself in a capacity of ruling public opinion, and ceased to dissemble.

The day after that on which the King had gone with so much frankness to deliver himself up to the National Assembly, they undertook to lay it down as a principle, that this assembly had a right to interfere in the formation of the ministry; and the two orators, who, upon this subject, directly attacked the royal authority, were Mirabeau and Barnave, both endowed with a popular eloquence; Mirabeau, with more vehemence and bursts of passion, and often also with artifice and deceit; Barnave, with more frankness, more nerve and more vigour. Both had supported the proposal of depriving the King of the free choice of his ministers; a right which Tolendal and Mounier had strongly defended, maintaining that, without this freedom of choosing the objects of his confidence, the King would have no power at all. The decree resulting from this discussion had left it undetermined; but this did not prevent the question, when once broached, from being the signal of a struggle between the two powers.

With a view to this combat, the Commons stood in need of a force which might be always active and threatening. Hence all the obstacles which Tolendal experienced in his motion of the 20th of July. We must hear him again :

"In the situation to which we were then reduced, it was evident," said he, "that the only dangers which threatened liberty arose from the projects of faction and the approach of anarchy. The National Assembly had to guard against nothing except the very excess of their own power. There was not a moment to lose for the re-establishment of public order. News had already arrived that the commotions experienced in the capital had been felt, not only in the neighbouring cities, but in distant provinces. They appeared in Brittany; they existed in Normandy and Burgundy; they threatened to spread themselves over the whole kingdom. Emissaries, who had evidently set out from a central point, ran over the high roads, and through the towns and villages, without stopping. Here they sounded the alarm, announced the arrival, sometimes of foreign troops and sometimes of robbers, cried everywhere, ' To arms ! ' and often dispensed money."—In fact, I myself saw them passing on horseback through the hamlet where I then was, calling out that hussars were spreading desolation around us, and were setting fire to our harvests ; that such a village was on fire, and such another deluged with blood. Nothing of all this was true; but fear roused the people to fury, and this was their whole aim.

Tolendal, with his hands full of letters, which bore witness to the excesses which were everywhere com-

mitted with impunity, went to the National Assembly
and proposed a proclamation, which, after presenting to
all Frenchmen a view of their situation, of their duties,
and of their hopes, invited them all to peace, and to
security of life and property; threatened the wicked,
protected the good, maintained the laws and tribunals
in vigour and activity. "This plan," said he, "was
overwhelmed with applause: a second reading was demanded, and the acclamations redoubled. But what
was my astonishment when I saw a party rise up and
oppose it? According to one, my sensibility had blinded
my judgment. These conflagrations, these imprison-
ments, these assassinations, were disagreeable circumstances which they must learn to endure, since they
might have been expected. According to another, my
imagination had conjured up dangers which had no
existence. There was no danger except in my motion.
Here there was danger for liberty, because the salutary
watchfulness of the people would thus be removed; there
was danger for the assembly, which would see Paris
declaring against them if they accepted the motion;
there was danger for the legislative power, which, after
having broken the formidable action of authority, was
about to restore to it an energy still more formidable."

The murder of Berthier, the intendant of Paris, and
that of his father-in-law Foulon, who were massacred
at La Grève, their heads carried round, and the body
of Foulon dragged through the Palais Royal, showed
that the populace, intoxicated with blood, still thirsted
for more, and seemed to call upon the assembly to
make no delay in adopting the motion of Tolendal.
He himself will now tell us how little impression was
made by this horrible event.

"Next day (the 21st of July) I was awakened by
cries of grief. A young man entered my room, pale, dis-
figured, threw himself upon me, and said, in a voice
broken by sobs, 'Sir, you have spent fifteen years of

your life in defending the memory of your father, save
the life of mine, and let him be brought to trial. Present
me to the National Assembly, and let me demand a trial
for my father.' This was the son of the unfortunate
Berthier. I conducted him immediately to the president
of the assembly. Unhappily, it did not meet in the
morning, and in the evening it was too late to do anything for this unhappy man. The father-in-law and son-
in-law had been torn in pieces.

"It may be well supposed," continued Tolendal,
"that at the next meeting I made haste to fix general
attention upon this horrible event. I spoke in the name
of a son whose father had been massacred; yet a son
who was in mourning for his own (it was Barnave),
dared to reproach me with feeling, when I ought only
to have thought. He added what I will not so much as
repeat,[1] and every time that he raised his arms amid
his sanguinary declamations, he showed to every eye
weepers, the mournful marks of his recent misfortune
and the undoubted evidence of his barbarous insensi-
bility."

But so completely depraved were the minds of the
promoters of faction, that a cold-blooded cruelty was accounted virtue, and humanity was accounted weakness.
Thirty-six country-seats demolished or burned in a single
province; in Languedoc, a gentleman of the name of
Barras cut in pieces before his wife, who was with child
and ready to lie in; in Normandy, a paralytic old man
thrown upon a burning pile; and so many other enormities committed were, in the assembly, either passed
over in silence, or treated as slight matters if anyone
brought them forward.

It was the policy of the seditious to allow the
people no time for reflection. A moment's coolness
would have shown them that they were deceived, that
these ambitious men made them accomplices only with

---

1 "Was the blood, then, which has been shed so very precious?"

the view of making them slaves, and that they wished
to drive them from crime to crime, till they could no
longer see any safety but in executing all their guilty
commands. Accordingly, the proclamation proposed by
Tolendal did not pass, after a long delay, until everything
had been expunged which could inspire the people with
moderation.   Again, from the fear of giving too much
authority to this pacific proclamation, even in its weakened state, they did not choose that it should be
sent by the King into the provinces, and read from
the pulpit ; but each of the deputies was entrusted
with the care of transmitting it to his constituents.

The 31st of July was a day distinguished by the
return of Necker, and by the species of triumph which
he obtained at the Hôtel de Ville.

He came from Basle, where he had received two
letters of recall—one from the King, and the other from
the National Assembly. On his road he had seen the
enormities to which the people abandoned themselves ;
he had attempted to tranquilize them, to infuse milder
sentiments, and to inspire everywhere a horror for
violence and injustice. He found the roads covered
with Frenchmen who were chilled with horror and
affright by the events that had happened at Paris, and
the assassinations committed near the Hôtel de Ville,
and who were going in search of another country. Informed of these bloody scenes, he conceived, from that
time, the most ardent wish to divert the people of Paris
from their blind cruelty, to recall them to sentiments of
humanity, and to make them wipe off the reproach with
which their criminal violence had stained the national
character. Here I only repeat the account given by
himself ; and, whatever errors or faults may be imputed
to him, no one, at least, will doubt his sincerity. In
assurance of this, I will give, in his own words, a relation
which will be, on that account, more interesting, and at
the same time, not less true.

"Great and happy day for me!" (the 28th of July, 1789), said he, "splendid and memorable era of my life! when, after receiving the most tender marks of affection from an immense people, I obtained from their numerous deputies assembled at the Hôtel de Ville, and then from themselves, with cries of joy, not only the entire freedom of the prisoner whom I defended (the Baron de Bezenval), but a general amnesty, a thorough oblivion of all grounds of complaint and distrust, a generous renunciation of those sentiments of hatred and vengeance with which they were so strongly inflamed—in short, a kind of peace and union between that great multitude of citizens, some of whom had already fled their country, and others were about to leave it. This honourable determination was the reward of my tears; I had asked it on account of the interest which, at that moment, I inspired—I had asked it as an acknowledgment of my last sacrifice—I had asked it as the sole and only reward which I would ever demand. I besought, I humbled myself in every possible manner, in order to succeed. I called into action all the powers of my soul, and being seconded by the eloquence of a feeling and generous citizen (Clermont-Tonnere), I gained the object of my wishes; and this first favour was granted unanimously, with bursts of enthusiasm and kindness which rendered it still more delightful."

The following, too, was the resolution of the general assembly of electors, who met at the Hôtel de Ville on the same day: "In consequence of the sincere, sublime and affecting discourse of M. Necker, the assembly of electors, deeply affected with the sentiments of justice and humanity which he breathes, has decreed that the day in which this beloved and necessary minister was restored to France should be a holiday. They therefore declare, in the name of the inhabitants of this capital, and with the certainty of their concurrence, that they pardon all their enemies, that they prohibit every act of violence contrary to the present decree, and that they henceforth regard those as the only enemies of the nation who shall in any manner disturb the public tranquility.

" They determine, besides, that the present decree shall be read in the parish churches, shall be published by sound of trumpet in all the streets and squares, and shall be sent to all the municipalities of the kingdom. To applaud it will be the distinguishing mark of a good Frenchman."

This was salvation to the State, but it was ruin to plans which could succeed only by means of trouble and terror.

" On the night of this memorable day," continues Necker, " all was changed. The chiefs of the democracy had other views. None of them wished either for kindness, or for oblivion, or for amnesty ; they stood in need of all the passions of the people ; they stood particularly in need of their mistrust ; and they wished, at any price, to prevent such a great and important event from being ascribed to my wishes and to my influence. The districts were therefore assembled, and were inflamed against a declaration, which their own representatives, the old electors named by themselves, which the general assembly at the Hôtel de Ville had unanimously adopted, and which the first wish of the people had ratified. My hope, amid this unfortunate opposition, was the National Assembly. But they approved of the opinion of the districts ; and I saw the edifice of my happiness overturned from its foundation. Yet, what was the object to which I had attached this happiness ? It was to retain in the midst of us those whose wealth and expenditure were the support of industry ; to see the ideas of persecution supplanted by a sentiment of confidence and magnanimity ; to prevent that exasperation which is the inevitable consequence of the fears which we disdain to tranquilize ; to preserve the French nation from those tremendous inquisitory tribunals which are marked by the name of committees of inquiry—in short, to render virtue more amiable by giving it a less fierce aspect, and by showing how it may be allied to sentiments of mildness, of indulgence, and of kindness : the noblest and best ornament of human nature. Ah ! how many misfortunes would have been prevented if the determination formed at the Hôtel de Ville had not been reversed, if the first wish of the people, if this sacred emotion had not been despised."

While Necker spoke thus, he was far from foreseeing the atrocities which were to fill up the measure of former crimes.

But, from that time, he must have felt how misplaced and how miserably useless he himself must be, amid men who disdained every principle of morality and every sentiment of justice and humanity.

It was by the exercise of the most violent despotism that the decree of the Hôtel de Ville had been annulled ; and Tolendal, that other witness whom no one dared to contradict, has loudly declared what Necker passed over in silence.

On the approach of night the promoters of faction had assembled in the Palais Royal, where history will be forced to say that morals were corrupted, that the troops were debauched, that the carcases of the dead were dragged along, and the heads of the living proscribed. There they had sworn to compel the decree of the Hôtel de Ville to be revoked, and had begun their march for that purpose. One terrified district had communicated its fear to several others ; the alarm-bell had sounded, the mob had swelled, the Hôtel de Ville had been threatened with a siege—in short, upon the mere remonstrance of a few districts, the assembled electors of Paris had been forced to yield ; and, by a new decree, pretending to explain that of the morning, had really retracted it.

On the 1st of August, the day appointed for the election of a president, Thouret was chosen by ballot ;

upon which the murmuring and threats of the seditious were instantly heard in the assembly. The election was stigmatized at the Palais Royal as treason ; Thouret was proscribed if he accepted the office; they threatened to assassinate him in his house. He resigned ; and this gave a mortal blow to the liberty of the assembly, which was chiefly composed of weak minds, whose silence, or whose votes, were commanded by fear.

The tribunals were themselves terrified ; the laws had no force, and were despised by the people. They had heard that the ancient edicts were annulled ; they refused to pay taxes previously established ; nobody dared to compel them, and the faction allowed them to believe that these taxes were taken off.

Meanwhile, the funds of the revenue were all exhausted, and their sources almost dried up. Necker laid before the assembly the distress in which he found himself, and asked authority to borrow £1,250,000 at five per cent. This moderate interest was malignantly cavilled at; a fifth was struck off, and the public viewing Necker now only as a minister thwarted and disliked by the Commons, the decline of his credit soon followed.

A patriotic contribution was the momentary resource of the assembly, and, for anything more, they allowed the minister to weary himself out with anxiety to supply the wants of the nation ; and began the work of a Constitution which was created by their own authority, not only without any power or consent from the nation, but in defiance of express prohibitions, which the nation themselves had given in their mandates, against touching any of the ancient and fundamental principles of the existing monarchy.

Till then, hopes had been always entertained of some termination to the usurpation of the Commons, and every means of conciliation had been employed. The evening sitting of the 4th of August had been distinguished by resolutions and by sacrifices which ought to have given

general satisfaction.   The Clergy and Nobility had made,
with acclamation, a resignation of their privileges.   These
renunciations, made with a kind of enthusiasm, had been
received in the same manner, and a very great majority
of the assembly had viewed them as the seal of a full and
lasting reconciliation.   The worthy Archbishop of Paris
had proposed that a *Te Deum* should be sung ; Tolendal,
who never lost sight of the safety of the State, had proposed that Louis XVI. should be proclaimed " The restorer of French liberty "—both proposals had been carried
unanimously.   In short, the King himself had consented
without reserve to all the renunciations which had been
decreed in the sitting of the 4th of August.   But he refused his simple acceptance to the ambiguous declaration
of the rights of man, and to nineteen articles of the Constitution which had been presented to him.   There were
even other articles, to which, it was foreseen, he would
refuse his sanction ; and although the veto which he retained had only the power to suspend a law, this was
enough to stop the revolutionary movement.   It was
necessary to overcome this obstacle, and the king, if they
should force him to resist, might assume a resolution of
which he had hitherto denied himself the exercise.

    This was really what led them to form the design
of having the King at Paris, and made them send to
Versailles, on the 5th of October, 1789, thirty thousand
of the seditious, with cannons at their head, and a crowd
of those abandoned women who are set foremost in every
mob.   The pretence of their mission was to complain of
the dearness of bread.

    I will not describe the brutality of this populace, led
to Versailles to carry off the King and his family.   The
proceedings of the Châtelet have revealed this horrible
mystery, this crime, of which the assembly vainly attempted to clear the Duke of Orleans and Mirabeau.
The facts are recorded in the memoirs of the time, which
my children will read.   They will shudder to see the faith-

ful guards, whom the King had forbidden to fire upon the people, massacred on the very threshold of the Queen's apartment, and their heads carried on pikes under the windows of the palace; they will see this Queen, distracted and trembling for the King and for her children, fly from her bed, which is soon after pierced with bayonets, and throw herself into the arms of the King, where she expected to die; they will see this august couple surrounded by a ferocious mob, to whose rage they opposed the most magnanimous mildness, whom they endeavoured to affect by the sight of their children, and asked what they wished them to do in order to appease them? "Let the King come with us to Paris!" This was the reply of the people, and the acknowledgment of the plot which they were employed to execute.

One thing which cannot be forgotten is, that on the night in which this sanguinary horde filled the apartments of the palace, some voices were raised in the assembly of deputies to propose that they should go in a body to protect the King and check the violence of the people. Mirabeau insolently repelled this motion, saying that "it would not become the dignity of the National Assembly to leave their places." He was careful not to oppose his own work.

The King had it still in his power to withdraw, and everything was prepared for his departure; his carriages, his guards waited for him and his family at the gates of the orangery; some faithful friends urged him to take advantage of the time in which the people should be dispersed through Versailles and immersed in sleep. But a greater number, trembling and weeping, besought him on their knees, not to abandon them. Deceived by the security of La Fayette, who assured him that everything would soon be tranquil, the King, by the fatality of his fortune or of his character, yielded to his destiny, and lost that moment which he was never more to find.

As soon as he had arrived at the Tuileries with his

family, the assembly declared that they could not remain separate from the person of the King; they came to establish themselves at Paris on the 19th of October, 1789; and the good people imagined these translations would be a pledge of their safety.

The first act of the King at Paris was, his acceptance of the first articles of the Constitution, and his sanction given to the rights of man.

These Memoirs are not the history of the Revolution. You will read it elsewhere, my children, and you will see from this era, the 19th of October, the sequel of so many memorable events, which might all have been easily foreseen after the first success of a conquering party—the property of the Clergy declared national on the 2nd of November; the creation of the *assignats* on the 21st of December; the form of this money, and the quantity to be issued, on the 17th of April, 1790; Nobility and all titles abolished on the 19th of June following; the flight of the King on the 21st of June, 1791; his return to Paris on the 25th; lastly, the acceptance of the whole Constitution by the King on the 3rd of December, and the promulgation of this Act on the 28th of the same month.

Here terminated the sitting of the Constituent Assembly; and then it was that I lost that friend, who, in the labours and dangers of a public assembly, had so amply fulfilled his duty and my hopes. The Abbé Maury, a man of the most singular ability, and of no less courage, had just been called to Rome, in order to be loaded with honours.

When I talked to you of him, my dear children, I only gave you the idea of a good friend, an agreeable man; I must now show him to you in the character of a public man, and as his enemies themselves could not avoid viewing him. Here he was invariably attached to the principles of justice and humanity; an intrepid defender of the throne and of the altar; contending every

day with the Mirabeaus and Barnaves; assailed with
clamorous threats by the people from the galleries; exposed to their insults and daggers without, and certain
that the principles for which he contended would sink
under the weight of numbers; yet, though every day
repulsed, he was every day under arms; nor did the
certainty of being overcome, the danger of being stoned,
the clamours, the insults of a frenzied populace, ever
discourage or weary him out. He laughed at the threats
of the mob; he answered with a jest or a vigorous re-
proof to the invectives from the galleries, and returned
to his adversaries with a coolness which nothing could
disturb. The arrangement of his speeches, which were
almost all extemporaneous and lasted for whole hours,
the connection of his ideas, the clearness of his reasonings,
his uninterrupted flow of correct and harmonious expression, made it hardly possible to believe that his eloquence
was not studied and prepared; yet the promptitude with
which he darted up and laid hold of an opportunity of
speaking, compelled us to believe that he spoke without
preparation.

I myself have more than once seen him dictate from
memory the speech that he had pronounced the evening
before, complaining that in his recollection its vigour
was weakened and its warmth extinguished. "Nothing,"
said he, "can render us so eloquent as the glow inspired
by a public assembly." This phenomenon, of which we
have seen so few instances, can be explained only by the
prodigious extent of his memory which comprehended
everything, and by the immense range of his study; indeed, besides that magazine of knowledge and of ideas,
which Cicero regarded as the arsenal of the orator,
Maury possessed a very general acquaintance with ora-
torical language—an inestimable advantage, which he had
derived from the pulpit.

With regard to the firmness of his courage, it was
founded on that contempt for death and that indiffer-

ence for life, without which, he used to say, a nation cannot have good representatives any more than good soldiers.

Such was the appearance made by the man who has been, who is, and who always will be my friend. No revolution, either in his fortune or mine, will cause any change in this mutual and lasting friendship.

The moment in which we embraced and took leave of each other, perhaps for the last time, had something of a religious and melancholy sadness. " My friend," said he, " I have done what I could to defend the good cause ; I have exhausted my strength, not to distinguish myself in an assembly where I was heard in vain, but in order to plant deep the ideas of justice and truth in the minds of the nation and of all Europe. I have even been ambitious of being heard by posterity. My heart is rent at the thought of leaving my country and my friends ; but I carry with me the firm hope that the revolutionary power will be destroyed."

I admired this indefatigable perseverance in my friend; but, after having seen him struggle in vain against that force which swept along or overthrew everything that opposed its rapid progress, I retained little hope of living long enough to see the end of our misfortunes.

The Legislative Assembly, which was opened on the 1st of October, 1791, imitated, and even exceeded, the spirit of the Constituent Assembly. I shall only give a few dates, and then come to what relates to myself.

On the 29th of November, the King is called upon, by a decree, to demand that the princes of the Empire should not allow any armaments to be made by the fugitive princes.

On the 14th of December, the King pronounces an applauded speech upon his declaration to these princes.

On the 1st of January, 1792, a decree of accusation is passed against the brothers of Louis XVI.

On the 1st of March, the death of the Emperor Leopold.

On the 29th of March, the assassination of Gustavus III., King of Sweden.

On the 20th of April, a declaration of war by France against the new King of Hungary and Bohemia.

In the month of June, the King refuses his sanction to two decrees; and this affords a pretence for the insurrection of the suburbs, who are sent in a tumultuous mass to the Tuileries.

The King, who hears them threatening with savage cries and horrible imprecations to break open the doors of his apartment, orders these doors to be opened. He appears and calmly listens to their petition. They require that he should sanction the decrees to which he had refused his acceptance. " My sanction," replied the King, " must be free; nor is this the time either to solicit or obtain it."

Two days later, in his proclamation against this act of violence, he declared that there should never be any necessity for extorting his consent to what he believed to be just and advantageous to the public good; but that he would risk, if necessary, his tranquility, and even his safety, in order to do his duty.

This resistance would have imposed a check on popular despotism. The free acceptance of the laws, and the right which the King had retained of suspending those which he should not approve of, were fundamental articles in a limited monarchy, and in the oath which had been freely given throughout the whole kingdom to the nation, to the law, and to the King; but that alone would have stopped the progress of the Revolution, and the faction wished no limits to be set to their power.

The 31st of July was distinguished by the arrival of the Marseillais at Paris—a kind of satellites, whom the faction kept by them at command for great occasions.

On the 3rd of August, Petion presents the assembly

with a petition from the sections of Paris for the deposition of the King.

On the 6th, a report is spread at the Tuileries that the King is attempting to fly.

Then it was that, from a too-faithful presentiment of what was to happen, my wife urged me to leave that country-house of which she had been so fond, and to seek, at a distance from Paris, an obscure retreat, where we might breathe in peace.

We knew not where to turn our steps. Our children's tutor determined our irresolution. He assured us that in his native province of Normandy we should find without difficulty a secure and peaceful asylum. But time was necessary in order to procure it, and we arrived at Evreux without knowing as yet where to rest our heads. The master of the inn at which we alighted had a very neat house near the city, in the hamlet of St. Germain, situated on the banks of the Iton, and at the gate of the gardens of Navarre. He offered it to us. Delighted with this situation we made it our temporary abode till the family of Charpentier should find us a suitable residence nearer his native place.

If any situation could be delightful in such a painful state of our minds, this would have been so. But, scarce were we arrived at Evreux when we learned the horrible event of the 10th of August.

At Paris, by break of day—of that day which was to usher in others so fatal—the squares and streets adjacent to the Tuileries were filled by armed men, with a train of artillery. They were the populace of the suburbs, supported by the band of Marseillais, who came for the purpose of besieging the King in his palace.

That unhappy Prince was defended only by a small number of Swiss Guards, and though it has been said that there were a multitude of brave men in the garden of the Tuileries who would have stationed themselves round his person had he chosen to appear, doubtless he did not think resistance either lawful or possible. He was advised to go with his family into the bosom of the National Assembly. There he took refuge.

Meanwhile his brave Swiss soldiers, who, faithful to their orders, were opposing the entrance of the populace into the courts of the palace, found themselves obliged to fire. They had repelled them, and were keeping firm to their post, when they learned that the King had withdrawn. They then lost courage, and, having dispersed, were almost all massacred in Paris.

The King was removed, and shut up with his wife, his children, and his sister, in the prison of the Temple (the 13th of August).

On the 31st of August, the mayor and *procureur syndic* (Petion and Manuel) appeared before the assembly at the head of a deputation, in whose name Tallien, their orator, declared that they had shut up a number of factious priests, of whose presence the soil of liberty should, in a few days, be purged.

On the 2nd of September, at the convent of the Carmelites in the Luxembourg ; at the seminary of St. Firmin, in the street of St. Victor ; and at the Abbey St. Germain-des-Pres, many prelates and a great number of priests were slaughtered. The carnage lasted till the 6th in the Hôtel de la Force.

On the 8th, the prisoners who had been sent from Orleans to Versailles were massacred there.

During these days of terror, a man, whom I did not at first recollect, came and lodged near us in the hamlet of St. Germain. His disguise made it so difficult for me to remember where I had seen him, that he was obliged to tell me his name. It was Lorry, the Bishop of Angers. Our recognition of each other was rendered affecting by his unfortunate situation, which, however, he supported with considerable fortitude.

At his desire we lived together and had a common table; indeed, during a happier period, this accidental connection would have been mutually agreeable. We were lodged together on the banks of a beautiful river, in the finest season of the year, with enchanting gardens and a magnificent forest to walk in. Our opinions, our tastes, our principles, were perfectly in unison; the recollection of a world in which we had lived supplied us with inexhaustible subjects of conversation, but all these pleasures were poisoned by the afflictions with which we were continually overwhelmed.

On the 21st of September, the convention took the place of the legislative body. Their first decree was the abolition of royalty.

Meanwhile, columns of volunteers flew to arms in the name of Republican liberty; we were in their way, and our repose was troubled by them. Besides, the approach of winter rendered the place where we were moist and unhealthy; we were obliged to quit it, and, not without regret, left the good bishop. My wife and I retired to Couvicourt.

On the 11th of December, the King appeared at the bar of the convention and underwent an examination. He demanded the two advocates, Tronchet and Target, as his counsel.

Target refused to undertake these responsible functions; the virtuous Malesherbes zealously offered to supply his place; he was allowed to do so.

Tronchet and Malesherbes asked permission to take, as their associate, the feeling and worthy De Seze; and this, too, was allowed.

On the 26th, the King appeared for the second time, with his three defenders. De Seze spoke, but the King had forbidden him to use any parade of eloquence. The obedience of De Seze made him only the more affecting.

On the 17th of January, 1793, the punishment of

death was decreed, with a majority of 366 votes against 355.

The King appealed to the nation.   The appeal was rejected.

On the 19th, it was determined by a majority—380 votes against 310—that the execution of the sentence should not be delayed ; and on the 21st, Louis XVI. was beheaded in the square of Louis XV.

His confessor, at the foot of the scaffold, said to him these ever-memorable words: " *Son of Saint Louis, ascend to heaven.*"

The King wished to speak to the people from the scaffold ; Santerre, who commanded the execution, and was one of those who raised disturbances in the suburb of St. Antoine, ordered the drums to beat, that his voice might not be heard.

This execution was followed, soon after, by that of the other prisoners in the Temple.   On the 21st of January the King had perished on the scaffold.   On the 16th of October the Queen experienced the same fate. On the 21st of Floréal, in the following year, Elizabeth, the King's sister, terminated her innocent life under the same axe ; and, on the 20th of Prairial, the same year, the Dauphin died at the Temple.

BOOK XIX

THE French Revolution might have found in ancient
Rome an honourable example to follow.   Louis XVI.
had none of the vices of the Tarquins, and could not
be accused of pride or violence.   France, for no other
reason than that of being weary of its kings, might
have banished them and their whole race.

But, on the 21st of January, the Reign of Terror
began, and could not but begin.

The vast, the infernal project seemed to have been
formed of corrupting the whole mass of the people, of
combining together all vices and crimes, of propagating
immorality by law, and of realising, in the general depravity, everything which is ascribed to the darkest
geniuses of humankind.

Religious opinions, the belief in a God, the idea of
a life to come, might check man in his career of guilt;
children might be restrained by the authority of their
fathers; morality, by principles of humanity, justice and
generosity, might regenerate a corrupted race.   The
scheme of seduction was formed to embrace all these
objects.   We heard proclamations in favour of unbelief
and blasphemy; we saw libertinism affecting contempt
for God, sacrilege insulting His altars, and guilt rendered
daring by the hope of annihilation; we saw all the ties
of subordination which Nature had formed broken;
children, being rendered by law independent of their
fathers, had only to wish their death in order to be
certain, even against their consent, of sharing their
spoils.   The conjugal tie still remained as a means of

handing down domestic virtues, and of uniting a married couple with themselves and with their children : this tie was allowed to be broken at will; marriage became only a legal prostitution, a transient connection, which libertinism, caprice and inconstancy might form and dissolve at pleasure. In short, honour, public faith, respect for themselves and for public opinion, the veneration inspired by the sacred image of virtue, still presented a point of union for minds susceptible of the emotions of repentance and of the impressions of good example. This was all destroyed. Impudence, licentiousness and the most abandoned profligacy were set up as maxims of Republican conduct ; and the system of Mirabeau and the Duke of Orleans—the system of spreading depravity through a whole generation—seemed to reign in France. Thus was formed that revolutionary despotism, that colossus of mire, kneaded and cemented with blood.

Retired as we were in our cottage of Abloville, to which we had gone after leaving Couvicourt, we could not but dread the effect of so corrupted an age upon our children; and we employed every care in fortifying them by a salutary and cautious education, when the almost sudden death of their faithful instructor added to our sorrows a domestic affliction which completely overwhelmed us. A putrid fever, of extreme malignity, deprived us of this excellent young man. Our children must recollect the grief we felt at losing him, and our fear at seeing them exposed to the contagion of an alarming malady.

Their mother and I knew not what was to become of us, and our last resource was to seek refuge in some inn at Vernon, when someone suggested the idea of asking a retreat from a venerable old man who lived in the village of Aubevoie, at a small distance from ours, and had a house large enough to accommodate us all without inconvenience. There is something romantic in this occurrence of my life.

The old man was affected by our situation, and gave us a most cordial reception. He was one of the monks who had been expelled from the neighbouring convent of Carthusians. His name was Dom Honorat. He was older than I. His character reminded us of the hermits of the Thebaid. This virtuous man seemed to be sent by Heaven to instruct and console us. His whole manner breathed piety, but of a mild, indulgent and charitable kind—a truly evangelical piety. He seldom allowed himself to dine with us; but, for an hour after dinner, and for a little longer in the evening, he came and talked to us of those great objects on which his mind dwelt without ceasing—of divine providence, of the immortality of the soul, of the life to come, of the morality of the Gospel; and all this flowed spontaneously and naturally from the bottom of his heart, with an affecting warmth and lively conviction. It would have been cruel to express any doubt on subjects which formed the consolation of his age and solitude. The soul of this good old man was constantly in heaven; and it was equally pleasing to us to ascend along with him, as it would have been inhuman to attempt bringing him down. He raised us from the dejection into which the death of the King had sunk us, and repeating the words of the confessor, "Son of Saint Louis, ascend to heaven," he said, with confidence: "Yes, he is now before God; and I am sure he is imploring forgiveness for his enemies." He thought the same of the virtuous martyrs who died on the 2nd of September.

The comfort which a pious hermit might derive from his intercourse with us vexed the mayor of Aubevoie. At the end of eighteen days he gave me to understand that it would be time for us to withdraw. Luckily, the air of our house was purified; and after having suitably expressed our gratitude to him who had given us so kind a reception, we returned to our own fireside.

This humble and moderate abode was my own;

I had purchased it; but what a decline did it mark of
our former fortune. I had just left, near Paris, a
country-house, which was our delight; a garden, where
everything was in plenty; and this smiling abode was
now, as by the stroke of a wand, changed into a very
small and decayed cottage. There it was that we were
obliged to attempt to suit ourselves to our situation, and,
if possible, to live as respectably in poverty as we had
done in abundance. The experiment was painful: my
literary appointments were suppressed: the French
Academy was on the point of being destroyed;[1] the
literary pension, which had been the fruit of my labours,
was no longer of any value. The only solid property
which I retained was a small farm at Paray, which the
prudent foresight of my wife had induced me to purchase.
I had been obliged to give up my carriage, and dismiss
even the servant who was necessary to my old age. But,
amid these privations, which scarcely left us the necessaries of life, my wife judiciously and skilfully lessened
our expense by rendering our wants more simple; and
I can truly say that our own uncomfortable situation
but affected us feebly, in comparison with the public
calamity. The attention which I bestowed on the
instruction of my children, the tender interest which
their mother took in their moral education, and, if I may
be allowed to say it, the natural goodness of their
character supplied us in our solitude with an inexpressible resource. They consoled us under a misfortune which was not the misfortune of their age. We
took care, at least, not to distress them with it. "The
storm," said we, "passes over their heads, and smiles
upon them; and we have the hope that their day may
be more calm and serene."

But the storm continued to increase: we saw it
extend over the whole nation; it was not a civil war, for

---

[1] It was destroyed on the 10th of August, 1793.

one of the two parties was disarmed and submissive; but, on one side, it was a jealous hatred, and on the other, a gloomy terror.

Millions of men who were to be paid in the armies, and a number of other enormous expenses, absorbed infinitely more wealth than could be furnished by the public contributions, or by selling the property of the Clergy and emigrants. Paper money, issued in millions, destroyed itself; its accelerated downfall carried credit along with it. Commerce was ruined. The resources supplied by war from the conquered countries were not sufficient. It was decreed (March 10, 1793) that the property of condemned persons should belong to the Republic; and this they called coining money with the guillotine, upon that square (Place de la Revolution) which was made to overflow with blood.

On this account riches became a cause of proscription, and not only men distinguished by their merit, such as Malesherbes, Nicolaï, Gilbert de Voisin, but those noted for wealth, such as Magon, Laborde, Duruey, Serilly, and a multitude of farmers-general, were put to death. Accordingly, when the old Magon was brought before the revolutionary tribunal, and was asked his name: " I am rich," replied he; he did not deign to say more.

In order to give more latitude to the tables of proscription, the accused were distinguished by vague appellations of "enemies to the people," "enemies to liberty," "enemies to the Revolution," and, lastly, by the name of "suspicious" persons; and all those were accounted suspicious whose conduct, whose connections, or whose conversation showed them to be partisans of tyranny (that is, of royalty), or enemies to the Republic, and, in general, those to whom certificates of civism had been refused. Now it was lawful to refuse these certificates without assigning any reason;[1] it was lawful also to

---

1 Decree of January 30th, 1793.

accuse and condemn without proof. In a decree, which subjects to capital punishment the "enemies of the people" (22nd of Prairial, year 2), it was said: "Those are accounted such who endeavour to destroy liberty by force or by fraud; to degrade the national convention and the revolutionary government, of which it is the centre; to mislead public opinion, and to prevent the instruction of the people; in short, to stain the purity of revolutionary principles. The proof necessary to condemn them," continued this decree, "shall be every kind of document, material or moral, which may naturally command the assent of a sound and reasonable mind. The rule of judgment is the conscience of juries enlightened by the love of their country. Their object is the triumph of their country and the ruin of its enemies. If there exist documents of the above-mentioned nature, no witnesses need be heard."

By means of this ambiguous and treacherous language, did an hypocritical quackery establish a system of arbitrary procedure in our criminal tribunals. No proofs, no witnesses, but merely the conscience of juries —and what juries were these? Organs and substitutes of Robespierre, of Lebon, of Carrier, of Francastel, and of so many other tigers, insatiable for human blood.

One of the itinerant executioners of the faction had caused a guillotine to be engraved as an emblem on his seal. Another had one on his table at dinner, with which he amused himself in cutting off the head of the chicken which had been served up to him; and whilst these sported with the instrument of their inhumanity, others boasted to the convention of the speedy and economical manner in which they executed its decrees. One of them wrote: "Shooting is too tedious, and it wastes powder and ball. We have fallen upon the plan of putting them (the prisoners) in large boats on the river; at a mile from the city we sink the boat. St. Florent and the other places," continued he, "are full of prisoners, who shall all receive the civic baptism." I need not describe the inexpressible horror which we felt at these cannibal jests. Things which made humanity shudder—the *noyades* of Carrier upon the Loire, the cannonades of Collot-d'Herbois at Lyons—obtained honourable mention in the bulletin. The atrocities of Lebon in the Pas de Calais were "rather harsh proceedings," which must just be winked at—and which were winked at!

A formidable party was suddenly formed in the heart of the convention against Robespierre; on the 9th of Thermidor, Tallien publicly accused him. He was instantly outlawed, surprised, torn from the Hôtel de Ville, in which he had taken refuge, and dragged, on the 10th, to that scaffold on which he made so many innocent men perish.

After the death of Robespierre, the committees, the revolutionary tribunal, were changed, and the convention disowned their former cruelty; but they declared[1] that they would receive no appeal from the judgments given by the criminal tribunals, and executed during the Revolution, by which property had been confiscated for the advantage of the Republic.

Meanwhile, the fermentation of men's minds was not at an end. The society of the Jacobins did not forget that they had been omnipotent; they saw themselves kept at a distance, and could not endure that the anarchical power, which was their own bloody work, should be usurped by a party different from their own. In vain were they checked in the gentlest manner; they felt the rein, and gnawed it in silence. Attempts were made to weaken by purifying them; and the committees were instructed to unite in suggesting the mode of this purification.[2] All correspondence, all connection between the popular assemblies was prohibited.[3] But the fire was

---

1 22nd of Frimaire, year 3.
2 13th of Vendémiaire.
3 25th of Vendémiaire.

slowly burning under the ashes, and it was yet a vain attempt to prevent it from spreading.

The convention defended itself against public accusations by a decree, regulating the manner in which the trial of a member should be conducted ;[1] but this decree was no security in the time of an insurrection, and the tumult began to threaten around the hall of the Jacobins.[2] Orders were given to shut that hall ; and this decree was sent to the armies and popular societies.[3] The movements of the people in the centre of Paris, and in the suburbs of St. Antoine, became only the more furious.

In order to strengthen the party which opposed the Jacobin combination, the sixty-six deputies who had been arrested on the 3rd of October, 1793, were again admitted into the convention on the 18th of Frimaire ; and three of the old Terrorists being found guilty of the enormities which they committed at Nantes, were condemned to death. A prosecution was raised against Fouquier-Tinville, the public accuser, and he was condemned, with fifteen of his accomplices. At the same time Collot-d'Herbois, Barrere and Billaud-Varenne were brought to trial.

At last, the whole convention entered into an oath to prosecute to death all the followers of Robespierre.

The Jacobins seemed at the last extremity. Some young persons, who had met in the garden of the Palais Royal, had burned an effigy in the costume of Jacobinism, and had carried the ashes into the sewer of Montmatre, with this inscription on the funeral urn : " The pantheon of the Jacobins of the 9th of Thermidor."

Yet, so little was the assembly at ease that, amid all these acts of vigour, it continued still to hold out a signal of alarm and distress. For such I call the decree, in which, providing for the event of its dissolution, it

1 8th of Brumaire.
2 19th of Brumaire.
3 20th of Brumaire.

stated that, if that should happen, all the representatives who might be able to escape the murderous sword,
should meet, as soon as possible, at Chalons-sur-Marne.
The event proved their apprehensions to have been well
founded.

On the 1st of Prairial, some women of the populace
having broken open the doors of the assembly hall, with
cries and insults which interrupted the deliberations,
crowds of men instantly rushed in along with them, and
the head of one of the deputies was laid upon the table.
All was over if the people had taken advantage of the
momentary terror which they had struck. But the insurgents began to amuse themselves with seizing upon
the seats which had been left vacant; and one of them,
called Romme, was so impudently vain as to seat himself in the president's elbow-chair and to lose time in
pronouncing decrees. By these decrees he ordained
that the members of the committees appointed by the
present government should be arrested; that all those
imprisoned since the 9th of Thermidor should be enlarged;
that Barrere, Billaud de Varenne and Collot-d'Herbois
should be recalled. This silly ostentation of authority
lulled asleep the rage of the people; and while he was
giving laws, one of the deputies entered the hall at
the head of an armed force, dispersed the multitude,
and restored courage and freedom to the assembly.

From that time the blood of the Terrorists began
to flow in torrents; and the movers of popular sedition were executed in presence of the people.

Armed force was thus the sole arbiter between
despotism and anarchy, and the leaders of the conquered party were destined to perish on the scaffold.

This was but a melancholy spectacle to the virtuous part of the nation, who dreaded equally anarchy
and despotism.

Men felt, at length, the necessity of altering, not
the fundamental principles, but the form of a govern-

ment, which, though Republican in name, was, in
reality, despotic.   They pretended to divide the powers
in order to balance them.   Such was the object and
the art of the new Constitution.   In this shadow of
fundamental laws, which a commission was instructed
to form, and which they presented on the 3rd of Mes-
sidor of the year 3, two legislative councils and an
executive Directory composed the body in which the
national power was to be lodged.

The two councils—consisting, the one of five hundred, and the other of two hundred and fifty deputies,
chosen every year by a majority of votes in the electoral assemblies—were invested with the power, one
of proposing, and the other of accepting, of sanctioning, or of refusing the laws ; being designed to regulate
and moderate that in which everything was to originate.
So far, the public interest, provided elections were free
and judicious, might be in good hands.

But to these two councils was added a Directory,
armed with the executive power for the maintenance of
order and law ; and thus was established a despotism,
absolute and tyrannical beyond any former example.

The five members who composed the Directory
were to be taken out of the number of fifty candidates,
who should be proposed by the council of five hundred ;
and the choice was to rest with the council of two
hundred and fifty, called the Council of Ancients.

These Pentarchs were to go out by rotation ; first,
one was to go out every year, and his place to be
supplied by lot ; and afterwards each was to continue
in office till the end of his five years, when they were
to go out in the order of succession.

Thence it happened, as we may observe by the
way, that able men were in no way urgent to be in the
number of those first elected, whom the lot might remove at the end of a year or two, and who, besides,
would run the risk attendant upon a first experiment.

But all had a right to aim at these eminent
dignities of the State, and might pass through them
more than once.   Accordingly, their first care had been
to fill up the commission for drawing up the Constitutional Act with the most ardent, the most able, the most
ambitious Republicans; and these had laboured to bestow on this rolling oligarchy the greatest possible
degree of strength and authority.

The conduct of the greatest affairs of the State,
political interests, the finances, foreign relations, commerce and alliances, war and peace, the formation and
management of armies, the appointment and dismissal
of generals, the nomination to all military employments,
were exclusively vested in this council of five.   In the
conduct of internal affairs, they had the police, the use
of the armed force, the right of inspection over the
treasury, and over those employed in the collection of
taxes, the management of the public money without the
least responsibility, the choice of ministers, who acted
under their orders and were removable at their pleasure,
the superintendence of the tribunals, the immediate command of the constituted authorities, and of the agents
whom they should employ in all the departments of
administration—in short, the right of having legal commissaries in all departments, even the smallest, and of
annulling the elections of magistrates and judges which
the people should have made.   Such were the pre-
rogatives lavished upon the Directory by the Constitutional Act, without including those which were afterwards
added.

Thus all the means of governing, of intimidating,
and of corrupting—the use of the armed force; the
disposal of the national treasure; the interest which
those employed in the armies, in the finances, in all
lucrative employments, would have to gain the favour
of these omnipotent Pentarchs ; the devotion of the
generals to the authors of their fortune ; the example

which they would set to the soldiers and subalterns;
the fear of being deposed and the desire of being continued which would be felt by the popular magistrates;
the ambition which would reign in the National Assembly
of gaining the favour of those who promoted to great
offices, and who held in their hands reward and punishment, according as they should have been well or ill
served — all these things, I say, bestowed upon the
Directory a power before which the councils were reduced to nothing.

But it was necessary, in the first place, that the
Constitution should be accepted; and the people might
discover that they were proposing to them only a tyranny
ably disguised and skilfully organised: it was necessary,
besides, to take care that no change should happen in
the spirit of the assembly which was to be formed by
the approaching elections; and for this they provided
in the most daring manner.

BOOK XX

THE events which I have just recalled to my memory have wholly occupied my thoughts, and amidst so many public calamities I have almost forgotten myself. The impression made upon me by seeing this multitude of sufferers was so strong and so deep as to make it natural that what affected myself only should often escape unnoticed. Still, however, I endeavoured, by composition and study, to keep off those painful reflections, the continuance of which might have led to a gloomy melancholy, or to a state of mind in which the ideas, always rivetted upon one object, produce still more dangerous effects upon the frail and feeble organ of good sense.

As long as my imagination could amuse me with agreeable reveries, I composed new tales, less gay than those which I had written during the happy days of my life and the smiling leisure of prosperity, but somewhat more philosophical, and in a tone better suited to my age and to the circumstances of the time.

When these reveries failed, I called my reason into exercise, and endeavoured to employ better the time of my retreat and solitude by composing, for the instruction of my children, a course of elementary study, in little treatises on Grammar, Logic, Metaphysics, and Morality, in which I carefully collected the substance of what I had read on these various subjects, in order that they might reap the fruits.

Sometimes, in order to amuse and instruct them by means of example, I employed our winter evenings in telling them little adventures which happened to me in my youth ; and my wife, perceiving that they were interested by these narratives, urged me to write out for them the events of my life.

In this manner I was led to write these volumes of my Memoirs. I must own, like Madame de Staël, that I have drawn a bust only of myself; but I was writing for my children.

These recollections were a real consolation to me, because they effaced, for the moment, at least, the gloomy images of the present by the pleasing reveries of the past.

I am now come to the period when public affairs took a stronger and closer hold of me than ever. In my capacity of citizen I was called to the primary assembly in the canton of Gaillon, in which the new Constitution was to be proposed. This was the time to observe the state of the national disposition, and it was an interesting time; for the question was to be proposed and determined by a majority of votes in all the primary assemblies at once.

In that where I was present it was evident that the two parties were equally balanced.

———

Here concludes the manuscript of the " Memoirs of Marmontel." We have seen, in the eighteenth and nineteenth books of this work, that, on the approach of the 10th of August, 1792, he had retired first into the neighbourhood of Evreux, in the department of l'Eure, and then to Abloville, a small village near Gaillon, where he had procured a little cottage and small garden.

There he devoted his whole attention to the education of his children, to some literary works for their instruction, and to a few historical pieces.

He continued to devote himself to these pleasing

occupations till the month of April, 1797 (Germinal, year 5), an era at which those electoral assemblies were held, by which, according to the regulations of the third Constitution, a third part of the National Assembly was to be renewed. He went to Evreux, and was unanimously elected by his department, who expressly charged him to defend, in the National Assembly, the cause of the Catholic religion, an engagement which he undertook and fulfilled, by pronouncing before the legislative body the discourse which will be found annexed.

Being then a member of the Council of Ancients, he returned to Paris, and lived there, fulfilling his functions, and connected with all the most distinguished characters in the two sections of the legislative body, till the 18th of Fructidor, year 5, when the department of l'Eure being one of those of which the elections were declared null, he took refuge anew in his rural retreat, and thus escaped the deportation to which most of his friends fell victims.

He there put the last hand to some works which will appear in succession.

Towards the close of the year 1799, he was struck with apoplexy, as he was preparing to go to spend some weeks at Rouen. Notwithstanding the care of his wife, and all the aid of medicine, he could not recover his speech, and seemed also to have lost his recollection. He died on the 31st of December. He was born on the 11th of July, 1723.

He was interred in his garden by ministers of the Catholic religion.

He left a widow and three sons, with scarcely any fortune, though he had spent his whole life in literary labours, and had published works which have become classical : such as his " Elements of Literature "; to which we shall, doubtless, have occasion to add his " Elements of Grammar," of " Logic," of " Metaphysics " and of " Morality."

OPINION

DELIVERED BY MARMONTEL

ON THE

FREEDOM OF RELIGIOUS WORSHIP

REPRESENTATIVES OF THE PEOPLE,—If the resolution which is proposed to you were only a result of the principle established by the Constitutional Act, nothing could be more just. Certainly, everyone should be at liberty to exercise that form of religion which he has chosen, so long as he respects public order and does not violate the laws. The rule is the same for all, and attaches to their liberty only one equal and necessary condition; but when we restrain by prohibitory laws this principle of liberty and equality, do we not impair it? and is the necessity for this restriction so great as to render it just? It is upon this subject that opinions are divided.

I do not enter the lists with the arms of eloquence: its vehemence, its force, its energy no longer belong to my age. But I can still employ the language of feeling and truth.

In order to reduce the question which is submitted to you to its most precise and simple terms, I shall distinguish, in religious worship, between thought and action. In religion, the thoughts possess an absolute liberty, because they belong to man, considered as an individual and as connected with God alone. But action

possesses only a constitutional and limited liberty, because it belongs, not only to the individual, but to the
social order for which he is responsible.

In this view, moral action, in general, is dependent
on human laws. But in what degree are human laws
entitled to restrain it ? This is the grand question, and
I find it determined in the second article of the " Rights
of Man." It is there said : " Liberty consists in being
able to do whatever does not injure the rights of others."
Now, what are the rights of others in the social com-
pact ? Liberty, property, security to each individual,
and tranquility to all. Whatever is innocent in these
respects ought, therefore, to be allowed ; and every
restriction imposed upon this freedom of action is unjust.

Let us apply this principle to the free exercise of
public worship, and let us see how far, in respect to it,
the precautions of police, the measures of security, ought
to extend. I remark, in the first place, that these precautions wear a character of inquietude, of mistrust, of
suspicion, and, perhaps, even of secret aversion, and
repugnance to allow what they would wish to prevent,
but dare not prohibit.

Our politicians treat religion like a jealous rival,
whom they are forced to treat with courtesy, but would
wish to weaken—a behaviour which appears to me unworthy of a powerful and supreme system of legislation,
the character of which ought to be grandeur and majesty.

I shall observe, besides, that our prohibitory laws,
these hostile dispositions, are not equally levelled against
every form of worship, and that, to speak openly, they
have one only in view. For instance, the prohibition of
external ceremonies can be aimed at no worship except
the Catholic. Philosophical deism has not even temples :
it is a pure contemplation, a mental, solitary, silent
adoration.

Oriental deism has temples, assemblies and public

solemnities; but it was not, probably, the religion of Confucius, nor that of Mahomet, nor even that of Moses, expressly, against which our laws are designed to operate.

Neither is it polytheism, nor the ceremonies of Ceres or Cybele, whose celebration they are afraid of seeing. Let us speak plainly : our prohibitory laws cannot even have in view Christianity in general, but the Catholic religion alone; for it alone has ceremonies and signs out of its temples ; it alone obliges its ministers to wear always a particular dress. No other sect has anything of that external appearance which is prohibited by our laws.

The apparent equality which is presented by a vague prohibition common to every kind of worship, is, therefore, only a vain formula ; and the prohibition of external signs and ceremonies falls, in reality, upon the Catholic religion alone. It is the Catholic religion, therefore, that was supposed dangerous when it was thought proper to guard against the "enterprises which might be made by the ministers of religion against the civil condition of the citizens," to borrow the express words of the law of the 7th of Vendémiaire.

Let me, therefore, be allowed to examine this policy, so hostile to the Catholic religion, and to ask, not as a zealot, but as a legislator, without any partiality, or any ostentation of my private sentiments, what causes of suspicion peculiar to this religion, or to its ministers, have given rise to such scrupulous and severe precautions ?

If, in the Catholic religion, as in idolatry, the objects of worship had been passions, vices and crimes exalted into deities, doubtless we ought to abolish, or, at least, confine, these licentious images.

But what can be scandalous or hurtful in the symbols of the most modest, the mildest virtues ? What alarm can be given, either to morals or to laws, by examples of humility, of patience, of indulgence, of self-denial, of universal beneficence ?

In particular, what is the symbol which Catholics are to be prevented from holding up in their solemnities and funerals ? The symbol of their faith and hope, their pledge of immortality, the sign of the love of God, and of His having devoted Himself for the salvation of men.

Ah! suppose that this mysterious symbol—the object of veneration to so many men distinguished by genius and understanding—is regarded with contempt by men who pretend to be more wise and enlightened; freedom of thought allows this; but, let these very men tell us what injury the world can sustain, although upon the front of a temple, upon the coffin of a Christian, or upon the tomb of a just man who has died the victim of the wicked, there be engraved the image of Him whose last sigh asked of His Father the forgiveness of his enemies ? What danger is there in that symbol of peace at a time when the spirit of conciliation and concord is so necessary—at a time when the only hope of rest and of public safety is founded, perhaps, on the oblivion of crimes and the forgiveness of injuries ?

Ought you, in particular, ye guilty men! whom the mercy of our laws permits to live—wretches who would have no refuge but annihilation if mercy were banished from heaven and earth—ought you to reject the worship of a God who forgives and teaches forgiveness ? Ah! rather seek to find everywhere this merciful religion; believe in a redeeming God; this is your only hope. By what other expiation could you quiet your remorse ? And what other victim would wash in its blood, the blood with which you are covered ?

A superstitious belief! say the sceptics, insulting the most sublime example of the most heroic of all virtues.

Well, suppose that the belief of the Chrysostoms, the St. Ambroses, the St. Augustins, the Newtons, the

Pascals, the Bossuets—suppose, if you will, that it is all folly ; for we are not now handling a theological controversy, nor am I defending the truth of this religion : I speak of its innocence, and I ask, which of its symbols would it be dangerous to present to the public eye— especially after they have been accustomed to them during so many ages?

This, it is said, would be a distinction in favour of the Catholic religion, and the law wishes none. If, by distinction, you mean only a visible difference, it will be vain to propose that there shall be none between different religions ; their temples will be opened, and the rites, the songs, the public prayers will sufficiently distinguish them. If, by distinction, you mean any prerogative, the Catholic religion will have none ; for all religions will be allowed equally with it to have their exterior symbols and signs. This is a visible and solemn profession of faith, which everyone will be allowed to make, and which no one will be allowed to insult. The crescent, the ark of the covenant, the tables of the law, will all be openly displayed, and from civil equality order and peace will result.

But, the signs of a belief which they no longer choose should be the reigning one, produce a stronger impression upon the senses, which increases its power over men's minds. Yes, this is the motive of those severe laws with which it has been supposed necessary to restrain the Catholic religion. Its solemnities, its duties, the pomp of its holidays, the commanding aspect of its mysteries, even its rural processions, which seem to render the blessings of heaven more abundant when the voice of the labourers in the fields calls them down upon the harvest, and, above all, the consolations which religion affords to Nature in the accidents of life, to the sick, the dying, in the pangs of suffering, in the last agonies—all this, I say, has been thought to have too powerful an influence on the mind and soul. This religion has been treated like a tree whose spacious shade is dreaded, and of which one attacks the root and another breaks the branches. In the same manner men have vied with each other, some in extirpating the Catholic religion, others in stripping it of whatever seemed likely to extend its influence; and, it must be allowed that, upon the depraved system which had been conceived, this measure was prudent. The scheme of a policy which should be destructive of all morality, could not be better contrived; our corrupters have been consistent.

It was well known that the Catholic religion consisted in the profession of all those maxims which they wished to make us abjure; that it was the friend of all the virtues which they wished to banish, and the enemy of all the vices which they wished licentiousness and impiety to engender.

It was well known, also, that, of all religions, the Catholic was the most popular, and the most attractive to that class of men whom they intended to corrupt. Its advantage consists in presenting them with consolatory objects, with friends who, from the highest heaven, take an interest in their labours, in their sorrows, in their disgraces; a God, in particular, a God, the example and model of those humble virtues which the people have need of in their laborious condition, and who has Himself suffered so much in order to teach them to suffer.

Proud minds, doubtless, feel repugnance to all this; but the people have not this unbelieving pride: whatever affects their heart takes easy possession of their understanding. A God, the friend of the unhappy, who wipes away their tears, who listens to their sighs; a God who supports their courage, and who exalts their hopes; a God who, after some moments of affliction and suffering, promises them endless felicity and glory. This consoling Deity is felt by them to be too necessary not to obtain their love and their faith; and more will be made Christians by the desire of believing than will be made unbelievers by a false philosophy. This was fully understood by those who formed the scheme of depraving a whole people; they could not banish humanity from men's minds so long as there should remain any traces of a compassionate and charitable religion; they have erected their scaffolds only on the ruins of the altars.

We need not wonder, therefore, if minds which are still animated by the ill-extinguished fire of the same passions that have been so fatal to us, should retain an invincible antipathy to a religion which opposes these passions. They wish to find among the people accomplices who resemble themselves. They would think themselves undone were they to see themselves everywhere surrounded by virtuous men. Peace is their scourge; justice, humanity, whose voice haunts, whose name terrifies them, are like furies in their eyes. Since they have called up hell, and chained it down upon the earth, they have begun to view heaven with horror; or, if urged by remorse, they have recourse to prayer, the hope of obtaining forgiveness suddenly fails them; and, like the Macbeth of the English poet, they are forced to exclaim, "I cannot pray."

There is another class of men, weaker and less violent, who, since they dare not propose to banish altogether the Catholic religion, wish, at least, that it should be invisible to them. All the deserters from this faith have not divested themselves of it so completely as they pretend. To meet with those religious symbols which their fathers have revered gives rise to tormenting recollections. They feel a repugnance to recognise, under their modest and simple dress, the ministers of a religion which they have abandoned. These mysterious ceremonies rekindle in their minds a certain involuntary feeling of respect and shame. The very sound of bells through the air recalls them as deserters, accuses them

as faithless, and, whether it announces a festival or a
funeral, is always to them either an afflicting reproach or
a threatening presage.

Accordingly we have seen, at all times, that the
Catholic who has renounced his religion becomes its
most cruel, its most implacable enemy; and we may say
of him what, in *Athalia*, Joad says of Mathan:

> " Ce temple l'importune, et son impieté
> Voudroit aneantir le Dieu qu'il a quitté." [1]

But, after all, according to the principles of good
legislation and sound policy, are there not reasons
founded upon equity, upon prudence, for preserving all
religions in a state of equality, which may prevent anyone from becoming too powerful? Nothing, it may be
said, can be more prudent than the maintenance of this
equality; no regulations can be more just than those
which, while on one side they repress political fanaticism, on the other keep within bounds the fanaticism of
religion; which even oppose the progress of a too ardent
proselytism, and allow no form of worship to acquire
the power of excluding or harassing another. Such, in
short, has been the spirit and plan of the prohibitory
laws, and particularly of that of Vendémiaire.

I do not attack this system; but I lay it down as a
principle, that the equality which the laws may justly
establish consists in granting to none of the permitted
forms of worship any privilege, precedence or prerogative whatever, and not in reducing them to a level in
point of natural advantages; for it is with religions as
with men: it is not in the power of the laws to prevent
an excellent man from obtaining the personal esteem of
his fellow-men; from exercising over them the superiority conferred by understanding and virtue, by the influence of beneficence, by the ascendency of genius and

---

[1] " This temple offends, and his impiety would annihilate the
God whom he abjur'd."

the charm of persuasion.   In the same manner it ought
not to be in the power of the laws to prevent a religion
from exercising its empire over thought, from employing
the means which it may possess of gaining over men's
minds, provided these means be innocent.   The right of
placing all religions on a level, is only the right of
favouring none whatever.

Nevertheless, if one of them could not be thoroughly
free without becoming really formidable, would it not be
a wise policy to provide against such a danger?   I agree;
I applaud this maxim of prudence; but I observe that
most of our revolutionary laws have proceeded upon
vague presumptions, jealous suspicions, gloomy mistrust
and chimerical terrors.   Nothing is easier than to throw
suspicion upon innocence itself; nothing more common
than to affect to dread what we wish to render odious.
Let us guard, legislators, against every opinion rashly
conceived or malignantly inspired.   Let us guard against
the impressions which the rumours of calumny too often
make upon the friends of truth.

Everything is liable to abuse, even the best things,
and religion itself.   But the abuse is made by men, who
must answer for themselves individually, and who are
all equally under the superintendence of the laws.

Our business, then, is to examine whether the spirit
of the Catholic religion authorises or condemns the evils
of which it is accused, the crimes committed in its name;
whether it would naturally induce its ministers to commit
them, and whether the passions, which raise its standard,
do not betray its interests while they affect to serve it.

I shall give a fair statement of the reasons which
we are supposed to have for being on our guard against
this religion.   These reasons follow, with all the force
that can be given to them.   France, since the time of
Clovis, has had a ruling religion, a church exclusively
favoured and protected, successively enriched and dignified, and holding the first rank in the State.   Now, say

they, contemplate its present ruin and decay! Stripped of its splendour, degraded from all its privileges and all its dignities, deprived of all its riches, how can it not be formidable to those who have robbed it of its all? How can it fail to be the irreconcilable enemy of a constitution which allows it no establishment, no provision, and which reduces its priests to the necessity of subsisting on private charity? Is it possible that it should not detest a revolution which has profaned, destroyed, and stained its altars with blood; which has banished it from its temples; which has caused its ministers to be proscribed, imprisoned, exiled, slain?— Yes, all this is doubtless calculated to embitter, to exasperate minds abandoned to the impulses of human passions. But these emotions are here opposed by the restraints of a religion which subdues Nature, and enjoins the sacrifice of all interests and all resentments; of a religion, which, from its birth, and after the example of its Model, has breathed nothing but humility, patience, mildness, obedience to the laws, peace with men, the most profound submission to the decrees of Providence, indulgence and love to enemies, even dread and contempt for earthly prosperity, and the sacrifice of everything which can gratify avarice and pride—for such is the Catholic religion; such has been its character—its unalterable character—since the time when a God (I speak His own language), since a God, *patient even unto death*, was its legislator.

The times, we are told, are changed.

Yes, the times are changed; but religion is not. Amid persecution, and in prosperity, she has remained incorruptible, and her maxims are the same as in the time of Tertullian.

But, if such was the spirit of its early disciples, has it always been that of its pontiffs—of its priests? Is it so still? And if they have been so often animated by ambition, by hatred, by vengeance, what security

have we that they will not be at all times susceptible
to these passions?

What would become of us, great God! were we to
reason thus on social policy? What would men retain of
their natural faculties if the laws should take away from
them the use of all those which they have sometimes,
nay, which they have often, abused. It is by this system
of merciless suspicion that we have seen the prisons filled
with innocent men, the scaffolds loaded—overloaded—with
victims; and it is well known to have been always the
maxim of tyranny to prefer what is safe to what is just:
to chain, to oppress all whom it suspects not to be its
willing slaves.

But, is this oppressive, is this Revolutionary police,
still ours? Yes, exclaim the factious, the Revolution requires these measures; for it is not finished. It is not
finished, indeed, to their wish; and when will it be so, to
those who never think that the measure of destruction is
full—to those who still call out for proscriptions and
massacres? It is not finished to ruffians still greedy of
plunder and thirsting for blood; in a word, it is not
finished to all who enjoy the public calamities and dread
nothing so much as their cessation. But the Revolution
is finished—it is fully finished—for that great majority of
virtuous men who wished only a legitimate liberty, an
equitable government, wisely arranged as to its form,
and rested it upon good laws. The foundation is laid,
the edifice is rising; it is already too firm to be overthrown, or even to be violently shaken.

Thanks to the trial of misfortune—thanks to the return of reason into men's minds, of humanity into their
hearts—almost the whole nation demands now only a
legislation which may render its rights sacred; and this
public and universal wish forms a rampart against faction,
under whose shelter Liberty rests, guarded by the laws.

Now, when laws are made by a free and generous
people, by a people who wish only to be peaceful and

just, their foresight is prudent without being suspicious;
their precautions, their watchfulness, presume the commission of no crimes which may not reasonably be
presumed, and in weighing what is probable, in making
the uncertain calculation of what is possible, they never
confound doubt with certainty and real facts with the
illusions and phantoms of fear.

Without recurring, then, to ages, of which the
annals would bear testimonies so uniformly glorious to
the ministers of the Gospel, I ask what has been their
spirit and character in our days, in the midst of ourselves, when exposed, under our eyes, to the rudest
trials? Is it in dungeons, where they were, in a manner,
heaped together without respect, without compassion
for the aged or the infirm? Is it in the hold of ships,
where, with greater barbarity still, they were left to
perish in crowds, shut out from the light and forced
to breathe only impure vapours and a stagnant air?
Is it at Nantes, in vessels which were to bury them
in the Loire? Is it at Marseilles, where they were
dragged, alive and mutilated, on hurdles to the scaffold?
Is it in any of these places, I say, that they have been
seen enraged, breathing vengeance, detesting their
country, or even impatient under the inhumanity which
was practised towards them?

What do I say? Whither am I led by so just a
defence? Ah! my colleagues, with reluctance do I speak
of those places for ever fatal, in which such multitudes
perished. Truth forces me to call to your recollection
these abominable massacres; but my design is not to
paint their horror. Far from our thoughts be those
ferocious murderers, who, with eyes on fire, their mouths
foaming with rage, the sword or the axe in their hands,
watched for their victims, and demanded prey with the
roarings of hungry tigers. Shuddering, let us pass them
over, and turn our eyes to a spectacle worthy of earth
and of heaven—to that multitude of injured virtuous men

shut up in the prisons of St. Firmin, of Carmes, and of St. Germain-des-Pres. Withdrawn into themselves, bent on their knees, with joined hands, and lifting their eyes to heaven, they implore the mercy of God for themselves, His compassion for their murderers. In vast and deep silence each waits till his name is pronounced ; he is called—he rises—he embraces his companions, recommends himself to their prayers, and goes to die, like the Lamb, without a murmur, a complaint, or a sigh. Is there anything here of that factious and rebellious spirit, that spirit of vengeance, of hatred, and treachery, of which I hear them accused ?

But do those who survive resemble them ? Will they resemble them ? What occasion is there that they should all possess the same degree of heroism ? Will their virtue again be tried by punishment ? . Are they all destined to be martyrs ? Some will be weak, some will feel too sensibly the loss of that property of which they are deprived ; others will lament having fallen into indigence. Surely it would be dealing too hardly were we to reproach the unhappy because they consoled themselves by lamentation ! But, if they have preserved the spirit of the Gospel, misfortune itself will neither render them revengeful, nor treacherous, nor factious, nor enemies of that authority to which Providence subjects them. This is what I affirm, and what no one can deny. On entering into the priesthood, they have sworn to follow the maxims, the example of their divine Legislator ; and on what grounds can they be presumed capable of a breach of faith, which would amount to apostacy ? On what grounds are they supposed to be no longer Christians ?

However, do you wish to ascertain if they be Christians at heart ? Ask of that nation which, ambitious of showing itself more magnanimous than ours, has so humanely received, so generously succoured and respected them in their misery. Ask in Italy, of those gallant French soldiers whom they served and relieved in the

VOL. II   22

hospitals with such affectionate piety ; and believe, at
least, the testimony of the warrior who has praised them
so loudly.

There is no conspiracy of which they are not suspected—no crime or misfortune of which they are not
accused ; but without proof, and always in the mass,
for no individual is ever named. What! among so
many informers, is there not one who can fix upon
a criminal ? They are " suspicious persons ! " Such,
even under the reign of guilt, was the form used in
personal accusations. Suspected persons ! Suspected of
what ? Of incivism—of Royalism ? Thus their thoughts,
their sentiments only are suspected, and suspicion itself
dares not go farther. What a triumph for innocence,
to make the calumny of its calumniators thus expire on
their lips !   •

" No, assuredly," pursue the calumniators of priests,
" it is not in public, it is not in the pulpit that they dare
to profess their seditious doctrine. They have a tribunal
within themselves, by the inviolable secrecy of which impunity is secured ; it is in the confessional that they
inculcate fanatical attachment to kings and hatred to the
Republic."

Against such an accusation defence appears impossible. In fact, where is the proof that the confessor does
not, in secret, do that of which he is accused ? No, he
does not ; even that is proved, and proved to demonstration.

The secrecy of confession is impenetrable on one
side only. If the penitent perceives that he who listens
to him abuses his office, in order to inspire him with a
spirit of revolt and sedition, he has a right to denounce
him as sacrilegious and treacherous. How, then, has it
happened that, since the Revolution, among so many
young enthusiasts for Republican maxims ; amid so many
spies and informers, to whom, as we have seen, nothing
was inviolable—who saw nothing sacred in friendship, in

gratitude, in Nature itself : who sought only pretexts to plunder and exterminate the priesthood—how, I say, has it happened, that not one should have appeared to denounce this species of seduction? No, in not one tribunal of revolutionary tyranny has it ever been heard of. You wish that the laws should suppose a crime to exist, which imposture itself dares not invent ! and the only security required against the presumption of such an enormous sacrilege is—a declaration of obedience to the laws! What a tie upon men, who should be at once dishonest and impious enough to contradict in secret what they had professed in public, what they had recommended from the pulpit ! What a tie upon men, who should carry this profound hypocrisy to the very foot of the altars of a God of truth!

No, in our treatment of priests we must adhere to the principle—the sacred principle—never to suppose guilt without proof, and to believe a man innocent so long as we have no authority to believe him guilty; or, if we except priests from this grand rule of natural equity, we ought to expatriate them all.

But, besides the negative proof in favour of their ministry, there is another, which is positive and completely authentic. This proof is the public, solemn, unanimous testimony of the people, whose voice rises and resounds on all sides. All demand their priests ; and trust me, my colleagues, they know them well. Those whom they demand are not deceitful, factious and impious ; they are not impostors, conspirators and disturbers of public tranquility. They are friends of peace, equitable arbiters, wise promoters of harmony, faithful depositaries of their most secret sorrows—in short, it is in them that they wish to find anew their morality and their religion. They feel deeply what a dissolution, what a corruption of morals, what impudence in every vice, what audacity in every crime which can escape the laws, what enmities, what dissensions in the interior of families, what a fatal relaxation even of the ties of Nature have ensued from the banishment of these evangelical pastors. They feel deeply the necessity of these guides, these advisers, these supporters, to instruct them to be just, to aid them to be good, even in the midst of the wicked. They have expressed it to us with an affecting candour.

" O you," said they, " whom we have elected to be the organs of our just petitions, obtain for us the restoration of our churches, our priests; obtain the restoration of those who teach us how to live, who teach us how to die"; and when we promised to justify their confidence, they shed tears of joy, and loaded us with blessings. These are true, irreproachable witnesses; they do not reason; they feel their wants and their interests.

Trust me, legislators, they would feel in like manner how injurious it would be to the spirit of their worship, and to the character of its ministers, that a distrustful law should thus surround them with embarrassing precautions.

In the council the vote has been carried to prohibit the ceremonies, the dress, and all the external symbols of the Catholic religion. But laws of which the people do not perceive the reason are bad laws for them. Now, what reasons, for example, can be given to the people of the country for the suppression of bells? What signal, equally public, can call from such a distance to the offices of religion? and what is there ridiculous in this mode of assembling them? The bell is precious to them from its use, and from habit; their ear is accustomed to it from their infancy; they have associated with it a religious sentiment; and, doubtless, they consider it as a misfortune to be deprived of it. Now, upon this point, how ill do we act up to our own maxims? How can a privation so needlessly afflicting be reconciled with the intention of making our laws the object of love?

But the sound of a bell may be a signal of sedition. Oh! will sedition be ever in want of signals? Say, rather, that this salutary sound may be a signal of distress, as it actually is in cases of fire, that it may announce to the neighbourhood the incursions of a robber, and in any imminent danger occurring at night, during the hours of sleep, may call the neighbouring villages to the aid of the one attacked. There is nothing, therefore, so childish as has been represented in the interest which men, instructed by misfortune, attach to a public safeguard, in the most sonorous instrument which the genius of the arts has ever invented.

The prohibition against the dress usually worn by priests will not appear to the people less wanton and arbitrary. They know well that it is not at the altar only that their pastor ought to be invested with a venerable character; they know well that the decorum and dignity of a minister of religion requires him to be warned by a dress simple and modest, but distinctive, of what he owes to his profession and to himself.

But the law, it is said, chooses to consider him in no other light than that of a citizen. And, pray, what has the law to do with the form and colour of the clothes he puts on? Can they make a distinction, an exception, in its eyes?

If the Government was distrustful of priests, it would, on the contrary, have been a measure of security to enjoin a difference of dress. What, then, has been the motive for prohibiting this distinction? Could it be the hope that, when mingled in the crowd of corrupt men, they might be more at liberty to adopt their morals, and thus degrade at once their person and their office. I can discover nothing, I must own, in these arbitrary laws but marks of aversion for the Catholic religion; and the more I think of them the less can I imagine any good reason which can be given for them.

The attachment to Royalty which is imputed to this

religion, the aversion which it is supposed to entertain for Republican government, is a charge which rests on no proof, and which facts have belied throughout all Europe. The grossest ignorance can alone give credit to the imputation. I do not deign to say a word more on the subject.

The deference, or, if you will, the obedience, of the Catholic priests to the authority of the Romish Church was, in the clergy of France, no more than a passive dependence. Civil order has been long distinct and separate from it. As to the complete uniformity of doctrine, it belongs to thought, on which our laws impose no restraint.

But this unity of doctrine is said to render the Catholic religion exclusive and intolerant. Yes, exclusive, so far as the persuasion goes, that, in point of doctrine and belief, truth is one, and that it is professed by the Catholic Church alone, without any alteration, any mixture of error; hence its intolerance, that is to say, a strict refusal to admit to its hopes anyone who does not hold its faith. This, apparently, is the best founded reproach made against the Catholic religion. I shall consider it at full length, in order completely to refute it.

When intolerance and proselytism are united in the same religion, must they not render it formidable and, as it were, a scourge to all other religions? What! say they, it is not enough to declare itself incompatible with them; it attacks, it pursues, it drives them from their domain, it carries off daily some of their votaries.

I dwell not upon the number of these conquests; but they are conquests made by persuasion, and therefore without reproach. I go farther, I allow it to be possible and probable that the Catholic religion, without aid and support, merely by virtue of its moral excellence, or by its adaptation to the disposition and character of the people, should make all the progress which is to be dreaded. I maintain that this indefinite power will still be only the innocent effect of a just liberty—the simple exercise of that freedom of thought which the laws ought to respect.

It is otherwise, I own, with that tyrannical and persecuting intolerance which a blind and outrageous fanaticism has practised, in the name of the Catholic religion, while it was in power; I have uniformly combated this abuse of force by which it attempts to govern thought. I combated it in presence of false doctors, who, dishonouring the Gospel, sought to employ in its name constraint and violence; I told them, to their face, that their dungeons, their faggots, their punishments, were abominable in the eyes of God as well as of man, and that they placed the tiger upon the altar of the Lamb. I only repeat, therefore, what I then said, that religious wars, and all crimes which an absurd zeal and an impious policy have prompted in the name of a God of peace, of mercy, and of love, have been the crimes of men, the errors and the faults of kings. And not the Gospel only, but all those who have professed it in its original purity and in its genuine spirit, have disavowed these crimes. Our arms, they have said, are neither sword nor fire; our religion has no power but that of persuasion; its characters are mildness and mercy; by these good fruits it ought to be known; we ought to defend it by suffering death in its cause, not by inflicting it. If we employ in its defence, prohibitions, torments, in short, any punishment whatever, it will not be defended, it will be polluted and shamefully profaned. Such, at all times, has been the language and spirit of its genuine disciples; any other was the mere frenzy of human passions, too often excited by the love of power, by the ambition of ruling the minds of men and holding them in subjection. If, under monarchs who were weak and easily misled, these abuses have become formidable, they will be otherwise under a government which numbers freedom of thought among the rights of man, to be inviolably maintained by the laws.

Citizens and colleagues, let us invest these laws with the dignity which belongs to them.

Mistrust, disquiet, timid precautions, are symptoms of weakness ; we must pity and forgive them. Assurance, firmness, a noble frankness, are the attributes of power ; it is unworthy of her to surround herself with suspicions.

Representatives of the People, I have already expressed sufficiently the repugnance I should feel to vote for the declaration which the ministers of religion are required to give—of submission to the government of the Republic. Not but that I regard this submission as an indispensable duty to which every good priest ought to bind himself without scruple. But, if citizens are all equal in the eye of the law, why is not the law itself equal towards all ? Why should there be restrictions or exceptions in any particular case ?

Priests, it is said, are allowed to exercise functions which require a special guarantee. But others before me have shown how needless the guarantee of a declaration was, on the supposition of these priests being good, and how useless if they were bad. It is to God alone that they have promised fidelity to the laws under which they live. Either they will keep this oath or they would not keep any. And to whom will not he be faithless who has been faithless to his God ?

And why, then, should they not promise to the law what they have promised to God ? *Why*, indeed ! — because they dread that the law, under the vague and indistinct term of submission, should tacitly imply something more than can be lawfully promised. I am aware that these alarms are false. But, legislators, scruples are natural to minds perhaps deficient in knowledge, and whose innocence, whose piety, dreads a fall—virtuous scruples, which it is generous, which it is just, which it is humane to respect!

At length, after long misfortunes and cruel persecutions, the man whose fears are not yet dissipated is allowed to look around him; and if, in the conditions imposed upon him, he thinks he perceives any symptom of ill-will, he is uneasy—he needs to be re-assured.

Yes, my colleagues, let us re-assure minds yet troubled by storms, yet stunned by the thunderbolts which they have seen falling around them. They dread snares; show them that there are none in our laws. They are humbled, afflicted by our mistrust; secure their fidelity by a noble and sincere esteem. Worn out with misfortune and calamity, they ask only for rest; but they wish it to be innocent; let us leave nothing which a timid conscience can dread. No, it is not upon hearts penetrated with the purest morality that indulgence and kindness can be bestowed in vain.

I vote that religious worship should enjoy all the liberty granted to it by the Constitutional Act.

NOTES TO VOL. II

NOTE 1, p. 134.

THIS melancholy event happened on the 27th April, 1785. The following account of it is given in the *Leyden Gazette:*

" We have, within these few days, experienced the greatest calamities by the overflowing of the Oder, which burst its banks in several places, and carried away houses, bridges, and everything that opposed its course. Numbers of people have lost their lives in this rapid inundation ; but of all the accidents arising from it, none is so generally lamented as the death of the good Prince Leopold of Brunswick. While this amiable Prince was standing at the side of the river, a woman threw herself at his feet, beseeching him to give orders for some persons to go to the rescue of her children, whom, bewildered by the sudden danger, she had left behind her in the house : some soldiers, who were also in the same place, were crying out for help. The Duke endeavoured to procure a flat-bottomed boat, but no one could be found to venture across the river, even though the Duke offered large sums of money, and promised to share the danger. At last, moved by the cries of the unfortunate inhabitants of the suburb, and led by the sensibility of his own benevolent heart, he took the resolution of going to their assistance himself. Those who were about him endeavoured to dissuade him from this hazardous enterprise ; but, touched to the soul by the distress of the miserable people, he replied in the following words, which so nobly picture his character : ' What am I more than either you or they ? I am a man like yourselves, and nothing ought to be attended to here but the voice of humanity.' Unshaken, therefore, in his resolution, he immediately embarked, with three watermen, in a small boat, and crossed the river ; the boat had almost reached the opposite bank, when it struck against a tree, and in an instant they all, together with the boat, disappeared. A few moments after, the Duke rose again, and supported himself a short time by taking hold of a tree ; but the violence of the current soon bore him down, and he never appeared more. The boatmen, more fortunate, were every one saved, and the Duke alone became the victim of his own humanity. The whole city is in affliction for the loss of this truly amiable Prince, whose humility, gentleness of manners, and compassionate disposition, endeared him to all ranks. He lived, indeed, as he died, in the highest exercise of humanity. Had not the current been so rapid, he would, no doubt, have been saved, as he was a remarkably good swimmer."

Note 2, p. 162.

The Council of State in France was not, in the same degree as our Privy Council, a mere honorary body; but was employed in deliberating upon the affairs belonging to all the different branches of administration. It was divided into five parts—one for foreign affairs, another for domestic regulation, a third for the finances, a fourth for the marine, and the fifth and last for private affairs, or those which respected the rights of individuals. All these sometimes deliberated together, and formed then what was properly called the Royal Council, or Council of State. That for foreign affairs was the most honourable, and it seems to be the branch to which the name of Cabinet is here given. Besides one or two of the ministers, it consisted of a few of the most distinguished nobility, whom the King, when he wished to pay peculiar honour to them, sent and desired them to attend a particular meeting, ever after which they were considered as cabinet ministers—a distinction which, like that of privy counsellor with us, seems often to have been, in a great measure, honorary.

Note 3, p. 165.

The French Parliaments were chiefly established for the administration of justice throughout the kingdom. They had a higher privilege, however, which was that of registering the royal edicts. Till this ceremony was performed, these edicts were not considered as laws. The Parliament thus possessed a sort of negative in legislative arrangements. When, however, it obstinately refused to register any particular edict which the

Court was determined to enforce, the King came in person to the assembly, and there, by his sovereign authority, ordered its registration. The meetings where this took place were called Beds of Justice. It was considered, however, a high stretch of power, and never failed to occasion discontent.

Note 4, p. 180.

A BED OF JUSTICE was the name given to those meetings of the Parliament at which the King attended in person for the purpose of enforcing the registration of any decree that had been rejected by the Parliament (*see* Note 3). As soon as the approach of the King was announced, a deputation of the Parliament went to meet him. He then entered, and seated himself on a throne of a peculiar construction, called *Lit de Justice*, from which the sitting took its name. The First President and all the other Presidents and Councillors then placed one knee on the ground till the King desired them to rise. The Sovereign used formerly to propose, himself, the subjects which were to be discussed in the meeting; but, of late, he merely said a few introductory words; upon which the Chancellor went up and received His Majesty's orders on his knees, came down and delivered them to the assembly, and then proceeded to take the opinions, which, unless by special permission, were always delivered in a low voice. The Chancellor then, after having again consulted with the King, pronounced these words : " The King has ordered, and does order, that we proceed to the registration of the letters upon which we have deliberated."

Note 5, p. 180.

LAMOIGNON.—This minister must not be confounded with M. Lamoignon de Malesherbes, so celebrated for his virtues and heroic devotion to his unfortunate master. They were both descended from the same ancient and highly-respected family ; but the Keeper of the Seals, of whom Marmontel here speaks, belonged to the eldest branch, which came directly from the First President de Lamoignon, who enjoyed that office under Louis XIV., and to whom Cardinal Mazarin said : " If the King had known a worthier man, or a better subject than you, you would not have been chosen." Malesherbes was the great-grandson of this celebrated magistrate.

THE events of Marmontel's life have been detailed at sufficient length in these Memoirs; from which the reader may also be enabled to form a correct idea of the leading features of his character. He may be curious, however, to learn the light in which he was viewed by his countrymen and contemporaries. The representation is, on the whole, favourable; yet, in point of manners, at least, it is somewhat different from what we might have been led to expect. One of his biographers says:

"To all the advantages of genius and talents, he joined those of external appearance. He was tall and well-proportioned; his expression was pleasing and dignified; it had a commanding character, which easily assumed the air of severity, and in which disdain was sometimes more strongly expressed than he could have wished; even in his gaiety there was gravity and dignity. So long as he lived unmarried he was considered as fortunate in love and a favourite of the fair sex. But, after marriage, he was the model of husbands; never was there a better or happier one; in proof of this I adduce the charms, the virtues, the bitter regrets, the deep affliction of his amiable widow. 'He believes,' said Saint-Lambert, 'that marriage and paternity were invented expressly for him; he enjoys them as if they were a good exclusively his own.'"[1]

Another writer expresses himself thus:

"He contracted, from his studies at Toulouse, a stiff and pedantic manner, of which the habit of living in the great world, and his long residence in the capital, could never entirely cure him. Destitute of those light graces which render a man agreeable in society, he possessed, at least, those talents which command the esteem of the reflecting, and those qualities of the heart which deserve friends. His conversation was mild, instructive, abounding in ideas, and enlivened by anecdote. He possessed that talent, so necessary, of respecting the self-love of others, and somtimes even of flattering it."[2]

With regard to his writings, the "Moral Tales" are undoubtedly those which have commanded the greatest and most general admiration. The following account is given by a late writer, of the enthusiasm with which they were read in France:

---

1 "Encyclopedie Methodique," Supplement.
2 "Dictionnaire Historique."

"This, of all modern works, is perhaps that which has been most universally read; there was not a country-house in which it was not found. Every person who went to breathe for a few days the air of the country, carried it with him to amuse his leisure, as Horace carried Plato, Menander, Eupolis and Archilochus. Was anyone alone? he found himself in good company with this book. Had he company? it was one of the most agreeable readings which could be made to them. It amused the most sedate, fixed the most frivolous, without requiring, either great ability in the reader, or great attention in the listeners; and these tales tended always to the correction of some fault, the suppression or diminution of some folly. They were so many little narrative-comedies, which were not restrained by any of the rules of the drama. They have, in fact, furnished many subjects for comedies and for comic operas; they were a copious mine, which was ransacked without ceasing. M. Marmontel appeared there at once as a man of the world and a man of letters."

His larger romances, "Belisarius" and "The Incas," are not less celebrated. He himself has informed us of the impression which was made by the former work throughout Europe. The Empress of Russia divided it into parts, which were given to be translated by the most distinguished persons of her Court; and she reserved one for herself. The following letter from the King of Sweden has appeared in the late collection of the works of that monarch:

"At the Castle of Carlberg,

"June 19th, 1797.

"Monsieur de Marmontel,—I should have thanked you sooner for the excellent work you were pleased to transmit to me, had I not been prevented by considerations concerning which you have received information from another quarter. The suffrages of all nations have already fixed the value of 'Belisarius': I shall not, therefore, say anything on that subject here. I could not, however, be silent as to my own private obligations, which are so much the greater, as my age and situation enable me the better to profit by the great lessons which you give to kings, as well as to those who are destined to mount the throne.

"The good which your work is calculated to produce, will endure beyond the pleasure which you yourself must experience in having contributed to the happiness of mankind. This consideration, sir, ought, I think, to recompense you for having consecrated your talents to the publication of the most useful truths which have ever been uttered, or, at least, which never were uttered before with an equal degree of force, or in so convincing a manner.

" If you continue, as I trust you will, to increase the lustre of the present age by means of your useful labours, I beseech you not to forget one who is only anxious for further instruction ; and who, with these sentiments, is, &c."

Even La Harpe, who lashes without mercy almost all Marmontel's other productions, is softened by these. Of " The Incas," he observes that " it is full of superior beauties ; there," says he, " we find the morality, the elevation, the pathetic eloquence which rendered ' Belisarius ' so successful ; and this work will be regarded as one of the most distinguished monuments of our literature."

His critical writings, of which the chief are the " Art of Poetry " and " Elements of Literature," are little known beyond the precincts of his native country ; but there they are held in considerable estimation. Yet La Harpe asserts that he was deficient in natural taste, and had conceived a number of critical paradoxes, of which he was not cured till after thirty years' intercourse with literary men and the Academy. One of these was his contempt for Boileau, whom he took every opportunity of depreciating. La Harpe mentions that Voltaire, on reading some verses of Marmontel, in which that writer was very roughly handled, said to him, " This is an unlucky whim which our friend Marmontel has taken. My good fellow, nothing does a man so much harm as speaking ill of Boileau." No less was his antipathy to Racine ; nay, he is said, at one time, when he found Madame Geoffrin reading the works of that writer, to have snatched them out of her hand, exclaiming, " Quoi ! vous lisez ce polisson-là."[1]

His tragedies, though some of them were applauded at the first representation, have never since been able to support themselves on the theatre. La Harpe treats them with extreme severity, and says that *Cleopatra* and the *Heraclides*,

---

[1] " What ! you read that blackguard ? "

which were so unfavourably received, are the only two which are tolerable.

His operas, though they are not considered as displaying any great powers, are still seen with pleasure. Some, indeed, thought that, after the eminence he had attained in higher branches of literature, he had demeaned himself by becoming the author of such compositions. To others, however, it appeared that he had raised this class to his own level.

Upon the whole, Marmontel appears to have ranked among the most distinguished writers who adorned the last age of French literature. His writings, peculiarly suited to the taste of the age, acquired a fame even more extensive, perhaps, than was strictly proportioned to their merit. His character appears also to have been highly esteemed. We find him possessing the regard and friendship of the most distinguished and virtuous characters of his time. His faults seem to have sprung less from any natural badness of disposition than from the easiness of his temper and the influence of prevailing example.

THE END

H. S. NICHOLS, PRINTER, 3 SOHO SQUARE, LONDON, W.